Teacher's Edition

Vocabulary
for Achievement

Fourth Course

Margaret Ann Ríchek

GREAT SOURCE
WILMINGTON, MA

Author

Margaret Ann Richek

Professor of Education Emerita, Northeastern Illinois University; consultant in reading and vocabulary study; author of The World of Words *(Houghton Mifflin)*

Classroom Consultants

Beth Gaby
English Chair, Carl Schurz High School, Chicago, Illinois

Chris Hausammann
Teacher of English, Central Mountain High School, Lock Haven, Pennsylvania

Malisa Cannon
Teacher of Language Arts, Desert Sky Middle School, Tucson, Arizona

Stephanie Saltikov-Izabal
Teacher of Reading and English, At-Risk Specialist, Huntington Beach High School, Huntington Beach, California

Patricia Melvin
District Secondary Reading Specialist, Duval County Public Schools, Jacksonville, Florida

Sean Rochester
Teacher of English, Parkway Central High School, St. Louis, Missouri

Acknowledgments

Editorial: Ruth Rothstein, Victoria Fortune, Dan Carsen, Amy Gilbert

Design and Production: Mazer Corporation

Text Design and Production: Mazer Creative Services

Illustrations: Chris Vallo/Mazer Creative Services; Barbara Samanich, Toby Williams of Wilkinson Studios, LLC; Jerry Hoare, Tim McWilliams, Jeff O'Conner, Ron Zalme of Langley Creative

Cover Design: Mazer Creative Services

Cover Photo: © John Downer/Getty Images & Mazer Creative Services

Definitions for the three hundred words taught in this textbook are based on Houghton Mifflin dictionaries—in particular, *The American Heritage High School Dictionary*—but have been abbreviated and adapted for instructional purposes.

All pronunciations are reproduced by permission from *The American Heritage Dictionary of the English Language, Fourth Edition*, copyright © 2000.

Printed in the United States of America

ISBN-13: 978-0-669-51765-1   ISBN-10: 0-669-51765-8

3 4 5 6 7 8 9 10 - DBH - 10 09

Contents

Why Study Vocabulary Systematically?

Teachers and researchers agree on the importance of vocabulary in refining language skills. The greater the store of words we have at our disposal, the better equipped we are to comprehend what we read and express what we think.

Vocabulary for Achievement is a systematic approach to word learning that helps students to

- understand and use words effectively and flexibly
- learn, retain, and apply a core of important words
- independently unlock the meanings of new words
- engage in lifelong vocabulary acquisition
- improve reading comprehension in all curriculum areas
- improve performance on standardized, state, and college entrance tests
- select words forcefully in speaking and writing
- continually increase vocabulary knowledge

A systematic program ensures the development of the large storehouse of words that is critical to achievement, both in the classroom and in the larger world.

Essential features of the program include:
- exercises and features based on changes in the SAT, standardized, and state tests
- a revised, improved word list
- increased concentration on Greek and Latin word elements
- increased review of Greek and Latin word elements
- lesson organization that ensures correspondence between skills and words
- increased assessment
- the addition of exercises that directly apply word usage and comprehension
- increased word enrichment
- illustrations of specific words
- word explanations and teacher notes
- emphasis on related, derivative words

How Were the Words Selected?

The principal source for word lists was SATs published by the College Entrance Examination Board. Authors and editors also consulted numerous scholarly works, including the *Educator's Word Frequency Guide*, the American Heritage *Word Frequency Book*, *Living Vocabulary*, and many standard thesauruses. Most important, the words were chosen for usefulness, appropriateness to grade level, and applicability to lesson themes and word elements.

Vocabulary for Achievement contains over 80 percent of a well-accepted list of SAT words. The words in *Vocabulary for Achievement* are representative of the difficulty level of vocabulary frequently used in sentence-completion and critical-reading test items on the verbal section of the SAT. Further, most are taught in the Fourth Course or earlier, providing students with ample time to master them before encountering them on the SAT.

Vocabulary for Achievement ensures success, not only on the SAT but in lifelong vocabulary acquisition, by offering students early and engaging instruction with critical and challenging words.

A Tour of the Program

Vocabulary for Achievement is a systematic program of vocabulary development that provides comprehensive instruction and application of word meanings. These four principles guide the program:

- Clearly structured lessons teach best.
- Application of meanings in rich contexts aids retention.
- Learning vocabulary acquisition skills promotes independent learning.
- Vocabulary instruction must be accessible and adaptable to classroom needs.

These four principles are reflected throughout the program, which provides the structure necessary for students to learn new words; to apply them in a variety of practice formats to ensure ownership; and to use dictionary, reasoning, context, test-taking, and word structure skills to independently build and incorporate their growing pool of words.

Teacher-Friendly Elements

- The clear and consistent structure of *Vocabulary for Achievement* makes it ideal for either direct classroom instruction or for independent use, allowing you to direct sound and successful vocabulary instruction.
- **Lessons** provide complete presentation of words, special notes on word usage, carefully scaffolded and abundant practice, numerous contexts, substantial application, and notes for the teacher. Six of the thirty lessons focus on Greek and Latin word roots.
- **Skill Features** facilitate independent vocabulary learning through dictionary skills, reading and reasoning, test-taking, and Greek and Latin word elements.
- **Flash Cards (in student book only)** enable students to review words independently. Each card shows a vocabulary word on one side, and phonetic spelling and definition on the other.
- **Tests** cover each two consecutive lessons. The fifteen reproducible multiple-choice tests (with answers) allow you to monitor student progress.
- **Bonuses** align with tests to provide review on every two lessons. These activities include engaging practice formats such as word searches, crossword puzzles, and scrambled words.
- **Teaching Suggestions** provide concrete ideas to help you extend the range of the program for special classroom needs as well as enrichment.

The Lessons

- There are thirty six-page lessons per level.
- Each theme- or root-related lesson has ten words.
- Entries for words are adapted from the *American Heritage Dictionary* series, and use a dictionary format. They include pronunciations, part-of-speech labels, multiple definitions, etymologies, illustrative sentences, and related words (derivatives) with part-of-speech labels and example sentences.
- There are four scaffolded exercises for practice in writing words that correspond with definitions, completing sentences in an SAT format, writing derived forms in appropriate sentences, and finding examples of the words in varied contexts. Additional word learning is facilitated through illustrations.
- There is an additional challenge exercise using the SAT format of two blanks.
- An engaging reading comprehension passage incorporates each of the ten words, followed by two exercises, one focusing on vocabulary and the other on passage comprehension. The passages cover all areas of the curriculum, and include history, science and nature, the arts, myths and legends, technology, and careers.
- A writing assignment relates to the theme. In alternate lessons, students are asked to use their words in an essay of varied genres or to use words creatively in sentence stems.
- Vocabulary enrichment focuses on word histories and information to spark students' interest as well as to facilitate independent word learning. Some lessons include analogy exercises.

Skill Features

- Ten skill features, one following every third lesson.
- Each feature focuses on fostering student independence in word learning.
- Four skill strands that are critical to independent word learning are covered:
  - using the dictionary
  - reading and reasoning
  - taking tests
  - prefixes, roots, and suffixes
- Clear explanation includes examples, tables of information, and strategies for learning and using new words independently.
- Immediate practice is provided to ensure mastery of the information and strategies.
- Review of Greek and Latin word elements are found in both lessons and skill features.

Dictionary Skills

- Lessons emphasize grade-appropriate skills, building on each other.

- Topics include understanding an entry, finding the right definition, using parts of speech, understanding etymologies, using biographical and geographical entries, reading labels and usage notes, differentiating among synonyms, and using a thesaurus.

- Exercises require students to immediately apply their knowledge to dictionary entries.

Reading and Reasoning Skills: Contextual Clues

- Lessons focus on guiding students to figure out unknown words as they read.

- Several different strategies—substitution, definition, opposition—are provided for students.

- Specific procedures present methods of reasoning to help students get maximum contextual information in a sentence.

- Students practice deriving word meanings from context and then check their working definitions with a dictionary.

- Skills application is graduated from sentence level in earlier books to passage level in more advanced grades; authentic passages are taken from historical sources and literature.

Test-Taking Skills

- Students are given strategies for successfully completing a variety of verbal tests—synonym, antonym, sentence completion, and reading comprehension and writing tests—often found on standardized tests, such as the SAT, ACT, and state tests.

- The two-blank sentence completion items found on the SAT receive focus in Second Course through Sixth Course.

- Guided strategies help students to understand the thought processes required to eliminate inappropriate answer choices and select the correct one.

- Immediate practice provides students the opportunity to apply the strategies they have learned.

Prefixes, Roots, and Suffixes

- Students are given specific cognitive strategies, using illustrative words, to determine meaning from Greek and Latin word roots, prefixes, and suffixes.

- These strategies are first applied in single words, and then in words within a sentence context. Students check their working definitions against dictionary definitions.

- Clear and concise explanation, including possible points of confusion, illuminate the use of word parts in unlocking word meaning.

- The features are carefully sequenced and organized to facilitate cumulative learning and application.

- Lessons featuring Greek and Latin word elements are sequenced near Skill Features on the same subject to provide consistent focus.

- Special review sections cover Greek and Latin word elements in both Word Lessons and Skill Features.

Practice Test for the New SAT

A two-part practice test is included on pages T43–T49. This test is based on the new SAT and provides practice with sentence completion and comprehension items.

Lessons are **theme-related** or **root-centered** to provide a context in which students can learn new words.

The **Word List** is a convenient reference for both students and teachers.

Introductions are motivational.

Pronunciations, definitions, and **etymologies** are from Houghton Mifflin dictionaries.

Word entries are presented **dictionary-style.**

Illustrations provide extra context for understanding the words.

Teaching Suggestions provide concrete ideas to extend the range of the program.

Example sentences illustrate each definition.

Related words were chosen for their usefulness and appropriateness to grade level.

Sidebars provide tips for using the words correctly or remembering them.

Enrichments and Analogies deepen reasoning skills and provide more practice for word use and understanding.

Lesson 23

The Root -cred-

WORD LIST

accredit	credence	credential	credibility	creditable
credulous	creed	discredit	incredulous	miscreant

The root *-cred-*, which means "to believe," is derived from the Latin verb *credere*. Many English words contain this root. For example, businesses extend *credit* to their customers because they *believe* that the debt will be repaid. When we find a story hard to believe, we may call it *incredible*. This lesson presents other words that are based on the root *-cred-*.

1. **accredit** (ə-krĕd´ĭt) *verb* from Latin *ad-*, "to" + *cred*, "believe"
   a. To officially recognize or approve as having met certain standards
      • A national board **accredits** teacher preparation programs at universities.
   b. To credit with; to attribute to
      • To **accredit** only Liz with the success of the project would be to overlook the valuable contributions of her assistants.
   accredited *adjective* To practice medicine in the United States, physicians have to graduate from an **accredited** medical school.

2. **credence** (krēd´ns) *noun* from Latin *cred*, "believe"
   Acceptance as true or valid; belief
      • I don't give any **credence** to common superstitions.

   > Credence is often used in the expression *give credence to.*

3. **credential** (krĭ-dĕn´shəl) *noun* from Latin *cred*, "believe"
   Something that gives one confidence or authority; evidence of one's qualifications
      • The judge's **credentials** included fifteen years on the Ohio Court of Appeals.

4. **credibility** (krĕd´ə-bĭl´ĭ-tē) *noun* from Latin *cred*, "believe"
   Believability; reliability; the power to inspire belief
      • The factual errors in the article damaged the writer's **credibility**.

   credible *adjective* Jury members believed that the defendant's alibi was **credible** because several witnesses had confirmed his whereabouts.

   credential

5. **creditable** (krĕd´ĭ-tə-bəl) *adjective* from Latin *cred*, "believe"
   a. Deserving of limited praise; sufficiently good
      • The substitute tenor gave a **creditable** performance, but I would have preferred to hear the singer who was originally scheduled.
   b. Worthy of belief
      • "The dog ate my homework" is hardly a **creditable** excuse.

Discuss with students the meanings of the prefixes that are added to the root *cred* to form the words *miscreant*, *discredit*, and *incredulous*.

Lesson 23 **147**

---

6. **credulous** (krĕj´ə-ləs) *adjective* from Latin *cred*, "believe"
   Easily deceived; believing too readily; gullible
      • The **credulous** man fell victim to yet another get-rich-quick scheme.

   credulity *noun* The woman's **credulity** led her to believe advertisements that made the most ridiculous claims.

   credulousness *noun* Young children who believe in the tooth fairy display a charming **credulousness**.

7. **creed** (krēd) *noun* from Latin *cred*, "believe"
   A system of beliefs, principles, or opinions
      • All members of the U.S. Army are expected to learn and live by the Soldier's Creed.

   > Creed is often used to refer to a system of religious beliefs.

8. **discredit** (dĭs-krĕd´ĭt) from Latin *dis-*, "deprive of" + *cred*, "believe"
   a. *verb* To damage in reputation; to disgrace
      • The company was **discredited** after its chief executive was charged with knowingly reporting inflated sales figures.
   b. *verb* To cause to be distrusted or doubted
      • The man's testimony was **discredited** by three witnesses.
   c. *noun* Lack of trust or belief; doubt
      • Her mismanagement of the project should cast no **discredit** on her coworkers.

9. **incredulous** (ĭn-krĕj´ə-ləs) *adjective* from Latin *in-*, "not" + *cred*, "believe"
   Disbelieving; showing disbelief; skeptical
      • They were **incredulous** when they heard that their shabbily dressed neighbor had made a fortune in the stock market.

   incredulity *noun* The student's insistence that she wrote the scholarly paper herself was met with **incredulity** by her teacher.

10. **miscreant** (mĭs´krē-ənt) *noun* from Latin *mis-*, "bad; wrong" + *cred*, "believe"
    An evildoer; a villain
      • At the end of the play, the **miscreant** was sent to prison, and the hero rode off into the sunset.

    > Miscreant once referred to a person who objected to or refused to follow religious beliefs.

ANALOGIES

On the answer line, write the letter of the answer that best completes each analogy. Refer to Lessons 21–23 if you need help with any of the lesson words.

___a___ 1. Objectionable is to acceptable as _____.
   a. dejected is to happy
   b. invincible is to strong
   c. discredited is to discarded
   d. accredited is to qualifications

___b___ 2. Credulous is to gullible as _____.
   a. jut is to harbor
   b. trajectory is to path
   c. fortitude is to weakness
   d. resilient is to fragile

___d___ 3. Stalwart is to fortitude as _____.
   a. incredulous is to belief
   b. invincible is to weakness
   c. abject is to uplifted
   d. believable is to credibility

148 The Root -cred-

A variety of **exercise formats** provides practice and aids in **recognition, recall,** and **application** of the words.

A **Write the Correct Word** exercise reinforces definitions and spelling.

A **Complete the Sentence** exercise provides application practice similar to that found on the SAT.

A **Challenge** activity provides practice with the two-blank format found on SATs and other standardized tests.

NAME _____   DATE _____

WRITE THE CORRECT WORD

Write the correct word in the space next to each definition.

credibility	**1.** believability		creed	**6.** a system of beliefs
incredulous	**2.** showing disbelief; skeptical		discredit	**7.** to cause to be doubted
credence	**3.** acceptance as true		credulous	**8.** easily deceived
creditable	**4.** deserving of limited praise		miscreant	**9.** a villain
accredit	**5.** to officially recognize		credential	**10.** a qualification that gives authority

COMPLETE THE SENTENCE

Write the letter for the word that best completes each sentence.

___b___ **1.** The politician tried to _____ his opponent in an effort to win the election.
  a. accredit   **b.** discredit   **c.** credential   **d.** creed

___c___ **2.** The thief who stole from the poor was the worst kind of _____.
  a. creed   **b.** credulity   **c.** miscreant   **d.** credence

___a___ **3.** I made a(n) _____ effort on my report, but I knew I could have done more.
  a. creditable   **b.** credulous   **c.** accredited   **d.** discredited

___d___ **4.** Morna was _____ when Harry told her that he saw aliens from outer space.
  a. creditable   **b.** accredited   **c.** discredited   **d.** incredulous

___c___ **5.** In order to get his real-estate license, he had to complete a(n) _____ program.
  a. discredited   **b.** incredulous   **c.** accredited   **d.** credulous

___b___ **6.** She politely refused the hamburger because her _____ prohibited consuming beef.
  a. credibility   **b.** creed   **c.** credence   **d.** credentials

___a___ **7.** Her _____ was in question after her boss learned that she had lied on her résumé.
  a. credibility   **b.** creed   **c.** credulousness   **d.** incredulity

___d___ **8.** My little brother was _____ enough to believe that my ghost stories were true.
  a. creditable   **b.** incredulous   **c.** credible   **d.** credulous

___b___ **9.** I don't usually give much _____ to the gossip I hear at school.
  a. credential   **b.** credence   **c.** discredit   **d.** creed

___c___ **10.** The doctor's diplomas and other _____ hung in the office where patients could see them.
  a. accredits   **b.** creeds   **c.** credentials   **d.** miscreants

Challenge: I didn't give _____ to the biography because its author's _____ had come into question when some information in his previous book proved to be fabricated.
___c___ **a.** accredits…creed   **b.** credulity…credence   **c.** credence…credibility

---

Reading passages incorporating the vocabulary words reinforce the important link between vocabulary and reading comprehension.

A **follow-up exercise** on the passage tests students' understanding of the vocabulary words in context.

READING COMPREHENSION

Raining Cats and Dogs?

(1) You would no doubt be *incredulous* if someone told you that, in England, it sometimes rains fish, or that in Kansas City, Missouri, a downpour of frogs once pelted the surprised residents. **(2)** Most people are not likely to give *credence* to such fantastic tales, especially when the tales travel by word of mouth. **(3)** After all, *credulity* is not a trait for which people wish to be known.

Amazingly, however, these stories are actually true! **(4)** *Creditable* sources, such as the national weather institutes of many countries, have reported that unusual weather events can cause rather unexpected precipitation. **(5)** Showers of tadpoles, fish, frogs, crabs, salamanders, and (perhaps most unpleasant) slimy jellyfish have all been reported by meteorologists with the most respected *credentials.*

(6) Scientists on the faculties of *accredited,* well-respected universities explain that fish storms may be caused by waterspouts, which are small tornadoes that form over water. A waterspout's powerful winds can suck up water, along with the creatures that live in it, and carry the creatures for miles before expelling them.

In 2000, the seaside resort of Great Yarmouth, England, was bombarded with sprats, a type of small fish. Sounds fishy, doesn't it? **(7)** Most people who heard about the event probably thought it was more likely that some *miscreants* had littered the town with smelly sea creatures.

But England's weather institute reported that this fish fall was a natural event. Such things, experts explained, are often reported around the world. In fact, accounts of fish and frogs falling from the sky date back to the first century. In the world's first encyclopedia, the Roman scientist Pliny the Elder wrote that the residents of one town fled when frogs began to rain down on them.

(8) Today, scientists cannot verify Pliny's claims, but many *credible* accounts of more recent fish showers can be found in respected newspapers. **(9)** Reputable news reporters follow a journalistic *creed* which states, among other core values, that "the public journal is a public trust." This means that reporters have an obligation to readers to make sure that what they report is both true and confirmed by reliable sources.

Still, don't believe everything that you hear or read. **(10)** Some accounts of bizarre weather, such as one tale of falling cows, have been *discredited.* The fishermen who claimed that the heavens pelted them with cattle were just repeating a story that originated in a Russian comedy show.

So there is no need to fear rain containing cows, dogs, or cats. But the next time it rains, you might want to bring an umbrella, just in case fish or frogs fall from the sky!

Each sentence below refers to a numbered sentence in the passage. Write the letter of the choice that gives the sentence a meaning that is closest to the original sentence.

___b___ **1.** You would no doubt be _____ if someone told you that, in England, it sometimes rains fish.
  a. horrified   **b.** skeptical   **c.** deceived   **d.** delighted

___a___ **2.** Most people are not likely to give _____ to such fantastic tales, especially when the tales travel by word of mouth.
  a. acceptance   **b.** praise   **c.** confidence   **d.** thought

___d___ **3.** After all, _____ is not a trait for which people wish to be known.
  a. recognition   **b.** bitterness   **c.** believability   **d.** gullibility

___b___ **4.** _____ sources, such as the national weather institutes of many countries, have reported that unusual weather events can cause rather unexpected precipitation.
  a. Questionable   **b.** Believable   **c.** Skeptical   **d.** Foreign

True or **False** questions check student comprehension of the passage.

A **Writing Extended Responses** activity, related to the lesson theme or passage topic, lets students apply new words. Assignments are designed to stimulate interest, enthusiasm, and creativity.

A **Write the Derivative** exercise helps students apply related words and provides practice in writing these forms.

A **Find the Example** exercise encourages creative and higher-level thinking.

---

a **5.** Showers of tadpoles, fish, frogs, and slimy jellyfish have all been reported by meteorologists with the most respected _____.
    a. qualifications   **b.** recognition   **c.** reputations   **d.** manners

c **6.** Scientists on the faculties of _____, well-respected universities explain that fish storms may be caused by waterspouts.
    a. national   **b.** praiseworthy   **c.** approved   **d.** truthful

c **7.** Most people who heard about the event probably thought it was more likely that some _____ had littered the town with smelly sea creatures.
    a. fishermen   **b.** townspeople   **c.** evildoers   **d.** authorities

d **8.** Today, scientists cannot verify Pliny's claims, but many _____ accounts of more recent fish showers can be found in respected newspapers.
    a. amusing   **b.** damaging   **c.** ordinary   **d.** reliable

b **9.** Reputable news reporters follow a journalistic _____ which states, among other core values, that "the public journal is a public trust."
    a. lifestyle   **b.** system of beliefs   **c.** style of language   **d.** set of qualifications

c **10.** Some accounts of bizarre weather, such as one tale of falling cows, have been _____.
    a. amazing   **b.** shown true   **c.** shown false   **d.** trustworthy

Indicate whether the statements below are TRUE or FALSE according to the passage.

F **1.** All reports of animals raining from the sky have been discredited by meteorologists as false.

T **2.** People in the ancient world recorded events of animals falling from the sky.

F **3.** Amazingly, the skies have sometimes rained cows.

WRITING EXTENDED RESPONSES

The passage you just read describes some seemingly fantastic weather events. Suppose a friend told you a similar type of story. In an essay of at least three paragraphs, tell how you would decide whether this story was true. Give examples of two reliable sources of information that you might consult to confirm the story, and tell why they are trustworthy. (Or, indicate why your friend's sources should not be trusted, and explain why.) Use at least three lesson words in your essay and underline them.

WRITE THE DERIVATIVE

Complete the sentence by writing the correct form of the word shown in parentheses. You may not need to change the form that is given.

discredited **1.** In the sixteenth century, Copernicus _____ the idea that the sun revolves around the earth. *(discredit)*

credible **2.** I found her argument to be persuasive and _____. *(credibility)*

---

accredits **3.** A special board _____ all the state's lawyers. *(accredit)*

creeds **4.** The _____ of many religions dictate that followers must donate money or time to those who are less fortunate than themselves. *(creed)*

credulity **5.** His _____ made him the perfect victim for the con man's scheme. *(credulous)*

incredulous **6.** I was _____ when I read about a man who survived alone on a desert island for years. *(incredulous)*

creditable **7.** Georgette made a _____ effort, and her name was mentioned in the acknowledgments. *(creditable)*

Miscreants **8.** _____ may often get more media attention than law-abiding people. *(miscreant)*

credence **9.** I didn't give too much _____ to the things he said in anger. *(credence)*

credentials **10.** After many years of schooling, he finally acquired the necessary _____ for his dream job. *(credential)*

FIND THE EXAMPLE

Choose the answer that best describes the action or situation.

c **1.** Something that might be *accredited*
    a. a play   **b.** the weather   **c.** a university   **d.** a villain

d **2.** Something that makes up a *creed*
    a. stones   **b.** a degree   **c.** actions   **d.** beliefs

a **3.** The subject of a story that would be most likely to cause *incredulity*
    a. monster   **b.** pet   **c.** bank   **d.** marriage

b **4.** An example of a *credential*
    a. credit card   **b.** college degree   **c.** term paper   **d.** shopping list

a **5.** Something one might say to someone who has done a *creditable* job
    a. Nice job.   **b.** Fantastic!   **c.** Unacceptable!   **d.** This is all wrong.

b **6.** Something that might cause one's reputation to be *discredited*
    a. an experiment   **b.** a nasty rumor   **c.** a portrait   **d.** an award

d **7.** An example of something that is *credible*
    a. gossip   **b.** tall tale   **c.** funny joke   **d.** evidence

a **8.** A fairy tale character who is an example of a *miscreant*
    a. Big Bad Wolf   **b.** Goldilocks   **c.** Cinderella   **d.** Snow White

c **9.** Something a *credulous* person might believe in
    a. gravity   **b.** Saturn   **c.** Martians   **d.** history

b **10.** Something you would probably NOT give *credence* to
    a. diploma   **b.** myth   **c.** bank statement   **d.** newspaper article

X

Teaching Suggestions

Review and Retention

Resources in *Vocabulary for Achievement* provide many opportunities for review.

1. Have students use **Flash Cards,** located on pages 201–220 of the student books, for individual drills or game-style classroom practice.

2. Assign the **Bonuses** as follow-up activities for the vocabulary lessons.

3. Many motivating and short games help students to both deeply process and gain automaticity with words. These are referenced in Richek, Margaret, (2005) "Words are Wonderful: Interactive, Time-efficient Strategies to Teach Meaning Vocabulary," *The Reading Teacher,* Vol. 58 (5, February). Each can be done in segments as short as five minutes.

- In **Find That Word,** students receive extra credit points for bringing in program words that they have found in their reading, in the media, or in speech. They are required to write the word and its sentence context, correctly spelled and punctuated, before receiving this credit. To encourage use in student speech, double credit can be given if one student overhears another using the word. If desired, students may be given a few minutes per week to read some sentences they have found. All sentences, whether read publicly or not, should be posted on a bulletin board. You might prefer to give cumulative class points rather than individual credit.

- In **Two in One,** students may be encouraged to write sentences containing two, three, or four lesson words. It is often helpful for students to work with partners or in groups of three when doing this.

- In **Connect Two,** the words from several lessons are written in two columns. Students are asked to find a similarity between the words in column one and those in column two. For example, in the following list, students could point out that an "imprudence" in spending might well lead "indigence." Or, students could notice that "deference" is a quality lacking in "flippancy." Similarly, when we "importune," our actions are not "surreptitious." Society tends to view "incorrigible" criminals with "repugnance."

apprehensive	importune
deference	imprudence
indigence	flippancy
incorrigible	derogatory
surreptitious	repugnance

- In **Anything Goes,** words are written on a board, overhead, or wall chart. For quick review, the teacher may simply point to a word and ask a question for a class member to answer. Sample questions include: What does _____ mean? What part of speech is _____? Use _____ and _____ in the same sentence. What is the difference between _____ and _____?

4. Students can also be encouraged to make connections among lessons and to learning in other areas.

EXAMPLES In what situations could you use *beguile* (Lesson 3), *imbue* (Lesson 7), and *indoctrinate* (Lesson 7)? How are *discursive* (Lesson 26) and *erudite* (Lesson 7) similar, and how are they different? How do *resilient* (Lesson 21) and *assertive* (Lesson 5) differ? How do *gauche* (Lesson 18) and *feral* (Lesson 3) differ? Refer to the **Complete Word List** on page xv to aid in making similarly related word groups.

5. Have students periodically review their own or others' compositions for word choice. Encourage them to replace overused words or phrases with vocabulary words. For example, in the sentence "Jasper didn't care about the test, "students might rewrite the sentence as "Jasper seemed *nonchalant* about the test" (Lesson 18). Or "Jasper was *apathetic* toward the test (Lesson 27).

Vocabulary and Reading

1. To help students master the literal level of comprehension, give them a series of quotations. Ask students first to underline the key words in each quotation. Then, based on their choices, have them write in their own words the gist of each statement.

EXAMPLES "In life courtesy and self-possession, and in the arts style, are the sensible impressions of the free mind, for both arise out of a deliberate shaping of all things and from never being swept away, whatever the emotion, into confusion, or dullness." (William Butler Yeats)

"The scientist takes off from the manifold observations of predecessors, and shows his intelligence, if any, by his ability to discriminate between the important and the negligible, by selecting here and there the significant stepping-stones that will lead across the difficulties to new understanding." (Hand Zinsser)

2. Another way to reinforce reading comprehension skills at the literal level is to provide students with a paragraph and ask them to identify the overarching idea and supporting material.

EXAMPLE As early as the 1830's, growing urbanization in the Northeast had made a substantial impression upon the nature of agriculture in that region. In the immediate vicinity of burgeoning factory towns and commercial centers, farmers were concentrating their energy upon supplying local markets with fresh vegetables, fruits, and dairy products. In outlying districts, farmers had begun to specialize in the raising of beef or pork, or in the production of wool for the region's new textile industry. Farmers who participated in this commercial economy soon abandoned the old practice of home manufacture which, in the past, had been an inseparable part of farm life. Store-bought cloth replaced homespun, and factory-made furniture and farm tools were substituted for home-made ones.

Possible Questions:
What are the key words in the passage?
What is the central idea of the passage?
Is it actually stated within the passage?
If so, where?
What material (facts and illustrations) supports the central idea?

Vocabulary and Word Analogies

1. Analogies in the second half of the student book reinforce vocabulary and provide critical thinking practice. To give students practice identifying word relationships, provide them with the first half of several analogies and have them work together to determine the types of analogies. You may want to draw from the following types of analogies:

degree	type of
part/whole	relative size
is used to	place where
characteristic of	part of
antonym	synonym

2. To help students practice their analogy-solving strategies, give them several word pairs and ask them to restate the relationship between the words in a simple sentence. For example, in the word pair "scrap/paper," a restated simple sentence could be, "A scrap is a small piece of paper."

Vocabulary, Grammar, and Usage

1. Remind students that a word may be used as several different parts of speech. Have students examine the multiple meanings of such words as *conduct, rebel, insult, digest, trim, subject, escort, compound, progress,* and so forth. Have students write sentences such as the following that illustrate the different meanings.

EXAMPLES Lucia will *conduct* a tour of the museum for visiting Argentinean dignitaries. *(verb)* Both speakers commented on the deplorable *conduct* of some members of the audience. *(noun)*

2. Have students write original sentences that both illustrate particular elements of grammar or rules of usage and incorporate vocabulary words. For example, when covering agreement problems, ask students to write sentences such as the following.

EXAMPLES Many a *vagary* has led to an important discovery or invention. (Rule: Use a singular verb with a single or compound subject modified by *every, many a, or many an.*) Neither his *willfulness* nor his *blandishments* affect my decision. (Rule: When a compound subject consists of a singular subject and a plural subject connected by *or* or *nor,* use a verb that agrees in number with the subject that is closer to the verb in the sentence.)

3. When discussing usage problems, have students examine the likelihood of confusion between pairs of homophones such as the following: *callous/callus, bale/bail, pour/pore, faze/phase, heel/heal, palette/palate/pallet, discreet/discrete, site/cite/sight,* and so forth. Then have them look up the definitions of each word and write a sentence for each word that illustrates its use.

As an alternative, have students examine the likelihood of confusion between groups of homographs (words spelled the same but which differ in meaning and pronunciation): *bow, compact, converse, invalid, lead, minute,* and so forth.

Vocabulary and Literature

1. To help students understand the rich nature of idioms, ask them to explain the difference between "at sea" and "confused." Help students to locate and explain the literal and figurative meanings of other expressions such as the following that may appear in short stories and novels. Examples are: *by the skin of one's teeth, miss the mark, head over heels, sow one's wild oats, strike while the iron is hot, through the grapevine, tooth and nail, take with a grain of salt,* and so forth.

2. When reading works of American literature, such as the fiction of John Steinbeck, Ring Lardner, Sinclair Lewis, Mark Twain, Willa Cather, and William Faulkner, point out how these authors use dialect as literary devices in their works.

3. Have students study the literary effects of rhetorical devices such as *oxymorons* (two contradictory terms used together for emphasis) and *hyperbole* (exaggeration). Examples of *oxymorons* include: *cruel kindness, proudly ignorant, wise folly, cheerful pessimist, sad joy, jumbo shrimp, old news, working vacation, justifiably paranoid, legal brief,* and *weather forecaster.* Examples of *hyperboles* are: *rivers of blood, millions of ships, all the sands of the sea, the waves were mountains high, sleep for a year,* and so forth.

Preparing for College-Entrance Examinations

Use the following suggestions to help students become cognizant of helpful approaches to completing the different types of test items on the verbal portions of college-entrance examinations. Three skill features within the student book give strategies and practice for taking the new SAT. These sections are the SAT Writing Tests, Sentence-Completion with Two Blanks, and SAT Critical Reading Tests. In addition, each of the thirty lessons contains sentence completion items with both one and two blanks.

VOCABULARY FOR ACHIEVEMENT
READING COMPREHENSION PASSAGES

An informative and entertaining Reading Comprehension passage appears in each of the thirty vocabulary lessons in each level. The passage contains all ten vocabulary words, giving students an opportunity to understand the new words in reading. The passages also lend depth, length, and variety to the abundant practice. Finally, they provide students with enriching information drawn from a wide variety of subject areas. *Vocabulary for Achievement* passages offer students a chance to read across the curriculum while they deepen understanding of newly learned words. For your convenience, the following is a level-specific list of content areas and passage titles.

COMPLETE WORD LIST FOR FOURTH COURSE

Words for this grade level found on two reputable SAT review lists are marked with an asterisk.

abhor, 127*
abject, 141
accredit, 147
acrimonious, 61
acronym, 1
adroit, 113
aegis, 47
affect, 33*
affinity, 127*
affix, 1*
aggrandize, 21
alacrity, 187*
amends, 47
analogous, 73
animosity, 127*
antithesis, 73
apathy, 173
apprehensive, 7
ardent, 127*
assail, 133
assent, 173
assertive, 27*
asylum, 133*
attenuate, 193
august, 101*
austerity, 53*
autocratic, 81
autonomy, 81
aversion, 153*
avert, 153

banter, 67*
beguile, 13*
benevolent, 13*
blasé, 113
brazen, 27
bulwark, 133

caricature, 67
caste, 81
categorical, 7
cede, 161
chastise, 61
citadel, 133
cliché, 113
clientele, 113
coinage, 1
colloquial, 1*
commensurate, 73
complaisant, 27
composure, 187
concede, 161
conciliatory, 47
conclusive, 7
concurrent, 167
condemn, 93*
condescend, 101*
conducive, 47
congruence, 73
conjecture, 141*
courier, 167
credence, 147
credential, 147
credibility, 147
creditable, 147

credulous, 148*
creed, 148
culpable, 93*
cursory, 167

debunk, 61*
deceased, 161
decorum, 13
deference, 101
dejected, 141
demeanor, 13
depreciate, 53
depredation, 33
deprivation, 33
derogatory, 61
despot, 81*
deviate, 73
diaphanous, 193
didactic, 41*
dilatory, 121*
diligence, 87*
diminutive, 2
discredit, 148*
discursive, 167
disdain, 127*
disinterested, 34
disparage, 61*
disparity, 74*
diversify, 153
diversion, 153
docile, 27
droll, 67
dubious, 7*

edify, 41
effect, 33
effulgent, 193
egress, 161
elucidate, 41
emigrate, 34*
empathy, 173
enamor, 127
encumber, 193
ennui, 187*
ensue, 181
entrepreneur, 113
ephemeral, 181*
equity, 53
erudite, 41
esoteric, 42*
estrange, 128
evanescent, 193
exonerate, 93
exorbitance, 21
extort, 93
extricate, 47*

facetious, 67*
fastidious, 87*
feral, 14*
feudal, 81
finicky, 87*
flagrant, 107*
flamboyant, 27
flippant, 67

forte, 114
fortitude, 133
frugal, 53
furtive, 107*

gauche, 114
gradation, 161
gradient, 162
grandiose, 21*
gratuitous, 21*
grovel, 101

harass, 62
harbinger, 181*
hegemony, 82*
heterogeneous, 74
hilarity, 68
homogeneous, 74

ignoble, 14
imbue, 42*
immigrate, 34
imminent, 181
imperturbable, 187
impetuous, 187*
importune, 47*
imprudent, 87
impugn, 62*
inadvertently, 154
incite, 187
incontrovertible, 154*
incorrigible, 93*
incredulous, 148
incur, 167
incursion, 167
indeterminate, 8
indigent, 54*
indoctrinate, 42
indolent, 188*
inertia, 188
innuendo, 62
intemperate, 22
interim, 181
interject, 141
interminable, 182
intrepid, 28*
invective, 62*
invert, 154
invincible, 134*
irreversible, 154

jettison, 141
jetty, 142
judicious, 87*
jut, 142

kudos, 128*

lackey, 101
languid, 121*
latent, 107*
lethargy, 121*
ludicrous, 68

malfeasance, 94*
mediate, 48
melancholy, 121*
mellow, 28
meticulous, 88*
metonymy, 2
mettle, 134
minutia, 88
mirth, 68*
miscreant, 148
misdemeanor, 94
mitigate, 48*
mores, 14
multifarious, 22*
munificent, 54*

naive, 114
nonchalant, 114
nuance, 74

objectionable, 142
oligarchy, 82
opulence, 22*
ostensible, 107
oxymoron, 2

pacific, 28
palindrome, 2
palpable, 193*
pandemonium, 188
pathetic, 173
pathology, 173
patronize, 48
pecuniary, 54
pedagogy, 42
pedantic, 42
pejorative, 128*
perennial, 182
permeate, 194*
pliant, 194*
ponderous, 194*
portmanteau word, 2
precarious, 8*
precede, 34
precipitate, 182
precursor, 168
predecessor, 162
predominate, 102
presentiment, 174
proceed, 34
profligate, 22*
projectile, 142
provincial, 14*
provisional, 182
pundit, 42*
purloin, 94

qualm, 8
quiescent, 121

recession, 54
recourse, 168
recurrent, 168
regress, 162
remunerate, 54

rendezvous, 114
renovate, 48
repose, 122
repugnance, 128
resilient, 134*
retrospective, 182
revert, 154
ruffian, 94

salient, 107*
satiate, 22
sensational, 174
sensibility, 174
sententious, 174
sentient, 174
sequester, 107
serenity, 188*
slavish, 102
sloth, 122
slovenly, 88*
solvent, 54*
somnambulate, 122
soporific, 122*
sovereign, 82
spoonerism, 2
stalwart, 134
stamina, 134
strident, 28*
stupor, 122
subjugation, 102
subterfuge, 108
succor, 168
supercilious, 102
surfeit, 22
surreptitious, 108*
sycophant, 102

tantamount, 74
tentative, 8
totalitarian, 82
trajectory, 142
transgress, 162
trepidation, 88*

unabashed, 28
unequivocal, 8*
uninterested, 34
unmindful, 88
unobtrusively, 108
unprecedented, 162
unscrupulous, 94*
unseemly, 14
usurp, 82*

vacillate, 8*
vaunt, 108
vertigo, 154
vilify, 62*
viscous, 194

whimsical, 68*
wily, 14*
witticism, 68

SCOPE AND SEQUENCE OF SKILLS

	INTRODUCTORY	FIRST	SECOND	THIRD	FOURTH	FIFTH	SIXTH
Using the Dictionary	Parts of Speech and Derivatives (pp. 19–20) Parts of a Dictionary Entry (pp. 39–40) Looking for the Right Definition (pp. 59–60)	Finding the Appropriate Definition (pp. 19–20) Using Parts of Speech Labels (pp. 39–40) Run-on Entries and Inflected Word Forms (pp. 59–60)	Finding the Appropriate Definition (pp. 19–20) Understanding Etymologies, Biographical Entries, and Geographical Entries (pp. 39–40)	Finding the Appropriate Definition (pp. 19–20)	Using Synonym Paragraphs (pp. 19–20)	Usage Notes (pp. 19–20)	Combining the Dictionary Synonym Paragraphs and a Thesaurus (pp. 19–20)
Reading and Reasoning	Context Clues (pp. 79–80)	Context Clues: Definition in the Sentence (pp. 79–80)	Context Clues of Substitution (pp. 59–60) Context Clues of Opposites (pp. 79–80) Analogies (pp. 99–100)	Three Types of Context Clues (pp. 39–40) Context Clues in Literature (pp. 59–60) Analogies (pp. 79–80)	Three Types of Context Clues (pp. 39–40) Using Context Clues to Read Primary Sources (pp. 59–60)	Three Types of Context Clues (pp. 39–40) Using Context Clues to Read Literature (pp. 59–60)	Three Types of Context Clues (pp. 39–40) Using Context Clues to Read Primary Sources (pp. 59–60)
Taking Tests	Synonym Tests (pp. 99–100) Antonym Tests (pp. 119–120)	Sentence-Completion Tests (pp. 99–100) Synonym and Antonym Tests (pp. 119–120)	Sentence-Completion Tests with Two Blanks (pp. 119–120)	Sentence-Completion with Two Blanks (pp. 99–100) SAT Critical Reading Tests (pp. 119–120)	SAT Writing Tests (pp. 79–80) Sentence-Completion Items with Two Blanks (pp. 99–100) SAT Critical Reading Tests (pp. 119–120)	SAT Writing Tests (pp. 79–80) Sentence-Completion Items with Two Blanks (pp. 99–100) SAT Critical Reading Tests (pp. 119–120)	SAT Writing Tests (pp. 79–80) Sentence-Completion Items with Two Blanks (pp. 99–100) SAT Critical Reading Tests (pp. 119–120)
Prefixes, Roots, and Suffixes	Identifying Prefixes, Roots, Suffixes (pp. 139–140) The Prefixes non- and un- (pp. 159–160) The Prefixes pre- and post- (pp. 179–180) The Prefixes sub- and super- (pp. 199–200)	Word Elements (pp. 139–140) The Prefixes in-, im-, ir-, and il- (pp. 159–160) The Prefixes ex- and en- (pp. 179–180) The Prefix trans- (pp. 199–200)	The Prefix re- (pp. 139–140) The Prefixes com-, con-, and cor- (pp. 159–160) Number Prefixes (pp. 179–180) Number Prefixes (pp. 199–200)	The Prefixes a- and an- (pp. 139–140) The Prefixes micro-, macro-, mini-, maxi-, and mega- (pp. 159–160) The Prefix de- (pp. 179–180) The Prefix dis- (pp. 199–200)	The Prefixes circum-, peri-, semi-, and hemi- (pp. 139–140) The Prefixes auto-, equi-, and iso- (pp. 159–160) The Prefixes sym-, syn-, and syl- (pp. 179–180) The Prefixes anti- and counter- (pp. 199–200)	The Prefixes inter-, intra-, and intro- (pp. 139–140) The Prefixes ambi- and para- (pp. 159–160) The Word Elements astro-, geo-, hydro-, -mar-, and -terra- (pp. 179–180) The Prefixes pan-, extra-, ultra-, and omni- (pp. 199–200)	The Word Elements archy-, -dem-, -ver-, and -cracy (pp. 139–140) The Prefixes bene-, eu-, and mal- (pp. 159–160) The Word Elements ante- and -ann- (pp. 179–180) The Word Elements hyper-, hypo-, and -dyn- (pp. 199–200)

Vocabulary

for Achievement

Fourth Course

Margaret Ann Ríchek

GREAT SOURCE
WILMINGTON, MA

Author

Margaret Ann Richek

Professor of Education Emerita, Northeastern Illinois University; consultant in reading and vocabulary study; author of The World of Words *(Houghton Mifflin)*

Classroom Consultants

Beth Gaby

English Chair, Carl Schurz High School, Chicago, Illinois

Chris Hausammann

Teacher of English, Central Mountain High School, Lock Haven, Pennsylvania

Malisa Cannon

Teacher of Language Arts, Desert Sky Middle School, Tucson, Arizona

Stephanie Saltikov-Izabal

Teacher of Reading and English, At-Risk Specialist, Huntington Beach High School, Huntington Beach, California

Patricia Melvin

District Secondary Reading Specialist, Duval County Public Schools, Jacksonville, Florida

Sean Rochester

Teacher of English, Parkway Central High School, St. Louis, Missouri

Acknowledgments

Editorial: Ruth Rothstein, Victoria Fortune, Dan Carsen, Amy Gilbert

Design and Production: Mazer Corporation

Text Design and Production: Mazer Creative Services

Illustrations: Chris Vallo/Mazer Creative Services; Barbara Samanich, Toby Williams of Wilkinson Studios, LLC; Jerry Hoare, Tim McWilliams, Jeff O'Conner, Ron Zalme of Langley Creative

Cover Design: Mazer Creative Services

Cover Photo: © John Downer/Getty Images & Mazer Creative Services

Definitions for the three hundred words taught in this textbook are based on Houghton Mifflin dictionaries—in particular, *The American Heritage High School Dictionary*—but have been abbreviated and adapted for instructional purposes.

All pronunciations are reproduced by permission from *The American Heritage Dictionary of the English Language, Fourth Edition,* copyright © 2000.

Printed in the United States of America

ISBN-13: 978-0-669-51758-3   ISBN-10: 0-669-51758-5

4 5 6 7 8 9 10 - DBH - 10 09

Contents

COMPLETE WORD LIST FOR FOURTH COURSE

abhor, 127
abject, 141
accredit, 147
acrimonious, 61
acronym, 1
adroit, 113
aegis, 47
affect, 33
affinity, 127
affix, 1
aggrandize, 21
alacrity, 187
amends, 47
analogous, 73
animosity, 127
antithesis, 73
apathy, 173
apprehensive, 7
ardent, 127
assail, 133
assent, 173
assertive, 27
asylum, 133
attenuate, 193
august, 101
austerity, 53
autocratic, 81
autonomy, 81
aversion, 153
avert, 153

banter, 67
beguile, 13
benevolent, 13
blasé, 113
brazen, 27
bulwark, 133

caricature, 67
caste, 81
categorical, 7
cede, 161
chastise, 61
citadel, 133
cliché, 113
clientele, 113
coinage, 1
colloquial, 1
commensurate, 73
complaisant, 27
composure, 187
concede, 161
conciliatory, 47
conclusive, 7
concurrent, 167
condemn, 93
condescend, 101
conducive, 47
congruence, 73
conjecture, 141
courier, 167
credence, 147
credential, 147
credibility, 147
creditable, 147

credulous, 148
creed, 148
culpable, 93
cursory, 167

debunk, 61
deceased, 161
decorum, 13
deference, 101
dejected, 141
demeanor, 13
depreciate, 53
depredation, 33
deprivation, 33
derogatory, 61
despot, 81
deviate, 73
diaphanous, 193
didactic, 41
dilatory, 121
diligence, 87
diminutive, 2
discredit, 148
discursive, 167
disdain, 127
disinterested, 34
disparage, 61
disparity, 74
diversify, 153
diversion, 153
docile, 27
droll, 67
dubious, 7

edify, 41
effect, 33
effulgent, 193
egress, 161
elucidate, 41
emigrate, 34
empathy, 173
enamor, 127
encumber, 193
ennui, 187
ensue, 181
entrepreneur, 113
ephemeral, 181
equity, 53
erudite, 41
esoteric, 42
estrange, 128
evanescent, 193
exonerate, 93
exorbitance, 21
extort, 93
extricate, 47

facetious, 67
fastidious, 87
feral, 14
feudal, 81
finicky, 87
flagrant, 107
flamboyant, 27
flippant, 67

forte, 114
fortitude, 133
frugal, 53
furtive, 107

gauche, 114
gradation, 161
gradient, 162
grandiose, 21
gratuitous, 21
grovel, 101

harass, 62
harbinger, 181
hegemony, 82
heterogeneous, 74
hilarity, 68
homogeneous, 74

ignoble, 14
imbue, 42
immigrate, 34
imminent, 181
imperturbable, 187
impetuous, 187
importune, 47
imprudent, 87
impugn, 62
inadvertently, 154
incite, 187
incontrovertible, 154
incorrigible, 93
incredulous, 148
incur, 167
incursion, 167
indeterminate, 8
indigent, 54
indoctrinate, 42
indolent, 188
inertia, 188
innuendo, 62
intemperate, 22
interim, 181
interject, 141
interminable, 182
intrepid, 28
invective, 62
invert, 154
invincible, 134
irreversible, 154

jettison, 141
jetty, 142
judicious, 87
jut, 142

kudos, 128

lackey, 101
languid, 121
latent, 107
lethargy, 121
ludicrous, 68

malfeasance, 94

mediate, 48
melancholy, 121
mellow, 28
meticulous, 88
metonymy, 2
mettle, 134
minutia, 88
mirth, 68
miscreant, 148
misdemeanor, 94
mitigate, 48
mores, 14
multifarious, 22
munificent, 54

naive, 114
nonchalant, 114
nuance, 74

objectionable, 142
oligarchy, 82
opulence, 22
ostensible, 107
oxymoron, 2

pacific, 28
palindrome, 2
palpable, 193
pandemonium, 188
pathetic, 173
pathology, 173
patronize, 48
pecuniary, 54
pedagogy, 42
pedantic, 42
pejorative, 128
perennial, 182
permeate, 194
pliant, 194
ponderous, 194
portmanteau word, 2
precarious, 8
precede, 34
precipitate, 182
precursor, 168
predecessor, 162
predominate, 102
presentiment, 174
proceed, 34
profligate, 22
projectile, 142
provincial, 14
provisional, 182
pundit, 42
purloin, 94

qualm, 8
quiescent, 121

recession, 54
recourse, 168
recurrent, 168
regress, 162
remunerate, 54
rendezvous, 114

renovate, 48
repose, 122
repugnance, 128
resilient, 134
retrospective, 182
revert, 154
ruffian, 94

salient, 107
satiate, 22
sensational, 174
sensibility, 174
sententious, 174
sentient, 174
sequester, 107
serenity, 188
slavish, 102
sloth, 122
slovenly, 88
solvent, 54
somnambulate, 122
soporific, 122
sovereign, 82
spoonerism, 2
stalwart, 134
stamina, 134
strident, 28
stupor, 122
subjugation, 102
subterfuge, 108
succor, 168
supercilious, 102
surfeit, 22
surreptitious, 108
sycophant, 102

tantamount, 74
tentative, 8
totalitarian, 82
trajectory, 142
transgress, 162
trepidation, 88

unabashed, 28
unequivocal, 8
uninterested, 34
unmindful, 88
unobtrusively, 108
unprecedented, 162
unscrupulous, 94
unseemly, 14
usurp, 82

vacillate, 8
vaunt, 108
vertigo, 154
vilify, 62
viscous, 194

whimsical, 68
wily, 14
witticism, 68

Our Evolving Language

WORD LIST

acronym	affix	coinage	colloquial	diminutive
metonymy	oxymoron	palindrome	portmanteau word	spoonerism

Modern English-speakers are constantly borrowing, changing, and inventing new words. Think of the sentence "Hip-hop bursting with funky jazz samples filled the room, as the laser read the digitally encoded disc." A hundred years ago, this would have been completely incomprehensible. The words in this lesson address some of the many ways our language continues to change.

affixing

1. **acronym** (ăk´rə-nĭm´) *noun* from Greek *acro,* "beginning" + *onym,* "word; name"
A word formed from the first letter of each word in a series
   • *PAC* is an **acronym** for *political action committee.*

   acronymic *adjective* *NAFTA* is the **acronymic** title for the *North American Free Trade Agreement.*

2. **affix** from Latin *ad,* "to" + *figere,* "to fasten"
   a. *noun* (ăf´ĭks´) A prefix or suffix
   • The word *reappearance* has two **affixes,** *re-* and *-ance.*
   b. *verb* (ə-fĭks´) To attach a part to the beginning or end of a word
   • We often **affix** *-ed* to a verb to form its past tense.
   c. *verb* (ə-fĭks´) To attach something
   • To help prevent birds from crashing into windows, **affix** noticeable stickers to the glass.

   > Remember that a *prefix* is attached to the beginning of a word, and a *suffix* is attached to the end.

3. **coinage** (koi´nĭj) *noun* from Latin *cuneus,* "wedge" (used to make coins)
   a. The invention of new words
   • The spread of computer technology has resulted in the **coinage** of words such as *blog* and *cyberculture.*
   b. An invented word or phrase
   • Another recent **coinage** is the verb *to google,* as in "I *googled* the author of the article to find out his background and credentials."
   c. The making of metal coins; metal currency
   • More zinc than copper is now used in the **coinage** of U.S. pennies.

4. **colloquial** (kə-lō´kwē-əl) *adjective* from *col-,* "together" + *loqui,* "to speak"
Typical of informal language usage; conversational
   • "Hi" and "What's up?" are **colloquial** expressions for "Hello" and "How are you?"

   colloquialism *noun* A "close call" is a **colloquialism** for a "narrow escape."

To ensure that students understand the format of the book, guide them through some of the entries. Students may need help locating the pronunciations, etymologies, or related word forms. Guide them through some of the exercises, as well. Also, have students think of examples for some of the terms, such as *colloquialisms, diminutives,* and *acronyms.*

5. diminutive (dĭ-mĭn´yə-tĭv) from Latin *deminuere*, "to lessen"

    a. *noun* A suffix that indicates small size, youth, familiarity, affection, or contempt
- Two common **diminutives** are *-ette* and *-let*.

    b. *noun* A nickname indicating affection or familiarity
- Did you know that *Peggy* is a **diminutive** of *Margaret?*

    c. *adjective* Extremely small; tiny
- The **diminutive** dollhouse furniture enchanted the youngsters.

> A word containing one of these suffixes, such as *kitchenette* or *booklet*, is also called a *diminutive.*

6. metonymy (mə-tŏn´ə-mē) *noun* from Greek *meta-*, "change" + *onym*, "name"

A figure of speech that substitutes a word with a different but closely associated word
- The sentence "Washington's official response was negative" includes a **metonymy;** the word *Washington* is substituted for *the U.S. government.*

metonymic *adjective* The **metonymic** expression "the hand that rocks the cradle" refers to a mother.

7. oxymoron (ŏk´sē-môr´ŏn´) *noun* from Greek *oxus*, "sharp" + *moros*, "foolish; dull"

An expression that contains contradictory terms
- A common **oxymoron** is "jumbo shrimp."

oxymoronic *adjective* Two examples of **oxymoronic** expressions are "good grief" and "fresh frozen."

> The plural of *oxymoron* is either *oxymora* or *oxymorons.*

8. palindrome (păl´ĭn-drōm´) *noun* from Greek *palin*, "again" + *dromos*, "running"

A word or an expression that is spelled the same backward and forward
- The words *rotor* and *civic* are **palindromes.**

9. portmanteau word (pôrt-măn´tō wûrd) *noun*

A word formed by combining the sounds and meanings of two different words
- *Chunnel*, a **portmanteau word** formed from *channel* and *tunnel*, is the name for the tunnel that runs underneath the English Channel.

> A *portmanteau* is a large, leather suitcase that opens into two compartments.

10. spoonerism (spōō´nə-rĭz´əm) *noun*

An often comical switching of the first sounds of two or more words
- "Lack of pies" is a **spoonerism** for "pack of lies."

WORD ENRICHMENT

Wonderland words

    Lewis Carroll, author of *Alice's Adventures in Wonderland* and its sequel, is famous for his inventive use of words. His poem *Jabberwocky,* which appears in the book *Through the Looking Glass and What Alice Found There,* is full of *portmanteau words*. The poem begins "'Twas brillig, and the slithy toves / Did gyre and gimble in the wabe; / All mimsy were the borogoves, / And the mome raths outgrabe." The word *slithy* is created from *lithe* and *slimy; mimsy* is a combination of *flimsy* and *miserable.* Another word in the poem, *chortle,* constructed from *chuckle* and *snort,* is now found in dictionaries of Standard English.

WRITE THE CORRECT WORD

Write the correct word in the space next to each definition.

metonymy   1. the use of a closely related word as a substitute

spoonerism   2. a comical switching of the first sounds of words

acronym   3. a word made from first letters

diminutive   4. a suffix indicating smallness

coinage   5. an invented word

palindrome   6. a word spelled the same backward and forward

oxymoron   7. an expression with contradictory words

portmanteau word   8. a word formed from two other words

affix   9. a prefix or suffix

colloquial   10. conversational

COMPLETE THE SENTENCE

Write the letter for the word that best completes each sentence.

b   1. An easy _____ to remember is *noon*.
     a. spoonerism   **b.** palindrome   **c.** oxymoron   **d.** coinage

a   2. The substitution of "sons of toil" for "tons of soil" is a(n) _____.
     a. spoonerism   **b.** diminutive   **c.** acronym   **d.** palindrome

d   3. The _____ -*less* and -*ful* have opposite meanings.
     a. coinages   **b.** acronyms   **c.** diminutives   **d.** affixes

c   4. Saying that the United States signed a treaty is a clear use of a _____.
     a. spoonerism   **b.** colloquialism   **c.** metonymy   **d.** coinage

d   5. Although _____ expressions are commonly used in everyday speech, they are usually not appropriate in formal writing.
     a. diminutive   **b.** affixed   **c.** oxymoronic   **d.** colloquial

b   6. Shakespeare is credited with the _____ of more than a thousand English words.
     a. metonymy   **b.** coinage   **c.** spoonerism   **d.** palindrome

c   7. *Slanguage* is a good example of a(n) _____.
     a. spoonerism   **b.** metonymy   **c.** portmanteau word   **d.** oxymoron

d   8. *MADD* is a(n) _____ for Mothers Against Drunk Driving.
     a. metonym   **b.** oxymoron   **c.** coinage   **d.** acronym

a   9. Taken literally, *silent scream* is a(n) _____.
     a. oxymoron   **b.** palindrome   **c.** diminutive   **d.** colloquialism

b   10. The _____ dachshund had the bark of a much larger dog.
     a. metonymic   **b.** diminutive   **c.** oxymoronic   **d.** coined

Challenge: The poet was always _____ new words, such as the _____ *craugh*, a combination of cry and laugh, meaning "to laugh so hard you cry."

c   **a.** spooning…diminutive   **b.** affixing…acronym   **c.** coining…portmanteau word

Our Changing Vocabulary

Few languages rival English in the richness, creativity, and flexibility of vocabulary. English has a long history of adopting words from other languages. Examples include *cliché* from French, *nadir* from Arabic, *pajamas* from Persian, and *kiosk* from Turkish.

(1) English *coinages* also arise from new technologies and from popular culture. Some recent additions to the English language include *cellie,* a cell phone, or a person who uses one in public; *bloviate,* to boast at length; and *drafter,* a racer who follows closely behind another to take advantage of reduced wind flow.

(2) Many additions to English vocabulary start as *colloquialisms.* Colloquialisms that are widely used are eventually entered into dictionaries and become part of Standard English. New words are popping up so fast that, each year, *Barnhart's Dictionary Companion* lists about 1,500 that haven't yet appeared in other reference sources.

(3) Adding *affixes* is another way to expand the vocabulary of the English language. Here are some *super-* examples: *superhero, superbug* (a strain of antibiotic-resistant bacteria), and *supercontinent* (a huge, ancient continent that some believe split into the seven continents that exist today). **(4)** The suffix *-y* is used to form *diminutives.* For example, take the first syllable of *Andrew* and add a *-y* to form *Andy.*

Many of our new words are shorter forms of old ones. We say *flu* instead of *influenza,* and *bus* instead of *autobus.* **(5)** *Acronyms* are another way of communicating by using abbreviations. *Scuba* comes from **s**elf-**c**ontained **u**nderwater **b**reathing **a**pparatus, while *radar* stands for **ra**dio **d**etecting **a**nd **r**anging. **(6)** *Portmanteau words* also make communication more efficient. The words *transfer* and *resistor* have been combined to give us *transistor. Motel* comes from *motor* and *hotel.*

(7) *Metonymies* allow us to speak and write figuratively about concepts. On a literal level, it is ridiculous to say that a pen is mightier than a sword. But when you consider the figurative intent of this phrase—that the "power of the written word" to inspire change is greater than the power of violence—it acquires new meaning. Shakespeare frequently used metonymies, as in his play *Julius Caesar,* when Marc Anthony says, "Friends, Romans, countrymen, *lend me your ears.*"

English also offers playful speakers and writers ample opportunity to amuse their audiences. **(8)** Reverend William Spooner was famous for a type of funny verbal mistake that became known as a *spoonerism.* The reverend had a tendency to switch sounds, often with comical results, as in "It is kisstomary to cuss the bride." **(9)** *Oxymorons* are another odd wrinkle in our language. Shakespeare used them effectively in lines such as "Parting is such sweet sorrow." You have probably used them, too. Have you ever said "exact estimate" or "pretty ugly"? **(10)** Finally, *palindromes* appear in many word puzzles. These can be as simple as *tot* and *Madam, I'm Adam,* or as long as the 17,259-word creation once made by a palindrome-generating computer program.

Backward or forward, English allows us to invent, experiment, and play with words, making it a versatile and dynamic language.

Each sentence below refers to a numbered sentence in the passage. Write the letter of the choice that gives the sentence a meaning that is closest to the original sentence.

____c____ **1.** English _____ also arise from new technologies and from popular culture.
   a. informal words   **b.** abbreviations   **c.** new words   **d.** nicknames

____b____ **2.** Many additions to English vocabulary start as _____.
   a. abbreviations   **b.** informal words   **c.** contradictions   **d.** sound-switches

____a____ **3.** Adding _____ is another way to expand the vocabulary of the English language.
   a. attachments   **b.** contradictions   **c.** nicknames   **d.** combinations

__c__ **4.** The suffix -*y* is used to form _____.
    a. slang   **b.** attachments   **c.** nicknames   **d.** abbreviations

__d__ **5.** _____ are another way of communicating by using abbreviations.
    a. Contradictions   **b.** Attachments   **c.** New words   **d.** First-letter words

__b__ **6.** _____ also make communication more efficient.
    a. New words   **b.** Combined words   **c.** Figurative words   **d.** Affectionate words

__d__ **7.** _____ allow us to speak and write figuratively about concepts.
    a. Slang words   **b.** Combinations   **c.** Attachments   **d.** Nonliteral substitutions

__a__ **8.** Reverend William Spooner was famous for a type of funny verbal mistake that became known as a(n) _____.
    a. sound-switch   **b.** backward word   **c.** attachment   **d.** self-contradiction

__c__ **9.** _____ are another odd wrinkle in our language.
    a. New words   **b.** Abbreviations   **c.** Contradictions   **d.** Nicknames

__d__ **10.** Finally, _____ words appear in many word puzzles.
    a. contradictory   **b.** attached   **c.** combined   **d.** backward-forward

Indicate whether the statements below are TRUE or FALSE according to the passage.

__F__ **1.** If a word is listed in *Barnhart's Dictionary Companion*, then it is accepted as Standard English.

__F__ **2.** Up until the last fifty years or so, English did not change much.

__T__ **3.** New words come into being as new needs and uses for them arise.

WRITING EXTENDED RESPONSES

Colloquial speech—including new words, *diminutives,* and *acronyms*—is increasingly used in formal-writing situations such as newspaper stories and magazine articles. Do you think this is an acceptable trend, or should only formal, Standard English be used in these settings? Write a three-paragraph persuasive essay explaining and defending your point of view. Your essay should contain at least two reasons for your position. Use at least three lesson words in your essay and underline them.

WRITE THE DERIVATIVE

Complete the sentence by writing the correct form of the word shown in parentheses. You may not need to change the form that is given.

__metonymic__ **1.** *Lend a hand* is a _____ expression meaning "to provide help." (*metonymy*)

__spoonerism__ **2.** "Wave the sails" is a _____ of the well-known environmental slogan used to encourage the protection of whales. (*spoonerism*)

portmanteau word	3.	The other day, I was trying to decide whether to say "fast" or "speedy," and I accidentally created a nonsensical _____: "feedy." (*portmanteau word*)
palindrome	4.	*A Man, a Plan, a Canal: Panama* is a _____ used as the title for a 1948 book by Leigh Mercer. (*palindrome*)
oxymoronic	5.	Some common examples of _____ expressions are "alone together," "virtual reality," and "a fine mess." (*oxymoron*)
diminutive	6.	The _____ of Daniel is *Danny*. (*diminutive*)
acronymic	7.	*NASA* is the _____ name of the U.S. government agency responsible for space exploration. (*acronym*)
coined	8.	At the age of nine, Milton Sirotta _____ the term *googol* to refer to the number 1 followed by one hundred zeros. (*coinage*)
affixes	9.	One of the longest words in the English language, *antidisestablishmentarianism*, has five _____. (*affix*)
colloquialism	10.	"Hang a right" is a _____ that means "turn right." (*colloquial*)

FIND THE EXAMPLE

Choose the answer that best describes the action or situation.

b   1. An example of a *metonym* for the planet Earth
     a. soil   **b.** globe   **c.** rock   **d.** moon

c   2. One kind of *affix*
     a. nix   **b.** Styx   **c.** suffix   **d.** matchsticks

a   3. The letter that appears at the beginning of a *palindrome* that ends with the letter *a*
     a. *a*   **b.** *b*   **c.** *c*   **d.** *z*

c   4. A *colloquial* expression
     a. Farewell.   **b.** Goodbye.   **c.** I'm outta here.   **d.** See you tomorrow.

d   5. *Spoonerism* of "ease my tears"
     a. fleas in years   **b.** tear my eyes   **c.** rip my fears   **d.** tease my ears

b   6. Something that is most *diminutive*
     a. moose   **b.** mouse   **c.** maple tree   **d.** mountain

a   7. A *portmanteau word* referring to a meal that is a combination of two other meals
     a. brunch   **b.** two meals   **c.** lunch   **d.** breakfast

b   8. The most recent *coinage*
     a. fire   **b.** e-mail   **c.** airplane   **d.** planet

d   9. An *oxymoron*
     a. ATM machine   **b.** University School   **c.** fit athlete   **d.** small fortune

d   10. *Acronym* for "Clean Energy Network Taskforce"
     a. EnvironmENT   **b.** Global Warming   **c.** TENT   **d.** CENT

Certainty and Uncertainty

WORD LIST

apprehensive	categorical	conclusive	dubious	indeterminate
precarious	qualm	tentative	unequivocal	vacillate

The quest for knowledge is, to a large degree, a quest for certainty. Institutions such as courts, universities, and science laboratories are dedicated to determining the truth. Individuals, too, have a strong desire to find concrete answers to their questions and doubts. The words in this lesson will help you discuss ideas of certainty and uncertainty.

1. **apprehensive** (ăp´rĭ-hĕn´sĭv) *adjective* from Latin *ad-*, "to" + *prehendere*, "grasp"
   Anxious or fearful about the future; uneasy
   • Many students are **apprehensive** about the first day of school.

   apprehension *noun* Despite his **apprehension,** Evelyn's father gave her the keys to his brand-new car.

> *Apprehension* can also mean "the capture or arrest of someone."

2. **categorical** (kăt´ĭ-gôr´ĭ-kəl) *adjective* from Greek *kategoria,* "accusation; charge"
   a. Without exception or qualification; absolute
   • His **categorical** denial of guilt left no room for doubt as to the plea that he would enter in court.
   b. Done according to types; arranged by categories
   • Knowing how organized he is, I was not surprised that his stamp collection has a **categorical** arrangement by country of issue.

   categorically *adverb* The teacher **categorically** refused to listen to the student's reason for being late to class.

categorical

3. **conclusive** (kən-klōō´sĭv) *adjective* from Latin *concludere,* "to end"
   Decisive; putting an end to doubt, question, or uncertainty
   • The medical test results were **conclusive:** Sally's operation had been successful.

4. **dubious** (dōō´bē-əs) *adjective* from Latin *dubitare,* "to doubt"
   Doubtful; uncertain; questionable as to quality or validity
   • The salesperson's claim—that the vacuum cleaner was so durable we would never need to buy another one—seemed **dubious.**

> The common phrase *dubious distinction* refers to being famous for something shameful.

Ask students to identify words in the list that deal with certainty (such as *categorical* and *conclusive*) and those that deal with uncertainty (such as *precarious* and *indeterminate*). Encourage students to explain their choices.

5. indeterminate (ĭn´dĭ-tûr´mə-nĭt) *adjective* from Latin *in-,* "not"
+ *determinare,* "to limit"
  a. Not capable of being determined or established; not precisely
    known
    • The antique amethyst necklace was of **indeterminate** age.
  b. Lacking clarity of precision; vague
    • The neighbors were disturbed by the developer's **indeterminate**
    answer regarding his plans for the newly purchased farmland.

6. precarious (prĭ-kâr´ē-əs) *adjective* from Latin *precari,* "to entreat"
  a. Dangerous; risky; lacking in security or stability
    • Realizing their situation was **precarious,** most people tried to stay
    in their homes during the political rebellion.
  b. Based on uncertain or questionable premises
    • To the average listener, his argument sounded reasonable, but
    knowledgeable listeners knew his conclusions were **precarious.**

> *Precarious* can also describe an object's lack of stability, as in "a *precarious* ladder."

7. qualm (kwäm) *noun*
A sense of doubt or uneasiness about a course of action
  • Since Janice rarely turned in assignments or paid attention in class,
  her teacher had no **qualms** about giving her a failing grade.

> *Qualms* often involve one's conscience, honor, or code of good behavior.

8. tentative (tĕn´tə-tĭv) *adjective* from Latin *tentare,* "to try"
Uncertain; not fully worked out or agreed upon; provisional
  • The two women could make only **tentative** plans to meet for dinner
  because they both had unpredictable work schedules.

9. unequivocal (ŭn´ĭ-kwĭv´ə-kəl) *adjective* from Old English *un-,*
"not" + Latin *equi-,* "equal" + *vocare,* "to call"
Perfectly clear; leaving no room for doubt or misunderstanding
  • Martin answered the question with an **unequivocal** "Yes!"

10. vacillate (văs´ə-lāt´) *verb* from Latin *vacillare,* "to waver"
  a. To swing indecisively from one opinion or action to another
    • I **vacillate** between choosing a career in medicine and pursuing
    my interest in music.
  b. To sway or hesitate in choice of actions or opinions
    • When the quarterback **vacillated** on the field, the coach lost
    confidence in his ability to lead the offense.

vacillation *noun* What the politician's opponents saw as **vacillation,**
his supporters saw as a reasonable revision of policy, based on new
evidence.

WORD ENRICHMENT

Singular or plural?

    Although the word *qualm* is defined here as a singular noun, it is most
often used as a plural in sentences such as "Her parents had no *qualms*
about allowing her to go to the movie with her friends," and "The band had
qualms about its song being used in a commercial."

WRITE THE CORRECT WORD

Write the correct word in the space next to each definition.

dubious	**1.** doubtful	apprehensive	**6.** nervous or uneasy
vacillate	**2.** to hesitate in choice of action or opinion	tentative	**7.** not fully worked out; provisional
qualm	**3.** a sense of doubt	categorical	**8.** absolute
precarious	**4.** dangerous; unstable	unequivocal	**9.** perfectly clear
indeterminate	**5.** vague; unclear	conclusive	**10.** decisive

COMPLETE THE SENTENCE

Write the letter for the word that best completes each sentence.

___c___ **1.** The critic didn't have any _____ about giving the horrible play a bad review.
    a. conclusions   **b.** precariousness   **c.** qualms   **d.** categories

___a___ **2.** We were surprised by our employer's _____ refusal to change any deadlines.
    a. categorical   **b.** tentative   **c.** apprehensive   **d.** dubious

___d___ **3.** That state has the _____ distinction of having the lowest voter turnout in the nation.
    a. categorical   **b.** precarious   **c.** conclusive   **d.** dubious

___d___ **4.** Unsure about whether I would have visitors from out of town, I _____ agreed to go to Jessica's dinner party.
    a. categorically   **b.** unequivocally   **c.** conclusively   **d.** tentatively

___b___ **5.** The results of the election were _____; Hiroshi won by a landslide.
    a. indeterminate   **b.** conclusive   **c.** dubious   **d.** apprehensive

___c___ **6.** At the ice-cream shop, Seth _____ between ordering chocolate or vanilla.
    a. had qualms   **b.** concluded   **c.** vacillated   **d.** apprehended

___a___ **7.** The fans showed their _____ support for the revered baseball team.
    a. unequivocal   **b.** indeterminate   **c.** precarious   **d.** dubious

___d___ **8.** The shy child was _____ about spending three weeks away from home while at camp.
    a. unequivocal   **b.** precarious   **c.** categorical   **d.** apprehensive

___d___ **9.** A rock climber who does not use the recommended safety gear could find herself in a(n) _____ situation.
    a. indeterminate   **b.** dubious   **c.** conclusive   **d.** precarious

___b___ **10.** It was obvious from Juan's _____ answer that he had not done his homework.
    a. categorical   **b.** indeterminate   **c.** conclusive   **d.** unequivocal

Challenge: At first, many of her colleagues were _____ about Sondra's hypothesis, but they changed their minds once they saw the _____ results of her experiments.
___c___   **a.** tentative…indeterminate   **b.** precarious…categorical   **c.** dubious…unequivocal

Lies: Are They Detectable?

Are you telling the truth? How do I know you're not lying? Much research has been devoted to answering questions such as these.

Researchers have found that people who are lying often provide hints about their dishonesty through their language and body movements. There are two signs of lying that have been well documented. **(1)** First, liars tend to *vacillate* in their positions or stories, indicating that they can't remember the last lie they told, or that they are telling a lie to cover another lie that is about to be exposed. They also tend to cover their mouths and avoid direct eye contact with listeners.

Other clues about lying are more subtle. **(2)** According to a study by physician Alan Hirsch, people making *dubious* statements often scratch their noses, as the stress of lying sends blood rushing to the nasal cavity, causing swelling and itching. People who are lying may also lean over, as though getting ready to flee the situation. In addition, they may use fewer contractions; for example, they tend to say "do not" instead of "don't." **(3)** Researchers theorize that liars try to cover up their *precarious* statements by using more formal language.

While such clues may be helpful in everyday situations, criminal investigations require more reliable methods for lie detection. The polygraph, or "lie detector" test, invented in 1921, brought technology into the quest for truth. **(4)** According to the theory underlying the machine's design, people who are lying are *apprehensive*, either about the wrongdoing that they are covering up, or about the possibility of being discovered. Fear and guilt usually result in physiological changes in breathing rate, pulse rate, and perspiration. The polygraph measures these three physical conditions. Unfortunately, there are ways to trick or manipulate the machine. **(5)** Some people experience no *qualms* about lying, so their physical responses do not change. Others try to use techniques to beat the test. There are even books available on this topic. In addition, the tests are fairly complicated to administer. Errors made by the technician giving the test can lead to inaccurate results. **(6)** Independent investigations have shown that polygraph tests do not give *unequivocal* results, but are accurate only 70 to 90 percent of the time.

(7) Because of these potential problems, many courts have decided that the results of polygraph tests are too *indeterminate* to be admitted as evidence. The state of California, for example, has outlawed the use of polygraph results in court, unless the defense agrees that the results can be admitted as evidence. **(8)** Federal law *categorically* forbids private-sector employers from requiring an employee or a job applicant to take a polygraph test. However, government agencies are allowed to require applicants or employees to take the tests.

Recently, Magnetic Resonance Imaging (MRI) has shown promise as a tool for detecting lies. This technology creates a digital picture of brain activity. Dr. Scott Faro and his team at Temple University School of Medicine have found that people's brain patterns are very different when they are lying than when they are telling the truth. Whereas telling the truth requires the use of four areas of the brain, lying requires seven areas. Dr. Faro and his colleagues believe that the MRI will eventually provide law enforcement with a technology that is not subject to tricks and is less susceptible to human error. **(9)** These claims remain *tentative*, however, until they are thoroughly investigated.

Perhaps the perfect lie detector will be developed soon. **(10)** In the meantime, we should bear in mind that our own judgments, and the results of current technologies, may not always be *conclusive* in detecting lies.

Each sentence below refers to a numbered sentence in the passage. Write the letter of the choice that gives the sentence a meaning that is closest to the original sentence.

___d___ **1.** Liars tend to _____ in their positions or stories.
    a. be uneasy   **b.** express doubt   **c.** be certain   **d.** swing back and forth

___c___ **2.** People making _____ statements often scratch their noses.
    a. fearful   **b.** public   **c.** doubtful   **d.** clear

___a___ **3.** Liars try to cover up their _____ statements by using more formal language.
    a. questionable   **b.** decisive   **c.** absolute   **d.** immoral

_a_   **4.** People who are lying are _____ about their wrongdoing.
       a. anxious   **b.** certain   **c.** unsure   **d.** conscious

_d_   **5.** Some people experience no _____ about lying.
       a. fear of the future   **b.** end to doubt   **c.** increased pulse   **d.** sense of uneasiness

_b_   **6.** Independent investigations have shown that polygraph tests do not give _____ results.
       a. doubtful   **b.** perfectly clear   **c.** well-tested   **d.** arranged by category

_b_   **7.** Because of these potential problems, many courts have decided that the results of polygraph tests are too _____ to be admitted as evidence.
       a. risky   **b.** unclear   **c.** absolute   **d.** unscientific

_d_   **8.** Federal law _____ forbids private-sector employers from requiring the test.
       a. with limits   **b.** temporarily   **c.** questionably   **d.** without exception

_c_   **9.** These claims remain _____ , however, until they are thoroughly investigated.
       a. secret   **b.** uneasy   **c.** uncertain   **d.** fearful

_b_   **10.** In the meantime, we should bear in mind that our own judgments, and the results of current technologies, may not always be _____ in detecting lies.
       a. uncertain   **b.** decisive   **c.** doubtful   **d.** objective

Indicate whether the statements below are TRUE or FALSE according to the passage.

_F_   **1.** Today's polygraph technology is completely reliable.

_T_   **2.** Most liars experience physiological changes when they are lying.

_T_   **3.** Generally speaking, lying requires more brain activity than does telling the truth.

FINISH THE THOUGHT

Complete each sentence so that it shows the meaning of the italicized word.

1. I am often *apprehensive* about _____ Answers will vary. _____

_____

2. I am *unequivocally* opposed to _____ Answers will vary. _____

_____

WRITE THE DERIVATIVE

Complete the sentence by writing the correct form of the word shown in parentheses. You may not need to change the form that is given.

precariously   **1.** The tightrope walker stepped _____ onto the high wire. *(precarious)*

qualms   **2.** Rosa had _____ about borrowing her sister's favorite sweater without permission. *(qualm)*

<u>conclusively</u> **3.** Research has _____ shown that fluoride helps prevent tooth decay. (*conclusive*)

<u>unequivocally</u> **4.** The Matisse exhibit was _____ the best art show I've ever seen. (*unequivocal*)

<u>apprehension(s)</u> **5.** The farther we ventured into the woods, the more our _____ grew. (*apprehensive*)

<u>tentatively</u> **6.** The toddler _____ dipped a toe into the cold water. (*tentative*)

<u>categorically</u> **7.** The author _____ refused to grant interviews to reporters. (*categorical*)

<u>dubiously</u> **8.** The children looked _____ at the magician when he promised to pull a rabbit out of his hat. (*dubious*)

<u>indeterminate</u> **9.** An _____ number of people were at the concert in the park. (*indeterminate*)

<u>vacillation</u> **10.** It was difficult to put up with the _____ of his moods. (*vacillate*)

FIND THE EXAMPLE

Choose the answer that best describes the action or situation.

_c_ **1.** An example of *conclusive* evidence at a crime scene
   a. a bag of money   **b.** some old clothes   **c.** DNA evidence   **d.** footprints

_c_ **2.** An event you would most likely feel *apprehensive* about
   a. a barbeque   **b.** a shopping spree   **c.** a final exam   **d.** a graduation party

_a_ **3.** Something a person is most likely to have *qualms* about doing
   a. lying to a friend   **b.** cooking a dinner   **c.** skating in a park   **d.** playing in a band

_b_ **4.** A *categorical* school rule
   a. no running   **b.** no cheating   **c.** no eating   **d.** no whispering

_d_ **5.** What you would most likely say if you were *dubious* about someone's statement
   a. Would I lie?   **b.** I'm anxious.   **c.** Of course!   **d.** Are you sure?

_c_ **6.** Something that is *indeterminate*
   a. length of a mile   **b.** distance to Mars   **c.** size of universe   **d.** today's weather

_d_ **7.** The way voters might view a political candidate who *vacillates* on his position
   a. opinionated   **b.** very sincere   **c.** likely to win   **d.** not trustworthy

_d_ **8.** A *precarious* place for a car
   a. in a parking lot   **b.** on a street   **c.** on a dirt road   **d.** hanging over a cliff

_c_ **9.** A *tentative* travel itinerary makes this easier to do
   a. make reservations   **b.** stick to a budget   **c.** change plans   **d.** relax and enjoy

_a_ **10.** An *unequivocal* answer to the question "May I go to the party?"
   a. Absolutely not.   **b.** Where is it?   **c.** We'll see.   **d.** Who else is going?

Behavíor

WORD LIST

beguile	benevolent	decorum	demeanor	feral
ignoble	mores	provincial	unseemly	wily

Say please and thank you! Share with your sister! Eat with your mouth closed! From the time we are children, we learn rules that govern our behavior. The words in this chapter will help you describe some aspects of behavior, such as maintaining *decorum,* adhering to social *mores,* and avoiding *unseemly* table manners.

1. **beguile** (bĭ-gīl´) *verb* from Middle English *be-,* "by" + *gilen,* "to deceive"
   a. To charm; to delight
      • The twelve-year-old **beguiled** his parents' guests with witty commentary about current events.
   b. To deceive skillfully
      • Don't let the friendly saleswoman **beguile** you into believing that the table is a valuable antique.

   beguiling *adjective* The adorable puppy's begging was so **beguiling** that we couldn't resist feeding him from the table.

2. **benevolent** (bə-něv´ə-lənt) *adjective* from Latin *bene-,* "good" + *velle,* "wish"
   a. Wishing to do good; kindly; characterized by helpful intentions
      • Breeding programs at many zoos have the **benevolent** goal of saving endangered species from extinction.
   b. Concerned with, or for the benefit of charity
      • In a **benevolent** act, Maggie gave all of her birthday money to a homeless shelter.

   benevolence *noun* Mark's **benevolence** shows in the many small deeds he does to help others.

3. **decorum** (dĭ-kôr´əm) *noun* from Latin *decor,* "beauty"
   Appropriateness of behavior; propriety
      • Diplomats must act with **decorum** or they risk offending foreign officials and jeopardizing international relations.

   decorous *adjective* The queen's **decorous** behavior contrasted sharply with the king's gruff manner.

4. **demeanor** (dĭ-mē´nər) *noun* from Old French *de-,* "completely" + *mener,* "to lead; conduct"
   The way one behaves or presents oneself; one's manner
      • Her carefree **demeanor** hid her deep anxiety about her mother's health.

The words in this list deal with behavior that is pleasant or well intentioned, such as *benevolent;* deceitful or unbecoming, such as *feral;* or neutral, such as *demeanor.* Ask students to classify words into these categories. Point out that some words, such as *beguile,* can be used positively or negatively. Ask students to explain their answers.

benevolent

The word *demean* can mean "to rob someone of dignity," usually through insults or criticism.

5. feral (fîr´əl) *adjective* from Latin *fera,* "wild animal"
   a. Wild and untamed; savage
   • The U.S. National Park System was established to ensure that
   wilderness areas remain **feral.**
   b. Having returned to an untamed state from domestication
   • The two **feral** cats in the shed scratched and hissed at the
   animal-shelter workers.

Feral can also refer to uncivilized human behavior.

6. ignoble (ĭg-nō´bəl) *adjective* from Latin *ig-,* "not" + *nobilis,* "noble"
   a. Mean, unethical, or dishonorable; not noble in character
   • The **ignoble** rider constantly whipped his gentle horse.
   b. Not of the nobility; common
   • Ancient laws forbade the prince from marrying a woman of
   ignoble birth.

7. mores (môr´āz´) *noun* from Latin *mores,* "customs"
   Accepted standards and customs of a social group
   • **Mores** of traditional southern society place great value on hospitality.

8. provincial (prə-vĭn´shəl) *adjective*
   a. Relating to areas that are far from large cities or capitals
   • The **provincial** governments controlled land use in their
   respective regions.
   b. Not sophisticated, fashionable, or informed; culturally limited
   • The **provincial** tourists were amazed by the hairstyles and clothing
   they saw in San Francisco.
   c. Limited or narrow in perspective
   • The **provincial** man didn't understand that there were billions of
   people in the world who did not share his belief system.

   province *noun* The slow pace of life in the **provinces** provided respite
   from the stress of the city.

   provincialism *noun* Mike was painfully aware of his **provincialism**
   whenever he spent time with the sophisticated European students.

Province also refers to a region of a country. Canada, for example, is divided into *provinces* (not states).

9. unseemly (ŭn-sēm´lē) *adjective* from Old English *un-,* "not"
   + Old Norse *soemr,* "fitting"
   Unfitting and inappropriate; grossly improper
   • It amazes me that some talk-show guests are willing to discuss their
   unseemly behavior on national television.

10. wily (wī´lē) *adjective* from Old Norse *vel,* "a trick"
   Cunning; full of trickery or intentions to deceive
   • The **wily** character Tom Sawyer not only tricked his friends into
   doing his work, but he also got them to pay for that "privilege."

   wiliness *noun* Known for their **wiliness,** the door-to-door salesmen
   of the past often deceived their customers.

WORD ENRICHMENT

Wily words

   Wily comes from the Old Norse word *vel,* which means "trick." Also
from this root is the word *wile,* which has a few different meanings. As a
noun, it means "a deceitful trick," but is generally used in the plural: She
had all the *wiles* of a skilled negotiator. As a verb, *wile* can mean either
"to entice" or "to pass agreeably."

WRITE THE CORRECT WORD

Write the correct word in the space next to each definition.

ignoble	**1.** dishonorable
wily	**2.** cunning
demeanor	**3.** one's manner
feral	**4.** untamed; wild
decorum	**5.** appropriateness of behavior

provincial	**6.** unsophisticated
unseemly	**7.** grossly improper
beguile	**8.** to charm
benevolent	**9.** with kind intentions
mores	**10.** accepted customs of a group

COMPLETE THE SENTENCE

Write the letter for the word that best completes each sentence.

___c___ **1.** Because of his _____ table manners, Jay was rarely invited to dinner parties.
    a. wily   **b.** demeanor   **c.** unseemly   **d.** benevolent

___a___ **2.** The _____ man was only kind to his elderly neighbor so that he could earn a place in her will.
    a. ignoble   **b.** feral   **c.** provincial   **d.** decorous

___d___ **3.** Eliana's happy and carefree _____ lifts the spirits of everyone around her.
    a. decorum   **b.** provincialism   **c.** wiliness   **d.** demeanor

___d___ **4.** The bus runs from the city center through several _____ towns.
    a. feral   **b.** ignoble   **c.** wily   **d.** provincial

___a___ **5.** Through clever arguments and shrewd bargaining, the _____ politician managed to gain the support of her colleagues.
    a. wily   **b.** feral   **c.** unseemly   **d.** decorous

___b___ **6.** _____ dictates that those entering a mosque must remove their shoes.
    a. Demeanor   **b.** Decorum   **c.** Provincialism   **d.** Benevolence

___b___ **7.** Every night, we hear the howling of the _____ dogs in the woods.
    a. ignoble   **b.** feral   **c.** benevolent   **d.** unseemly

___a___ **8.** Fascinated by ancient customs, the anthropologist explored the _____ of medieval societies by studying their writings and burial practices.
    a. mores   **b.** benevolence   **c.** demeanor   **d.** wiles

___c___ **9.** In a Greek myth about vanity, Narcissus was completely _____ by his own reflection.
    a. ignoble   **b.** provincial   **c.** beguiled   **d.** feral

___c___ **10.** Our _____ neighbor volunteers for several charitable organizations.
    a. ignoble   **b.** beguiling   **c.** benevolent   **d.** wily

Challenge: The _____ dinner guest, knowing little about the _____ of high society, was embarrassed to discover that using the wrong fork was considered unseemly.
___a___   **a.** provincial…mores   **b.** feral…ignobility   **c.** ignoble…provincialism

Medieval Manners

When we think of medieval times in Europe, we usually picture kings, queens, knights, jesters, and jousts. **(1)** But we might also imagine what are now seen as rather *unseemly* table manners.

Today, etiquette guides warn against putting your elbows on the table or speaking with your mouth full. But those who campaigned for good manners during the late Middle Ages wrestled with far greater challenges. "Courtesy books" from the years 1000 to 1500 instructed diners to keep their fingers out of their ears and noses, not to spit across the table, and not to put their thumbs in their drinks.

(2) Some historians theorize that these courtesy guides do not reflect the *mores* of the entire society. The nobility most likely adhered to higher standards of etiquette. **(3)** The books, the researchers argue, may have been aimed at *provincial* folk who wanted to be accepted into polite society.

But other experts think that the texts paint a hair-raising picture of the table manners of the era. Why, they ask, would warnings against such behaviors as scratching oneself at the table be written, if they were not common practice? **(4)** Besides, the experts point out, even if all the rules were widely followed, what passed for *decorum* in the Middle Ages would shock most diners today.

Seated at long wooden tables, diners commonly tossed bones to the floor and spat out fruit pits. For dogs and cats, though, dinnertime was paradise. **(5)** Unlike *feral* animals, pets ate what people ate. **(6)** No *wily* schemes were needed to nab a scrap of food. Pets were allowed in the dining rooms to scavenge for leftovers that had been tossed onto the floors. Still, some guides advised that, during dinner, it was impolite to pet the animals scrounging at one's feet.

Knives were used for cutting and spoons were used for eating soup, but forks were not commonly used until the 1600s, so diners ate everything, except soup, with their fingers. There was a strong emphasis on keeping one's knife clean, though the guide books advised diners to wipe their knives on a piece of bread, not the tablecloth.

Washbasins were usually set near the tables, and each diner took a turn washing up before the meal. But even this well-meaning attempt to promote sanitation required some guidance. In 1235, the Bishop of Lincoln advised that, "if you spit while washing, wisest is to spit outside the bowl." **(7)** Of course, today, spitting anywhere in a host's dining room would be considered highly *ignoble* behavior and would probably earn the offender a quick trip to the door!

Order did reign when it came to seating, though. Important guests were put at the best places, meaning above the saltcellar (a dish for holding and dispensing salt) at the middle of the table. **(8)** Less important visitors were seated "below the salt" and were expected to maintain a respectful *demeanor* toward their superiors. **(9)** No matter how *beguiling* a guest might be, stepping out of place in the social order was frowned upon.

Instead of using plates, diners ate off thick slices of stale bread called trenchers. It was impolite to eat one's trencher. Guests were expected to leave their sauce-soaked bread on the table. **(10)** In an act of *benevolence*, the used trenchers were gathered at the end of the meal and given to the poor, who were waiting outside.

Each sentence below refers to a numbered sentence in the passage. Write the letter of the choice that gives the sentence a meaning that is closest to the original sentence.

___d___ **1.** But we might also imagine what are now seen as _____ table manners.
   a. courtly   **b.** unusual   **c.** primitive   **d.** inappropriate

___a___ **2.** These courtesy guides do not reflect the _____ of the entire society.
   a. social customs   **b.** moral laws   **c.** good intentions   **d.** table manners

___d___ **3.** The books, the researchers argue, may have been aimed at _____ folk.
   a. sophisticated   **b.** well-intentioned   **c.** well-behaved   **d.** culturally unaware

_____c_____ **4.** What passed for _____ in the Middle Ages would shock most diners today.
    a. rudeness   **b.** charitable acts   **c.** suitable behavior   **d.** standards of ethics

_____b_____ **5.** Unlike _____ animals, pets ate what people ate.
    a. jungle   **b.** wild   **c.** farm   **d.** domesticated

_____a_____ **6.** No _____ schemes were needed to nab a scrap of food.
    a. tricky   **b.** inappropriate   **c.** charming   **d.** unsophisticated

_____c_____ **7.** Today, spitting anywhere in a host's dining room would be considered highly _____ behavior.
    a. appropriate   **b.** shocking   **c.** dishonorable   **d.** tricky

_____d_____ **8.** Less important visitors were seated "below the salt" and were expected to maintain a respectful _____ toward their superiors.
    a. smile   **b.** kindness   **c.** flattery   **d.** manner

_____a_____ **9.** No matter how _____ a guest might be, stepping out of place in the social order was frowned upon.
    a. charming   **b.** inappropriate   **c.** sophisticated   **d.** unworthy

_____b_____ **10.** In an act of _____, the used trenchers were gathered at the end of the meal and given to the poor, who were waiting outside.
    a. custom   **b.** goodwill   **c.** trickery   **d.** good manners

Indicate whether the statements below are TRUE or FALSE according to the passage.

_____F_____ **1.** In the Middle Ages, people attending banquets could sit wherever they wanted.

_____T_____ **2.** In the Middle Ages, spitting on the floor was acceptable behavior during meals.

_____T_____ **3.** The passage indicates that standards of behavior change over time.

WRITING EXTENDED RESPONSES

"Courtesy books" advised people on the *mores* of the Middle Ages. Suppose that you are writing a manual on table manners for a modern audience. In an expository essay, address at least two types of manners that you think are important. Describe how you think people should or should not behave at the table. Your essay should be at least three paragraphs long. Use at least three lesson words in your essay and underline them.

WRITE THE DERIVATIVE

Complete the sentence by writing the correct form of the word shown in parentheses. You may not need to change the form that is given.

_____decorous_____ **1.** At the coronation ceremony, everyone behaved in a _____ manner. (*decorum*)

_____ignobly_____ **2.** The baron behaved _____ when he sold the property and expelled the peasants, who had farmed the land for generations. (*ignoble*)

provincialism	**3.** The _____ of the professor's views surprised his colleagues. (*provincial*)
unseemly	**4.** The girl's _____ behavior at the party embarrassed her mother. (*unseemly*)
mores	**5.** Nicolas was eager to learn more about the _____ of South Pacific island societies. (*mores*)
benevolently	**6.** The police officer smiled _____ and asked the crying boy if he was lost. (*benevolent*)
feral	**7.** The _____ goats had survived in the wild for generations. (*feral*)
wiliness	**8.** Despite his _____, the coyote in the cartoon can never outwit the roadrunner. (*wily*)
demeanor	**9.** She maintains a calm _____, even in stressful situations. (*demeanor*)
beguiling	**10.** The _____ music captivated the entire audience. (*beguile*)

FIND THE EXAMPLE

Choose the answer that best describes the action or situation.

__c__   **1.** A quality most likely to be *beguiling*
    a. dishonesty   **b.** cruelty   **c.** humor   **d.** jealousy

__c__   **2.** An example of *decorum* while attending a lecture
    a. restless stretching   **b.** angry shouting   **c.** attentive silence   **d.** joyful dancing

__b__   **3.** An example of *ignoble* behavior
    a. attending a court   **b.** insulting an elder   **c.** giving to charity   **d.** holding open a door

__d__   **4.** An animal often characterized as *wily*
    a. mule   **b.** pig   **c.** chicken   **d.** fox

__d__   **5.** A *benevolent* act
    a. practicing piano   **b.** studying for a test   **c.** making your bed   **d.** visiting a sick relative

__a__   **6.** Possible topic of a paper on nineteenth-century American *mores*
    a. rules of dating   **b.** political parties   **c.** utopian ideals   **d.** advances in medicine

__c__   **7.** Most likely to be found in a *provincial* area
    a. traffic   **b.** smog   **c.** tranquility   **d.** skyscrapers

__d__   **8.** A person most likely to deal with a *feral* animal
    a. accountant   **b.** child   **c.** pet-store owner   **d.** animal-control officer

__b__   **9.** Behavior that would be *unseemly* at a dinner party
    a. eating slowly   **b.** sneezing on food   **c.** reciting a poem   **d.** passing the peas

__d__   **10.** Description of someone with a friendly *demeanor*
    a. sarcastic   **b.** hard-working   **c.** fashionable   **d.** easy to talk to

Using the Dictionary

Using Synonym Paragraphs

Words with similar meanings, such as *kind, benevolent, gracious,* and *compassionate,* are called *synonyms.* Each of these four adjectives describes a person who shows concern for others. However, synonyms often have slight differences in meaning. *Kind* describes an individual who is considerate of and sympathetic to others. *Benevolent* describes one who is charitable, while *gracious* suggests a courteous, warm manner. Finally, *compassionate* describes someone who feels pity for others.

Strategies

Many dictionaries have *synonym paragraphs* that differentiate among the related synonyms in a cluster. First, the paragraph explains the similarities in meaning. Then, the small but important differences in the meanings of the words are given. A synonym paragraph usually appears at the end of the entry for the most common word in the cluster. The paragraph is usually labeled "synonyms" or "syns" in boldface type. You can use these paragraphs to choose the best word when you are writing. Or they can help you to expand and refine your vocabulary.

Below is a synonym paragraph for *vent.* Read it and then answer the question below. As you read it, note that example sentences are included to help you understand differences in shades of meaning. These are printed in italics. If authors have been quoted, their names are enclosed in parentheses.

SYNONYMS *vent, express, utter, voice, air* These verbs mean to give outlet to thoughts or emotions. To *vent* is to unburden oneself of a strong pent-up emotion: *"She was jealous…and glad of any excuse to vent her pique"* (Edward G.E.L. Bulwer-Lytton). *Express* refers to both verbal and nonverbal communication: *"expressing emotion in the form of art"* (T.S. Eliot). *Utter* involves vocal expression: *"The words were uttered in the hearing of Montezuma"* (William Hickling Prescott). *Voice* denotes the expression of an outlook or viewpoint: *voiced her satisfaction with the verdict.* To *air* is to show off one's feelings, beliefs, or ideas: *They aired their differences during dinner.*

Read the following sentence and try to determine the best word to use from the synonyms above.

Her hand movements _____ her sentiments.

The best word would be *express,* since only this word involves nonverbal communication.

Practice

Read the synonym paragraphs below. Then decide which of the italicized synonyms best fits into each sentence. Write your choice on the line labeled "Best synonym."

SYNONYMS *fast, rapid, swift, fleet, speedy, quick, hasty, expeditious* These adjectives refer to something marked by great speed. *Fast* and *rapid* are often used interchangeably, though *fast* is more often applied to the person or thing in motion, and *rapid* to the activity or movement involved: *a fast runner; rapid strides. Swift* suggests smoothness and sureness of movement (*a swift current*), and *fleet* lightness of movement (*The cheetah is the fleetest of animals*). *Speedy* refers to velocity (*a speedy train*) or to promptness or hurry (*a speedy resolution to the problem*). *Quick* most often applies to what takes little time or to what is prompt: *a quick snack; your quick reaction. Hasty* implies hurried action (*a hasty visit*) and often a lack of care or thought (*regretted the hasty decision*). *Expeditious* suggests rapid efficiency: *sent the package by the most expeditious means.*

SYNONYMS *intelligent, bright, brilliant, knowing, quick-witted, smart, intellectual* These adjectives mean having or showing mental keenness.

Intelligent usually implies the ability to cope with new problems and to use the power of reasoning and inference effectively: *The intelligent math students excelled in calculus. Bright* implies quickness or ease in learning: *The bright child learned the alphabet quickly. Brilliant* suggests unusually impressive mental acuteness: "*The dullard's envy of brilliant men is always assuaged by the suspicion that they will come to a bad end*" (Max Beerbohm). *Knowing* implies the possession of knowledge, information, or understanding: *Knowing collectors bought all the auctioned paintings. Quick-witted* suggests mental alertness and prompt response: *quick-witted emergency medical staff. Smart* refers to quick intelligence and often a ready capability for taking care of one's own interests: *Smart lawyers can effectively manipulate juries. Intellectual* implies the capacity to grasp difficult or abstract concepts: *intellectual philosophers.*

1. Lee proposed a(n) (*expeditious, fleet*) way of conducting the debate that was both fair to everyone and sensitive to the time limits.

   Best synonym _____**expeditious**_____

2. The (*bright, knowing*) sixteen-year-old was easily able to learn the principles of calculus.

   Best synonym _____**bright**_____

3. The transportation service was known for its (*rapid, hasty*) service.

   Best synonym _____**rapid**_____

4. The (*intelligent, quick-witted*) soldier immediately changed his platoon's route when he saw that the enemy was waiting to ambush them.

   Best synonym _____**quick-witted**_____

5. Though the restaurant's food was good, the service was a bit (*fast, hasty*).

   Best synonym _____**hasty**_____

6. The (*bright, brilliant*) boy graduated from college at the age of twelve and had a Ph.D. by the time he was fifteen.

   Best synonym _____**brilliant**_____

7. We knew Harry was a (*rapid, fast*) runner, but were surprised he won the race.

   Best synonym _____**fast**_____

8. My (*intellectual, bright*) father enjoys spending time in his study comparing the literary traditions of Germany and France.

   Best synonym _____**intellectual**_____

Excess

WORD LIST

aggrandize	exorbitance	grandiose	gratuitous	intemperate
multifarious	opulence	profligate	satiate	surfeit

Have you ever eaten an entire chocolate cake in one sitting? Or have you spent an entire day lounging around, doing nothing? These are examples of what might be considered excess. The vocabulary in this lesson will give you additional ways to understand and express this concept.

1. **aggrandize** (ə-grăn′dīz′) *verb* from Latin *ad-*, "to" + *grandire*, "large"
   a. To make greater in power, influence, stature, or reputation
   • Sheldon **aggrandized** his business by acquiring another company.
   b. To exaggerate, or make something seem greater than it is
   • Roberta **aggrandized** her accomplishments by claiming that she was the top seller in the company.

   aggrandizement *noun* Tall tales, such as those about the giant lumberjack Paul Bunyan, developed as a result of the **aggrandizement** of stories passed down over many generations.

   > The hyphenated word *self-aggrandizement* is used quite commonly.

2. **exorbitance** (ĭg-zôr′bĭ-təns) *noun* from Latin *ex-*, "out of" + *orbita*, "path"
   Extreme, unreasonable expense or price; being beyond reasonable or proper limits
   • My dad was shocked by the **exorbitance** of the prices at the fancy French restaurant.

   exorbitant *adjective* The newspaper editorial criticized banks that charged farmers **exorbitant** interest rates to borrow money during the drought.

   > Point out that *exorbitance, opulence,* and *profligate* deal with excessive expenditures of money.

3. **grandiose** (grăn′dē-ōs′) *adjective* from Latin *grandis*, "great"
   a. Trying to seem important; characterized by pretended grandeur
   • Mario's **grandiose** talk of his high-powered connections in Hollywood couldn't hide the fact that he was a struggling actor.
   b. Grand; magnificent in size, beauty or scope; impressive
   • Perry admired the **grandiose** doorway of the mansion, with its huge, carved pillars and ornate stonework.

   grandiosity *noun* Coworkers got tired of the **grandiosity** of their manager, who boasted that the company president listened only to him.

grandiose

4. **gratuitous** (grə-tōō′ĭ-təs) *adjective* from Latin *gratis*, "free"
   Unnecessary; unjustified
   • According to the critic, the film was filled with **gratuitous** violence that served no purpose in the plot.

   > Although *gratuitous* can also mean "free; without cost," the word *gratis* is more commonly used to express this meaning.

5. **intemperate** (ĭn-tĕm′pər-ĭt) *adjective* from Latin *in-*, "not" + *temperare*, "to temper; to moderate"
Excessive; lacking moderation
- Mom tried to discourage Luz's **intemperate** consumption of chocolate.

intemperance *noun* Steven's **intemperance** as a sports fan was evidenced by the amount of his income that he spent on tickets and memorabilia.

6. **multifarious** (mŭl′tə-fâr′ē-əs) *adjective* from Latin *multifariam*, "in many places"
Having great variety; diverse
- Alicia's **multifarious** talents include acting, writing, playing the piano, and directing.

7. **opulence** (ŏp′yə-ləns) *noun* from Latin *opulentus*, "rich; wealthy"
a. Wealth; affluence
- We were astonished by the **opulence** of King Louis XIV's palaces at Versailles.
b. Great abundance, often to excess; lavishness
- The **opulence** of the buffet was overwhelming; we didn't know where to begin.

opulent *adjective* Andrew Lloyd Weber's **opulent** musical compositions are often filled with elaborate orchestration.

8. **profligate** (prŏf′lĭ-gĭt) *adjective* from Latin *profligare*, "to ruin"
Recklessly wasteful; wildly extravagant
- Shareholders were shocked to learn that the **profligate** executive had spent three million dollars on his wife's birthday party.

profligacy *noun* Reporters criticized the movie star's **profligacy** when she bought a new gown for a hundred thousand dollars.

> *Profligate* can also be used as a noun meaning "a reckless or an extravagant consumer."

9. **satiate** (sā′shē-āt′) *verb* from Latin *satis*, "sufficient"
To fully satisfy an appetite or a desire
- The enormous picnic lunch left me completely **satiated.**

10. **surfeit** (sûr′fĭt) from Old French *surfaire*, "to overdo"
a. *noun* An excessive amount
My Internet search provided such a **surfeit** of information that I had to spend hours combing through it all.
b. *verb* To feed or supply to excess or disgust; to overindulge
- Parents who **surfeit** their children with food run the risk of encouraging bad eating habits.

WORD ENRICHMENT

A prefix that goes "above and beyond"

The prefix *sur-*, found in *surfeit*, comes from Old French and means "over; above; beyond." This prefix is used in such words as *surtax, surmount, surpass, surveillance,* and *surname.* The twentieth-century artistic movement *surrealism* was named for the tendency of its artists to depict subject matter that is "above and beyond" reality. This style of art is marked by fantastic images and the inclusion of seemingly unrelated subjects. *Surrealism* is also found in literary and theatrical works.

WRITE THE CORRECT WORD

Write the correct word in the space next to each definition.

__multifarious__ **1.** diverse

__intemperate__ **2.** lacking moderation

__satiate__ **3.** to fully satisfy

__exorbitance__ **4.** extreme expense

__grandiose__ **5.** trying to seem important

__profligate__ **6.** wildly extravagant

__opulence__ **7.** great abundance

__surfeit__ **8.** to overindulge

__aggrandize__ **9.** to exaggerate

__gratuitous__ **10.** unnecessary; unjustified

COMPLETE THE SENTENCE

Write the letter for the word that best completes each sentence.

__b__ **1.** Fearing widespread panic, the public health official cautioned reporters not to _____ the minor outbreak of the disease.
   a. surfeit   **b.** aggrandize   **c.** profligate   **d.** satiate

__c__ **2.** Chantal's _____ spending habits got her deep into debt.
   a. satiated   **b.** grandiose   **c.** profligate   **d.** multifarious

__d__ **3.** A long and varied police report listed the convict's _____ criminal activities.
   a. satiated   **b.** exorbitant   **c.** opulence   **d.** multifarious

__c__ **4.** I refuse to pay such a(n) _____ price for a pair of shoes.
   a. grandiose   **b.** aggrandized   **c.** exorbitant   **d.** opulent

__a__ **5.** The billionaire built a _____ home so large that it overshadowed all the other houses in the neighborhood.
   a. grandiose   **b.** multifarious   **c.** surfeit   **d.** satiated

__d__ **6.** The antique furniture and fine rugs reflected the homeowners' _____.
   a. aggrandizement   **b.** intemperance   **c.** profligacy   **d.** opulence

__b__ **7.** There was such a(n) _____ of grain that it didn't all fit in the farmer's grain silos.
   a. exorbitance   **b.** surfeit   **c.** intemperance   **d.** profligacy

__b__ **8.** After guzzling the entire quart of juice, my thirst was finally _____.
   a. aggrandized   **b.** satiated   **c.** intemperate   **d.** gratuitous

__a__ **9.** Jamie has a(n) _____ appetite for sushi; she can eat one plateful after another.
   a. intemperate   **b.** opulent   **c.** satiated   **d.** multifarious

__c__ **10.** The long-winded professor threw some _____ personal anecdotes into her lecture.
   a. profligate   **b.** intemperate   **c.** gratuitous   **d.** exorbitant

Challenge: The press delighted in revealing the latest _____ expenditure of the _____ rock star in his endless efforts at self-aggrandizement.
__c__   **a.** exorbitant…surfeited   **b.** intemperate…satiated   **c.** gratuitous…profligate

Not Just a Fashion Statement

What object has served as a fashion statement, a symbol of liberation, and a weapon? Give up? It's that lovely accessory, the hatpin. **(1)** At the height of their popularity, between 1830 and 1920, hatpins were used for these *multifarious* purposes.

English women seemed to have had a special affection for hatpins. At first, the pins were merely functional items that held one's hat in place. **(2)** But in the 1800s, as women's hats grew larger and more *opulent,* so did the pins that secured them. **(3)** Handmade, *exorbitantly* priced pins, as long as fourteen inches, were fashioned from jade, silver, and gold and decorated with jewels. **(4)** Wearing fancy hatpins, like wearing expensive jewelry, soon became a method of *aggrandizing* one's social standing. **(5)** And like other symbols of *grandiosity,* they were criticized.

(6) Because these handmade accessories took a long time to produce, demand could not be *satiated* by craftsmen in Britain. So women began to buy pins imported from France. **(7)** By the mid-nineteenth century, alarmed by what it considered a *surfeit* of foreign imports, the British Parliament passed a law that limited the sale of hatpins to the first two days of January. This may have been the origin of the term *pin money,* or money saved for extra expenses. Women saved pin money all year to buy the expensive hatpins. In 1832, the invention of an automatic pin-making machine brought down the prices of most pins. These lower prices led to the pins' increased popularity among most of the classes, not just the wealthy.

Unlikely as it seems, hatpins also became a symbol of women's liberation. Before hatpins came into use, women were forced to fasten their hats, or bonnets, with ribbons tied under their chins. Eager to free themselves from the nuisance of ribbons, more and more women wore decorated hatpins. **(8)** This accessory, once considered an expenditure of the *profligate,* became a mark of freedom.

Then, in the early 1900s, as labor rights activism and the women's suffrage (voting rights) movement became popular, hatpins took on yet another purpose—that of a weapon. Women had long been slyly advised that their hatpins could be used for self-defense. Soon, determined women with both political agendas and hatpins were considered especially dangerous. In 1908, a British judge banned hatpins from his courtroom, afraid that the women might use them as weapons.

(9) Was this simply a *gratuitous* insult to women who were attempting to gain the right to vote, or was the threat real? Some reports indicate that hatpins could, indeed, be effective weapons. In one incident in Australia, a seventy-three-year-old woman, named Emma Miller, led a group of women on a march to help organize unions. The police attacked the women, who defended themselves with umbrellas and hatpins. **(10)** In what was, perhaps, an *intemperate* moment, Mrs. Miller dug her hatpin into the horse of the police commissioner, who was thrown from his horse and thereafter walked with a limp.

As luxuries, symbols of liberty, and weapons, hatpins have had a variety of uses. Today, however, they are as out of fashion as the hats they once held on women's heads. Now, they are mainly collector's items.

Each sentence below refers to a numbered sentence in the passage. Write the letter of the choice that gives the sentence a meaning that is closest to the original sentence.

____d____ **1.** At the height of their popularity, hatpins were used for these _____ purposes.
    a. fashionable   **b.** excessive   **c.** outrageous   **d.** diverse

____c____ **2.** But as women's hats grew larger and more _____, so did the pins that secured them.
    a. stylish   **b.** enormous   **c.** lavish   **d.** awkward

____a____ **3.** Handmade, _____ priced pins, as long as fourteen inches, were fashioned from jade, silver, and gold, and decorated with jewels.
    a. outrageously   **b.** reasonably   **c.** unfairly   **d.** uniformly

___d___ **4.** Wearing fancy hatpins soon became a method of _____ one's social standing.
   a. intermingling   **b.** wasting   **c.** fitting in   **d.** making greater

___d___ **5.** Like other symbols of _____, they were criticized.
   a. silly luxury   **b.** wasteful spending   **c.** high fashion   **d.** seeming importance

___a___ **6.** Demand could not be _____ by craftsmen in Britain.
   a. satisfied   **b.** wasted   **c.** exceeded   **d.** justified

___b___ **7.** Alarmed by what it considered a(n) _____ of foreign imports, the British Parliament passed a law that limited the sale of hatpins to the first two days of January.
   a. expense   **b.** excess   **c.** influence   **d.** limitation

___d___ **8.** This accessory was once considered an expenditure of the _____.
   a. average consumer   **b.** rich and famous   **c.** fashion conscious   **d.** recklessly wasteful

___a___ **9.** Was this simply a(n) _____ insult to women, or was the threat real?
   a. unjustified   **b.** mean   **c.** huge   **d.** exaggerated

___d___ **10.** In what was, perhaps, a(n) _____ moment, Mrs. Miller dug her hatpin into the horse of the police commissioner.
   a. defensive   **b.** strategic   **c.** magnificent   **d.** uncontrolled

Indicate whether the statements below are TRUE or FALSE according to the passage.

___T___ **1.** Women sometimes used hatpins as a form of self-defense.

___F___ **2.** Only the very wealthy wore hatpins.

___T___ **3.** Hatpins were seen as symbols of liberty because they freed women from a more constricting style of hat.

FINISH THE THOUGHT

Complete each sentence so that it shows the meaning of the italicized word.

1. An *exorbitant* expenditure might be _____ **Answers will vary.**

_____

2. An *opulent* home might have _____ **Answers will vary.**

_____

WRITE THE DERIVATIVE

Complete the sentence by writing the correct form of the word shown in parentheses. You may not need to change the form that is given.

__satiated__ **1.** We were all _____ after the five-course meal. *(satiate)*

__intemperance__ **2.** When it came to video games, Connor's _____ forced his parents to set limits on how often he could play them. *(intemperate)*

profligacy	**3.**	The loan officer distrusted customers who were prone to _____. (*profligate*)
exorbitant	**4.**	We couldn't imagine who would pay the _____ price of $10,000 for a bicycle. (*exorbitance*)
aggrandizement	**5.**	The fisherman's _____ of his prize catch continued with each telling of the story, until the fish became bigger than a small boat. (*aggrandize*)
gratuitous	**6.**	The movie would have been much better if the director had cut all the _____ scenes. (*gratuitous*)
surfeit	**7.**	When only half of the invited guests showed up at the party, we were left with a _____ of food. (*surfeit*)
grandiosity	**8.**	C. J.'s _____ in talking about his royal ancestors annoyed his friends rather than impressing them. (*grandiose*)
multifarious	**9.**	Lorraine was promoted to office manager because of her work ethic and _____ skills. (*multifarious*)
opulent	**10.**	Sigalle was dazzled by the _____ interior of the theater. (*opulence*)

FIND THE EXAMPLE

Choose the answer that best describes the action or situation.

d   **1.** Of the ones listed, the most *grandiose* structure
     a. hut   **b.** grocery store   **c.** townhouse   **d.** skyscraper

b   **2.** A *gratuitous* part of a report
     a. introduction   **b.** joke   **c.** conclusion   **d.** supporting details

d   **3.** The way to most effectively *aggrandize* your position in school
     a. do homework   **b.** clean erasers   **c.** study harder   **d.** become class president

d   **4.** An *exorbitant* price for a pair of blue jeans
     a. $10   **b.** $20   **c.** $35   **d.** $350

c   **5.** A meal that would probably *satiate* a hungry teenager
     a. three crackers   **b.** an apple   **c.** two hamburgers   **d.** a scoop of ice cream

d   **6.** Something a musician with *multifarious* skills might be able to do
     a. sing opera   **b.** compose a song   **c.** play a solo   **d.** play several instruments

a   **7.** A place you would most likely find *opulence*
     a. castle   **b.** factory   **c.** office building   **d.** community center

c   **8.** Something a *profligate* would most likely collect
     a. stamps   **b.** baseball cards   **c.** sports cars   **d.** teapots

b   **9.** An *intemperate* reaction to a simple criticism
     a. shrug   **b.** lawsuit   **c.** silence   **d.** sneer

b   **10.** The likely result of a *surfeit* of skilled workers
     a. prices go up   **b.** wages go down   **c.** jobs stay the same   **d.** profits go down

Boldness and Mildness

WORD LIST

assertive	brazen	complaisant	docile	flamboyant
intrepid	mellow	pacific	strident	unabashed

Some people are shy or easygoing; others are loud and *flamboyant*. Some are *complaisant*, always wanting to please others, and some are *assertive*, never hesitating to voice their views and ideas. The words in this lesson will help you describe the qualities of boldness and mildness.

1. **assertive** (ə-sûr´tĭv) *adjective* from Latin *ad-*, "toward" + *serere*, "to join"
   Acting with confidence and force; sure of one's self
   • The **assertive** woman stood up at the town meeting and spoke for a full twenty minutes.

   assert *verb* While babysitting for us, our oldest sister **asserted** her right to decide our bedtimes.

2. **brazen** (brā´zən) *adjective* from Middle English *brasen*, "made of brass"
   Extremely bold; shamelessly rude or defiant
   • The rebel group was **brazen** enough to kidnap the respected leader in front of many of the villagers.

   brazenness *noun* We were horrified by the **brazenness** of the men who dumped trash into the pond as people fished nearby.

3. **complaisant** (kəm-plā´sənt) *adjective* from Latin *complacere*, "to please"
   Wanting to please; willing to do what pleases others; cheerfully obliging
   • The **complaisant** six-year-old played every game her friend suggested.

   complaisance *noun* Known for his **complaisance**, Gerald constantly ran errands for others.

4. **docile** (dŏs´əl, dŏs´īl´) *adjective* from Latin *docere*, "to teach"
   Gentle; easily manageable or teachable; tame
   • We usually give the most **docile** horse to the youngest rider.

5. **flamboyant** (flăm-boi´ənt) *adjective* from Latin *flamma*, "flame"
   Showy, flashy, vivid or dramatic
   • The **flamboyant** hip-hop star arrived wearing gobs of jewelry and a five-thousand-dollar outfit.

   flamboyance *noun* Theresa's **flamboyance** gives her a special flair for selling luxury items.

docile

Have students classify the words into those that signal boldness, such as *assertive, brazen,* and *intrepid,* and those that suggest mildness, such as *pacific* and *mellow.* Allow students to defend their classifications.

A similar word, *complacent,* usually means "self-satisfied to a fault; unconcerned," but it can also mean "*complaisant.*"

6. intrepid (ĭn-trĕp´ĭd) *adjective* from Latin *in-*, "not" + *trepidus*, "alarm"

Fearless; having unwavering courage
- The **intrepid** explorer ventured alone into the depths of the jungle.

7. mellow (mĕl´ō)
   a. *adjective* Relaxed and unhurried; easygoing
   - The soft music put me in such a **mellow** mood that I stopped worrying about my test.
   b. *verb* To become more relaxed or pleasant
   - Mrs. Herrera used to be tense all the time, but in the last few weeks, she seems to have **mellowed** a bit.

> *Mellow* can also mean "smooth or soft," as in *mellow* music or a *mellow* flavor.

8. pacific (pə-sĭf´ĭk) *adjective* from Latin *pax-*, "peace" + *facere*, "to do"

Of a peaceful nature; calm
- The water was astonishingly **pacific** the day after the hurricane had blasted through the area.

pacify *verb* The principal tried to **pacify** the students after they learned that the school dance had been canceled.

> To calm babies, parents often give them *pacifiers* to suck on.

9. strident (strīd´nt) *adjective* from Latin *stridere*, "to make harsh sounds"

Loud, harsh, grating, or shrill
- When she sang, Malika's high notes sounded sharp and **strident** rather than smooth.

stridency *noun* The **stridency** of the children's voices gave Grandma a headache.

10. unabashed (ŭn´ə-băsht´) *adjective* from Middle English *un-*, "not" + *abaishen*, "to lose one's composure"
   a. Not embarrassed; composed
   - Completely **unabashed,** Michelle introduced herself to the celebrity.
   b. Not hidden or disguised; obvious
   - Sam showed **unabashed** disgust at the thought of gutting a fish.

WORD ENRICHMENT

Fiery words

What is something that is bright, vivid, and eye-catching? One answer to that question might be a *flame*. Another answer might be a *flamboyant* costume. As you learned earlier in the lesson, the word *flamboyant* is derived from a word meaning "flame." Other "fiery" words include *flambé* (to drench in liquor and ignite), *flamingo* (think of this bird's appearance), *flammable* (easily ignited and capable of burning rapidly), and *inflammable*, which, strangely enough, means the same thing as *flammable*.

WRITE THE CORRECT WORD

Write the correct word in the space next to each definition.

__complaisant__ 1. eager to please

__mellow__ 2. easygoing

__intrepid__ 3. fearless

__brazen__ 4. shameless and bold

__assertive__ 5. confident; forceful

__docile__ 6. gentle; tame

__pacific__ 7. peaceful; calm

__flamboyant__ 8. flashy; vivid

__strident__ 9. harsh; shrill

__unabashed__ 10. not embarrassed

COMPLETE THE SENTENCE

Write the letter for the word that best completes each sentence.

__d__ 1. As the speaker grew angry, a _____ tone crept into his voice.
a. complaisant   b. docile   c. pacific   d. strident

__c__ 2. One way to relieve stress is to imagine yourself in a beautiful, _____ place, such as a deserted beach or a hammock in a garden.
a. assertive   b. flamboyant   c. pacific   d. unabashed

__a__ 3. Next to all of the dark business suits, Anna's bright green dress seemed _____.
a. flamboyant   b. mellow   c. docile   d. complaisant

__b__ 4. Chris is so _____ that he always agrees to his friends' crazy plans.
a. strident   b. complaisant   c. unabashed   d. assertive

__b__ 5. The _____ reporter continued to disclose the misdeeds of very powerful people.
a. pacific   b. intrepid   c. mellow   d. docile

__c__ 6. Terrance hoped to find a job with a _____ work environment because he felt that he was more productive in a less stressful setting.
a. strident   b. flamboyant   c. mellow   d. brazen

__a__ 7. The _____ student debated with her professor about the meaning of the poem.
a. assertive   b. mellow   c. docile   d. complaisant

__d__ 8. How can you be so _____ about your unethical behavior?
a. pacific   b. complaisant   c. docile   d. unabashed

__d__ 9. Her _____ behavior alienated many of her coworkers and family members.
a. mellow   b. pacific   c. docile   d. brazen

__c__ 10. In the 1800s, women were expected to be _____ and obedient to men.
a. flamboyant   b. brazen   c. docile   d. assertive

Challenge: The sisters made a good team: Jamie was _____ and willing to go along with her _____ older sister, who insisted on taking the lead in everything they did.
__c__ a. unabashed…intrepid   b. pacific…docile   c. complaisant…assertive

Crocs Rule!

Imagine that you are on an exciting vacation, exploring the Florida Everglades by airboat. Suddenly, you spot an ominous shape in the water. Oh no—it's a crocodile! Do you panic?

Actually, crocodiles are more timid than you might think. They generally won't bother human beings who keep their distance. **(1)** Of course, crocodiles are not *docile,* but with appropriate caution and respect, humans have little to fear from them.

Crocodiles have existed for about 200 million years, thanks to their hardiness and effective survival strategies. Crocodiles can even recover from very serious injuries, including losing a limb! They are quite intelligent for reptiles, and they are excellent at capturing prey and avoiding danger. And they are surprisingly involved parents, another trait that is unusual in reptiles. Mother crocodiles carefully guard their eggs and carry their young to the water after they hatch. In some species, the young remain with their mother for two to three years.

Despite these survival techniques, crocodiles have much to fear from humans. Crocodile hunting has reduced about seven of the twenty-three species to the verge of extinction. **(2)** Fortunately, *assertive* wildlife advocates have pushed for legislation to protect these animals. Hunting crocodiles is now illegal in several countries, including the United States and Australia.

(3) Some poachers *brazenly* defy the law and continue to hunt crocodiles because a hefty profit can be made, especially from the skin, which is used to make leather goods such as shoes, belts, and handbags. In many countries, there are regulations against making leather from hunted crocodiles; only the skins of farm-raised crocodiles are legal to sell for this purpose. **(4)** Unfortunately, some manufacturers, *unabashed* by the harm they may be causing, continue to buy crocodile skins from poachers. Overall, however, hunting bans have enabled the crocodile population to gradually increase.

(5) A more *pacific* pursuit has largely replaced traditional crocodile hunting. Television and movie personality Steve Irwin is an example of a new breed of crocodile "hunter." Steve wrestles the animals in hand-to-mouth combat. **(6)** On his television program, *Crocodile Hunter,* Irwin provokes the creatures, which causes them to display a temperament that is anything but *mellow.* **(7)** Irwin and his equally *intrepid* wife, Terri, often expose themselves to considerable danger. **(8)** The camera operator follows *complaisantly* as the Crocodile Hunter wrestles the animals to the ground. As Irwin holds a crocodile's mouth closed, you might hear him exclaim, "Isn't she a beauty? Crocs rule!" He never harms the creatures. In fact, he has spent much of his life rescuing crocodiles and other animals.

(9) Steve Irwin's *flamboyance* has gained him much popularity. **(10)** Although some may find his style a bit *strident,* he has used his fame to promote wildlife preservation. His concern for animal welfare led him and Terri to found the Steve Irwin Conservation Foundation, which, among other activities, rescues animals and educates the public about animal and environmental conservation. Steve says, "We want to make people aware, all over the world, about the environment and just how precious it is— all of it!"

Each sentence below refers to a numbered sentence in the passage. Write the letter of the choice that gives the sentence a meaning that is closest to the original sentence.

_____a_____ **1.** Of course, crocodiles are not _____.
    a. tame   **b.** fearless   **c.** forceful   **d.** quiet

_____b_____ **2.** _____ wildlife advocates have pushed for legislation to protect these animals.
    a. Timid   **b.** Forceful   **c.** Unembarrassed   **d.** Easygoing

_____d_____ **3.** Some poachers _____ defy the law and continue to hunt crocodiles.
    a. dauntlessly   **b.** peacefully   **c.** secretly   **d.** shamelessly

_____d_____ **4.** Unfortunately, some manufacturers are _____ by the harm they may be causing.
    a. not swayed   **b.** not pleased   **c.** not confident   **d.** not ashamed

_____c_____ **5.** A more _____ pursuit has largely replaced traditional crocodile hunting.
  a. entertaining   **b.** reckless   **c.** peaceful   **d.** aggressive

_____a_____ **6.** On his television program, *Crocodile Hunter,* Irwin provokes the creatures, which causes them to display a temperament that is anything but _____.
  a. mild   **b.** flashy   **c.** fearless   **d.** embarrassed

_____c_____ **7.** Irwin and his equally _____ wife, Terri, often expose themselves to considerable danger.
  a. peaceful   **b.** eager-to-please   **c.** fearless   **d.** committed

_____b_____ **8.** The camera operator follows _____ as Steve wrestles the animals to the ground.
  a. hesitantly   **b.** willingly   **c.** boldly   **d.** defiantly

_____c_____ **9.** Steve Irwin's _____ has gained him much popularity.
  a. gentleness   **b.** shamelessness   **c.** showiness   **d.** harshness

_____a_____ **10.** Although some may find his style a bit _____, he has used his fame to promote wildlife preservation.
  a. loud and grating   **b.** pleasant and nice   **c.** showy and bright   **d.** peaceful and cool

Indicate whether the statements below are TRUE or FALSE according to the passage.

_____T_____ **1.** Crocodiles are still hunted today.

_____T_____ **2.** Steve Irwin is dedicated to educating the public about the importance of wildlife conservation.

_____F_____ **3.** Crocodiles have evolved into very docile animals.

WRITING EXTENDED RESPONSES

The reading passage shows how Steve and Terri Irwin must alternate their behavior between boldness and mildness as they work toward their various goals. Think of another person (or type of person) who is capable of acting boldly and mildly, depending on the situation. In an essay of at least three paragraphs, describe the scenarios that bring out these alternate behaviors in your subject. Also describe how he or she acts in these different situations. Use at least three lesson words in your essay and underline them.

WRITE THE DERIVATIVE

Complete the sentence by writing the correct form of the word shown in parentheses. You may not need to change the form that is given.

_____assert_____ **1.** If the decision has already been made, it's a waste of time to _____ your opinion. (*assertive*)

_____stridency_____ **2.** The _____ of the talk-show host's voice discouraged many listeners from tuning in to his show. (*strident*)

unabashedly   **3.** The convict smiled _____ as he told the story of how he had robbed the store. (*unabashed*)

flamboyance   **4.** Elsa Schiaparelli (1890–1973) was a fashion designer known for the _____ of her creations. (*flamboyant*)

intrepidly   **5.** In 1953, Sir Edmund Hillary's expedition _____ made it to the top of Mt. Everest. (*intrepid*)

pacific   **6.** Cheryl's _____ temperament makes her a perfect babysitter for siblings who often argue. (*pacific*)

brazenly   **7.** Anxious to talk to the coach before the game, Sarina _____ barged into the teacher's lounge looking for him. (*brazen*)

docilely   **8.** Hoping for a tasty treat, the trained seal _____ clapped his flippers three times. (*docile*)

mellowed   **9.** Harry has _____ over the years. (*mellow*)

complaisantly   **10.** The tour guide _____ allowed the tourists to ask him some personal questions. (*complaisant*)

FIND THE EXAMPLE

Choose the answer that best describes the action or situation.

d   **1.** A *complaisant* action
    a. starting a fight   **b.** spreading rumors   **c.** angering easily   **d.** agreeing to plans

d   **2.** An action that is *unabashedly* patriotic
    a. attending a university   **b.** writing love poetry   **c.** driving a foreign car   **d.** displaying a huge flag

a   **3.** A *pacific* step a government might take
    a. negotiate a treaty   **b.** declare war   **c.** activate troops   **d.** make threats

c   **4.** A *brazen* response to a teacher who tells students to write a short essay
    a. On what topic?   **b.** I love essays!   **c.** Why should I?   **d.** How many pages?

b   **5.** An animal that makes a *strident* sound
    a. butterfly   **b.** monkey   **c.** fish   **d.** snake

d   **6.** Something an *assertive* employee would be likely to say to her boss
    a. Yes, sir.   **b.** Nice tie.   **c.** I'll be right there.   **d.** I deserve a raise.

a   **7.** An animal that is usually *docile*
    a. cow   **b.** crocodile   **c.** lion   **d.** shark

b   **8.** Something a *mellow* person would be likely to say
    a. I'm in charge.   **b.** Fine with me.   **c.** I disagree.   **d.** No way!

d   **9.** Someone likely to wear *flamboyant* clothes to work
    a. librarian   **b.** accountant   **c.** nurse   **d.** rock star

d   **10.** Something only an *intrepid* person would choose to do
    a. relax by pool   **b.** visit museums   **c.** play tennis   **d.** go skydiving

Easily Confused Words

WORD LIST

affect	effect	depredation	deprivation	disinterested
uninterested	emigrate	immigrate	precede	proceed

The rich vocabulary of the English language includes many words that are easily confused because they look or sound similar. This lesson covers five pairs of these words. Study the differences between each pair of words carefully so that you will be less likely to confuse them.

1. **affect** from Latin *ad-,* "toward; to" + *facere,* "to do"
   a. *verb* (ə-fĕkt´) To influence; to change
      • Teachers can **affect** their students' lives in many ways.
   b. *verb* (ə-fĕkt´) To put on a false show or display of
      • He **affected** a British accent to impress the crowd at the party.
   c. *noun* (ăf´ĕkt´) Feeling or emotion, especially as shown in facial expressions or body language
      • Sammy showed no **affect,** so we couldn't tell how she felt about the news.

2. **effect** (ĭ-fĕkt´) *noun* from Latin *ex-,* "outside; away from" + *facere,* "to make"
   a. *noun* A result
      • One **effect** of raising a vehicle's height is a loss of stability or control when making turns.
   b. *verb* To bring about
      • He **effected** an overhaul of the registration system.

   effective *adjective* This ointment provides **effective** relief for itchy bug bites.

3. **depredation** (dĕp´rĭ-dā´shən) *noun* from Latin *de-,* "from; out of" + *praedari,* "to plunder"
   a. A predatory attack; a raid
      • A **depredation** by an army of ants spoiled our picnic.
   b. Damage, destruction, or loss
      • The **depredation** of the Amazon rain forest has harmed many species.

depredation

4. **deprivation** (dĕp´rə-vā´shən) *noun* from Latin *de-,* "from; out of" + *privare,* "to rob"
   The state of lacking or doing without something; loss
   • The drought caused a **deprivation** of food and clean water in the region.

   deprive *verb* By law, people accused of a crime in the United States cannot be **deprived** of due process, including their right to an attorney.

> The first meaning of *affect* and the second meaning of *effect* are often confused.

For a challenging activity that will help students grasp the distinctions between the often-confused words, have students write five proper sentences, each including one of the five *pairs* of words.

5. disinterested (dĭs-ĭn′trĭ-st′ĭd) *adjective*
Impartial; free of bias or self-interest in an outcome
• We want a **disinterested** judge when our case goes to court.

6. uninterested (ŭn-ĭn′trĭ-st′ĭd) *adjective*
Without interest; having no interest or concern in a matter
• By the time that ridiculous movie ended, I was completely **uninterested** in what happened to the characters.

> A *disinterested* person does not take sides in an issue; an *uninterested* person simply doesn't care.

7. emigrate (ĕm′ĭ-grāt′) *verb* from Latin *e-*, "outside; away from" + *migrare*, "to move"
To leave one country or region and settle in another
• During the early 1900s, millions of people **emigrated** from Europe to America.

emigrant *noun* **Emigrants** often have to leave friends and family behind.

emigration *noun* High unemployment sparked a wave of **emigration.**

> Remember that the meaning of *emigrate* focuses mainly on the place that was left, whereas *immigrate* refers mainly to the destination.

8. immigrate (ĭm′ĭ-grāt′) *verb* from Latin *in-*, "into" + *migrare*, "to move"
To settle in a country or region where one is not a native
• My parents **immigrated** to the United States twenty years ago.

immigrant *noun* Many **immigrants** from Vietnam live in Los Angeles.

immigration *noun* **Immigration** has helped build the economy and increase the diversity of the population in the United States.

9. precede (prĭ-sēd′) *verb* from Latin *prae-*, "before; in front" + *cedere*, "to go"
To come before
• A sudden drop in atmospheric pressure **preceded** the storm.

precedence *noun* In an emergency room, a patient suffering from a heart attack takes **precedence** over someone with a minor burn.

10. proceed (prō-sēd′) *verb* from Latin *pro-*, "forward" + *cedere*, "to go"
To go forward or onward
• Turn right on Main Street and then **proceed** to the next intersection.

procession *noun* The **procession** of limousines moved ever so slowly.

WORD ENRICHMENT

Types of confusing words

Homographs are words that have the same spelling, but different meanings and origins, and sometimes different pronunciations. Examples include *bow* (the front of a ship) and *bow* (a decorative knot). The roots of the word *homograph* mean "same" and "writing."

Homonyms, or "same names," are words that have the same sound and sometimes the same spelling, but different meanings. Examples include *boar* and *bore*, *meet* and *meat*, and *air* and *heir*. The word *homophone*, or "same sound," is often used as a synonym of *homonym*.

WRITE THE CORRECT WORD

Write the correct word in the space next to each definition.

effect	**1.** a result	affect	**6.** to influence
immigrate	**2.** to settle in a new country	emigrate	**7.** to leave one's country
proceed	**3.** to go forward	depredation	**8.** an attack
precede	**4.** to come before	disinterested	**9.** impartial; unbiased
uninterested	**5.** not interested	deprivation	**10.** lack of something

COMPLETE THE SENTENCE

Write the letter for the word that best completes each sentence.

d **1.** Some of the results of severe sleep _____ resemble depression.
  a. depredation   **b.** effects   **c.** affectation   **d.** deprivation

a **2.** You might want to talk to an outside party to get a(n) _____ point of view.
  a. disinterested   **b.** deprived   **c.** affected   **d.** uninterested

b **3.** _____ in professional sports, Jo decided to read rather than watch the game.
  a. Deprived   **b.** Uninterested   **c.** Affected   **d.** Disinterested

b **4.** When the path ended, we were unsure how to _____.
  a. precede   **b.** proceed   **c.** deprive   **d.** affect

c **5.** Suki's plan was a success; it was more _____ than anyone could have imagined.
  a. affective   **b.** affected   **c.** effective   **d.** uninterested

d **6.** Arriving late, we missed the orchestral performance that _____ the musical.
  a. proceeded   **b.** uninterested   **c.** disinterested   **d.** preceded

d **7.** During the potato famine, many families _____ from Ireland to settle in countries where food was more abundant.
  a. immigrated   **b.** preceded   **c.** deprived   **d.** emigrated

a **8.** We wondered how the forest fire would _____ the animals' habitat.
  a. affect   **b.** effect   **c.** precede   **d.** proceed

d **9.** After _____ to France, Josh immediately worked on improving his French-speaking skills.
  a. preceding   **b.** affecting   **c.** emigrating   **d.** immigrating

b **10.** Many homes were destroyed by the _____ of the soldiers.
  a. deprivations   **b.** depredations   **c.** disinterest   **d.** immigration

Challenge: She _____ with her plan to graduate from college early by taking the maximum number of classes each quarter, but she was unhappy about the _____ that this had on her social life.
  c
  a. preceded…effect   **b.** proceeded…affect   **c.** proceeded…effect

Dream On

Why do people dream? What is actually happening in the brain while a person is experiencing a dream? Do our dreams mean anything? If so, what? **(1)** It is hard to be *uninterested* in these fascinating mysteries. After all, dreaming is something that humans and many animals do every night, if they get enough sleep.

(2) For more than one hundred years, scientists have been investigating the ways in which dreaming *affects* our minds and bodies. In recent decades, specialists have made great advances in dream research. Using brain scans and other new technology, scientists have found that the part of the brain that regulates emotions is more active during sleep than it is during waking hours. This helps explain why dreams can be so emotionally charged.

Interestingly, one recent study found that just three emotions—anxiety, elation, and anger—accounted for 70 percent of the feelings experienced by dreamers. **(3)** One *effect* of this study is to show that people across the planet regularly have dreams that are similar in emotional content. **(4)** In one study, *disinterested* researchers gathered 50,000 dream reports from around the world, including accounts from remote places and isolated cultures. **(5)** As the researchers *proceeded*, they found that people from every culture had more bad dreams than they had good ones. Anxiety dreams about being unprepared were very common, but the setting changed depending on the person and his or her

background. For example, students might dream about showing up for an exam, without any of the required knowledge, or worse, without that knowledge and without any clothing!

Intense and often negative emotions are frequently "let loose" in our minds while we sleep. **(6)** For better or for worse, we are more likely to dream about hiding during a military *depredation* than we are about folding the laundry.

Because the part of the brain that handles long-term memory is active during dreaming, another common aspect of dreams arises—memories from childhood are likely to appear in dreams. **(7)** An elderly *immigrant* may have lived in her adopted country for decades. **(8)** Yet her dreams may bring her right back to the homeland she *emigrated* from as a child.

As you have probably realized, the logical part of the brain is not in control during dreaming. **(9)** While awake, our minds are dutifully making sense of the day's experiences that *precede* a night of dreaming. But once we are asleep, our minds do not impose order or "sense" on the content of our dreams. Random impressions often swirl together in a vivid symphony of nonsense.

As to why we dream, some researchers believe that dreaming helps us to "hard-wire" memories and knowledge, similar to how a computer might record information and "back it up." **(10)** That interpretation is supported by research showing that people who suffer from sleep *deprivation* often have memory and learning deficits. But researchers still don't know precisely what our individual dreams mean. That may always be a mystery.

Each sentence below refers to a numbered sentence in the passage. Write the letter of the choice that gives the sentence a meaning that is closest to the original sentence.

_____c_____ **1.** It is hard to be _____ these fascinating mysteries.
   a. not biased about   **b.** not attacked by   **c.** not curious about   **d.** not lacking for

_____b_____ **2.** Scientists have been investigating the ways in which dreaming _____ our minds and bodies.
   a. brings about   **b.** influences   **c.** comes before   **d.** moves

_____b_____ **3.** One _____ of this study is to show that people across the planet regularly have dreams that are similar in emotional content.
   a. influence   **b.** result   **c.** interest   **d.** combination

_____c_____ **4.** In one study, _____ researchers gathered 50,000 dream reports.
   a. foreign-born   **b.** unpaid   **c.** unbiased   **d.** bored

_c_ **5.** As the researchers _____, they found that people from every culture had more bad dreams than they had good ones.
   a. lacked necessities   **b.** came before   **c.** went on   **d.** was published

_c_ **6.** We are more likely to dream about hiding from a military _____ than we are about folding the laundry.
   a. journey   **b.** result   **c.** attack   **d.** shortage

_a_ **7.** An elderly _____ may have lived in her adopted country for decades.
   a. nonnative settler   **b.** traveler   **c.** foreign agent   **d.** native

_d_ **8.** Yet her dreams may bring her right back to the homeland she _____ as a child.
   a. raided   **b.** loved   **c.** changed   **d.** left

_d_ **9.** While awake, our minds are dutifully making sense of the day's experiences that _____ a night of dreaming.
   a. influence   **b.** follow up   **c.** enhance   **d.** come before

_a_ **10.** That interpretation is supported by research showing that people who suffer from a(n) _____ of sleep often have memory and learning deficits.
   a. lack of   **b.** attack on   **c.** result of   **d.** bias about

Indicate whether the statements below are TRUE or FALSE according to the passage.

_F_ **1.** Modern technology has allowed specialists to decipher exactly what dreams mean.

_F_ **2.** The logical part of the brain is in full control of our dreams.

_T_ **3.** People across the world often experience dreams that have strong emotional content.

FINISH THE THOUGHT

Complete each sentence with a phrase that shows the meaning of the italicized word.

1. A *disinterested* person is needed to _____ Answers will vary. _____

_____

2. I am *uninterested* in _____ Answers will vary. _____

_____

WRITE THE DERIVATIVE

Complete the sentence by writing the correct form of the word shown in parentheses. You may not need to change the form that is given.

effectively **1.** Shawna _____ presented her side of the argument. *(effect)*

immigration **2.** Many countries have limits on _____. *(immigrate)*

<u>__procession__</u>   **3.** Fiona cried as she watched the beautiful wedding _____. *(proceed)*

<u>__precedence__</u>   **4.** *Triage* is a process or system used to determine who gets _____ in receiving medical care or other scarce necessities. *(precede)*

<u>__Affecting__</u>   **5.** _____ an air of sophistication, Matilda strutted across the ballroom floor. *(affect)*

<u>__uninterested__</u>   **6.** About halfway through the long play, the young children became _____ and restless. *(uninterested)*

<u>__Depredation__</u>   **7.** _____ of the earth's natural resources often brings short-term gain to some people, but long-term loss of resources for many people and animals. *(depredation)*

<u>__emigrant__</u>   **8.** The _____ needed to obtain the proper paperwork before leaving his country. *(emigrate)*

<u>__disinterested__</u>   **9.** How could the judge even claim to be a _____ party in the case when he owns a substantial amount of stock in the company being sued? *(disinterested)*

<u>__deprive__</u>   **10.** You cannot _____ me of my Constitutional rights! *(deprivation)*

FIND THE EXAMPLE

Choose the answer that best describes the action or situation.

<u>c</u>   **1.** A *deprivation* that would cause the most suffering
     a. no TV   **b.** too many tests   **c.** no food   **d.** a police raid

<u>d</u>   **2.** A subject in which most teenagers are *uninterested*
     a. movies   **b.** music   **c.** sports   **d.** taxes

<u>b</u>   **3.** Situation most likely to include cruel *depredations*
     a. peaceful meeting   **b.** war   **c.** school assembly   **d.** high five

<u>c</u>   **4.** The likely *effect* of a hurricane
     a. global warming   **b.** smarter goats   **c.** property damage   **d.** light breeze

<u>c</u>   **5.** Something that tells a driver to *proceed*
     a. parked vehicle   **b.** crosswalk   **c.** green light   **d.** ambulance

<u>d</u>   **6.** A reason one might *emigrate*
     a. to remain sick   **b.** to stay home   **c.** to keep old friends   **d.** to escape persecution

<u>c</u>   **7.** A factor that would most *affect* your final grade in math class
     a. rapping skills   **b.** muscle mass   **c.** exam scores   **d.** essay grades

<u>c</u>   **8.** Something with which a speaker would likely *precede* a talk
     a. a conclusion   **b.** a water balloon   **c.** a joke   **d.** audience questions

<u>b</u>   **9.** Something you would probably need if you were in the process of *immigrating*
     a. high-heeled shoes   **b.** a passport   **c.** a diary   **d.** a pet

<u>d</u>   **10.** The person LEAST likely to give you *disinterested* advice
     a. doctor   **b.** mediator   **c.** counselor   **d.** car salesperson

Reading and Reasoning

Three Types of Context Clues

The words, sentences, or paragraphs surrounding an unfamiliar word often provide clues to the meaning of that word. These *context clues* can be helpful in determining meaning.

Strategies

Three types of context clues are common: **definition clues, opposite clues,** and **substitution clues.**

1. *Look for definition clues.* An author might actually define the word in the text. Several methods may be used.

    *   Words or phrases set off by commas, parentheses, or dashes:
        Ruminants, animals that chew cud, are often found in flocks.
        (A *ruminant* is an animal that chews cud.)
        This comma construction is called an *appositive.*

    *   The use of *or* or *and:*
        An *iman,* or religious leader, is an important in the Muslim community.
        (An *iman* is a religious leader)

    *   Defining by a list of examples:
        Avian characteristics include feathers, hollow bones, laying eggs, and flying.
        (Since these are all characteristics of birds, you can guess *avian* means bird-like.)

    *   Definition by inclusion in a list of examples:
        We visited London, Paris, and *Baku.*
        (Since London and Paris are cities, you can guess *Baku* is also a city.)

2. *Look for opposite clues.* Sometimes an author defines a word by giving its opposite.

    *   The use of *not* or *no:*
        With no thought of settling down, Sasha continued to be an *itinerant* actor.
        (*Itinerant* means traveling from place to place.)

    *   Words, phrases, or prefixes signaling opposites, such as *but, nevertheless, despite, rather than, unless, despite, although, in spite of, regardless, in-, non-,* and *un-:*
        The agent's manner suggested *duplicity* rather than honesty.
        (*Duplicity* is dishonesty, and misleading others.)
        Marissa seemed unfriendly, but her friend was most *congenial.*
        (*Congenial* means friendly.)

    *   Words with negative senses, like *barely, only, never, hardly, nothing,* and *merely:*
        Claudius, known for his *boorishness,* was hardly ever polite.
        (*Boorishness* is very rude and uncivilized.)

3. *Try substituting simpler words.* The meanings of some unfamiliar words can be determined by substituting simpler words in the sentence to see if they make sense.
        Your outfit is completely *outlandish.* Go change at once!
        (*Outlandish* means very inappropriate and strange.)

Practice

Read each sentence to determine the meaning of the italicized word. Write the meaning you obtain from the context clues. Then look up the word in the dictionary and write the most suitable formal definition.

1. Although we think her art is beautiful, her status as a great artist is *equivocal*.

   My definition _____

   Dictionary definition _____ of a doubtful or uncertain nature _____

2. The fishing boats returned with a catch of salmon, tuna, and *menhaden*.

   My definition _____

   Dictionary definition _ any of several species of fish of the genus *Brevoortia* _

3. His past mistakes made Griffon more *circumspect* when he encountered similar situations.

   My definition _____

   Dictionary definition _ heedful of circumstances and potential consequences _

4. "The Constitution of the United States was made not merely for the generation that then existed, but for *posterity*—unlimited, undefined, endless, perpetual posterity." (Henry Clay)

   My definition _____

   Dictionary definition _____ future generations _____

5. At the Renaissance Fair, each performer wore a *jerkin*, a kind of sleeveless jacket.

   My definition _____

   Dictionary definition _ a short, close-fitting, often sleeveless coat or jacket _

6. Despite the *gravity* of the issue that Margaret was discussing with her father, she had a light-hearted smile.

   My definition _____

   Dictionary definition __ grave consequence: seriousness or importance __

7. He *regaled* his friends with fabulous tales about his travels in the Far East.

   My definition _____

   Dictionary definition _____ to provide with great enjoyment; entertain _____

8. The city engineer was accused of *nepotism,* after he put his wife on the payroll and granted high-paying positions to a friend and two nephews.

   My definition _____

   Dictionary definition __ favoritism shown or patronage granted to relatives __

Teaching and Explaining

WORD LIST

didactic	edify	elucidate	erudite	esoteric
imbue	indoctrinate	pedagogy	pedantic	pundit

The American philosopher and historian Henry Adams once said, "A teacher affects eternity. He can never tell where his influence stops." Imparting knowledge is not only one of the most common uses of communication, but one of the most important. The words in this lesson will help you describe different kinds of teachers and teaching styles.

1. **didactic** (dī-dăk´tĭk) *adjective* from Greek *didaskein,* "to teach"
   a. Intended to teach
   • We listened with some impatience to my aunt's **didactic** life stories.
   b. Overly moralistic; preachy
   • Children's books of the 1800s were quite **didactic,** often amounting to little more than lectures on behavior.

   > Point out that *didactic, indoctrinate,* and *pedantic* have negative connotations.

2. **edify** (ĕd´ə-fī´) *verb* from Latin *aedificare,* "to build"
   To instruct for intellectual, moral, or spiritual improvement
   • Studying literary classics **edifies** us about the ways human beings react to universal problems such as jealousy and grief.

   edification *noun* The professor assigned additional readings for the **edification** of her students.

3. **elucidate** (ĭ-lōō´sĭ-dāt´) *verb* from Latin *ex-,* "out" + *lucere,* "to shine"
   To explain or make clear
   • The textbook's chapter on calculus wasn't helpful, but our teacher **elucidated** the principles quite clearly.

   elucidation *noun* These strange-looking graphs need some **elucidation.**

   > Complex or difficult subjects often require *elucidation.*

4. **erudite** (ĕr´yə-dīt´) *adjective* from Latin *ex-,* "out" + *rudis,* "untaught"
   Possessing great knowledge and scholarship
   • The **erudite** language specialist could read Latin, ancient Greek, Hebrew, and Aramaic.

   erudition *noun* Shannon could not have given her lecture on Irish culture without drawing on a high degree of **erudition.**

5. **esoteric** (ĕs´ə-tĕr´ĭk) *adjective* from Greek *esoterikos,* "inward; within"
   Understood only by an elite, scholarly, or exclusive group; obscure
   • The difference between 32-bit and 64-bit hardware seems **esoteric** to most people, but it dramatically affects computer games.

   esoterica *noun* Antique cameras, lenses, filters, and other **esoterica** of the photographer's trade littered the back room of the shop.

elucidate

6. **imbue** (ĭm-byōō´) *verb* from Latin *imbuere*, "to moisten; to stain"
   a. To inspire or influence thoroughly
   • His older sister's success in soccer **imbued** Pablo with a love for the game.
   b. To stain or dye thoroughly
   • When washed with the navy sweater, the white clothes became **imbued** with blue.

7. **indoctrinate** (ĭn-dŏk´trə-nāt´) *verb* from Latin *in-*, "in" + *doctrina*, "teacher"
   To instruct in or impart certain principles or ideology
   • Good art schools seek not to **indoctrinate** their students with specific styles, but rather to inspire them to develop their own creative visions.

   indoctrination *noun* The dictator decided that weekly sessions of political **indoctrination** should be a requirement for all schoolchildren.

> Another definition of *indoctrinate* is "to *imbue* with a partisan or ideological point of view."

8. **pedagogy** (pĕd´ə-gō´jē, pĕd´ə-gŏ´jē) *noun* from Greek *paido*, "boy" + *agein*, "to lead"
   a. The art or profession of teaching
   • **Pedagogy** is an ancient and honorable profession.
   b. The body of knowledge related to education and teaching
   • Mathematical **pedagogy** in the United States has benefited from adopting strategies that are used in Russia and Eastern Europe.

   pedagogical *adjective* The English teacher's creative **pedagogical** methods made Shakespeare's sonnets fascinating to her students.

   pedagogue *noun* The Swiss **pedagogue** Jean Piaget influenced educators all over the world with his insights into the development of logic in children.

9. **pedantic** (pə-dăn´tĭk) *adjective*
   Overly concerned with or narrowly focused on book learning or formal rules
   • Lively debate and relevant experience often teach more about poetry than **pedantic** lectures do.

   pedantry *noun* Having students recite geometry proofs repeatedly could be considered counterproductive **pedantry**.

10. **pundit** (pŭn´dĭt) *noun* from Sanskrit *panditah*, "learned; scholar"
    a. A person of great learning about a particular topic; an expert
    • The president asked a small group of distinguished **pundits** to review his foreign policy.
    b. A source of opinion; a critic
    • The music **pundit** wrote an article about the new album.

> The media often feature *pundits* who comment on events or give their opinions on issues.

WORD ENRICHMENT

Words from Sanskrit

Sanskrit, an ancient language of India and of Hinduism, is the source of many English words, including *pundit*. The words *cheetah*, *loot*, *orange*, and *sugar* also come from Sanskrit.

WRITE THE CORRECT WORD

Write the correct word in the space next to each definition.

___pedagogy___   **1.** the art of teaching

___edify___   **2.** to instruct in order to improve

___pedantic___   **3.** too concerned with book learning

___pundit___   **4.** a person of great learning

___indoctrinate___   **5.** to instruct in a set of specific beliefs

___didactic___   **6.** teaching in a moralizing manner

___imbue___   **7.** to influence thoroughly

___erudite___   **8.** possessing extensive knowledge

___elucidate___   **9.** to make clear

___esoteric___   **10.** understood by few

COMPLETE THE SENTENCE

Write the letter for the word that best completes each sentence.

___a___   **1.** _____ professors risk losing their students' interest.
    a. Pedantic   **b.** Edifying   **c.** Imbued   **d.** Erudite

___c___   **2.** The moral of a fable is _____; it tries to teach a life lesson.
    a. esoteric   **b.** imbued   **c.** didactic   **d.** pedantic

___c___   **3.** Hannah attends lectures on diverse topics to _____ herself.
    a. indoctrinate   **b.** elucidate   **c.** edify   **d.** imbue

___d___   **4.** The article's explanatory footnotes help _____ the author's argument.
    a. indoctrinate   **b.** imbue   **c.** edify   **d.** elucidate

___b___   **5.** The antique collector had much _____ knowledge of rare lamps.
    a. edified   **b.** esoteric   **c.** pedagogical   **d.** didactic

___a___   **6.** There are many new _____ theories about how to teach literacy.
    a. pedagogical   **b.** pundit   **c.** esoteric   **d.** pedantic

___a___   **7.** Was it a harmless public service announcement, or a subtle way to _____ viewers?
    a. indoctrinate   **b.** edify   **c.** elucidate   **d.** erudite

___d___   **8.** Many parents try to _____ their children with ethics and values.
    a. didactic   **b.** pedagogue   **c.** elucidate   **d.** imbue

___c___   **9.** The sports _____ was asked to comment on the tennis match.
    a. pedantry   **b.** pedagogue   **c.** pundit   **d.** esoterica

___b___   **10.** The _____ scholar could quote any number of literary works at a moment's notice.
    a. esoteric   **b.** erudite   **c.** didactic   **d.** edifying

Challenge: When the scholar tried to _____ the topic she was studying, her language was so _____ that none of her friends could understand her.
___a___   **a.** elucidate…esoteric   **b.** edify…pedagogical   **c.** imbue…didactic

English Everywhere

What is the official language shared by Botswana, Cameroon, Gambia, India, Ghana, Belize, and Singapore? You might be surprised to learn that it is English.

The impact of the English language has been felt around the world. A Chinese businessperson speaks English with an airline receptionist in Nigeria. A Polish-born pope, who lived in Italy, traveled to Israel and gave a speech—in English. Over half of the world's newspapers are written in English. It is also the international language of air-traffic controllers.

One reason why English is so pervasive is the popularity of American culture. **(1)** People across the planet have been *imbued* with images from American pop culture through movies, television programming, and music. In Africa, more than half of the films shown are produced in the United States. **(2)** Not surprisingly, this has raised concerns that young Africans are being *indoctrinated* with values different from those of their traditional cultures.

English has even worked its way into other languages. Germans talk about *die Soundtrack* and *chatten* (to chat). **(3)** Although *guddobai, faitingu supiritto,* and *hottodoggu* may seem *esoteric*, they are simply Japanese "Anglicisms" for *goodbye, fighting spirit,* and *hot dog.*

When words like *le drugstore, le weekend, l'Internet,* and *le Big Western* became popular in France, some national politicians became worried. **(4)** Articles, some rather *didactic* in tone, urged the French people to protect their language. In fact, in 1994, a law was passed to prevent advertisers from using English words.

Because English is so widely used, people across the globe have been rushing to learn it. According to one estimate, a billion people currently study the language you are now reading. **(5)** The *pedagogical* methods that people use to learn English vary widely. **(6)** Some rely on *pedantic* routines, which focus on memorizing words and learning formal grammar. Other methods, such as Total Physical Response, use body movements to act out English commands. **(7)** More *erudite* methods include learning English by reading English literature. Still other programs require students to study American media. In China, hundreds of millions of people are learning English by watching television.

HOTTODOGGU

In one way, English is considered a relatively easy language. Unlike Spanish and German, English attaches no gender to common nouns. **(8)** So, unlike teachers of many other languages, teachers of English do not have to *elucidate* the gender of nouns.

On the other hand, English has an enormous vocabulary, general rules with many exceptions, and a large number of idioms, or nonliteral phrases, such as "brownie points," "keep your eye on the time," and "put up with." Finally, to speak a language well, one must know the culture of its users. **(9)** Therefore, good teachers must *edify* their students about the customs of the English-speaking world.

It is difficult to tell how long English will retain its worldwide status. **(10)** Language *pundits* predict an increase in the global importance of Mandarin Chinese, Hindu-Urdu, Spanish, and Arabic. With languages, as with anything else, nothing lasts forever.

Each sentence below refers to a numbered sentence in the passage. Write the letter of the choice that gives the sentence a meaning that is closest to the original sentence.

_____a_____ 1. People across the planet have been _____ with images from American pop culture.
  a. strongly influenced   **b.** tried to moralize   **c.** spread throughout   **d.** not had an effect on

_____d_____ 2. This has raised concerns that young Africans are being _____ nontraditional values.
  a. self-righteous with   **b.** made expert on   **c.** bored with   **d.** taught to adopt

_____a_____ 3. The words *guddobai, faitingu supiritto,* and *hottodoggu* may seem _____.
  a. known by few   **b.** meant to teach   **c.** foreign   **d.** expert

_a_ **4.** Some _____ articles urged the French people to protect their language.
   a. preachy   **b.** irate   **c.** complacent   **d.** explanatory

_d_ **5.** The _____ methods that people use to learn English vary widely.
   a. preachy   **b.** expert   **c.** ideological   **d.** educational

_b_ **6.** Some rely on _____ routines, which focus on memorizing.
   a. scholarly   **b.** formal   **c.** unconventional   **d.** comical

_b_ **7.** More _____ methods include learning English by reading English literature.
   a. spiritual   **b.** scholarly   **c.** linguistic   **d.** teacher's

_c_ **8.** Teachers of English do not have to _____ the gender of nouns.
   a. write   **b.** inspire   **c.** explain   **d.** influence

_c_ **9.** Good teachers must _____ their students about the customs of the English-speaking world.
   a. narrowly show   **b.** moralize to   **c.** enlighten   **d.** introduce

_a_ **10.** Language _____ predict an increase in the global importance of Mandarin Chinese, Hindu-Urdu, Spanish, and Arabic.
   a. experts   **b.** teachers   **c.** writers   **d.** students

Indicate whether the statements below are TRUE or FALSE according to the passage.

_T_ **1.** Some non-English speakers are unhappy about the filtering of English terms into their languages.

_F_ **2.** Most experts agree that English will hold its worldwide position of dominance forever.

_T_ **3.** American television and movies are influential around the globe.

WRITING EXTENDED RESPONSES

What is it like to learn a language? Based on personal experience or speculation, write about how it feels to learn another language. Your essay should be at least three paragraphs long. Use at least three lesson words in your piece and underline them.

WRITE THE DERIVATIVE

Complete the sentence by writing the correct form of the word shown in parentheses. You may not need to change the form that is given.

pedagogue **1.** In his later years, Samuel Johnson had a brilliant career as a _____. *(pedagogy)*

indoctrination **2.** Is mass _____ required to get a whole population to behave as a cohesive unit? *(indoctrinate)* _erudition_   **3.** Many scholars of great _____ lived in Medieval Spain. (*erudite*)

didactic   **4.** Lakisha's short stories are generally an interesting blend of _____ lessons and satire. (*didactic*)

edification   **5.** The museum curator's primary goal was the _____ of all patrons. (*edify*)

imbued   **6.** The magazine article was _____ with comic references to various historical figures. (*imbue*)

pedantry   **7.** After many years of lecturing, the professor's teaching has deteriorated into mere _____ . (*pedantic*)

pundits   **8.** The senator consulted with a team of political _____ for campaign advice. (*pundit*)

esoteric   **9.** The significance of the _____ title was understood only by the students who knew Armenian history. (*esoteric*)

elucidation   **10.** Your cryptic answer requires more _____ if you want me to understand it. (*elucidate*)

FIND THE EXAMPLE

Choose the answer that best describes the action or situation.

_c_   **1.** The person most likely to benefit from *pedagogy*
     a. pediatrician   **b.** teacher   **c.** student   **d.** plumber

_d_   **2.** Something you would most likely say if you needed *elucidation*
     a. Please leave.   **b.** Thank you.   **c.** I get it!   **d.** I don't understand.

_d_   **3.** Something a *didactic* story often ends with
     a. question   **b.** surprise   **c.** shouting   **d.** moral

_c_   **4.** Something a film *pundit* would most likely be asked to do
     a. star in a movie   **b.** produce a film   **c.** write a review   **d.** direct a show

_a_   **5.** An activity in which you would *imbue* fabric with something
     a. tie-dying   **b.** knitting   **c.** dressing   **d.** weaving

_b_   **6.** The object you would most associate with an *erudite* person
     a. hat   **b.** book   **c.** toothbrush   **d.** sandwich

_c_   **7.** Something a *pedantic* person is most likely to be concerned with
     a. motivation   **b.** experience   **c.** rules   **d.** typing

_a_   **8.** Something that should always be *esoteric*
     a. secret code   **b.** encyclopedia   **c.** scholar   **d.** speeches

_a_   **9.** The activity most likely to provide *edification*
     a. reading an article   **b.** watching a cartoon   **c.** playing a sport   **d.** e-mailing a friend

_b_   **10.** Something that is NOT a key ingredient for *indoctrination*
     a. students   **b.** onion   **c.** teacher   **d.** beliefs

Help and Improvement

WORD LIST

aegis	amends	conciliatory	conducive	extricate
importune	mediate	mitigate	patronize	renovate

Despite having less strength and speed than many of the animals on earth, human beings have managed to survive, advance, and thrive. This is largely because we have learned to use our intelligence to improve our lives. The words in this lesson will help you understand and discuss issues related to helping ourselves and others.

Point out common prefixes and their meanings in the lesson words. Examples include *con-*, *ex-*, *im-*, and *re-*.

1. **aegis** (ē´jĭs) *noun* from Greek *aigis*, "goatskin; skin shield"
   Protection; sponsorship; guidance
   • Ruben attended college under the **aegis** of the Public Arts Foundation, which gave him a scholarship and money to cover his living expenses.

   > The word *aegis* is often used in the phrase "under the *aegis* of." It can also be spelled *egis*.

2. **amends** (ə-mĕndz´) *noun* from Latin *ex-*, "out of" + *mendum*, "fault"
   Something done to make up for a wrong, an injury, or a mistake; compensation
   • To make **amends** for missing her championship soccer game, Jayna's uncle offered to take her to a theme park.

   > The word *amends* is always plural and is usually used in the phrase "make *amends*."

3. **conciliatory** (kən-sĭl´-ə-tôr´ē) *adjective* from Latin *concilium*, "meeting"
   Peacemaking; appeasing; intended to overcome distrust, animosity, or conflict
   • To end the argument, Maggie made a **conciliatory** gesture by offering to loan the CD to her little brother twice a week.

   conciliate *verb* The teacher tried to **conciliate** the dispute between the two students.

   conciliator *noun* Former president Jimmy Carter acted as a **conciliator** between the government and rebels in Venezuela.

4. **conducive** (kən-dōō´sĭv) *adjective* from Latin *com-*, "together" + *ducere*, "to lead"
   Tending to cause or bring about; favorable to
   • Quiet places are **conducive** to studying.

5. **extricate** (ĕk´strĭ-kāt´) *verb* from Latin *ex-*, "out of" + *tricae*, "hindrances"
   To free from difficulty or entanglement
   • Faye reached into the knotted seaweed and **extricated** a small starfish.

   extrication *noun* The quick work of the rescue team resulted in the successful **extrication** of all twenty workers from the collapsed mine.

extricate

6. **importune** (ĭm´pôr-tōōn´) *verb* from Latin *in-*, "not" + *portus*, "refuge; port"
To annoy with repeated and insistent requests; to ask for urgently or repeatedly
- Street vendors **importuned** passing tourists to buy souvenirs.

importunate *adjective* With their constant begging for gifts, **importunate** children can annoy even the most patient adult.

7. **mediate** (mē´dē-āt´) *verb* from Latin *mediare*, "to be in the middle"
To help opposing sides reach an agreement; to intervene in a conflict in order to improve the situation
- The chairman tried to **mediate** the disagreement between the two committees.

mediator *noun* Cary was a born **mediator**; he knew instinctively how each side felt and what was most important to them.

mediation *noun* Both the union and the management realized that **mediation** was the best hope of reaching an acceptable agreement.

> A *mediator* helps opposing sides reach an agreement and does not become party to the disagreement.

8. **mitigate** (mĭt´ĭ-gāt´) *verb* from Latin *mitis*, "soft" + *agere*, "to drive; do"
To make less severe; to soften, lessen, or moderate
- Grandpa **mitigated** the sting of his critical words with a wink and a pat on the shoulder.

mitigation *noun* Sometimes the best thing that hospital patients with incurable diseases can hope for is pain **mitigation.**

9. **patronize** (pāt´rə-nīz´, păt´rə-nīz´) *verb* from Latin *pater*, "father"
   a. To support or sponsor
   - Through the years, the family **patronized** several Mexican artists, bringing their work into the United States for exhibition.
   b. To go as a customer; to shop at regularly
   - Jo does not **patronize** stores that sell goods made by child laborers.
   c. To treat as inferior
   - Some people think it is wrong for politicians to **patronize** the public by assuming people know nothing about science or history.

patron *noun* **Patrons** of the store get mailings that offer special discounts.

patronage *noun* Thanks to the **patronage** of the private foundation, the afterschool program was able to continue its work.

> Note that *patronize* has both positive and negative meanings.

> *Patron* can mean either "customer" or "sponsor."

10. **renovate** (rĕn´ə-vāt) *verb* from Latin *re-*, "again" + *novare*, "to make new"
To restore something to an earlier condition, by repairing or remodeling
- When we **renovated** our house, we removed the tile from the kitchen floor and refinished the original wood flooring.

renovation *noun* The subway station is closed temporarily due to long-needed **renovations.**

WRITE THE CORRECT WORD

Write the correct word in the space next to each definition.

__mitigate__	**1.** to make less severe	
__conciliatory__	**2.** appeasing; peacemaking	
__extricate__	**3.** to release from entanglement	
__renovate__	**4.** to restore	
__conducive__	**5.** tending to cause or bring about	

__aegis__	**6.** protection; guidance	
__patronize__	**7.** to treat as inferior	
__amends__	**8.** compensation for a wrong	
__mediate__	**9.** to help sides agree	
__importune__	**10.** to annoy with repeated requests	

COMPLETE THE SENTENCE

Write the letter for the word that best completes each sentence.

d **1.** Regular exercise, adequate sleep, and a varied diet are _____ to good health.
   a. patronizing   **b.** extricated   **c.** conciliatory   **d.** conducive

a **2.** Harvey _____ himself from the meeting to take an important phone call.
   a. extricated   **b.** importuned   **c.** mitigated   **d.** mediated

a **3.** Vince made _____ with his neighbor by paying for the broken window.
   a. amends   **b.** aegis   **c.** extrication   **d.** patronage

b **4.** Much medical research is conducted under the _____ of the federal government.
   a. renovation   **b.** aegis   **c.** extrication   **d.** amends

b **5.** The secretary of state was asked to _____ the dispute between the two neighboring nations.
   a. importune   **b.** mediate   **c.** extricate   **d.** patronize

c **6.** Salvatore's weekly allergy shots helped _____ his symptoms.
   a. extricate   **b.** renovate   **c.** mitigate   **d.** patronize

d **7.** Realizing how angry she sounded, Ilana adopted a more _____ tone of voice.
   a. renovated   **b.** importunate   **c.** patronizing   **d.** conciliatory

a **8.** During the Italian Renaissance, members of the powerful and wealthy Medici family _____ many artists.
   a. patronized   **b.** renovated   **c.** mitigated   **d.** mediated

c **9.** Diane _____ her dad for weeks until he gave in and said she could go to the dance.
   a. mediated   **b.** extricated   **c.** importuned   **d.** patronized

c **10.** Sheila's business is _____ old houses.
   a. mitigating   **b.** conciliating   **c.** renovating   **d.** importuning

Challenge: The _____ did everything in her power to set a(n) _____ tone for the discussions so that the two parties would be more likely to compromise.
b
   a. patron…conducive   **b.** mediator…conciliatory   **c.** renovator…importunate

Remembering Their Homes

Picture a small, rural, impoverished village in Mexico. There is little access to clean water, education, or medical care. Residents receive little or no aid from their government, and wealthy donors and foundations ignore their needs. **(1)** It seems that no one will *mediate* on their behalf. But sometimes help does arrive, thanks to the hard work of villagers who have left these towns in search of jobs elsewhere.

(2) Thousands of rural Mexicans and Central Americans have *extricated* themselves from severe poverty by finding work in the United States. Though the jobs they work are often labor intensive and low paying, they still manage to carefully save money and send it back to their hometowns. **(3)** This plays an important role in *mitigating* poverty in these small towns and villages.

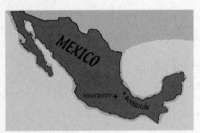

One example of this kind of support-from-afar can be found in the Mexican town of Boquerón, which is divided into five sections. So many of its people have moved to Newburgh, New York, that their neighborhood there is known as the "Sixth Section." **(4)** Under the *aegis* of an organization called "Grupo Union," U.S. residents originally from Boquerón have assisted their hometowns in countless ways.

(5) What kinds of projects were considered the most *conducive* to improving life in Boquerón? Surprisingly, Grupo Union began by funding the construction of a 2,000-seat baseball stadium. **(6)** *Patronizing* their own stadium has become an important affirmation of dignity and pride for Boquerón residents. **(7)** Without any *importunate* petitioning of the government for recreational facilities, Boquerón has become an important regional gathering place. Now, the town also has electricity, an ambulance, and a basketball court.

Filmmaker Alex Rivera documented the efforts of Grupo Union in his film *The Sixth Section*. Rivera notes that workers who scrounge and save money to support people in their hometowns gain much from doing so. Although many of these immigrants may work at jobs that seem menial, and they may feel somewhat invisible or powerless in their roles in America, Rivera notes that, "by organizing here and sending money back, they find dignity and power."

According to a World Bank study, the amount of money sent to Mexico in 2002 by Mexican-American workers exceeded the amount that Mexico amassed from either tourism or foreign investments. There are countless organizations like Grupo Union in the United States. **(8)** Their members hope to not only help relatives and friends directly, but to also play a role in *renovating* needed housing and medical facilities for the benefit of all villagers.

(9) Perhaps to make *amends* for previous neglect, the Mexican government has begun to get involved in aiding impoverished communities. Some of its programs are providing rural villagers with two or three dollars for every dollar raised by hometown assistance organizations like Grupo Union. **(10)** Such *conciliatory* and generous gestures have gone far to foster good relationships between the residents of small towns and their local and federal governments.

Each sentence below refers to a numbered sentence in the passage. Write the letter of the choice that gives the sentence a meaning that is closest to the original sentence.

_____b_____ **1.** It seems that no one will _____ on their behalf.
    a. provide support   **b.** intervene   **c.** give charity   **d.** compensate

_____b_____ **2.** Thousands of rural Mexicans have _____ themselves from severe poverty.
    a. negotiated   **b.** freed   **c.** renewed   **d.** avoided

_____c_____ **3.** This plays an important role in _____ poverty in these small towns and villages.
    a. increasing   **b.** compensating   **c.** reducing   **d.** calming

_____a_____ **4.** Some former residents have helped their hometowns under the _____ of an organization called "Grupo Union."
    a. sponsorship   **b.** conditions   **c.** managers   **d.** remodeling

___d___ **5.** What kinds of projects were considered the most _____ improving life in Boquerón?
    a. friendly about   **b.** unnecessary for   **c.** condescending to   **d.** favorable to

___d___ **6.** _____ their own stadium has become an important affirmation of dignity and pride for Boquerón residents.
    a. Begging for   **b.** Playing in   **c.** Restoring   **d.** Supporting

___c___ **7.** Without any _____ the government for recreational facilities, Boquerón has become an important regional gathering place.
    a. freeing   **b.** supporting   **c.** begging   **d.** paying

___b___ **8.** Their members hope to also play a role in _____ needed housing and medical facilities for the benefit of all villagers.
    a. protecting   **b.** rebuilding   **c.** requesting   **d.** intervening

___a___ **9.** Perhaps to _____ previous neglect, the Mexican government has begun to get involved.
    a. make up for   **b.** lessen the effects of   **c.** shed light on   **d.** provide evidence for

___d___ **10.** Such _____ gestures have gone far to foster good relationships.
    a. favorable for life   **b.** political and shrewd   **c.** kind and smart   **d.** friendly and appeasing

Indicate whether the statements below are TRUE or FALSE according to the passage.

___F___ **1.** It is impossible to spread wealth from one country to another.

___T___ **2.** Sports are important to the economy and social life of Boquerón.

___T___ **3.** The Sixth Section is actually a neighborhood in New York State.

FINISH THE THOUGHT

Complete each sentence so that it shows the meaning of the italicized word.

1. To make *amends*, I _____ Answers will vary. _____

_____

2. Your arrogant behavior is not *conducive* to _____ Answers will vary. _____

_____

WRITE THE DERIVATIVE

Complete the sentence by writing the correct form of the word shown in parentheses. You may not need to change the form that is given.

___mitigation___ **1.** Environmental groups want Congress to take steps that will result in the _____ of industrial pollution. (*mitigate*)

___aegis___ **2.** The foreign scientists toured the facility under the _____ of the U.S. State Department. (*aegis*)

<u>mediator</u>　**3.** It's better to call in a _____ than to become locked in a vicious cycle of conflict. *(mediate)*

<u>amends</u>　**4.** Andre was ashamed of his behavior and wanted to make _____ with his parents. *(amends)*

<u>conducive</u>　**5.** Droughts are _____ to forest fires. *(conducive)*

<u>renovation</u>　**6.** As the head of the _____ project, Yvonne hired the painters, carpenters, and electricians. *(renovate)*

<u>patronizing</u>　**7.** The intern handled the _____ remarks from his boss fairly well. *(patronize)*

<u>conciliatory</u>　**8.** "Pointing in someone's face is not exactly a _____ gesture," retorted Armen. *(conciliatory)*

<u>extricate</u>　**9.** The commander came up with a plan to _____ her troops from the valley. *(extricate)*

<u>importuning</u>　**10.** Your _____ will not change my mind about letting you drive on icy roads. *(importune)*

FIND THE EXAMPLE

Choose the answer that best describes the action or situation.

<u>b</u>　**1.** The thing most *conducive* to athletic excellence
　a. overeating　　**b.** training regularly　　**c.** high-tech cleats　　**d.** wheezing lungs

<u>d</u>　**2.** Usually NOT a good way to make *amends*
　a. fixing the damage　　**b.** giving a gift　　**c.** apologizing　　**d.** hurling insults

<u>a</u>　**3.** A *conciliatory* statement
　a. I'm sorry.　　**b.** It's not my fault.　　**c.** How dare you?　　**d.** I'll never forgive you.

<u>c</u>　**4.** Something an *importunate* child would do
　a. play　　**b.** steal　　**c.** pester　　**d.** juggle

<u>c</u>　**5.** Something that would most likely *mitigate* a headache
　a. a flu shot　　**b.** a loud noise　　**c.** a pain reliever　　**d.** a long concert

<u>b</u>　**6.** An organization that falls under the *aegis* of the federal government
　a. a restaurant chain　　**b.** the FBI　　**c.** a town library　　**d.** a football team

<u>d</u>　**7.** Something a *patron* of Burger Shack would most likely do
　a. seek knowledge　　**b.** seek sponsorship　　**c.** buy art　　**d.** buy fries

<u>a</u>　**8.** Something a person would most likely *renovate*
　a. a bathroom　　**b.** an argument　　**c.** a friendship　　**d.** an improvement

<u>c</u>　**9.** Something most likely to require *extrication*
　a. a lost pen　　**b.** a decrepit house　　**c.** a trapped animal　　**d.** a difficult essay

<u>d</u>　**10.** A situation in which a teacher might have to *mediate*
　a. sports team's victory　　**b.** power outage　　**c.** car wash　　**d.** dispute in class

Wealth and Poverty

WORD LIST

austerity	depreciate	equity	frugal	indigent
munificent	pecuniary	recession	remunerate	solvent

Words related to wealth or the lack of it are commonly used in the world of business and the media. The details of economic events and financial transactions are important for everyone to comprehend. The words in this lesson will help you understand wealth-related issues.

Point out that *depreciate, indigent,* and *recession* imply decreasing wealth or a lack of wealth.

1. **austerity** (ô-stĕr´ĭ-tē) *noun* from Greek *austeros,* "harsh"
   a. Severe and rigid restrictions, especially those brought about by difficult economic times
   • During World War II, wartime **austerity** included limits on the amount of gas and food people could buy.
   b. The quality of lacking luxury or ornamentation; bareness; simplicity
   • Monks live a life of **austerity.**
   c. The quality of being severe or stern in appearance or manner
   • Their great-aunt's **austerity** frightened the young children.

   austere *adjective* Employees were careful not to offend the **austere** bank manager.

austerity

2. **depreciate** (dĭ-prē´shē-āt´) *verb* from Latin *de-,* "reduce" + *pretium,* "price"
   To decrease or cause to decrease in value or price
   • The house **depreciated** in value because the owners did not keep up with yearly maintenance.

   depreciation *noun* **Depreciation** of a new car begins the moment you drive it off the lot.

3. **equity** (ĕk´wĭ-tē) *noun* from Latin *aequus,* "even; fair"
   a. Net value; the value of a business or property minus debt owed
   • The Watsons had accumulated enough **equity** in their home that they were able to refinance their mortgage at a better interest rate.
   b. Fairness; justice
   • Most people think that it is important to treat others with **equity.**

   equitable *adjective* Many civil rights laws were written with the goal of ensuring **equitable** treatment for all people, regardless of their backgrounds or beliefs.

The *equity* an owner has in a property is the total property value minus any mortgage owed.

4. **frugal** (frōō´gəl) *adjective* from Latin *frug,* "virtue"
   Economical; thrifty; careful or strict in avoiding unnecessary spending
   • People who live through hard times usually learn to be **frugal.**

   frugality *noun* The couple's **frugality** enabled them to save enough money to send all their children to college.

5. **indigent** (ĭn´dĭ-jənt) *adjective* from Latin *in-*, "within" + *egere*, "to lack"
Extremely poor; impoverished; lacking basic necessities
• As the mill laid off more and more workers, the number of **indigent** families in the area increased rapidly.

indigence *noun* **Indigence** usually goes hand in hand with poor nutrition and the lack of medical care.

Don't confuse the word *indigent* with *indignant*, which means "angry about an injustice."

6. **munificent** (myōō-nĭf´ĭ-sənt) *adjective* from Latin *munus*, "gift" + *facere*, "to make"
Generous; liberal in giving
• The chaos and pain inflicted by the terrible earthquake inspired people around the world to make **munificent** donations to aid the victims.

munificence *noun* Her **munificence** was well known throughout the city, for she had given millions of dollars to local charities.

7. **pecuniary** (pĭ-kyōō´nē-ĕr´ē) *adjective* from Latin *pecunia*, "wealth"
Having to do with money
• While social work may not bring large **pecuniary** rewards, it provides the satisfaction that comes from helping people.

8. **recession** (rĭ-sĕsh´ən) *noun* from Latin *recedere*, "to move back"
a. A general decline in business activity
• During the **recession,** my uncle lost his job and went into debt.
b. The act of withdrawing or going back
• In a tsunami, the sudden **recession** of the sea is followed by large, destructive waves.

recessional *noun* The organist played the **recessional** as the choir filed out of the church.

recede *verb* In 2005, when water **receded** from the canals in Venice, Italy, some gondolas ran aground.

Recessional means "a hymn played as people exit a church" or simply "the process of exiting in an orderly manner."

9. **remunerate** (rĭ-myōō´nə-rāt´) *verb* from Latin *re-*, "back" + *munus,* "gift"
To pay for goods provided, services rendered, or losses incurred; to compensate for
• Are professional athletes excessively **remunerated** for what they do?

remuneration *noun* The insurance company provided **remuneration** to the landlord for the extensive fire damage.

10. **solvent** (sŏl´vənt) *adjective* from Latin *solvere*, "to loosen"
Capable of meeting financial obligations; able to pay debts
• Cost cutting is one way to keep a company **solvent.**

insolvent *adjective* Unable to pay debts
• Charles Dickens's novels often feature characters who are **insolvent.**

solvency *noun* To maintain **solvency,** the small theater needed to sell fifty additional season tickets.

Solvent also means "a substance in which another substance is *dissolved,* forming a *solution.*"

WRITE THE CORRECT WORD

Write the correct word in the space next to each definition.

frugal	1. thrifty	recession	6. a decline in the economy
pecuniary	2. having to do with money	solvent	7. able to meet financial obligations
munificent	3. generous	remunerate	8. to pay for something
equity	4. net value	depreciate	9. to decrease in value
indigent	5. impoverished; lacking necessities	austerity	10. severe restrictions

COMPLETE THE SENTENCE

Write the letter for the word that best completes each sentence.

__c__ 1. Cheryl's _____ gift surprised and delighted me.
   a. frugal   b. indigent   c. munificent   d. solvent

__c__ 2. During the _____, the unemployment rate increased while salary rates decreased.
   a. remuneration   b. depreciation   c. recession   d. frugality

__d__ 3. Because the store is no longer _____, it will be having a going-out-of-business sale next week.
   a. depreciated   b. indigent   c. pecuniary   d. solvent

__a__ 4. The value of our stock _____ to the point that it was basically worthless.
   a. depreciated   b. remunerated   c. receded   d. solved

__b__ 5. Accustomed to restaurants and electricity, Harris was slow to adapt to the _____ of the primitive conditions on the island.
   a. munificence   b. austerity   c. equity   d. recession

__b__ 6. The motto "Waste not, want not" encourages _____ behavior.
   a. munificent   b. frugal   c. equitable   d. pecuniary

__a__ 7. He said, "There is much more to life than _____ concerns, my friend; money isn't everything."
   a. pecuniary   b. indigent   c. solvent   d. munificent

__a__ 8. It can take years to build up _____ in one's house and property.
   a. equity   b. munificence   c. depreciation   d. austerity

__d__ 9. Gustav was upset that he was not _____ for his work.
   a. indigent   b. depreciated   c. solvent   d. remunerated

__b__ 10. The refugees were utterly _____ and relied on charity for food and clothing.
   a. solvent   b. indigent   c. munificent   d. pecuniary

Challenge: Shortly after Darlene was laid off from her job, her family fell into _____, and they were forced to live a completely _____ lifestyle.

__b__   a. austerity…solvent   b. indigence…austere   c. munificence…frugal

Teens on Trains

The Great Depression changed the lives of millions of Americans, many of them teenagers. The 1920s had been a decade of great prosperity in the United States, and people expected this good fortune to continue in future decades. **(1)** Even after the stock market crash of 1929, many believed that the economic downturn would only be a brief *recession.*

What followed, however, was a worldwide financial crisis. In the United States, banks had heavily invested their patrons' money in the stock market. **(2)** After the banks lost those funds due to the crash, they were no longer *solvent.* Many banks closed and were unable to return people's money.

This sudden lack of money slowed the demand for goods, putting millions out of work. **(3)** At the same time, *equity* in real estate disappeared, as property values fell below the amount of debt that people owed on their mortgages. People began losing their homes.

With their savings and equity wiped out, families that had lived comfortably now faced serious financial challenges. **(4)** Those households that still had incomes relied on strict *frugality.* Others were not so fortunate.

(5) Often, people who lost their jobs became completely *indigent.* **(6)** Their families were forced to adopt *austere* lifestyles; many could barely afford to eat. **(7)** Some people sold their furniture or jewelry to get by, but its value had so *depreciated* that they received little for it.

When the head of a household was unable to find work, teenagers were expected to help in any way they could. In some cases, the only hope was for teens to look for work in other towns.

(8) During the Depression, more than 250,000 teens rode the railroad lines in search of work, hoping to lessen their families' *pecuniary* troubles. Some teens hopped on the trains in order to lessen their families' burdens by reducing the number of people who needed to be fed; others were simply seeking adventure.

Searching for work by roaming the country on trains was a hard life. **(9)** When teens managed to find some work, they often did the same jobs as adults for less *remuneration.* A day's work that earned a dollar for an adult might yield just a dime or two—or perhaps a piece of fruit—for a teenager. These young wandering workers faced hunger and illness. They often went several days without food, and if they became weak or ill, they usually went without medical treatment. **(10)** Many who rode the rails depended on the *munificence* of others for survival.

In 1933, President Franklin D. Roosevelt created the Civilian Conservation Corps, which offered jobs and room and board to unmarried men between the ages of seventeen and twenty-seven. These men were paid $30 each month and were required to send $25 of it back to their families. At its peak in 1935, the Corps employed a half million workers, many of them teens, glad to leave the trains for safer and more secure living quarters. The work they did both improved the nation's parks and forests and allowed the teens to send sorely needed funds home to their families.

Each sentence below refers to a numbered sentence in the passage. Write the letter of the choice that gives the sentence a meaning that is closest to the original sentence.

___c___ **1.** Many believed that the downturn would only be a brief _____.
    a. financial need   **b.** net value   **c.** economic decline   **d.** fair event

___d___ **2.** After the banks lost those funds due to the crash, they were no longer _____.
    a. economical, thrifty   **b.** liberal in giving   **c.** investing money   **d.** able to pay debts

___a___ **3.** At the same time, _____ real estate disappeared.
    a. values of   **b.** sales of   **c.** loans for   **d.** payments on

___c___ **4.** Those households that still had incomes relied on strict _____.
    a. generosity   **b.** poverty   **c.** thriftiness   **d.** jobs

_c_ **5.** Many people who lost their jobs became completely _____.
a. restricted   b. severe   c. impoverished   d. greedy

_c_ **6.** Their families were forced to adopt _____ lifestyles; many could barely afford to eat.
a. luxurious   b. declining   c. simple, bare   d. monetary, rich

_d_ **7.** Some people sold their furniture or jewelry to get by, but its value had so _____ that they received little for it.
a. rusted   b. gone up   c. held steady   d. decreased

_a_ **8.** Many teens left home hoping to lessen their families' _____ troubles.
a. financial   b. housing   c. medical   d. professional

_b_ **9.** Teens often did the same jobs as adults for less _____.
a. necessities   b. compensation   c. training   d. insurance

_b_ **10.** Many depended on the _____ of others for survival.
a. jobs   b. generosity   c. trains   d. families

Indicate whether the statements below are TRUE or FALSE according to the passage.

_T_ **1.** Many teenagers left home during the Depression.

_F_ **2.** During the Depression, teenagers were usually treated just like adults by most employers.

_T_ **3.** President Roosevelt's Civilian Conservation Corps did not offer jobs and room and board to elderly men or to women.

WRITING EXTENDED RESPONSES

Suppose that you are a teenager struggling through the Great Depression. Write an essay describing the challenges that you and your family face and how you are trying to meet them. Be sure to describe specific situations. Your essay should be at least three paragraphs long. Use at least three lesson words in your essay and underline them.

WRITE THE DERIVATIVE

Complete the sentence by writing the correct form of the word shown in parentheses. You may not need to change the form that is given.

solvency **1.** The business went from _____ to bankruptcy in just a few months. (*solvent*)

austere **2.** The defendant trembled as she entered the cold, _____ courtroom. (*austerity*)

equitably **3.** The new policy was meant to ensure that all employees would be treated _____. (*equity*)

indigence **4.** A sharp fall in crop prices left many farmers teetering on the verge of _____. (*indigent*) _pecuniary_ **5.** It is generally considered rude to ask someone about the details of their _____ circumstances. *(pecuniary)*

depreciation **6.** Kirsten calculated the _____ of her car to be roughly 20 percent per year. *(depreciate)*

frugally **7.** Every Sunday morning, Mom clips coupons from the newspaper so she can shop more _____ . *(frugal)*

remuneration **8.** After laboring in the hot sun all day, Kirk demanded _____ for his work. *(remunerate)*

receded **9.** As we drove off, our house _____ into the distance. *(recession)*

munificence **10.** The director of the museum thanked the patron for her _____ in donating the priceless paintings. *(munificent)*

FIND THE EXAMPLE

Choose the answer that best describes the action or situation.

_c_ **1.** The most *frugal* meal
   a. steak and potatoes   **b.** chicken and rice   **c.** bread and water   **d.** eggs and bacon

_d_ **2.** Something that a lawyer would likely be *remunerated* for
   a. brushing her teeth   **b.** reading a book   **c.** washing dishes   **d.** giving legal advice

_d_ **3.** Something that a *munificent* person would most likely do
   a. make predictions   **b.** melt pennies   **c.** hoard gold   **d.** make donations

_c_ **4.** Something that an *indigent* American would be most likely to have
   a. health insurance   **b.** a big house   **c.** hunger pangs   **d.** a sports car

_b_ **5.** Something that would make it more difficult for a pizza shop to remain *solvent*
   a. better tomatoes   **b.** rent increase   **c.** yummy toppings   **d.** fewer employees

_c_ **6.** Something that typically increases during a *recession*
   a. salaries   **b.** jobs   **c.** unemployment   **d.** bank accounts

_d_ **7.** The storage place where a car's value would be LEAST likely to *depreciate*
   a. garbage dump   **b.** lake bottom   **c.** war zone   **d.** indoor garage

_c_ **8.** A *pecuniary* birthday gift
   a. necklace   **b.** computer   **c.** check   **d.** sweater

_d_ **9.** The one that is LEAST likely to be a part of an *austere* lifestyle
   a. bread   **b.** water   **c.** shelter   **d.** chocolate

_c_ **10.** A person whose job involves fighting for or preserving *equity*
   a. hairdresser   **b.** astronaut   **c.** civil rights lawyer   **d.** mechanical engineer

Reading and Reasoning

Context Clues in Primary Sources

As your history courses become more advanced, you will probably read more primary sources, or works written during the periods you are studying. You have already studied some techniques for determining the meaning of unfamiliar words by using context clues. These additional strategies will help you read and understand primary sources.

Strategies

1. *Consider the date of the work.* This will alert you to the fact that some words may be used in unfamiliar ways. In the eighteenth century, for example, enthusiasm meant something closer to *fanaticism*.

2. *Consider the type of writing and the subject.* A personal letter will have a different level of vocabulary than a formal speech. Scientific writing and political tracts often use specific vocabulary. Keeping in mind the literary form and subject will help you make more accurate determinations of the meanings of unfamiliar words.

3. *Find out what you can about the author.* Knowing who wrote a work will provide additional clues to word meanings.

4. *Consult a dictionary.* If you can't figure out the meaning of a critical word, use a reference source. In some cases, a rare or obsolete word can only be found in an unabridged dictionary.

Practice

The following excerpt is from a work by Thomas Jefferson and John Dickinson. Addressed to the British government, it was approved by the Second Continental Congress on July 6, 1775, a full year before the Declaration of Independence. It makes many of the points that are found in that more famous document. Read the entire passage once to get a general idea of what it is about. Then slowly reread the passage, writing your own definition for each italicized word. Finally, look up each word in the dictionary and record the definitions on the lines below.

But why should we (1) *enumerate* our injuries in detail? By one statute it is declared that parliament can "of right make laws to bind us in all cases whatsoever." What is to defend us against so enormous, so unlimited a power? Not a single man of those who assume it, is chosen by us; or is subject to our control or influence; but, on the contrary, they are all of them exempt from the operation of such laws . . . We saw the misery to which such (2) *despotism* would reduce us. We for ten years (3) *incessantly* and ineffectually (4) *besieged* the throne as (5) *supplicants*; we reasoned, we remonstrated with parliament, in the most mild and decent language.

Administration (6) *sensible* that we should regard these (7) *oppressive* measures as freemen ought to do, sent over fleets and armies to enforce them. The indignation of the Americans was roused, it is true; but it was the indignation of a virtuous, loyal, and affectionate people. A Congress of delegates from the United Colonies was assembled at Philadelphia, on the fifth day of last September. We resolved again to offer an humble and dutiful petition to the King, and also addressed our fellow-subjects of

Great Britain. We have pursued every (8) *temperate*, every respectful measure; we have even proceeded to break off our [commerce] with our fellow-subjects, as the last peaceable (9) *admonition,* that our attachment to no nation upon Earth should (10) *supplant* our attachment to liberty. This, we flattered ourselves, was the ultimate step of the controversy.

1. enumerate

My definition _____

Dictionary definition _____ to count off or name one by one; to list _____

2. despotism

My definition _____

Dictionary definition _____ the actions of a despot; tyranny _____

3. incessantly

My definition _____

Dictionary definition _____ continuing without interruption _____

4. besieged

My definition _____

Dictionary definition _____ to harass or importune, as with requests · _____

5. supplicants

My definition _____

Dictionary definition _____ people who ask humbly or earnestly _____

6. sensible

My definition _____

Dictionary definition _____ having a perception of something _____

7. oppressive

My definition _____

Dictionary definition _____ difficult to bear; burdensome _____

8. temperate

My definition _____

Dictionary definition _____ exercising moderation and self-restraint _____

9. admonition

My definition _____

Dictionary definition _____ cautionary advice or warning _____

10. supplant

My definition _____

Dictionary definition _____ to displace and substitute for (another) _____

Criticism

WORD LIST

acrimonious	chastise	debunk	derogatory	disparage
harass	impugn	innuendo	invective	vilify

Criticism can be hard to accept, especially when delivered harshly, but it can also help us improve. The words in this lesson will help you distinguish various types of criticism.

1. acrimonious (ăk´rə-mō´nē-əs) *adjective*
from Latin *acrimonia,* "sharpness"
Bitter or sharp in language or tone
• The students' disagreement over the theme of the dance became so **acrimonious** that the faculty adviser called an end to the meeting.

acrimony *noun* During the final round of competition, the **acrimony** between the rival debate teams intensified dramatically.

acrimonious

> *Acrimony* is related to the word *acrid,* meaning "smelling or tasting sharp and strong."

2. chastise (chăs´tīz´, chăs-tīz´) *verb*
To punish or criticize severely
• The parents **chastised** their child for running across the street without looking both ways first.

chastisement *noun* Marie filed a complaint against her manager in response to his public **chastisement.**

3. debunk (dē-bŭngk´) *verb*
To expose or make fun of a false claim or an exaggeration
• The professor immediately **debunked** her colleague's new theory, pointing out the many false assumptions underlying his thesis.

4. derogatory (dĭ-rŏg´ə-tôr´ē) *adjective* from Latin *de-,* "away" + *rogare,* "to ask"
Insulting; belittling
• Not realizing that Dwayne was standing behind her, Ella made a **derogatory** comment about his taste in clothes.

5. disparage (dĭ-spăr´ĭj) *verb* from Latin *dis-,* "opposite of" + Old French *parage,* "high birth"
To speak of in a disrespectful or slighting way; to belittle
• The novice golfer felt discouraged after the instructor **disparaged** his first efforts to hit the ball.

disparaging *adjective* The student made **disparaging** remarks about the professor's requirement of rigid discipline in his classes.

6. **harass** (hə-răs´) *verb*
To irritate or torment repeatedly
   • The bullies who **harassed** the smaller children on the playground by ruining their games were finally caught and punished.

   harassment *noun* The landlord was charged with **harassment** for appearing at his tenants' places of employment to collect rent payments.

7. **impugn** (ĭm-pyōōn´) *verb* from Latin *in-*, "against" + *pugnare*, "to fight"
To attack or challenge as false or questionable
   • In an effort to win the race, the congressional candidate **impugned** his opponent's voting record, calling it favorable to special interests.

> To *impugn* someone's character is to call into question the ethics of their actions or beliefs.

8. **innuendo** (ĭn´yōō-ĕn´dō) *noun* from Latin *innuendo*, "by hinting"
An indirect or subtle expression of something, usually negative; a hint
   • Through masterful **innuendo,** she managed to make everyone think that Mr. Mattheiu was the culprit, without ever accusing him directly.

9. **invective** (ĭn-vĕk´tĭv) *noun* from Latin *in*, "against" + *vehere*, "to carry"
Abusive or strongly critical language
   • For weeks after their big fight, every exchange between the two sisters was filled with **invective.**

10. **vilify** (vĭl´ə-fī´) *verb* from Latin *vilificare*, "to hold cheap"
To make vicious insulting comments about; to slander
   • While some hailed the rebels as saviors, others **vilified** them as violent and brutal.

   vilification *noun* The athlete was upset by the journalist's **vilification** of his behavior, claiming she hadn't explained the whole story.

Point out that the words *vilify, impugn,* and *acrimonious* imply a very strong and critical emotional tone.

WORD ENRICHMENT

Hunting words

The word *harass* may come from the Old French word *harer*, meaning "to set dogs on." In the sport of hunting, hounds were sent ahead by owners to locate the prey, often a fox, using their keen sense of smell. The hounds then chased the prey, leading the hunters to it.

Other English words and expressions also come from hunting. A *red herring*, a type of fish, was used in the hunt to distract hounds from a scent. The term is now used to refer to something that draws attention away from a central issue. The word *venison,* which means "deer meat," originally referred to the flesh of any game animal used for food. The word is taken from Latin *venare,* "to hunt."

The expression *eat humble pie,* which means "to be humbled or proven wrong, usually after boasting," also originated in this sport. After an animal was killed in the hunt, nobles and aristocrats dined on the meat. The *umbles,* organs such as the heart, liver, and entrails of the animal, were often baked into a pie for the servants and huntsmen to eat. Those who ate "umble pie" were considered inferior.

WRITE THE CORRECT WORD

Write the correct word in the space next to each definition.

___debunk___	**1.** to expose as false	___harass___	**6.** to torment constantly
___chastise___	**2.** to punish severely	___acrimonious___	**7.** bitter in tone
___vilify___	**3.** to slander	___derogatory___	**8.** insulting; belittling
___invective___	**4.** abusive language	___innuendo___	**9.** a subtle hint at something negative
___impugn___	**5.** to attack as false or questionable	___disparage___	**10.** to speak of disrespectfully

COMPLETE THE SENTENCE

Write the letter for the word that best completes each sentence.

___d___ **1.** We were shocked by the stream of _____ she let loose on the referee.
    a. debunking   **b.** acrimonious   **c.** harassment   **d.** invective

___a___ **2.** Their dispute was so _____ that they stopped talking to one another.
    a. acrimonious   **b.** chastising   **c.** harassing   **d.** debunking

___a___ **3.** By questioning the authenticity of the painting, Roberto _____ the reputation of the gallery owner.
    a. impugned   **b.** invective   **c.** harassed   **d.** chastised

___c___ **4.** The architect _____ his competitors' designs, calling them "cluttered and meaningless."
    a. harassed   **b.** chastised   **c.** disparaged   **d.** debunked

___c___ **5.** Many gossip columnists spread scandal by _____, hinting at celebrities' misconduct.
    a. chastisement   **b.** invective   **c.** innuendo   **d.** harassment

___b___ **6.** Mrs. Garner _____ her son for tracking mud all over the new carpet.
    a. disparaged   **b.** chastised   **c.** vilified   **d.** impugned

___a___ **7.** The biographer wanted to _____ the myth surrounding the actor's illness.
    a. debunk   **b.** chastise   **c.** vilify   **d.** harass

___c___ **8.** Isabel reported her coworker's _____ comments about others to the manager.
    a. invective   **b.** chastising   **c.** derogatory   **d.** vilified

___d___ **9.** The young puppies _____ the old dog by nipping at him and climbing on him.
    a. debunked   **b.** disparaged   **c.** impugned   **d.** harassed

___d___ **10.** The corrupt CEO _____ employees who agreed to testify against him, claiming they were lying to cover up their own illegal conduct.
    a. innuendo   **b.** invective   **c.** debunked   **d.** vilified

Challenge: When the scandalous _____ about the politician proved to be true, he was completely _____ by the press and forced to resign his position.
___b___   **a.** acrimony...disparaged   **b.** innuendo...vilified   **c.** invective...chastised

Paid to Pry

(1) Of all the members of the media, the most *vilified* are the celebrity photographers, known as paparazzi. Wherever the rich and famous go, the paparazzi seem close behind, snapping candid photos to sell to the tabloid press.

Like detectives on a stakeout, camera-ready paparazzi watch the homes of stars and follow the stars when they run simple errands. **(2)** It's no surprise that many celebrities have nothing but *invective* to offer when asked about these photographers.

This relationship between the media and the rich and famous did not always exist. Until the 1950s, the only celebrity photographs that the public saw were those selected by movie studio publicists. Entertainment editors were content to print posed images that painted a rosy image of the stars. **(3)** No one seemed interested in casting these stars in a *derogatory* light.

Eventually, some editors became bored with these staged photos and began to demand candid shots of celebrities. One night, an Italian photographer in Rome got lucky. He managed to photograph a former king knocking over a table in a restaurant. After those unflattering photos were printed, the unspoken rules of etiquette regarding photographing celebrities fell by the wayside. **(4)** The media discovered that it could sell more papers and magazines with *disparaging* stories and photos of stars than it ever did with flattering material. In 1960, the Italian director Federico Fellini produced a film featuring a ruthless photographer named Paparazzo, thus giving the new breed of celebrity photo hounds their now common nickname.

The paparazzi began to behave like hunters. Stars could no longer go about their private lives without fear that a photographer would pop out from behind a bush at any moment. **(5)** Some tabloids have used these candid photos to *impugn* stars' reputations. **(6)** Along with *innuendo* and outright lies, innocent pictures have been used to create nasty rumors. For example, if an actor is caught with messy hair, a tabloid might claim she is having a nervous breakdown. If a rock star is photographed with a scowl, the tabloid might invent a story suggesting that he is having marital problems.

(7) Paparazzi continue to *harass* celebrities, and there is an increase in the use of dangerous tactics to obtain candid photos. Sometimes, the paparazzi chase superstars on highways at dangerous speeds. In 1997, when Princess Diana of Wales died in a fatal car accident in Paris, France, many blamed her death on the seven paparazzi that were pursuing her car when it crashed.

Some stars have gone to court to sue the paparazzi and their publishers. **(8)** There, the stars have *debunked* the outrageous stories invented by the press. **(9)** Other celebrities have simply chosen to *chastise* the paparazzi publicly and implore them to print only the truth. Still others have tried to outwit the stalking photographers by using look-alikes as a decoy tactic, or by sending out false press information to lure the paparazzi to the wrong events.

In response, the paparazzi argue that they are just trying to do their jobs. They also point out that celebrities may complain, but that, ultimately, the stars need exposure. As one Hollywood saying goes, "There's no such thing as bad publicity."

(10) The debate, however, remains highly *acrimonious*. Some of the accusations have also been aimed at the public. Publishers argue that if fans were not so hungry for candid photos of celebrities, the paparazzi would not take them.

Each sentence below refers to a numbered sentence in the passage. Write the letter of the choice that gives the sentence a meaning that is closest to the original sentence.

___d___ **1.** The most _____ members of the media are the paparazzi.
    a. beloved   **b.** famous   **c.** critical   **d.** insulted

___d___ **2.** Many celebrities have nothing but _____ to offer about these photographers.
    a. helpful comments   **b.** praise   **c.** ill will   **d.** insulting words

___a___ **3.** No one seemed interested in casting these stars in a _____ light.
    a. negative   **b.** questionable   **c.** praiseworthy   **d.** glowing

___b___ **4.** The media could sell more papers and magazines with _____ stories and photos of stars.
  a. tell-all   **b.** disrespectful   **c.** subtle   **d.** flattering

___b___ **5.** Some tabloids have used these candid photos to _____ stars' reputations.
  a. expose   **b.** attack   **c.** disprove   **d.** torment

___a___ **6.** Along with _____ and outright lies, innocent pictures have been used to create nasty rumors.
  a. subtle hints   **b.** false attacks   **c.** insults   **d.** doctored photos

___a___ **7.** Paparazzi continue to _____ celebrities.
  a. torment   **b.** photograph   **c.** insult   **d.** expose

___d___ **8.** There, the stars have _____ the outrageous stories invented by the press.
  a. strongly criticized   **b.** helped to establish   **c.** largely ignored   **d.** proved as false

___c___ **9.** Other celebrities have simply chosen to _____ the paparazzi publicly.
  a. appeal to   **b.** reward   **c.** criticize   **d.** spread rumors about

___c___ **10.** The debate, however, remains highly _____.
  a. respectful   **b.** subtle   **c.** bitter   **d.** apologetic

Indicate whether the statements below are TRUE or FALSE according to the passage.

___F___ **1.** Today, most celebrities enjoy the attention of the paparazzi.

___T___ **2.** Tabloids often distort the truth, using photos to support their stories.

___F___ **3.** The public bears no responsibility for the actions of the paparazzi.

FINISH THE THOUGHT

Complete each sentence so that it shows the meaning of the italicized word.

1. Your *derogatory* remarks _____ Answers will vary. _____

_____

2. She *impugned* her neighbor by _____ Answers will vary. _____

_____

WRITE THE DERIVATIVE

Complete the sentence by writing the correct form of the word shown in parentheses. You may not need to change the form that is given.

___disparagingly___ **1.** The unprofessional clerk was fired for speaking _____ about her manager in front of coworkers in the lunchroom. *(disparage)*

___harassment___ **2.** The man was taken to court on charges of _____. *(harass)* acrimoniously

3. The cranky siblings argued _____ all day. (*acrimonious*)

chastising or chastisement

4. Fran's teacher's _____ did no good; Fran still turned in her assignments late. (*chastise*)

invective

5. Feeling sorry about his _____ toward his sister the previous day, Lewis made a special effort to compliment her today. (*invective*)

innuendoes

6. The article was full of insinuations and _____ that cast doubt on the singer's reputation. (*innuendo*)

vilified

7. Crime suspects are sometimes _____ by the press before they are proven guilty. (*vilify*)

impugned

8. Mary Queen of Scots _____ Elizabeth I's right to the English throne. (*impugn*)

debunking

9. Cassie made a big show of arriving at work early and leaving later than everyone else, thereby _____ the rumor that she was a slacker. (*debunk*)

derogatory

10. The sensitive actor was devastated when the critic used _____ words like "terrible" and "dreadful" to describe her performance. (*derogatory*)

FIND THE EXAMPLE

Choose the answer that best describes the action or situation.

c **1.** An example of *innuendo:* Don't you think that she _____
  a. dances well? **b.** has nice clothes? **c.** looks ill? **d.** did a great job?

b **2.** A *derogatory* comment
  a. You look great! **b.** How dumb! **c.** Is that true? **d.** My birthday is today.

d **3.** A way that a child might *harass* his or her big sister
  a. share ice cream **b.** keep a messy room **c.** clean her room **d.** mimic her words

b **4.** A way that a parent might *chastise* a rebellious son
  a. give him a gift **b.** ground him **c.** clean his room **d.** lend him money

a **5.** The person most likely to be *vilified* by a community
  a. corrupt mayor **b.** school teacher **c.** registered nurse **d.** hyperactive toddler

d **6.** An *acrimonious* statement
  a. Let's compromise. **b.** Isn't that clever? **c.** Never mind. **d.** You arrogant fool!

c **7.** A way to describe a person who uses a lot of *invective*
  a. neutral **b.** generous **c.** abusive **d.** intelligent

a **8.** Something you might try to *debunk*
  a. nasty rumor **b.** bad novel **c.** bad game **d.** annoying habit

c **9.** A person whose job sometimes requires *impugning* others
  a. flight attendant **b.** singer **c.** lawyer **d.** athlete

c **10.** How you might feel if your efforts were *disparaged*
  a. optimistic **b.** accomplished **c.** discouraged **d.** critical

Humor

WORD LIST

banter	caricature	droll	facetious	flippant
hilarity	ludicrous	mirth	whimsical	witticism

Humor makes life fun and helps us connect with others. As entertainer Victor Borge once said, "Laughter is the shortest distance between two people." The words in this lesson will help you describe different styles and aspects of humor.

Ask students to describe a *caricature* they have seen, a *flippant* comment or some *banter* they have heard, or something *ludicrous* they have observed.

1. **banter** (băn´tər)
   a. *verb* To converse in a playful or teasing way
   • Talk-show hosts often **banter** with their guests.
   b. *noun* An exchange of good-humored, playful remarks
   • When a woman told Winston Churchill, who was famous for his **banter**, "If I were your wife, I'd put poison in your coffee," he replied, "If I were your husband, I'd drink it."

2. **caricature** (kăr´ĭ-kə-choͮor´) from Italian *caricare*, "to exaggerate"
   a. *noun* A representation in which distinctive traits are exaggerated or distorted for comic effect
   • **Caricatures** of the late Soviet leader Leonid Brezhnev usually included ridiculously bushy eyebrows.
   b. *verb* To represent or imitate in an exaggerated or distorted manner
   • Luckily, Principal Weiss laughed when she saw herself being **caricatured** on stage in the student talent show.

   caricaturist *noun* Becky is a great **caricaturist**; in just a few seconds, she can make a funny, recognizable sketch of any celebrity.

Caricatures often appear in cartoons, articles, books, and performances.

caricature

3. **droll** (drŏl) *adjective*
   Amusingly odd
   • My **droll** uncle showed up at the family barbecue wearing overalls and an upside-down hat full of ears of corn.

4. **facetious** (fə-sē´shəs) *adjective* from Latin *facetus*, "witty"
   Playfully joking; humorous; not meant to be taken seriously
   • I was being **facetious** when I said that, in the future, people who can spell will not be allowed to use the Internet.

5. **flippant** (flĭp´ənt) *adjective*
   Humorous in a disrespectful, casual way; rudely witty
   • While frantically asking neighbors if they had seen her lost dog, Lynn didn't appreciate the **flippant** question, "Is he the one with the tail?"

6. **hilarity** (hĭ-lăr´ĭ-tē) *noun* from Greek *hilaros*, "cheerful"
   Great merriment; extreme amusement
   • The silly costumes and jokes added to the **hilarity** of the gathering.

   hilarious *adjective* The comedian's jokes were so **hilarious** that we laughed until we were gasping for air.

7. **ludicrous** (loo´dĭ-krəs) *adjective* from Latin *ludus*, "game"
   Ridiculously, laughably absurd
   • At a fundraiser, the soccer dads dressed up as honey bees and did a **ludicrous** dance, buzzing up and down the aisles and pretending to gather honey.

   ludicrousness *noun* Imagine the **ludicrousness** of a sixty-year-old, overweight, bearded actor playing the lovely, young Juliet!

8. **mirth** (mûrth) *noun* from Old English *myrgth*, "merriment"
   Good spirits; happiness and merriment, especially as expressed by laughter
   • The wedding guests were full of **mirth** and excitement.

   mirthful *adjective* The court jester's constant jokes and imitations made the king's dinner a **mirthful** occasion.

9. **whimsical** (hwĭm´zĭ-kəl) *adjective*
   Playful or unpredictable
   • My **whimsical** aunt Harriet regularly traveled to exotic places on the spur of the moment.

   whimsy *noun* In an act of pure **whimsy,** the teacher did a back-flip before starting the lecture.

10. **witticism** (wĭt´ĭ-sĭz´əm) *noun*
    A clever remark or saying
    • Oscar Wilde is famous for his **witticisms;** my favorite is "I can resist anything but temptation."

    witty *adjective* We enjoyed the speaker's **witty** remarks.

> *Witticism* is a portmanteau word created from the words *witty* and *criticism*. The poet John Dryden coined it in the late 1600s.

WORD ENRICHMENT

Odd two-part words

Some two-part words sound funny, but can be used in both humorous and serious contexts. For example, *wishy-washy* means "lacking in strength of purpose or character." *Hoity-toity* means "pretentiously self-important." *Dilly-dally* means "to waste time, especially in indecision; to dawdle."

Some examples without hyphens include *hodgepodge,* "a mixture of dissimilar ingredients; a jumble," and *claptrap,* "pretentious, insincere, or empty language."

WRITE THE CORRECT WORD

Write the correct word in the space next to each definition.

___mirth___	**1.** good spirits	___whimsical___	**6.** unpredictable
___hilarity___	**2.** great merriment	___caricature___	**7.** a comic exaggeration
___banter___	**3.** playful conversation	___witticism___	**8.** a clever remark
___droll___	**4.** amusingly odd	___ludicrous___	**9.** utterly absurd
___flippant___	**5.** disrespectfully humorous	___facetious___	**10.** not meant to be taken seriously

COMPLETE THE SENTENCE

Write the letter for the word that best completes each sentence.

___b___ **1.** Where did you get the _____ idea that I'd changed my name to "Bumbelina"?
   a. caricatured   **b.** ludicrous   **c.** flippant   **d.** facetious

___c___ **2.** Some people call my sense of humor odd, but I prefer to call it _____.
   a. flippant   **b.** banter   **c.** droll   **d.** facetious

___a___ **3.** The winning team was so full of _____ that the three-hour bus ride seemed to fly by.
   a. mirth   **b.** facetiousness   **c.** caricature   **d.** witticism

___a___ **4.** I hope Jack realized that my comment about his presentation being "canceled due to lack of interest" was _____.
   a. facetious   **b.** droll   **c.** mirthful   **d.** ludicrous

___d___ **5.** We were amused by the clever _____ between the show's characters.
   a. hilarity   **b.** caricature   **c.** witticism   **d.** banter

___d___ **6.** Every chapter of the _____ book contained some delightful new twist.
   a. flippant   **b.** ludicrous   **c.** facetious   **d.** whimsical

___b___ **7.** I was embarrassed after tripping, but I could understand the _____ that followed.
   a. whimsy   **b.** hilarity   **c.** caricature   **d.** witticism

___c___ **8.** One of Mark Twain's many great _____ is, "The man who doesn't read good books has no advantage over the man who can't read them."
   a. hilarities   **b.** banters   **c.** witticisms   **d.** caricatures

___c___ **9.** Because of Peter's _____ answers during the interview, he did not get the job.
   a. hilarious   **b.** witty   **c.** flippant   **d.** caricatured

___c___ **10.** Maria's role in the comedy was a _____ of a lovesick teenager.
   a. hilarity   **b.** whimsy   **c.** caricature   **d.** mirth

Challenge: At first, the _____ between the colleagues was good-natured, but after a few veiled insinuations, their comments soon became more _____ and biting.
___a___ **a.** banter…flippant   **b.** witticisms…ludicrous   **c.** whimsy…droll

Not Your Average Clown

(1) The majority of today's clowns rely on silly physical acts to create *hilarity*. "When you think of clowns today, you might think of people in a big three-ring circus, bopping each other over the head with pies and then running away," says Barbara Michaels, a member of the all-women's clown troupe Only Fooling. "But that's not the whole story of where clowns came from." Not all clowns are like the ones who entertain circus audiences.

The art of clowning originates in the traditions of court jesters who once entertained kings and queens. Much of a jester's humor was verbal rather than the physical, slapstick variety used by many of today's clowns. **(2)** Jesters uttered *droll* comments about life in the royal court. **(3)** Often, their *facetious* remarks pointed out the faults of others—including the monarchs—in a humorous way.

"The jester was the only person allowed to contradict the king. It was an important role because only the jester was able to stand up to authority fearlessly and make fun of situations in order to set people straight," says Michaels.

By the sixteenth century, jester characters had made appearances in plays. In Italy, a form of theater called the *Commedia del Arte* featured comic characters who undermined authority figures. Many Shakespearean plays also include such characters.

Eventually, jesters became known as clowns. **(4)** At first, they performed in small circuses, where their *flippant* remarks about life amused their audiences. But clowns still played the role of social commentator.

(5) Audiences were able to appreciate the clown's observations about life in an atmosphere of *mirth*. "There's an old saying that people's minds are more open after they've laughed," says Michaels.

(6) With the advent of huge circuses, however, clowns could no longer *banter* with the audience. Their voices were simply not loud enough to be heard. "The things they had to do to get attention changed," says Michaels. **(7)** No longer able to tell jokes verbally, clowns shifted to visual humor, creating *ludicrous* situations such as five large people trying to squeeze into a tiny car.

In recent years, however, a revival of classic clowning has taken hold. Michaels is part of a wave of humorists seeking to return to the theatrical roots and social mission of clowning. **(8)** Their acts are still full of *whimsical*, lighthearted routines, but some of the clowns now talk and joke about serious matters such as loneliness or dishonesty. Many perform without makeup in small theaters and parks where they can better connect with the crowd.

"Basically, it's about taking the truth that being a human being is a vulnerable activity and making fun of that," says Michaels. Often, the clowns use their own personal failings in their performances. "For example, if you're somewhat conceited, your clown's character might be really vain, and the act will revolve around that," she says. **(9)** So, in a way, the clowns become *caricatures* of themselves.

Whether Michaels is prancing around with a duck on her head or exploring common problems such as insensitive bosses, her goals remain the same: She aims to entertain, teach, and bond with her audience.

"I feel like laughter is a social service because we all need it so badly," she says. **(10)** As the old *witticism* goes, "A clown isn't a serious person trying to be funny; it's a funny person trying to be serious."

Each sentence below refers to a numbered sentence in the passage. Write the letter of the choice that gives the sentence a meaning that is closest to the original sentence.

____a____ **1.** The majority of today's clowns rely on silly physical acts to create _____.
    a. amusement   **b.** remarks   **c.** ridiculousness   **d.** performances

____a____ **2.** Jesters uttered _____ comments about life in the royal court.
    a. odd and funny   **b.** rude and mean   **c.** teasingly playful   **d.** much exaggerated

____b____ **3.** Often, their _____ remarks pointed out the faults of others in a humorous way.
    a. totally serious   **b.** playfully funny   **c.** unpredictable   **d.** absurd

___c___ **4.** The clowns' _____ remarks about life amused their audiences.
    a. good-humored   **b.** sharply insightful   **c.** rudely witty   **d.** playfully impulsive

___d___ **5.** Audiences were able to appreciate the clown's observations about life in an atmosphere of _____.
    a. bafflement   **b.** exaggeration   **c.** casualness   **d.** merriment

___c___ **6.** Clowns could no longer _____ with the audience.
    a. act impulsively   **b.** talk seriously   **c.** playfully converse   **d.** provide entertainment

___c___ **7.** Clowns shifted to visual humor, creating _____ situations.
    a. oddly funny   **b.** greatly amusing   **c.** crazily absurd   **d.** unpredictably silly

___a___ **8.** Their acts are still full of _____, lighthearted routines.
    a. playful   **b.** clever   **c.** ridiculous   **d.** distorted

___d___ **9.** In a way, the clowns become _____ of themselves.
    a. odd amusements   **b.** good spirits   **c.** silly types   **d.** comic exaggerations

___b___ **10.** As the old _____ goes, "A clown isn't a serious person trying to be funny; it's a funny person trying to be serious."
    a. light conversation   **b.** clever saying   **c.** famous quotation   **d.** funny comment

Indicate whether the statements below are TRUE or FALSE according to the passage.

___T___ **1.** Historically, clowns have often undermined authority figures.

___F___ **2.** The court jester's only function was to amuse the king's court.

___T___ **3.** Barbara Michaels aims to teach and entertain at the same time.

WRITING EXTENDED RESPONSES

Choose a person whom you consider to be especially funny. The person can be real, such as an actor or a comedian, or a fictional character from a book, movie, or television show. In an essay, give at least two reasons why you find this person so hilarious. (Explain and support your reasons, but do not include details that would be inappropriate for the classroom.) Your essay should be at least three paragraphs long. Use at least three lesson words in your essay and underline them.

WRITE THE DERIVATIVE

Complete the sentence by writing the correct form of the word shown in parentheses. You may not need to change the form that is given.

___facetiously___ **1.** Eliana was not amused when Jorge told her _____ that his car had a flat tire so he couldn't take her to the dance. (*facetious*)

___mirthful___ **2.** The children were _____ when the clown hit himself with a pie. (*mirth*)

flippant   **3.** Mrs. Yung was shocked by her son's _____ answers to her serious questions. *(flippant)*

caricaturist   **4.** Tammi got a job as a _____ because she is a talented artist with a good sense of humor. *(caricature)*

hilarious   **5.** The movie's dialogue was so _____ that everyone we knew repeated the lines over and over. *(hilarity)*

whimsy   **6.** Some people carefully plan their lives, but others prefer to act on _____. *(whimsical)*

ludicrousness   **7.** "The _____ of your theory makes me question your sanity," said the judgmental astrophysicist. *(ludicrous)*

bantering   **8.** "You two stop _____ in class," the teacher scolded. *(banter)*

witty   **9.** Shakespeare's comedies contain many _____ comments about life and love. *(witticism)*

droll   **10.** The street performer's _____ act drew a large crowd. *(droll)*

FIND THE EXAMPLE

Choose the answer that best describes the action or situation.

d   **1.** The most likely reason a lecturer would begin a talk with a *witticism*
    a. to offend students   **b.** to state the thesis   **c.** to express anger   **d.** to interest the audience

c   **2.** A way to express *mirth*
    a. walk slowly   **b.** whisper softly   **c.** laugh loudly   **d.** sit quietly

c   **3.** A *ludicrous* item to wear to the beach on a hot summer day
    a. bathing suit   **b.** sandals   **c.** snow boots   **d.** floppy hat

d   **4.** A word that would NOT describe a *facetious* comment
    a. playful   **b.** sarcastic   **c.** humorous   **d.** serious

b   **5.** Something that would NOT inspire *hilarity*
    a. comedy routine   **b.** chemistry test   **c.** sitcom   **d.** romantic comedy

d   **6.** The person most likely to have a *flippant* attitude
    a. romantic poet   **b.** businessman   **c.** caring parent   **d.** rebellious teen

c   **7.** The genre of literature most likely to include *whimsical* plot twists
    a. poetry   **b.** nonfiction essay   **c.** fantasy   **d.** historical fiction

a   **8.** An audience reaction most likely caused by a *droll* character
    a. surprised laughter   **b.** eternal boredom   **c.** fiery anger   **d.** terrible fear

c   **9.** The LEAST appropriate place for *banter*
    a. ball game   **b.** party   **c.** library   **d.** street corner

c   **10.** A feature that would most likely be included in a *caricature* of a scholarly professor
    a. buzz cut   **b.** broad shoulders   **c.** thick glasses   **d.** slick suit

Similarities and Differences

WORD LIST

analogy	antithesis	commensurate	congruence	deviate
disparity	heterogeneous	homogeneous	nuance	tantamount

Many common words and expressions refer to similarities or differences. The words in this lesson will add to your ability to describe how things are alike and how they vary.

1. **analogy** (ə-năl´ə-jē) *noun* from Greek *analogos*, "proportionate"
   A comparison highlighting a similarity between otherwise dissimilar things
   • To explain how a camera works, the photography teacher made an **analogy** between the eye and a camera lens.

   analogous *adjective* The reporter thought that the World's Fair and the Super Bowl were **analogous** in their ability to excite wide interest.

2. **antithesis** (ăn-tĭth´ĭ-sĭs) *noun* from Greek *anti-*, "against" + *tithenai*, "to set"
   a. The direct or exact opposite
   • With his sloppy work habits and poor people skills, Norman was the **antithesis** of a good office assistant.
   b. A figure of speech in which contrasting ideas are placed side by side in parallel phrases
   • An example of an **antithesis** is Alexander Pope's famous quotation "To err is human; to forgive, divine."

   antithetical *adjective* Good and evil are **antithetical** concepts.

3. **commensurate** (kə-měn´sər-ĭt) *adjective* from Latin *com-*, "together" + *mensurare*, "to measure"
   Corresponding in size or degree; proportionate
   • His large office was **commensurate** with the power of his position as chief executive.

4. **congruence** (kŏng´grōō-əns) *noun* from Latin *congruere*, "to agree"
   Agreement, harmony, or correspondence
   • There is often a lack of **congruence** between the amount of money a movie makes and the quality of the reviews it gets.

   congruent *adjective* The speaker's flippant jokes and colloquial style were not **congruent** with the solemnity of the ceremony.

5. **deviate** (dē´vē-āt´) *verb* from Latin *de-*, "away" + *via*, "road"
   To depart or turn aside from a path, direction, or course of action
   • When the scientists **deviated** from previous approaches used to solve the problem, they made an important discovery.

   deviation *noun* Evan's father would not allow the slightest **deviation** from the route he had planned for the family trip.

In biology, the term *analogous* indicates similarity in function, but not in structure or origin. The fins of fish are *analogous* to the wings of birds.

Have students classify lesson words into those that imply similarities, such as *homogeneous* and *tantamount,* and those that imply differences, such as *disparity* and *heterogeneous.* Ask students to explain their classifications.

The plural of *antithesis* is *antitheses.*

In math, the term *congruent* refers to things that are the exact same shape and size.

congruent

6. **disparity** (dĭ-spăr´ĭ-tē) *noun* from Latin *dis-*, "not" + Late Latin *paritas,* "equality"
   The condition or fact of being unequal or different; inequality
   • The **disparity** between the wealth of the French nobility and the poverty of the masses eventually led to the French Revolution of 1789.

   disparate *adjective* Containing many differences in kind
   • The poll claimed to represent the opinions of a **disparate** group of workers, from manual laborers to CEOs.

7. **heterogeneous** (hĕt´ər-ə-jē´nē-əs) *adjective* from Greek *hetero,* "other" + *genos,* "kind"
   Consisting of many different elements or types; varied
   • The **heterogeneous** range of music at the festival included classical, folk, and hip-hop.

   heterogeneity *noun* The **heterogeneity** of modern urban populations makes for a fascinating mix of dress, customs, food, and languages.

8. **homogeneous** (hō´mə-jē´nē-əs) *adjective* from Greek *homo,* "same; like" + *genos,* "kind"
   Similar in kind or nature; uniform
   • The strip mall's **homogeneous** gray buildings contrasted sharply with the variety of colors and designs in the downtown storefronts.

   homogenize *verb* To make uniform or the same throughout
   • Milk is **homogenized** so that thick cream will not rise to the top.

   homogeneity *noun* The parents disliked the school's **homogeneity** because they wanted their children to be in a multicultural setting.

   > *Homogeneous* and *heterogeneous* are direct opposites. *Homogenous* (hə-mŏj´ə-nəs) is a variant form of *homogeneous.*

9. **nuance** (nōō´äns´) *noun* from Latin *nubes,* "cloud"
   A subtle or slight degree of difference
   • Bethany's talent for capturing **nuances** of voice and gesture enabled her to do wonderful imitations of famous people.

   nuanced *adjective* Her **nuanced** performance conveyed the subtle changes in her character's attitudes as the play progressed.

10. **tantamount** (tăn´tə-mount´) *adjective* from Anglo-Norman *tant amunter,* "to amount to as much"
    Equivalent in significance, effect, or value
    • The attack on the territory was **tantamount** to a declaration of war.

WORD ENRICHMENT

Cloudy words

The word *nuance* comes from the Latin word *nubes,* which means "cloud." The word *nebulous* has the same origin, and means both "cloudy; misty" and "lacking in definite form."

WRITE THE CORRECT WORD

Write the correct word in the space next to each definition.

disparity	**1.** inequality	tantamount	**6.** equivalent to
homogeneous	**2.** similar in kind	analogy	**7.** a comparison
deviate	**3.** to vary from a path	congruence	**8.** agreement; harmony
antithesis	**4.** the exact opposite	heterogeneous	**9.** mixed; varied
nuance	**5.** a slight degree of difference	commensurate	**10.** corresponding in size or degree

COMPLETE THE SENTENCE

Write the letter for the word that best completes each sentence.

d **1.** The _____ in their ages did not prevent the sixty-year-old woman and her thirty-year-old neighbor from becoming close friends.
   a. deviation   **b.** homogeneity   **c.** congruence   **d.** disparity

a **2.** Her extensive qualifications were _____ with the requirements of the important job.
   a. commensurate   **b.** heterogeneous   **c.** homogeneous   **d.** analogous

b **3.** The pilot _____ from the flight path, hoping to avoid storm activity.
   a. nuanced   **b.** deviated   **c.** homogenized   **d.** disparate

a **4.** The unanimous vote reflected the _____ of the committee members' opinions.
   a. congruence   **b.** antithesis   **c.** disparity   **d.** heterogeneity

b **5.** The way he left out important details about what happened was _____ to lying.
   a. heterogeneous   **b.** tantamount   **c.** disparate   **d.** homogeneous

c **6.** With his style and charm, the actor was the _____ of the slob he played on TV.
   a. homogeneity   **b.** nuance   **c.** antithesis   **d.** analogy

b **7.** The flying instructor drew a(n) _____ between playing a video game and operating a flight simulator.
   a. disparity   **b.** analogy   **c.** nuance   **d.** antithesis

a **8.** _____ of color from light pink to deep purple made the sunset especially beautiful.
   a. Nuances   **b.** Antithesis   **c.** Homogeneity   **d.** Deviations

d **9.** The businessmen were a(n) _____ bunch; they all wore dark suits and ties.
   a. heterogeneous   **b.** disparate   **c.** analogous   **d.** homogeneous

b **10.** The wide variety of cultures represented at the block party revealed the _____ of the neighborhood.
   a. deviation   **b.** heterogeneity   **c.** analogy   **d.** homogeneity

Challenge: Although the school paper stated that it published _____ opinions, the editors' lack of tolerance for any ideas that deviated from their own was _____ to censorship.
b   **a.** deviate...congruent   **b.** disparate...tantamount   **c.** homogeneous...analogous

Cell-Phone Designer

People use cell phones for dozens of functions that range from sending instant messages and reading news to taking photos and playing games. Yet cell phones continue to become smaller. How can this be?

Richard Schatzberger, a user interface engineer, works on the challenging issues of cell-phone design. **(1)** Born in England, he attended Staffordshire University, where he received a degree *tantamount* to a B.A. in the United States. Staffordshire, England, has a long tradition of visual design; famous makers of fine china, such as Wedgewood and Royal Spode, have been operating there for centuries. **(2)** So Schatzberger's education included *heterogeneous* experiences such as designing pottery, studying the psychology of visual design, and exploring computer typography. Every aspect of his varied education has served Schatzberger well. **(3)** It might seem that decorating fine china is the *antithesis* of designing modern cell phones, yet both fields address human concern with the appearance of functional items.

Today, Schatzberger works in the United States for a major cell-phone company. Fitting lots of stuff into a small space is one problem he confronts daily. People expect everything that appears on their computers to be on their cell phones, Schatzberger explains. **(4)** Yet there is a tremendous *disparity* in the size of the two types of screens. In fact, a cell-phone screen is only one-eighth the size of a typical computer screen. And as cell phones get smaller, there is even less room for the screen because the phone buttons must remain large enough so that our fingers can press one without touching another. **(5)** In fact, any *deviation* below a minimum of eight millimeters makes buttons unusable. This leads to challenges when designing smaller cell phones.

Schatzberger has also worked on cell-phone designs for use in China. This is very complex because entering text in Chinese can be problematic. In the Chinese writing system, each character is a word. **(6)** Thus, instead of our twenty-six-letter alphabet, Chinese has thousands of complex characters, and every *nuance* that differentiates them is important. Yet Chinese users must work with our Roman alphabet keyboard. **(7)** The situation is perhaps *analogous* to trying to write English using just four or five different letters. In response to this challenge, Schatzberger developed a "graffiti" system that allows users to draw Chinese characters over a normal keypad and then choose from options that pop up on a screen. This dramatically speeds up text entry.

(8) Cell phones are designed for users around the world and, as we all know, human beings are a *heterogeneous* bunch. Perhaps this is why "skinning," or customizing one's cell phone, has become so popular. Using skinning technology that Schatzberger has helped to develop, customers can transform their phones to match their favorite sports team, cartoon character, or TV show. **(9)** In Asia, where people often swap or borrow cell phones, a push of a button gives the phone a design *congruent* with the preferences of the current user.

(10) Although he started out as a designer, Schatzberger's position is now more *commensurate* with his creativity and record of success: He is already leading a creative design team, even though he is only in his twenties. Solving problems certainly has its rewards.

Each sentence below refers to a numbered sentence in the passage. Write the letter of the choice that gives the sentence a meaning that is closest to the original sentence.

___b___ **1.** Schatzberger received a degree _____ a B.A. in the United States.
    a. opposite to   **b.** equivalent to   **c.** varied from   **d.** different from

___a___ **2.** Schatzberger's education included _____ experiences.
    a. varied   **b.** tedious   **c.** uniform   **d.** harmonious

___c___ **3.** It might seem that decorating fine china is the _____ designing modern cell phones.
    a. same as   **b.** equivalent of   **c.** opposite of   **d.** closest to

__b__ **4.** Yet there is a tremendous _____ in the size of the two types of screens.
   a. comparison   **b.** difference   **c.** agreement   **d.** similarity

__c__ **5.** Any _____ below a minimum of eight millimeters makes buttons unusable.
   a. equation   **b.** enlargement   **c.** variation   **d.** agreement

__d__ **6.** Every _____ that differentiates Chinese characters is important.
   a. shape   **b.** agreement   **c.** figure of speech   **d.** slight difference

__b__ **7.** The situation is perhaps _____ to trying to write English using just four or five different letters.
   a. confusing   **b.** comparable   **c.** dissimilar   **d.** unequal

__d__ **8.** As we all know, human beings are a _____ bunch.
   a. uniform   **b.** curious   **c.** harmonious   **d.** diverse

__a__ **9.** One push gives the phone a design _____ the preferences of the current user.
   a. in agreement with   **b.** opposed to   **c.** in contrast with   **d.** differing from

__c__ **10.** Schatzberger's position is now more _____ with his creativity.
   a. measurable   **b.** envied   **c.** proportionate   **d.** varied

Indicate whether the statements below are TRUE or FALSE according to the passage.

__T__ **1.** There are some basic limits on how small a cell phone can get.

__F__ **2.** The Chinese language has twenty-six letters in its alphabet.

__F__ **3.** Richard Schatzberger has been designing cell phones for more than thirty years.

FINISH THE THOUGHT

Complete each sentence so that it shows the meaning of the italicized word.

1. There is a *disparity* between _____ Answers will vary.

_____

2. If you *deviate* from _____ Answers will vary.

_____

WRITE THE DERIVATIVE

Complete the sentence by writing the correct form of the word shown in parentheses. You may not need to change the form that is given.

__homogeneity__ **1.** The _____ of the band's parade uniforms was very pleasing to the eye. *(homogeneous)*

__nuances__ **2.** Being unaware of the _____ of the language, President Kennedy actually told the crowd, "I am a jelly donut." *(nuance)* __analogous__   **3.** On a planetary scale, rain forests and wetlands are _____ to lungs and kidneys. (*analogy*)

__deviation__   **4.** Any _____ from the assembly directions will result in the pieces not fitting together properly. (*deviate*)

__congruent__   **5.** Because their opinions were so often _____, the couple rarely argued. (*congruence*)

__commensurate__   **6.** Hat size is not _____ with intelligence. (*commensurate*)

__antithetical__   **7.** The playful comedy was completely _____ in tone to the somber tragedy. (*antithesis*)

__disparate__   **8.** The International Club was made up of a _____ group of students. (*disparity*)

__heterogeneity__   **9.** True music lovers enjoy the _____ of styles played on most university radio stations. (*heterogeneous*)

__tantamount__   **10.** Borrowing something without asking the owner's permission is _____ to stealing. (*tantamount*)

FIND THE EXAMPLE

Choose the answer that best describes the action or situation.

__c__   **1.** Things in a classroom that are most likely to be *homogeneous*
     a. students' hair   **b.** pictures   **c.** desks   **d.** students' shoes

__b__   **2.** The one most likely to notice *nuances* in music
     a. toddler   **b.** conductor   **c.** pilot   **d.** chef

__a__   **3.** What you do when you *deviate* from the rules
     a. break them   **b.** follow them   **c.** read them   **d.** explain them

__a__   **4.** The *antithesis* of working hard
     a. loafing   **b.** persevering   **c.** writing   **d.** listening

__d__   **5.** A reply *tantamount* to saying yes
     a. Maybe.   **b.** No way.   **c.** I think not.   **d.** Certainly.

__c__   **6.** Two things that are *congruent*
     a. a cup and a spoon   **b.** a stick and a tree   **c.** a pair of dice   **d.** a grape and an orange

__b__   **7.** Something that is *heterogeneous*
     a. distilled water   **b.** snack mix   **c.** pure oxygen   **d.** maple syrup

__a__   **8.** A vehicle *commensurate* with a luxurious lifestyle
     a. limousine   **b.** economy car   **c.** pickup truck   **d.** commuter bus

__c__   **9.** Two things that are *analogous* in function
     a. desk, chair   **b.** hammer, nail   **c.** gills, lungs   **d.** fire, extinguisher

__a__   **10.** The greatest *disparity* in emotions
     a. elated vs. depressed   **b.** mad vs. furious   **c.** scared vs. terrified   **d.** shocked vs. surprised

Taking Tests

SAT Writing Tests

The new SAT, first administered in 2005, has a Writing section that includes an essay question and a set of multiple-choice questions on grammar, usage, and composition. There are three different kinds of multiple-choice questions. Each kind is described below.

Strategies

1. The **identification of sentence error** questions require you to look at four underlined parts of a sentence and determine whether one of them is faulty.

   First, read the entire sentence. Then reread the sentence and choose the part that has an error in grammar, usage, or syntax. (No more than one part can be incorrect.) If you find no errors, choose E.

2. **Sentence correction** items also present a sentence with underlined words. Here, your task is to choose the correct version of the underlined part in order to improve the sentence.

   Note that choice A is the same as the underlined version.

3. **Paragraph improvement** items present a paragraph with several sentences. Each item asks how a specific sentence or part of the paragraph can be improved. Your task is to choose the correct change needed to improve the paragraph.

   To answer these kinds of questions, read through the paragraph and all of the answer choices first. The key is to choose the answer that combines the sentences—or makes another kind of change—without changing the meaning of the sentences. Decide what the sentences mean, and then choose the answer that is best written and retains the same meaning.

Practice

In questions 1–3, choose the underlined part of the sentence that contains an error in grammar, usage, or word choice. If there is no error, choose answer E.

d   **1.** I <u>knew</u> that Jesse <u>was</u> a better writer <u>than</u> <u>me</u>. <u>No error</u>
        A   B   C   D   E

a   **2.** "<u>Whom</u> <u>shall</u> I say <u>is calling</u>?" <u>asked</u> Carla. <u>No error</u>
       A   B   C   D   E

e   **3.** Jeannie's twin sister, <u>Melinda</u>, is <u>taller</u>, but Jeannie is <u>more</u> conspicuous
                                   A   B   C
<u>because of</u> her brilliant red hair. <u>No error</u>
    D   E

In questions 4–6, the underlined part of the sentence may need to be corrected. Choice A is the same as the original underlined part; the other answer choices are different. Choose the answer that best expresses the meaning of the original sentence.

_____ b _____ 4. Coming down the hill, my house is the first one on the right.
    a. Coming down the hill, my house
    b. Coming down the hill, you will find that my house
    c. My house, coming down the hill,
    d. Coming down the hill, and my house
    e. You will find my house, coming down the hill,

_____ a _____ 5. The uniforms that they wore were bright green.
    a. uniforms that they wore
    b. uniforms that they wearing
    c. uniforms, that they wore,
    d. uniforms they are wearing
    e. uniforms, which they wore,

_____ b _____ 6. The Roman Empire fell in the late fifth century, and it left an enduring legacy of culture and law.
    a. The Roman Empire fell in the late fifth century, and
    b. Although the Roman Empire fell in the late fifth century,
    c. Since the Roman Empire fell in the late fifth century,
    d. The Roman Empire fell in the late fifth century
    e. The fall of the Roman Empire occurred in the late fifth century, and

For questions 7–8, read the paragraph. Some parts of the paragraph need to be improved. Choose the best answer to each question about the way the paragraph is written.

(1) Today, Australia is one of the world's wealthiest nations. (2) Australia has very little land suitable for farming. (3) It has an abundance of natural resources. (4) Because it has huge supplies of bauxite, coal, and iron ore, Australia's main industry is mining. (5) Australia produces numerous metals and chemicals, gems, diamonds, petroleum products, and steel. (6) Ranching and fishing are also important parts of the economy. (7) The leading producer of wool in the world is this country, Australia.

_____ c _____ 7. Which is the best way to combine sentences 2 and 3?
    a. Australia has very little land suitable for farming and natural resources.
    b. Australia has very little land suitable for farming or an abundance of natural resources.
    c. Although Australia has very little land suitable for farming, it has an abundance of natural resources.
    d. Because Australia has very little land suitable for farming, it has an abundance of natural resources.
    e. If Australia has very little land suitable for farming, then it has an abundance of natural resources.

_____ d _____ 8. Which is the best version of sentence 7?
    a. The leading producer of wool in the world is this country, Australia.
    b. This country, Australia, is the leading producer of wool in the world.
    c. In the world, the leading producer of wool is this country, Australia.
    d. Australia is the world's leading producer of wool.
    e. The leading producer of wool is Australia, this country in the world.

Governing and Authority

WORD LIST

autocratic	autonomy	caste	despot	feudal
hegemony	oligarchy	sovereign	totalitarian	usurp

Over the course of history, nations have been governed by monarchs, small powerful groups, and elected officials. Today, there are still many different forms of government functioning throughout the world. This translates into varying degrees of political choices and personal freedoms among the governed. The words in this lesson refer to ways in which governments or people rule and hold authority.

1. **autocratic** (ô´tə-krăt´ĭk) *adjective* from Greek *auto*, "self" + *krates*, "ruler"
   Ruling with unlimited power or authority
   • The **autocratic** CEO wielded total control over her company.

   autocrat *noun* The king's use of his unlimited power for his own gain made him the most mistrusted **autocrat** in the nation's history.

   autocracy *noun* A country ruled by a dictator is an **autocracy**.

2. **autonomy** (ô-tŏn´ə-mē) *noun* from Greek *auto-*, "self" + *nomos*, "rule; law"
   Independence; self-determination or self-governance
   • The people in the northern part of the country gained **autonomy** by waging a fierce civil war against the ruler in the south.

   autonomous *adjective* Judges are supposed to be **autonomous** and uninfluenced by others' opinions.

3. **caste** (kăst) *noun* from Latin *castus*, "pure"
   A social class separated from others by profession, wealth, or hereditary rank
   • India's **caste** system was one of the many institutions that Mahatma Gandhi fought against.

4. **despot** (dĕs´pət) *noun* from Greek *despotes*, "master"
   a. A ruler with absolute power
   • Although portrayed as cruel in *The King and I*, King Monghut of Siam, was an enlightened **despot**.
   b. A person who wields power oppressively; a tyrant
   • The **despot** imprisoned anyone who criticized him.

   despotic *adjective* People took desperate measures to escape the **despotic** regime.

despot

Point out that two lesson words, *autocratic* and *autonomy*, contain the prefix *auto-* ("self"). Ask students to explain how the meaning of each word is related to "self."

The word *caste* can also be used to refer specifically to the *caste* system of traditional Hindu society.

The first definition of *despot* is synonymous with *autocrat*.

5. feudal (fyoō´l) *adjective* from Latin *feudum*, "fee"
Relating to a system in which people (called "vassals") were given
protection and the use of land, in return for loyalty, payments, and
services to a lord
• In **feudal** systems, vassals had to provide military service to their lord.

feudalism *noun* From about 1100–1400, **feudalism** was the dominant
governing system in Japan.

> *Feudalism* was a common
> political and economic
> system in Europe during the
> Middle Ages.

6. hegemony (hĭ-jĕm´ə-nē) *noun* from Greek *hegemon*, "leader"
Dominance, especially that of a country, region, or group over others
• Historians point out that, just as with anything else, the economic
and military **hegemony** of the United States will not last forever.

7. oligarchy (ŏl´ĭ-gär´kē) *noun* from Greek *oligos*, "few" + *-arch*, "rule"
a. Government by a few, especially by a small faction of people
or families
• An **oligarchy** does not grant the rights of democracy to the
common people.
b. A state governed by a few people or families
• For more than a thousand years, Venice was an **oligarchy** governed
by a group of nobles.

oligarch *noun* By definition, an **oligarch** must share power
with others.

8. sovereign (sŏv´ər-ĭn) from Old French *soverain*, "superior; ruler"
a. *adjective* Self-governing; independent
• Many former British colonies became **sovereign** nations during the
middle part of the twentieth century.
b. *adjective* Having supreme rank or power
• Although he possessed **sovereign** powers, the prince routinely
consulted his advisers.
c. *noun* A king, queen, or other noble person who serves as head of
state; a ruler or monarch
• As time wears on, fewer nations are ruled by **sovereigns**.

9. totalitarian (tō-tăl´ĭ-târ´ē-ən) *adjective* from Latin *totus*, "all;
whole" + (*author*)-*itarian*
Relating to a form of government with absolute and centralized control
over every aspect of people's lives
• George Orwell's novel *1984* depicts a **totalitarian** state, in which even
people's thoughts are controlled.

10. usurp (yoō-sûrp´) *verb* from Latin *usurpare*, "to take into use"
a. To take and hold power or rights by force and without legal
authority
• The rebels **usurped** control by taking over the palace, the main
roads, and the airwaves.
b. To take the place of or occupy without right
• The man **usurped** his neighbor's land by building on it.

usurper *noun* The crafty **usurper** seized the king's throne.

WRITE THE CORRECT WORD

Write the correct word in the space next to each definition.

_____feudal_____ **1.** relating to a system of lords and vassals

_____usurp_____ **2.** to take power by force

_____sovereign_____ **3.** a king or queen

_____autocratic_____ **4.** ruling with unlimited power

_____caste_____ **5.** a social class of rank, wealth, or profession

_____totalitarian_____ **6.** relating to an all-controlling government

_____autonomy_____ **7.** independence; self-determination

_____oligarchy_____ **8.** government by a few

_____hegemony_____ **9.** dominance

_____despot_____ **10.** a tyrant

COMPLETE THE SENTENCE

Write the letter for the word that best completes each sentence.

___c___ **1.** After being ruled by the same family for centuries, the former _____ became a democracy.
a. sovereign   **b.** caste   **c.** oligarchy   **d.** despot

___b___ **2.** Some remote regions, though technically not _____, are all but self-governing.
a. oligarchic   **b.** sovereign   **c.** feudal   **d.** totalitarian

___c___ **3.** "You may not marry someone of a lower _____," declared the noble.
a. despot   **b.** sovereign   **c.** caste   **d.** oligarchy

___a___ **4.** The Roman Empire's _____ was military, cultural, and political.
a. hegemony   **b.** sovereign   **c.** caste   **d.** autonomy

___b___ **5.** The insurgent _____ seized political power from the elected leaders.
a. caste   **b.** usurpers   **c.** feuds   **d.** hegemony

___d___ **6.** The _____ regime was so oppressive that it even dictated official music.
a. feudal   **b.** autonomous   **c.** sovereign   **d.** totalitarian

___a___ **7.** The _____ cruelly punished all who did not greet him correctly.
a. despot   **b.** caste   **c.** autonomy   **d.** hegemonies

___b___ **8.** _____ people are independent and make their own life choices.
a. Feudal   **b.** Autonomous   **c.** Usurped   **d.** Caste

___c___ **9.** Since _____ systems of government maintain control through the use of land, they are often based on agriculture.
a. oligarchic   **b.** sovereign   **c.** feudal   **d.** autonomous

___d___ **10.** She ran her company as a(n) _____, insisting on total control.
a. autonomy   **b.** oligarchy   **c.** usurpation   **d.** autocracy

Challenge: The _____ headed a _____ government that had complete control over the politics, economy, and culture of the country.
___b___ **a.** caste…sovereign   **b.** despot…totalitarian   **c.** autonomy…feudal

What Was Feudalism?

We often hear the word *feudal* in conversations about the Middle Ages, but what does it really mean?

Feudalism was a system that arose partly because of a lack of central government power. In the 400s, the Roman Empire began to break apart. **(1)** In the East, it continued under a series of *despots* who governed from Constantinople (now called Istanbul). In the West, however, Europe fragmented into hundreds of different territories. **(2)** The larger, *autonomous* nations of today had not yet arisen.

Under the Roman Empire, independent farmers had been protected and provided with services—mail and water, for example—in return for paying taxes. As the Roman system collapsed, however, people began to fight for more land. **(3)** Strong leaders *usurped* power from simple farmers. **(4)** Unable to protect themselves, these farmers constantly came under the rule of new, increasingly powerful and *autocratic* neighbors. **(5)** The *feudal* system arose out of this chaos, providing some order in this era of change. In this system, lords granted land and protection to vassals. In return, the vassals owed the lords military service, taxes, labor, and crops. Vassals either worked the land themselves or organized peasants, or serfs, to do so. **(6)** Sometimes, loose *oligarchies* of lords controlled a large region, but often, a single lord was at the top of a *pyramid* of power. But this lord, in turn, might owe military service to an even more powerful overlord. That overlord might have yet another lord above him. **(7)** At the very top of this chain of pyramids, a *sovereign* king often ruled over all. **(8)** In theory, the sovereign's *hegemony* covered a vast area; in practice, he had little power without the cooperation of his lords and their underlings.

Knights were also an integral part of the feudal system. Originally, a knight was simply a professional soldier who lived with a lord. Because a horse and armor were required, only rich people could be knights. **(9)** Although knighthood was originally defined simply by service to a lord, it gradually became a *caste*, with membership passed from father to son.

Feudalism declined as centralized governments gradually spread. Many historians, legal experts, and workers' rights advocates consider the decline of feudalism to be a positive change. From the point of view of a free, tolerant democracy, they are undoubtedly right. **(10)** But seen from the vantage point of a modern *totalitarian* state, things may not be so clear-cut: In Hitler's Germany or Stalin's Russia, for example, greater numbers of people were controlled, manipulated, and mistreated than in feudal societies. In addition, feudal lords did not have the technology that modern tyrants use to control people today.

Making value judgments about the past can be tricky, but one thing is certain: Feudalism represents a long and important chapter in European history.

Each sentence below refers to a numbered sentence in the passage. Write the letter of the choice that gives the sentence a meaning that is closest to the original sentence.

__a__ **1.** In the East, it continued under a series of _____ .
 a. powerful rulers   **b.** polite lords   **c.** groups of rulers   **d.** military takeovers

__d__ **2.** The larger, _____ nations of today had not yet arisen.
 a. iron-fisted   **b.** medieval   **c.** all-powerful   **d.** independent

__c__ **3.** Strong leaders _____ power from simple farmers.
 a. shared   **b.** gave up   **c.** seized   **d.** built up

_c_ **4.** Farmers constantly came under the rule of new, increasingly powerful and
_____ neighbors.
    a. cruel   **b.** kind   **c.** authoritarian   **d.** persecuted

_d_ **5.** The _____ system arose out of this chaos.
    a. all-powerful   **b.** exploitive   **c.** independent   **d.** lord-and-vassal

_b_ **6.** Sometimes, loose _____ of lords controlled a large region.
    a. social classes   **b.** governing groups   **c.** military alliances   **d.** armies

_a_ **7.** At the very top of this chain of pyramids, a _____ king often ruled over all.
    a. supreme   **b.** weak   **c.** British   **d.** hateful

_b_ **8.** In theory, the sovereign's _____ covered a vast area.
    a. society   **b.** dominance   **c.** independence   **d.** social class

_a_ **9.** Knighthood gradually became a _____, with membership passed from father
to son.
    a. social class   **b.** small kingdom   **c.** governing group   **d.** dominant crew

_b_ **10.** But seen from the vantage point of a modern _____ state, things may not be
so clear-cut.
    a. group-led   **b.** all-controlling   **c.** medieval   **d.** tolerant

Indicate whether the statements below are TRUE or FALSE according to the passage.

_F_ **1.** Feudalism is a common economic and political system today.

_F_ **2.** All modern societies have been more respectful of human rights than feudal
societies were.

_T_ **3.** Feudalism arose out of a period of drastic change in Europe after the Roman
Empire broke apart.

WRITING EXTENDED RESPONSES

The reading passage describes a form of political and economic
organization called feudalism. In an expository essay of at least three
paragraphs, choose another form of government (such as democracy,
oligarchy, monarchy, totalitarianism, or socialism) and compare what
you know about it with feudalism. Use at least three lesson words in your
essay and underline them.

WRITE THE DERIVATIVE

Complete the sentence by writing the correct form of the word shown in
parentheses. You may not need to change the form that is given.

hegemony   **1.** The analyst predicted that the company's _____ over the widgets market would
be short-lived. *(hegemony)*

usurped   **2.** Yesterday, my neighbor _____ my parking space. *(usurp)* __sovereigns__   **3.** The _____ of some modern countries are figureheads whose positions are mainly ceremonial. *(sovereign)*

__autocrat__   **4.** The coach behaved like an _____, refusing to let the players have a say in the decisions that affected the team. *(autocratic)*

__caste__   **5.** She was enraged by the notion that her _____ determined what she could do with her life. *(caste)*

__Feudalism__   **6.** _____ was the dominant system of societal organization in Europe in the Middle Ages. *(feudal)*

__autonomous__   **7.** Mom's decision to let the children be completely _____ in choosing their clothes resulted in some strange outfits. *(autonomy)*

__oligarch__   **8.** The power-hungry noble dreamed of the day when he would no longer be an _____, but a monarch with complete control. *(oligarchy)*

__totalitarian__   **9.** Aldus Huxley's novel *Brave New World* paints a chilling portrait of a _____ state. *(totalitarian)*

__despot__   **10.** The _____ imprisoned people whose political views differed from his own. *(despot)*

FIND THE EXAMPLE

Choose the answer that best describes the action or situation.

__b__   **1.** An example of a *sovereign*
     a. circus   **b.** king   **c.** cheetah   **d.** mountain

__a__   **2.** Someone who is likely to be a member of an *oligarchy*
     a. noble   **b.** cook   **c.** mechanic   **d.** jester

__d__   **3.** The amount of aspects of life controlled by a *totalitarian* government
     a. none   **b.** a few   **c.** several   **d.** all

__c__   **4.** A group that often tries to *usurp* power
     a. hikers   **b.** fish   **c.** rebels   **d.** grandmothers

__b__   **5.** Something that is likely to be influenced by a *caste* system
     a. moon's orbit   **b.** career paths   **c.** jump shot   **d.** cat's vision

__a__   **6.** A word that describes an *autocratic* government
     a. powerful   **b.** open   **c.** democratic   **d.** wishy-washy

__a__   **7.** A word most associated with the *feudal* system
     a. vassal   **b.** radio   **c.** caveman   **d.** voting

__b__   **8.** Something that would most likely lead to military *hegemony*
     a. peaceful times   **b.** a huge army   **c.** disorganization   **d.** new buildings

__d__   **9.** Someone who does NOT have *autonomy*
     a. star athlete   **b.** department head   **c.** lone reporter   **d.** prison inmate

__c__   **10.** Something that a *despot* would NOT do
     a. eat food   **b.** make rules   **c.** ask permission   **d.** protect himself

Care and Precision

WORD LIST

diligence	fastidious	finicky	imprudent	judicious
meticulous	minutia	slovenly	trepidation	unmindful

The degree of care and precision you demand from yourself can be the difference between an A and an F, or between contentment and stress. The words in this lesson will help you express and understand descriptions of situations in which those things are important.

Have students classify lesson words into those that denote a high degree of care or precision (for example, *fastidious, meticulous*) and those that denote a low degree of care or precision (for example, *imprudent, unmindful*).

1. **diligence** (dĭl´ə-jəns) *noun* from Latin *dis-,* "apart" + *legere,* "to choose"
   a. Steady effort; persistent hard work
   • Becoming a doctor requires intelligence, **diligence,** and a caring nature.
   b. Attentive care; carefulness
   • Her **diligence** as a copyeditor made her an important asset to the school newspaper.

   diligent *adjective* The college graduate was **diligent** in the pursuit of a job, sending out resumes daily and going to several job fairs.

2. **fastidious** (fă-stĭd´ē-əs) *adjective* from Latin *fastidium,* "squeamishness; haughtiness"
   a. Possessing or displaying careful attention to detail
   • He was so **fastidious** about keeping his room clean that his mother had to tell him, "One sock in the wrong place won't kill you."
   b. Picky; difficult to please
   • My cousin Arielle was such a **fastidious** eater that our grandmother worried whether Arielle was getting enough nutrition.

   fastidiousness *noun* The row of pencils, sorted by size and color and laid out perfectly on the desk, hinted at her **fastidiousness.**

3. **finicky** (fĭn´ĭ-kē) *adjective*
   Difficult to please; insisting on getting exactly what one wants
   • Young children are often **finicky** eaters, uncomfortable with trying different kinds of food.

4. **imprudent** (ĭm-prōōd´nt) *adjective* from Latin *im-,* "not" + *providere,* "to provide for"
   Unwise; doing things without careful thought or judgment
   • It is **imprudent** to spend more than you earn.

   imprudence *noun* One obvious example of **imprudence** is riding in a car without wearing a seatbelt.

Note that the second definition of *fastidious* is a synonym of *finicky.*

highly imprudent

5. **judicious** (jōō-dĭsh´əs) *adjective* from Latin *iudicium*, "judgment"
Having or exhibiting good, sound judgment
- **Judicious** reporters thoroughly check their sources of information before submitting a story for publication.

Judicious is an antonym of *imprudent* (and a synonym of *prudent*).

6. **meticulous** (mĭ-tĭk´yə-ləs) *adjective* from Latin *meticulosus*, "timid"
Extremely careful and precise
- Plotting a large ship's course through narrow, hazardous waterways requires **meticulous** work.

meticulousness *noun* Though known for **meticulousness,** Pat accidentally included several factual errors in his big presentation.

7. **minutia** (mĭ-nōō´-shē-ə) *noun* from Latin *minutus*, "small"
A small, minor, or trivial detail
- The **minutiae** of the company's financial report were listed in the appendix.

minute (mī-nōōt´) *adjective* Extremely small; tiny
- As a good director, he knew the film's script down to the most **minute** detail.

The plural of *minutia* is *minutiae*. *Minute* (tiny) is pronounced differently from *minute* (60 seconds).

8. **slovenly** (slŭv´ən-lē) *adjective* from German *sloven*, "to dress carelessly"
   a. Untidy; sloppy in dress or appearance
   - With her shirt half tucked in and her wrinkled pants, she looked rather **slovenly.**
   b. Marked by carelessness or negligence; shoddy
   - "You should be embarrassed by the **slovenly** job you did on that report," said the teacher.

9. **trepidation** (trĕp´ĭ-dā´shən) *noun* from Latin *trepidus*, "anxious"
   a. Anxiety; a state of alarm, dread, or fear
   - Unfortunately, many students approach college entrance exams with **trepidation.**
   b. Involuntary trembling or quivering
   - No matter how hard I tried, I couldn't control my **trepidation** at the thought of delivering the speech.

10. **unmindful** (ŭn-mīnd´fəl) *adjective*
Failing to give due care or attention; inattentive
- **Unmindful** of the darkening sky and falling barometer, the inexperienced sailors headed out to sea.

WORD ENRICHMENT

Imprudent words

There are many ways to be *imprudent,* as evidenced by that word's many synonyms, most of which have slightly different connotations. Some of those synonyms are *careless, hasty, improvident, incautious, irresponsible, rash, reckless, thoughtless,* and *unwise.*

WRITE THE CORRECT WORD

Write the correct word in the space next to each definition.

__slovenly__	**1.** untidy		__finicky__	**6.** difficult to please
__trepidation__	**2.** anxiety		__unmindful__	**7.** inattentive
__diligence__	**3.** hard work; steady effort		__judicious__	**8.** having good, sound judgment
__meticulous__	**4.** very precise		__imprudent__	**9.** unwise; thoughtless
__fastidious__	**5.** showing careful attention to detail		__minutia__	**10.** trivial details

COMPLETE THE SENTENCE

Write the letter for the word that best completes each sentence.

__d__ **1.** Some colleges can be very _____ about whom they choose to admit.
  a. slovenly   **b.** minute   **c.** unmindful   **d.** finicky

__a__ **2.** NASA flight-engineers have to be _____ in their calculations.
  a. meticulous   **b.** unmindful   **c.** slovenly   **d.** imprudent

__b__ **3.** It is unwise to present a _____ appearance on job interviews.
  a. fastidious   **b.** slovenly   **c.** finicky   **d.** judicious

__c__ **4.** The nervous child proceeded into the "haunted house" with _____.
  a. minutia   **b.** diligence   **c.** trepidation   **d.** meticulousness

__a__ **5.** Deciding to cut class and go to the mall was a very _____ decision.
  a. imprudent   **b.** slovenly   **c.** meticulous   **d.** judicious

__a__ **6.** Supreme Court justices are supposed to be _____ in their legal reasoning.
  a. judicious   **b.** imprudent   **c.** slovenly   **d.** unmindful

__b__ **7.** Here's some bad advice: "Don't worry about the _____ of your new contract."
  a. meticulousness   **b.** minutiae   **c.** diligence   **d.** trepidation

__d__ **8.** He was so insanely _____ about his clothes that a raindrop hitting his shoe sent him running inside to get a paper towel.
  a. judicious   **b.** imprudent   **c.** slovenly   **d.** fastidious

__c__ **9.** Unfortunately, she seemed completely _____ of the number of people whose feelings she was hurting.
  a. judicious   **b.** fastidious   **c.** unmindful   **d.** meticulous

__b__ **10.** She wondered if her boss's words "Your _____ won't be forgotten" meant "You will get a raise."
  a. slovenliness   **b.** diligence   **c.** imprudence   **d.** minutia

Challenge: One way to avoid pre-exam _____ is to make _____ use of your study time.
__c__   **a.** minutia…finicky   **b.** imprudence…unmindful   **c.** trepidation…judicious

Scalpel, Scissors, Robot

(1) Patients who see the da Vinci surgical robot for the first time sometimes react with *trepidation*. Its four mechanical arms look like the tentacles of some monster from a science-fiction movie. **(2)** Though it might seem *imprudent* to let such an evil-looking thing into an operating room, this new robot is actually helping to make surgery safer and more effective.

The robot, named for fifteenth-century inventor and artist Leonardo da Vinci, has extremely tiny "fingers" that can be inserted through equally tiny incisions in a patient's body. **(3)** This makes the da Vinci robot a *judicious* choice for delicate operations.

Attached to each of the robot's "arms" are different surgical tools, including a tiny knife (or scalpel), forceps for holding tissue, a pair of scissors, and a special camera called an endoscope. The robot's actions are controlled by a surgeon who sits at a console located a few feet away. There, the surgeon looks through a high-powered eyepiece and works the robot's controls. The actions of the surgeon's arms, wrists, and fingers are mimicked by the robot working inside the patient. But the robot's work is more precise than that of any human surgeon. All human hands shake, at least a little bit; in contrast, the robot's "hands" are perfectly steady. **(4)** This increase in stability allows even the most *fastidious* surgeons to operate with more precision than ever before.

At one time, heart-valve surgery required chest incisions large enough for a surgeon's hands. **(5)** Fortunately, doctors and medical engineers have *diligently* pursued strategies to reduce incision sizes. The da Vinci robot requires openings no larger than a fingertip. This decreases the overall danger of the operation, the recovery time, and the amount of scarring for patients. Also, the three-dimensional images that the surgeon sees through the eyepiece are magnified ten times. **(6)** This enhanced view helps surgeons avoid damaging *minute* nerves and veins.

During some cancer operations, patients undergoing conventional surgery lose lots of blood. **(7)** But with the *meticulous* care that doctors can take using the da Vinci robot, patients undergoing these operations lose far less blood. This reduces patients' risks on the operating table and shortens their recovery time significantly.

Finally, with a machine, patients and doctors know what to expect. **(8)** No one need fear *slovenly* work by overly tired or overworked doctors or nurses. **(9)** The da Vinci robot is never *unmindful* of a surgeon's commands. **(10)** Even the most *finicky* patient would find it hard to reject such competent abilities.

Each sentence below refers to a numbered sentence in the passage. Write the letter of the choice that gives the sentence a meaning that is closest to the original sentence.

___b___ **1.** Patients who see the da Vinci surgical robot for the first time sometimes react with _____.
    a. foolishness   **b.** anxiety   **c.** care   **d.** judgment

___c___ **2.** It might seem _____ to let such an evil-looking thing into an operating room.
    a. picky   **b.** cautious   **c.** unwise   **d.** uninformed

___d___ **3.** This makes the da Vinci robot a _____ choice for delicate operations.
    a. metallic   **b.** careless   **c.** lazy   **d.** sound

___a___ **4.** This increase in stability allows even the most _____ surgeons to operate with more precision than ever before.
    a. careful   **b.** clumsy   **c.** wise   **d.** trivial

b   **5.** Fortunately, doctors and medical engineers have _____ pursued strategies to reduce incision sizes.
      a. never   **b.** steadily   **c.** wisely   **d.** sometimes

b   **6.** This enhanced view helps surgeons avoid damaging _____ nerves and veins.
      a. sixty-second   **b.** very tiny   **c.** taste-sensitive   **d.** hard-working

c   **7.** Doctors can take _____ care using the da Vinci robot.
      a. random   **b.** trivial   **c.** precise   **d.** haphazard

d   **8.** No one need fear _____ work by overly tired or overworked doctors or nurses.
      a. too precise   **b.** unwise   **c.** surgical   **d.** sloppy

a   **9.** The da Vinci robot is never _____ a surgeon's commands.
      a. inattentive to   **b.** aware of   **c.** picky about   **d.** excited by

c   **10.** Even the most _____ patient would find it hard to reject such competent abilities.
      a. clumsy   **b.** frightened   **c.** picky   **d.** injured

Indicate whether the statements below are TRUE or FALSE according to the passage.

F   **1.** Leonardo da Vinci drew up the first plans for a surgical robot.

T   **2.** The da Vinci surgical robot can operate without being affected by hand tremors.

T   **3.** Certain features of surgical robots can lead to a reduction in scarring and recovery time.

FINISH THE THOUGHT

Complete each sentence so that it shows the meaning of the italicized word.

1. She was so *finicky* that _____ Answers will vary. _____

_____

2. We watched with *trepidation* as _____ Answers will vary. _____

_____

WRITE THE DERIVATIVE

Complete the sentence by writing the correct form of the word shown in parentheses. You may not need to change the form that is given.

diligent   **1.** The _____ sentry remained at his post, intently scanning the horizon. *(diligence)*

trepidation   **2.** The new student approached the school with great _____. *(trepidation)*

Imprudence | 3. _____ is often punished by its results. (*imprudent*)

meticulously | 4. The _____ crafted plan was virtually foolproof. (*meticulous*)

minute | 5. Computers have all sorts of _____ parts. (*minutia*)

Finicky | 6. _____ people hold up cafeteria lines. (*finicky*)

judiciously | 7. The council acted _____ by distributing funds equally to the groups. (*judicious*)

slovenly | 8. If my appearance is _____, please understand that a delayed flight forced me to sleep in the airport. (*slovenly*)

unmindful | 9. The knight entered the castle _____ of the trap his enemies had set. (*unmindful*)

fastidious | 10. Interior decorators are often _____ people who care about each color and aspect of design in a house or an office. (*fastidious*)

FIND THE EXAMPLE

Choose the answer that best describes the action or situation.

b   **1.** Something that a *finicky* person would be most likely to do
  a. gobble anything   **b.** reject food   **c.** try new things   **d.** look sloppy

a   **2.** Something that would cause most airline passengers to feel *trepidation*
  a. turbulence   **b.** safety precautions   **c.** in-flight movies   **d.** a long vacation

d   **3.** Something requiring *fastidious* planning
  a. trip to mall   **b.** bad accident   **c.** strange coincidence   **d.** space mission

b   **4.** A group that is LEAST likely to make *judicious* decisions
  a. judges   **b.** angry mob   **c.** city council   **d.** professors

a   **5.** A situation in which a knowledge of *minutiae* would be most helpful
  a. trivia competition   **b.** movie marathon   **c.** college application   **d.** resting comfortably

a   **6.** A place that should NEVER have a *slovenly* appearance
  a. operating room   **b.** garbage dump   **c.** dorm room   **d.** tool shed

c   **7.** An example of *imprudent* behavior
  a. studying for test   **b.** voting for mayor   **c.** teasing a lion   **d.** driving carefully

c   **8.** A likely result of adequate *diligence*
  a. failure   **b.** shame   **c.** success   **d.** embarrassment

b   **9.** The opposite of *unmindful*
  a. confused   **b.** aware   **c.** oblivious   **d.** inattentive

d   **10.** Something that requires *meticulous* attention
  a. silly show   **b.** comic book   **c.** midday stroll   **d.** research paper

Crime and Wrongdoing

WORD LIST

condemn	culpable	exonerate	extort	incorrigible
malfeasance	misdemeanor	purloin	ruffian	unscrupulous

Most of us have heard the adage "crime doesn't pay." The words in this lesson deal with wrongdoing and its consequences. Many of the words also have more general meanings. This vocabulary is widely used in the fields of law and of current events and will add depth to your understanding of these topics.

Point out that several words in the lesson use common prefixes. *Ex-* ("out of") is found in *exonerate* and *extort*. *In-* ("not") appears in *incorrigible*. *Un-* ("not") appears in unscrupulous.

1. **condemn** (kən-dĕm´) *verb* from Latin *condemnare*, "to sentence"
   a. To express strong disapproval of
   • The mayor **condemned** the sloppy police work that led to the convictions of innocent people.
   b. To give a judgment against; to sentence
   • The judge **condemned** the repeat offender to twenty years in prison.
   c. To declare to be unfit for use, often by official order
   • Local residents pressured the city to **condemn** the old building.

   condemnation *noun* The dictator received **condemnation** from the United Nations for the brutal acts he committed.

2. **culpable** (kŭl´pə-bəl) *adjective* from Latin *culpare*, "to blame"
   Deserving of blame or punishment for being wrong, evil, or harmful
   • The editorial insisted that armed-forces personnel who are **culpable** for the mistreatment of prisoners should face severe punishment.

   culpability *noun* The firm denied **culpability** for the accounting errors discovered by the auditors.

3. **exonerate** (ĭg-zŏn´ə-rāt´) *verb* from Latin *ex-*, "out of" + *onus*, "burden"
   a. To free from blame
   • The defendant was **exonerated** when the true culprit confessed.
   b. To free from a responsibility, an obligation, or a task
   • The resident was **exonerated** from paying condo fees, in exchange for serving as the chairman of the condo association.

   exoneration *noun* The innocent man was certain that a thorough investigation would lead to his **exoneration.**

4. **extort** (ĭk-stôrt´) *verb* from Latin *ex-*, "out of" + *torquere*, "to twist"
   To obtain by force or threat
   • The detective tried to **extort** a confession from the suspect.

   extortion *noun* Neighborhood businesspeople united to combat **extortion** by local criminals.

condemned

The word *extortion* typically refers to obtaining money through threats.

5. incorrigible (ĭn-kôr´ĭ-jə-bəl) *adjective* from Latin *in-*, "not"
+ *corrigere*, "to correct"
  a. Incapable of being corrected or reformed
  • Once again, the **incorrigible** criminal was back in court.
  b. Difficult or impossible to control
  • The **incorrigible** child was sent home because the teachers became
  concerned for the safety of the other students.

  incorrigibility *noun* Despite the teenager's apparent **incorrigibility**,
  the officer still held out hope for his reform.

> *Incorrigible* can also be used as a noun to refer to a person who cannot be reformed.

6. malfeasance (măl-fē´zəns) *noun* from Latin *male-*, "ill" + *facere*,
"to do"
  Wrongdoing or misconduct, especially by a public official
  • The cover story in the local paper accused the governor of
  malfeasance, charging that he had accepted bribes in return for
  awarding contracts.

7. misdemeanor (mĭs´dĭ-mē´nər) *noun* from Old French *mis-*, "bad;
wrong" + *demener*, "to conduct"
  A minor offense; a misdeed
  • Some people don't realize that, in many places, littering is a
  misdemeanor, punishable by a fine or possibly jail time.

> A *misdemeanor* is a minor violation of the law; a *felony* is a more serious crime.

8. purloin (pər-loin´) *verb* from Anglo-Latin *pur-*, "away" + *loign*, "far"
  To steal, often in a violation of trust; to commit theft
  • The employee at the computer help desk **purloined** customer
  passwords, and then accessed and sold confidential customer
  information.

9. ruffian (rŭf´ē-ən) *noun*
  a. A gangster or thug
  • The city councilors demanded better police protection from
  ruffians who threatened and stole from local residents and store
  owners.
  b. A tough or rowdy person; a troublemaker
  • Mrs. Kovorsky worried that the **ruffians** her son had been
  associating with were going to get him into trouble.

10. unscrupulous (ŭn-skrōō´pyə-ləs) *adjective* from Middle English
un-, "not" + Latin *scrupus*, "sharp stone"
  Lacking moral restraint; scornful of what is right or honorable
  • The **unscrupulous** car salesman did not reveal that the car had
  engine problems.

> The adjective *scrupulous* can mean both "moral; principled" and "conscientious; exact."

  scruple *noun* An uneasy feeling about doing something that is wrong
  • With the answers left by mistake in plain view, he was tempted to
  cheat, but his **scruples** kept him from doing it.

WORD ENRICHMENT

A pebble of conscience

The word *scruple* comes from the Latin *scrupus*, meaning "sharp stone;
pebble." The origin of the word suggests that someone with *scruples* is
bothered by his or her conscience, much the way one would be irritated
by a pebble in one's shoe.

94 **Crime and Wrongdoing**

WRITE THE CORRECT WORD

Write the correct word in the space next to each definition.

purloin	**1.** to steal	ruffian	**6.** a thug or gangster
culpable	**2.** deserving of blame	extort	**7.** to obtain by threat
exonerate	**3.** to free from blame	misdemeanor	**8.** a minor crime
incorrigible	**4.** not capable of being reformed	condemn	**9.** to pass judgment against
unscrupulous	**5.** without moral restraint	malfeasance	**10.** misconduct by an official

COMPLETE THE SENTENCE

Write the letter for the word that best completes each sentence.

a **1.** Roman was accused of taking the cookies, but he was _____ when his mother found crumbs in his sister's room.
   a. exonerated   **b.** extorted   **c.** condemned   **d.** purloined

d **2.** The _____ began throwing punches for no apparent reason.
   a. misdemeanor   **b.** scruple   **c.** malfeasance   **d.** ruffian

c **3.** The _____ students hacked into the teacher's computer to change their grades.
   a. purloined   **b.** exonerated   **c.** unscrupulous   **d.** extorted

a **4.** The mayor was found guilty of _____ for going on lavish vacations at taxpayers' expense.
   a. malfeasance   **b.** extortion   **c.** condemnation   **d.** exoneration

b **5.** Blackmail involves _____ money from others by threatening to reveal their secrets.
   a. exonerating   **b.** extorting   **c.** condemning   **d.** purloining

d **6.** People convicted of _____ usually do not receive long prison sentences.
   a. incorrigibility   **b.** unscrupulousness   **c.** extortion   **d.** misdemeanors

a **7.** The shady lawyer _____ millions of dollars from the trust fund that she was hired to manage.
   a. purloined   **b.** condemned   **c.** extorted   **d.** exonerated

b **8.** The Hans were clearly _____, considering that the stolen goods were found in their truck.
   a. exonerated   **b.** culpable   **c.** incorrigible   **d.** extorted

c **9.** People were once _____ to long prison sentences if they couldn't pay their debts.
   a. extorted   **b.** exonerated   **c.** condemned   **d.** purloined

d **10.** The _____ arsonist plotted to strike again.
   a. extorted   **b.** exonerated   **c.** purloined   **d.** incorrigible

Challenge: The _____ youths were referred to derisively as "those _____" by all the neighbors whose property had been vandalized.
a
   a. incorrigible…ruffians   **b.** extorted…culpable   **c.** exonerated…malfeasance

The Slovak Robin Hood

(1) What is the name of a well-known *ruffian* who hid in the forest, robbing the rich and giving to the poor? If you live in Eastern Europe, the answer would be Juraj Janosik. Not surprisingly, he is known as the Slovak Robin Hood. Like Robin Hood, Janosik's story is a mixture of fact and fiction that casts light on the disparity of the social conditions of the time.

Janosik was born in 1688, in what is now northern Slovakia. While still a teenager, he joined a Hungarian revolt against the Hapsburg Empire. After the revolt was suppressed, he then joined the emperor's army and was sent to a castle to guard prisoners. One of them, Thomas Uhorcik, would later become an important influence in Janosik's life.

Janosik returned home when he received news that his mother was ill. **(2)** Then, as the story goes, his life was abruptly changed by an *unscrupulous* nobleman. Legend has it that the lord of the manor ordered Janosik's father to abandon the bedside of his dying wife and go back to work in the fields. When the father refused, the nobleman had him killed. Outraged, Janosik left the lord's estate to live in the forest. There, he met Uhorcik, who had recently escaped from prison. Uhorcik persuaded Janosik to join his band of robbers.

Janosik's daring exploits soon brought him fame. Due to his fearless leadership, he became captain of a fraternal band of thieves. With them by his side, he expanded his operations into several provinces, as well as into neighboring Poland. He robbed rich nobles, often with the cooperation of the peasants who lived on their estates. He generally took sheep from their folds, but he also seized more valuable items, particularly from people who were traveling through the forest. According to legend, Janosik robbed Lord Jan Radvansky on the road, took his jewels, and distributed them to the poor. There are numerous accounts of Janosik's gang stealing from rich people and parceling out the valuables to the less fortunate. It is also said that when poor people walked along the roads, the gang let them pass freely.

(3) Janosik's activities were limited to *misdemeanors* and simple robbery. **(4)** They did not include more sophisticated strategies, such as kidnapping people to *extort* a ransom. **(5)** Nor did Janosik use *purloined* documents to blackmail his victims.

Janosik was ultimately betrayed by his sweetheart and captured. He escaped but was soon recaptured, confined in chains, and put on trial. **(6)** By today's standards, the authorities involved in his trial would be accused of *malfeasance;* some of the crimes for which Janosik was charged actually took place while he was in prison! **(7)** Although Janosik admitted *culpability* for theft, he denied he was guilty of killing anyone. **(8)** He asked for mercy, stating that he was not an *incorrigible* villain and would give up his life of crime, but he refused to reveal the locations of his accomplices. **(9)** Ignoring Janosik's pleas, the court *condemned* him to death at the age of twenty-five. **(10)** One version of the story recounts that a courier came with a letter of *exoneration* from the emperor—but it arrived too late.

Today, travelers to Slovakia can still see the farm where Janosik was born. His feats are celebrated in songs, stories, and poems. His likeness appears in paintings, pottery, and glassware. Several places are named for him. Janosik's hat, hatchet, and pipe are in national museums. People still hunt for the treasure that he supposedly buried. Whether legends of his generosity are true or not, the Slovak Robin Hood is an important symbol of resistance to oppression.

Each sentence below refers to a numbered sentence in the passage. Write the letter of the choice that gives the sentence a meaning that is closest to the original sentence.

___a___ **1.** What is the name of a well-known _____ who robbed the rich and gave to the poor?
     a. troublemaker   **b.** politician   **c.** physician   **d.** lawyer

___d___ **2.** His life was abruptly changed by a(n) _____ nobleman.
     a. good-hearted   **b.** wealthy   **c.** judgmental   **d.** immoral

___b___ **3.** Janosik's activities were limited to _____ and simple robbery.
     a. major crimes   **b.** minor crimes   **c.** threats   **d.** hobbies

_____a_____ **4.** Janosik did not kidnap people to _____ a ransom.
   a. obtain by threat   **b.** disapprove of   **c.** make fun of   **d.** steal

_____c_____ **5.** Nor did Janosik use _____ documents to blackmail his victims.
   a. engraved   **b.** official   **c.** stolen   **d.** forged

_____d_____ **6.** By today's standards, the authorities involved in his trial would be acccused of _____.
   a. unfair delays   **b.** long speeches   **c.** entertainment   **d.** official misconduct

_____a_____ **7.** Although Janosik admitted _____ for theft, he denied he was guilty of killing anyone.
   a. deserving blame   **b.** conspiracy   **c.** admiration   **d.** strong disapproval

_____d_____ **8.** He asked for mercy, stating that he was not a(n) _____ villain.
   a. talented   **b.** willing   **c.** convicted   **d.** unreformable

_____b_____ **9.** Ignoring Janosik's pleas, the court _____ him to death.
   a. flogged   **b.** sentenced   **c.** bored   **d.** cursed

_____d_____ **10.** One version of the story recounts that a courier came with a letter of _____ from the emperor.
   a. greetings   **b.** regret   **c.** disapproval   **d.** pardon

Indicate whether the statements below are TRUE or FALSE according to the passage.

_____T_____ **1.** According to legend, Janosik turned to a life of crime after his father was unjustly murdered.

_____F_____ **2.** The courts that tried Janosik had very high standards, compared with current international standards of justice.

_____T_____ **3.** Janosik is a national hero in Slovakia, symbolizing resistance to oppression.

WRITING EXTENDED RESPONSES

The passage describes Janosik as a person who, at least in legend, stole from the rich and gave to the poor. Consider whether criminal acts done in such a spirit should be punished less severely than those motivated by more selfish concerns. Then, in a persuasive essay, defend your point of view. You should give and defend at least two points. Your essay should be a minimum of three paragraphs long. Use at least three lesson words in your essay and underline them.

WRITE THE DERIVATIVE

Complete the sentence by writing the correct form of the word shown in parentheses. You may not need to change the form that is given.

___misdemeanor___ **1.** Failing to stop at a stop sign is a _____. (*misdemeanor*)

___purloined___ **2.** The dishonest trustee had _____ funds from the estate. (*purloin*)

culpability   3. His _____ became evident when the police pulled him over while he was driving the stolen car. *(culpable)*

incorrigibility   4. The report stated that prisoners' _____ will most likely continue as long as the prison system focuses on punishment instead of reform. *(incorrigible)*

extortion   5. The attorney claimed that the pharmacy had committed _____ by threatening to withhold the patient's medication until he paid off all his charges. *(extort)*

scruples   6. Studies show that people tend to have less _____ about wrongdoing if they think they will never be caught. *(unscrupulous)*

exoneration   7. Twenty years after their conviction, new evidence led to the rebels' _____. *(exonerate)*

ruffians   8. In the musical *Westside Story*, the Sharks and the Jets are two gangs of _____ who are constantly battling over turf. *(ruffian)*

condemned   9. The city _____ the bridge because it was unsafe. *(condemn)*

malfeasance   10. The large highway project created opportunities for _____ and corruption. *(malfeasance)*

FIND THE EXAMPLE

Choose the answer that best describes the action or situation.

b   1. Someone who is *incorrigible*
    a. brilliant teacher   **b.** hardened criminal   **c.** tax attorney   **d.** experienced accountant

b   2. A word that does NOT describe a *ruffian*
    a. rugged   **b.** gentle   **c.** tough   **d.** unruly

d   3. A crime that is NOT a *misdemeanor*
    a. speeding   **b.** petty theft   **c.** jaywalking   **d.** murder

a   4. The phrase that would most likely be used to describe an *exoneration*
    a. At last she's free.   **b.** So she did do it.   **c.** What a bad alibi.   **d.** Justice is finally served.

c   5. How you might feel if something dear to you was *purloined*
    a. amused   **b.** justified   **c.** betrayed   **d.** indifferent

c   6. Someone or something that is LEAST likely to be *condemned*
    a. guilty prisoner   **b.** vacant building   **c.** brand-new home   **d.** unsafe bridge

d   7. How you might feel if you are *culpable*
    a. proud   **b.** indignant   **c.** angry   **d.** guilty

c   8. Someone who is NOT likely to be accused of *malfeasance*
    a. senator   **b.** mayor   **c.** cab driver   **d.** town manager

a   9. Someone who is LEAST likely to be *unscrupulous*
    a. superhero   **b.** terrorist   **c.** gangster   **d.** bank robber

b   10. How you would probably feel if someone were *extorting* funds from you
    a. gratified   **b.** powerless   **c.** reassured   **d.** relaxed

Taking Tests

Sentence-Completion with Two Blanks

Standardized tests may contain sentence-completion items with either one or two blanks. You practice answering two-blank items in this book when you do the Challenge that is found in each lesson.

Strategies

You can apply what you have already learned about context to sentence-completion test items. Following these steps will help you to choose answers for two-blank items.

1. *Read the directions carefully.* You can lose credit if you don't follow the directions.

2. *Read the sentence completely.* Because "two-blank" items involve different parts of the sentence, it is wise to get an overview by carefully reading the entire sentence. Substitute the word *blank* for the empty spaces as you read.

3. *Look for words that fit the first blank.* To start, try to narrow your choices down to words that fit the first empty space. Make sure the word is the correct part of speech and fits in the context. Eliminate the other choices. Here is an example:

   The results of their _____ spending were seen in their _____ mansion, but maintaining this lifestyle eventually bankrupted them.

       a. ignoble . . . grandiose   **d.** pacific . . . whimsical

       b. profligate . . . uninterested   **e.** frugal . . . grandiose

       c. intemperate . . . opulent

   By focusing on the first blank, you can eliminate (a) *ignoble* and (d) *pacific* immediately. Neither fits in the sentence. One cannot spend *ignobly.* Nor can spending be *pacific.*

4. *From the remaining choices, look for words that fit into the second blank.* Eliminate any remaining choices in which the second word doesn't fit in the second blank. In the example above, try the second word for choices (b) and (e) in the second blank. *Profligate* spending would not result in an *uninterested* mansion. Nor would *frugal* spending result in a *grandiose* mansion. The correct answer is (c): "The results of their *intemperate* spending were seen in their *opulent* mansion, but maintaining this lifestyle eventually bankrupted them."

5. *Reread the sentence with your choices inserted.* Two-item tests are difficult. Make certain to check your choices. At times, a few choices may fit, and you must choose the one that fits best.

Also, notice that in the following example below, the two missing words are related.

Although just about everyone was _____ to the agreement, one political party remained _____ and refused to cooperate.

The word *although* signals that the first blank and the second blank are opposites in some way. So you can check your answer by making sure that the two words you've chosen are opposing. Some other key words that might indicate a relationship include:

       • *not, but, never, hardly,* and *in spite of* (signaling opposites)

       • *and, as well as,* or *in addition to* (signaling agreement)

Practice

Each sentence below has two blanks, each blank indicating that a word has been omitted. Beneath the sentence are five lettered sets of words labeled a through e. Choose the pair of words that, when inserted in the sentence, <u>best</u> fits the meaning of the sentence as a whole.

_____a_____ **1.** Sensible and _____ students realize that handing in _____ work will not gain them the respect of their teachers.
   a. prudent . . . slovenly
   b. indigent . . . erudite
   c. uninterested . . . edifying
   d. judicious . . . meticulous
   e. whimsical . . . remuneration

_____b_____ **2.** Extremely embarrassed, Jerome tried valiantly to make _____ to the hostess for what he considered his brother's _____ behavior at the party.
   a. decorum . . . wily
   b. amends . . . unseemly
   c. mediation . . . judicious
   d. invective . . . ignoble
   e. witticisms . . . pacific

_____b_____ **3.** The wise _____ exercised control _____, realizing that a position of power was held only through the continuing goodwill of the people.
   a. autocrat . . . esoterically
   b. sovereign . . . judiciously
   c. pedagogue . . . conclusively
   d. lackey . . . patronizingly
   e. caste . . . whimsically

_____e_____ **4.** After long months of nutritional _____, the refugees enjoyed a meal that finally left them feeling _____.
   a. depredation . . . docile
   b. indeterminacy . . . patronized
   c. intemperance . . . apprehensive
   d. harassment . . . diligent
   e. deprivation . . . satiated

_____d_____ **5.** The _____ professor lived simply, knowing that _____ gain was not the natural result of a life spent studying ancient languages.
   a. pedantic . . . purloined
   b. flippant . . . unequivocal
   c. finicky . . . meticulous
   d. erudite . . . pecuniary
   e. austere . . . homogeneous

_____c_____ **6.** They had all observed his _____ behavior at social gatherings, so they were very surprised to learn about his _____ white-water rafting trips.
   a. unscrupulous . . . feral
   b. gratuitous . . . totalitarian
   c. meek . . . intrepid
   d. tentative . . . decorous
   e. nuanced . . . renovated

_____c_____ **7.** The idea of people walking on the ceiling was a _____ topic for a movie, and his suggestion that we try to film it was the source of much _____ amongst our circle of friends.
   a. hilarious . . . deviation
   b. nuanced . . . unscrupulousness
   c. ludicrous . . . mirth
   d. benevolent . . . qualm
   e. brazen . . . stridency

_____d_____ **8.** At first, the jury member thought that the defendant was _____, but when she heard the eyewitness's testimony, it _____ the accused.
   a. incorrigible . . . beguiled
   b. unscrupulous . . . vilified
   c. feral . . . usurped
   d. culpable . . . exonerated
   e. indigent . . . aggrandized

Exerting and Yielding Power

WORD LIST

august	condescend	deference	grovel	lackey
predominate	slavish	subjugation	supercilious	sycophant

The will of some people to exert power over others has led to much oppression and injustice. As Lord Acton said, "Power tends to corrupt; absolute power corrupts absolutely." The words in this lesson deal with relationships that involve exerting and yielding power.

Discuss the meanings of the prefixes *sub-* (under), *super-* (above), and *pre-* (before) and have students locate the lesson words that contain them.

1. **august** (ô-gŭst´) *adjective* from Latin *augustus*, "majestic"
   Majestic; inspiring awe or admiration
   • The Federal Court judge looked dignified and **august** with his silver hair and dark robe.

an august judge

Augustus was an honorary title granted to the first Roman emperor, Augustus Caesar, by the Roman senate. Later, it renamed the eighth month, *August*, in his honor.

2. **condescend** (kŏn´dĭ-sĕnd´) *verb* from Latin *con-*, "with" + *descendere*, "to descend; to go down"
   a. To lower oneself to the level of one considered inferior
   • The concert pianist refused to **condescend** to teaching students who did not demonstrate exceptional talent.
   b. To treat others as though they are inferior; to patronize
   • Gayle offended her coworkers when she **condescended** and acted as if she was the only one who could do the job correctly.

   condescension *noun* The waiter at the expensive restaurant addressed the high-school students with an air of **condescension.**

3. **deference** (dĕf´ər-əns) *noun* from Latin *de-*, "away" + *ferre*, "to carry"
   Respectful yielding to the opinion or wishes of another; courteous respect
   • The actors showed **deference** to their director's judgments about how to play the characters.

   defer *verb* The lawyer said she would **defer** to her client's decision.

Defer can also mean "to postpone."

4. **grovel** (grŏv´əl) *verb* from Middle English *grufe*, "face downward"
   a. To behave so humbly that it is demeaning
   • When you meet the rock star, don't **grovel**; try to act naturally.
   b. To lie or creep face downward, as in humility
   • The man **groveled** before the throne of the tyrant.

5. **lackey** (lăk´ē) *noun* from Old French *laquais,* "servant"
   One who does lowly jobs for another; one who follows all orders
   without questioning them
   • The judge treated his interns as **lackeys,** requiring them to serve
     coffee and do endless duplicating of documents.

6. **predominate** (prĭ-dŏm´ə-nāt´) *verb* from Latin *pre-,* "before"
   + *dominari,* "to rule"
   a. To be greatest in number or importance
      • French Canadians **predominate** in the province of Quebec.
   b. To have or gain the greatest power or influence; prevail
      • It often seems that Hollywood **predominates** as the cinema capital
        of the world.

   predominant *adjective* Yellow is the **predominant** color in my garden.

7. **slavish** (slā´vĭsh) *adjective* from Medieval Latin *sclavus,* "Slav"
   a. Acting completely under the will of another; like a slave; servile
      • In his **slavish** devotion, the personal assistant followed every one
        of his boss's orders, no matter how ridiculous.
   b. Showing no originality; blindly imitating
      • The artist's painting was a **slavish** copy of a work from Picasso's
        blue period.

   slavishness *noun* David's **slavishness** to his older brother was sad.

   > The word *slave* comes
   > from *Slav* because of the
   > widespread enslavement of
   > Slavic-speaking people of
   > eastern Europe during the
   > Middle Ages.

8. **subjugation** (sŭb´jə-gā´shən) *noun* from Latin *sub-,* "under"
   + *iugum,* "yoke"
   The act of conquering or bringing under control; enslavement
   • Hernando Cortez's **subjugation** of the Aztec Empire took only
     two years.

   subjugate *verb* Dictators often **subjugate** people through fear and
   intimidation.

   > Just as an ox is put under
   > a yoke for farm work,
   > *subjugated* people are treated
   > as slaves under a yoke.

9. **supercilious** (soō´pər-sĭl´ē-əs) *adjective* from Latin *supercilium,*
   "eyebrow; pride"
   Proudly scornful; disdainful
   • The hotel clerk's **supercilious** look made Mrs. Gray feel that she was
     not welcome.

   superciliousness *noun* The literary agent treated the author
   with **superciliousness**—until she wrote a bestseller.

10. **sycophant** (sĭk´ə-fənt) *noun* from Greek *sukophantes,* "an informer"
    A person attempting to win favor by flattering important people
    • After a while, the movie star became impatient with the constant
      attention of **sycophants.**

    sycophantic *adjective* A weak ruler often seeks **sycophantic** aides.

WORD ENRICHMENT

The eyebrows have it

The word *supercilious* comes from the well-known mannerism of
raising one's eyebrows in disapproval. The word is formed by combining
super-, "above," and *cilium,* "lower eyelid." Other expressions that refer to
facial features to characterize emotional states include *two-faced, nosy,*
and *bug-eyed.*

WRITE THE CORRECT WORD

Write the correct word in the space next to each definition.

condescend	**1.** to treat others as inferior	**august**	**6.** inspiring awe	
grovel	**2.** to behave too humbly	**lackey**	**7.** one who does lowly jobs for another	
predominate	**3.** to be greatest in number or power	**supercilious**	**8.** proudly scornful	
sycophant	**4.** a flatterer	**slavish**	**9.** acting like a slave	
subjugation	**5.** the act of conquering	**deference**	**10.** respectful yielding	

COMPLETE THE SENTENCE

Write the letter for the word that best completes each sentence.

d **1.** Not wanting to disappoint the boss, Carl paid _____ attention to detail.
   a. august   **b.** supercilious   **c.** predominant   **d.** slavish

a **2.** The designer wanted earth tones to _____ in the color plan for the apartment.
   a. predominate   **b.** condescend   **c.** subjugate   **d.** defer

b **3.** The leader wanted all of his close advisers to be adoring _____.
   a. predominant   **b.** sycophants   **c.** supercilious   **d.** subjugations

a **4.** Rochelle's constant _____ for the teacher's approval annoys her classmates.
   a. groveling   **b.** condescending   **c.** deference   **d.** superciliousness

c **5.** The petty tyrant entered the town on horseback, his _____ walking behind, carrying the baggage.
   a. deference   **b.** superciliousness   **c.** lackey   **d.** condescension

d **6.** The _____ ruler had led the country wisely for fifty years.
   a. groveling   **b.** slavish   **c.** supercilious   **d.** august

b **7.** As a sophomore, Mark wouldn't _____ to associate with a mere freshman.
   a. grovel   **b.** condescend   **c.** defer   **d.** predominate

c **8.** At first, the new student seemed _____, but once we got to know her, we learned she was really very modest and humble.
   a. slavish   **b.** predominant   **c.** supercilious   **d.** subjugating

a **9.** Leah usually _____ to her friends to choose what video to rent.
   a. defers   **b.** condescends   **c.** grovels   **d.** subjugates

d **10.** The rebels fought against their country's _____ by its powerful neighbor.
   a. sycophant   **b.** superciliousness   **c.** deference   **d.** subjugation

Challenge: Without ever turning his head to look at the man, the _____ butler condescended to interview the _____ lackey who was begging for a position in the household.
b
   a. slavish…august   **b.** supercilious…groveling   **c.** predominant…slavish

Prometheus

Disease, lightning, floods, and other uncontrollable acts of nature have frightened people throughout the ages. People in ancient times often attributed such misfortunes to the cruel acts of the gods. But some of the gods were protectors. **(1)** Prometheus, an immortal Titan, refused to *grovel* before the gods who sought to destroy Earth.

According to ancient Greek mythology, the Titans once ruled the world. **(2)** Zeus and the gods revolted, defeated the Titans, and *subjugated* them. Although most of the Titans were sent to the underworld for punishment, Prometheus was spared because he had sided with Zeus.

Zeus then assigned Prometheus the task of making men from clay. **(3)** In *deference* to the wishes of his new king, he created them in the image of the gods. Prometheus also wanted to give mankind everything it needed to survive.

Zeus, however, did not share Prometheus's kind feelings. **(4)** His increasingly *august* presence did not mean he had concern for his subjects. **(5)** He refused to *condescend* to improving the lives of the primitive people that he had ordered to be created. He feared that, if people became too powerful, they would no longer worship the gods. He insisted that knowledge, particularly knowledge of fire, would only bring suffering to mankind.

(6) However, Prometheus was no mere *lackey* for the king of the gods. **(7)** He was increasingly upset by Zeus's *supercilious* attitude toward his subjects. **(8)** Prometheus felt that the new king was surrounded by *sycophants,* rather than those who shared real concern for the welfare of the king's subjects.

So Prometheus decided to take matters into his own hands. First, he stole fire from a bolt of Zeus's lightning,

wrapped it in a fennel leaf, and gave it to mankind. This was followed by other gifts: the secrets of brickwork and woodworking, numbers, the alphabet, healing drugs, mining, and art. Finally, he tricked Zeus into giving mankind meat to eat. **(9)** Soon, peace and prosperity *predominated* among the people of Earth.

Angered beyond measure, Zeus wanted to punish both Prometheus and mankind. With the help of the other gods, Zeus created a gift for mankind—a beautiful woman named Pandora. Although Prometheus had warned humans not to accept Zeus's gifts, Pandora's charm was so great that she was immediately welcomed. Her curiosity, however, led her to open a forbidden box given to her by the gods. Out flew illness, violence, famine, and all the other miseries now known on Earth. Only one thing remained in the box—hope. Zeus had his revenge on humanity.

But Zeus still had Prometheus to punish, and he did so by chaining him to a rock. Each night, an eagle would descend and feed on Prometheus's body. And because he was immortal, his body would regenerate during the day. **(10)** And so he was tortured, day and night, as a punishment for refusing to be *slavish* to Zeus.

The valiant figure that championed mankind inspired a trilogy by the ancient Greek playwright Aeschylus and a poem by the English poet Percy Bysshe Shelley. Many paintings and sculptures also honor his heroism.

Each sentence below refers to a numbered sentence in the passage. Write the letter of the choice that gives the sentence a meaning that is closest to the original sentence.

_____ a **1.** Prometheus refused to _____ before the gods who sought to destroy Earth.
    a. humble himself   **b.** show off   **c.** be defeated   **d.** perform

_____ c **2.** Zeus and the gods revolted, defeated the Titans, and _____ them.
    a. governed   **b.** enriched   **c.** enslaved   **d.** respected

_____ c **3.** _____ the wishes of his new king, he created them in the image of the gods.
    a. Because of   **b.** In opposition to   **c.** Out of respect for   **d.** Unrelated to

___d___ **4.** His increasingly _____ presence did not mean he had concern for his subjects.
    a. patronizing   **b.** respectful   **c.** scornful   **d.** majestic

___b___ **5.** He refused to _____ improving the lives of mankind.
    a. aspire to   **b.** lower himself to   **c.** be interested in   **d.** join in

___b___ **6.** However, Prometheus was no mere _____ for the king of the gods.
    a. adviser   **b.** follower   **c.** leader   **d.** relative

___d___ **7.** He was increasingly upset by Zeus's _____ attitude toward his subjects.
    a. charitable   **b.** majestic   **c.** respectful   **d.** scornful

___a___ **8.** Prometheus felt that the new king was surrounded by _____ .
    a. flatterers   **b.** team leaders   **c.** tireless workers   **d.** terrorists

___b___ **9.** Soon, peace and prosperity _____ among people of Earth.
    a. were influential   **b.** prevailed   **c.** were scorned   **d.** failed

___d___ **10.** And so he was tortured, day and night, as a punishment for refusing to be _____ to Zeus.
    a. creative   **b.** corrupt   **c.** humble   **d.** servile

Indicate whether the statements below are TRUE or FALSE according to the passage.

___F___ **1.** Zeus was a warm and loving god.

___T___ **2.** Prometheus was a good friend and ally to humans.

___F___ **3.** Zeus and Prometheus agreed about how humans should be treated.

FINISH THE THOUGHT

Complete each sentence so that it shows the meaning of the italicized word.

1. The artist would not *condescend* to _____ Answers will vary. _____

_____

2. In *deference* to the teacher, _____ Answers will vary. _____

_____

WRITE THE DERIVATIVE

Complete the sentence by writing the correct form of the word shown in parentheses. You may not need to change the form that is given.

___condescension___ **1.** In a tone of _____ , Jeremy's older sister agreed to help him with his homework. (*condescend*)

___lackeys___ **2.** The dictator's three _____ carried out all his dirty work. (*lackey*) defer, deferred   3. The children usually _____ to their grandfather's wishes. *(deference)*

slavishness   4. The critic pronounced the new musician's style boring and imitative to the point of _____. *(slavish)*

superciliousness   5. Kennedy's _____ was evident from her disdainful expression. *(supercilious)*

sycophants   6. It must get tiring to be surrounded by _____ and never have the honest advice of a true friend. *(sycophant)*

groveling   7. The leader soon grew tired of his subjects' _____. *(grovel)*

august   8. The _____ king was honored with a grand banquet. *(august)*

predominant   9. Dominic credited Frank Sinatra as the _____ influence on his music. *(predominate)*

subjugated   10. After their defeat, the _____ citizens were enslaved by their conquerors. *(subjugation)*

FIND THE EXAMPLE

Choose the answer that best describes the action or situation.

c   **1.** Someone most likely to attract *sycophants*
  a. a bus driver   **b.** a tax collector   **c.** a famous athlete   **d.** an undertaker

b   **2.** An *august* person might be described this way
  a. silly   **b.** awe-inspiring   **c.** bankrupt   **d.** clumsy

d   **3.** An example of a likely task that a *lackey* would undertake
  a. writing a novel   **b.** judging a trial   **c.** acting in a movie   **d.** fetching lunch

a   **4.** A characteristic of something that *predominates*
  a. most common   **b.** most scarce   **c.** least annoying   **d.** least obvious

a   **5.** The most likely reason one would *grovel*
  a. for mercy   **b.** for applause   **c.** to be noticed   **d.** for respect

b   **6.** One form of *slavishness*
  a. helpfulness   **b.** imitation   **c.** threat   **d.** independence

c   **7.** Something that would most suggest *superciliousness*
  a. physical size   **b.** attention   **c.** tone of voice   **d.** choice of clothing

b   **8.** Something a person who is being *condescending* would be likely to do
  a. have lunch   **b.** act superior   **c.** be helpful   **d.** arrive early

d   **9.** A likely precursor to the *subjugation* of a group of people
  a. the Olympics   **b.** a competition   **c.** a fair   **d.** a battle

c   **10.** A synonym for *deference*
  a. ignorance   **b.** hatred   **c.** respect   **d.** dislike

Openness and Concealment

WORD LIST

flagrant	furtive	latent	ostensible	salient
sequester	subterfuge	surreptitious	unobtrusively	vaunt

Openness and concealment have many dimensions. The words in this lesson will help you understand and express a range of meanings related to these broad areas. You will be able to write about a *surreptitious* plan, a *salient* point, or a *flagrant* violation of the law.

1. **flagrant** (flā´grənt) *adjective* from Latin *flagrare,* "to burn"
Noticeably bad; conspicuously offensive; glaring
   • In many sports, **flagrant** fouls bring higher penalties than regular fouls do.

   flagrancy *noun* The **flagrancy** of Lilian's lies astonished her friends.

2. **furtive** (fûr´tĭv) *adjective* from Latin *furtum,* "theft"
Sneaky and secretive; characterized by stealth; sly
   • The detective noticed the **furtive** looks exchanged by the suspects.

   furtiveness *noun* The **furtiveness** of May's behavior made us suspicious of her intentions.

3. **latent** (lāt´nt) *adjective* from Latin *latere,* "to lie hidden"
Present or capable of coming into existence, but not visible, evident, or active
   • Nathan's **latent** talent was discovered when he took an art class.

   latency *noun* Some diseases have a **latency** period during which the infected person shows no symptoms.

4. **ostensible** (ŏ-stĕn´sə-bəl) *adjective* from Latin *ostendere,* "to show"
Apparent; represented as true; possibly or seemingly true on the surface
   • The **ostensible** purpose of Ms. Meader's trip to Miami is business, but she may be planning to spend some time at the beach, too.

5. **salient** (sā´lē-ənt) *adjective* from Latin *salire,* "to leap"
Strikingly conspicuous; prominent or significant
   • Jordana summarized the **salient** points of her proposal.

6. **sequester** (sĭ-kwĕs´tər) *verb* from Latin *sequestrare,* "to give up for safekeeping"
   a. To isolate someone or something; to seclude
   • The prisoner was **sequestered** in the Tower of London.
   b. To seize or gain possession of property
   • The invaders **sequestered** the estate and used it as their military headquarters.

   sequestration *noun* If you are serving on a jury, **sequestration** may not be convenient, but it might be the key to a fair verdict.

Have students group lesson words into those that pertain to openness (*flagrant* or *salient,* for example) and those that pertain to concealment (such as *latent* or *sequester*). Allow students to defend their choices.

a furtive burglar

Jurors are sometimes *sequestered* so that they aren't influenced by personal contact or media coverage.

7. **subterfuge** (sŭb´tər-fyōōj´) *noun* from Latin *subter*, "secretly" + *fugere*, "to flee"
   A deceptive strategem or trick
   • The spy used **subterfuge** to get past the guards and into the top-secret area.

Resort to subterfuge is a common phrase.

8. **surreptitious** (sûr´əp-tĭsh´əs) *adjective* from Latin *surripere*, "to take away secretly"
   Obtained, done, or made by secret or stealthy means
   • The guest **surreptitiously** put the expensive silverware in her purse.

9. **unobtrusively** (ŭn´əb-trōō´sĭv-lē) *adverb*
   Acting in a manner that does not attract attention
   • Dennis **unobtrusively** slipped the money into his mother's purse after she refused to allow him to pay for lunch.

   unobtrusive *adjective* The experienced waiter was **unobtrusive** as he filled our water glasses.

   obtrusive *adjective* Undesirably noticeable
   • A loud person in a library is certainly **obtrusive**.

Unobtrusive is usually a positive word; *obtrusive* is usually negative.

10. **vaunt** (vônt) from Latin *vanus*, "empty"
    a. *verb* To boast of; to brag about
    • Ingrid blushed as her parents **vaunted** her academic and athletic awards.
    b. *noun* A boastful remark; speech of extravagant self-praise
    • People rolled their eyes at the retiring partner's **vaunts** about his achievements with the law firm.

ANALOGIES

On the answer line, write the letter of the answer that best completes each analogy. Refer to Lessons 15–17 if you need help with any of the lesson words.

___c___ **1.** Culpable is to blame as _____.
    a. vaunt is to modest   **c.** august is to admire
    b. angry is to furious   **d.** misdemeanor is to felony

___b___ **2.** Flagrant is to surreptitious as _____.
    a. foul is to penalty   **c.** malfeasance is to wrongdoing
    b. brazen is to hidden   **d.** supercilious is to scornful

___a___ **3.** Slavish is to grovel as _____.
    a. gluttonous is to overeat   **c.** incorrigible is to obey
    b. pen is to paper   **d.** deference is to disrespect

___d___ **4.** Exonerate is to condemn as _____.
    a. subjugate is to control   **c.** purloin is to steal
    b. eat is to drink   **d.** set free is to confine

WRITE THE CORRECT WORD

Write the correct word in the space next to each definition.

latent **1.** present, but not evident

surreptitious **2.** done secretly

flagrant **3.** obvious and offensive

salient **4.** conspicuous

sequester **5.** to isolate someone or something

furtive **6.** sneaky; sly

vaunt **7.** to boast

unobtrusively **8.** without attracting attention

subterfuge **9.** trickery

ostensible **10.** apparent

COMPLETE THE SENTENCE

Write the letter for the word that best completes each sentence.

___a___ **1.** Marvin _____ came by to visit Doug, but he really wanted to meet Doug's sister.
a. ostensibly **b.** surreptitiously **c.** furtively **d.** unobtrusively

___d___ **2.** Everyone noticed Amy's _____ violations of the school dress code.
a. subterfuge **b.** furtive **c.** latent **d.** flagrant

___d___ **3.** People often get annoyed when braggarts _____ their achievements.
a. sequester **b.** latent **c.** subterfuge **d.** vaunt

___b___ **4.** My _____ plan to play a joke on Jamal was spoiled by his cousin.
a. latent **b.** furtive **c.** ostensible **d.** flagrant

___c___ **5.** _____ feelings can influence our behavior even if we're not aware of them.
a. Flagrant **b.** Salient **c.** Latent **d.** Vaunted

___b___ **6.** While Ronda performed, her parents sat _____ at the back of the auditorium so they would not make her more nervous.
a. furtively **b.** unobtrusively **c.** ostensibly **d.** flagrantly

___a___ **7.** The _____ of infected people likely saved many lives.
a. sequestration **b.** latency **c.** subterfuge **d.** vaunt

___a___ **8.** A clever _____ by the POWs enabled them to escape from the prison camp.
a. subterfuge **b.** vaunt **c.** sequestration **d.** latency

___d___ **9.** A(n) _____ feature of Impressionist paintings is the depiction of the effect of light on objects.
a. latent **b.** flagrant **c.** ostensible **d.** salient

___b___ **10.** Without leaving a trace, the spy _____ photographed the confidential documents.
a. flagrantly **b.** surreptitiously **c.** latently **d.** ostensibly

Challenge: The _____ goal of the diplomatic mission was to gain support for a new treaty, but some shady business deals were _____ arranged along the way.
___c___ **a.** flagrant...latently **b.** vaunted...saliently **c.** ostensible...surreptitiously

Treasure Ahoy!

Experts believe that hundreds of thousands of shipwrecks dot the ocean floor. They also suspect that much of the precious cargo that sank along with these ships remains intact. Billions of dollars worth of gold, jewels, and ancient objects are likely buried in these ghostly hulks.

But who owns this treasure? **(1)** *Salient* in the debate is whether the artifacts belong to the treasure hunters who find them, or to the nations that have rights to the waterways in which the ships rest. Some experts even argue that the wrecks should be left undisturbed as a sort of underwater museum.

Until the 1970s, treasure hunters announced their discoveries openly. **(2)** They *vaunted* the lost gold and jewels they found, like proud fishermen returning from sea. They then sold or displayed the treasures for their own gain. Few treasure hunters thought they were doing anything wrong. Since they sometimes spent decades in search of just one ship, a "finder's-keeper's" rule seemed to make sense.

But as new technology has made shipwrecks easier to find, more disputes over their ownership have arisen. In 1986, marine archaeologist Robert Ballard designed an underwater robot and put it to work in the waters off eastern Canada. By using the robot, Ballard discovered the remains of the *Titanic,* the luxury passenger ship that sank on April 15, 1912.

Ballard was interested in the history that had been preserved on the famous ship, rather than financial gain. **(3)** He took nothing from the *Titanic* because he recognized the *latent* potential of the site to shed light on another time. **(4)** He took photos and made videos to share with the public and with researchers, but he worked *unobtrusively* and left every last item in place.

(5) Regrettably, once news of the *Titanic's* discovery got out, treasure seekers *furtively* made their way to the wreck site, taking valuables and claiming ownership of them in the courts. Unfortunately, maritime law states that the first person to bring a piece of a shipwreck to court owns that wreck site. Ironically, though Ballard discovered the wreck of the *Titanic,* he can no longer visit it without permission from the legal owner.

(6) *Ostensibly,* those who lay claim to shipwrecks and then sell the cargo are helping to share underwater treasures with the public. These treasure seekers also argue that if they did not find the ships, no one would. **(7)** But archaeologists consider them to be looters who *flagrantly* violate historical sites.

(8) For this reason, some would like shipwrecks to be, in effect, *sequestered* from the public. **(9)** This would keep deep-sea-diving treasure hunters from *surreptitiously* stealing from the sunken ships. The United Nations is currently working to revise international maritime laws to help protect historically significant shipwrecks and to determine who owns their contents.

Law enforcement on the high seas, however, is difficult. Treasure hunters can easily clean out shipwrecks without anyone noticing. **(10)** One common form of *subterfuge* is for divers to locate a sunken ship, take the cargo and sell it secretly, and never report finding the wreckage to authorities. In some ways, these treasure hunters have become a new breed of pirates.

Each sentence below refers to a numbered sentence in the passage. Write the letter of the choice that gives the sentence a meaning that is closest to the original sentence.

___c___ **1.** _____ the debate is whether the located artifacts belong to the treasure hunters who find them, or to the nations that have rights to the waterways.
   a. Hidden in   **b.** Excluded from   **c.** Significant to   **d.** Separate from

___b___ **2.** They _____ the lost gold and jewels they found.
   a. sold   **b.** boasted of   **c.** traded   **d.** wrote about

___a___ **3.** He took nothing from the *Titanic* because he recognized the _____ potential of the site.
   a. hidden   **b.** obvious   **c.** unlikely   **d.** minor

___b___ **4.** He worked _____ and left every last item in place.
    a. flamboyantly   **b.** unnoticed   **c.** sneakily   **d.** obviously

___d___ **5.** Treasure seekers _____ made their way to the wreck site.
    a. illegally   **b.** boastfully   **c.** publicly   **d.** sneakily

___c___ **6.** _____, those who lay claim to shipwrecks and then sell the cargo are helping to share underwater treasures with the public.
    a. Nevertheless   **b.** Unlikely   **c.** Seemingly   **d.** Probably

___c___ **7.** But archaeologists consider them to be looters who _____ violate historical sites.
    a. sneakily, secretly   **b.** subtely, quietly   **c.** terribly, obviously   **d.** greedily, nastily

___b___ **8.** Some would like shipwrecks to be, in effect, _____ the public.
    a. sold to   **b.** isolated from   **c.** toured by   **d.** controlled by

___a___ **9.** This would keep deep-sea-diving treasure seekers from _____ stealing from the ships.
    a. secretly   **b.** publicly   **c.** legally   **d.** frequently

___d___ **10.** One common form of _____ is for divers to locate a sunken ship, take the cargo and sell it secretly, and never report finding the wreckage to authorities.
    a. navigation   **b.** bragging   **c.** marketing   **d.** trickery

Indicate whether the statements below are TRUE or FALSE according to the passage.

___T___ **1.** The high value of sunken cargo provides strong incentive for treasure hunters to find and retrieve it.

___F___ **2.** Robert Ballard is the legal owner of the *Titanic*'s wreckage.

___T___ **3.** The public historical interest in shipwrecks is in opposition to the personal financial interests of the treasure hunters.

WRITING EXTENDED RESPONSES

The passage outlines some of the problems and conflicts involved in establishing ownership of shipwrecks. In an essay at least three paragraphs long, propose a solution that you think would be fair to the various interests and parties involved. Be sure to support your proposal with arguments. Use at least three lesson words in your essay and underline them.

WRITE THE DERIVATIVE

Complete the sentence by writing the correct form of the word shown in parentheses. You may not need to change the form that is given.

___subterfuge___ **1.** Ella's aches and pains were only a _____ to avoid going shopping. (*subterfuge*)

___latent___ **2.** Jason's _____ anger, though under control and well disguised, occasionally burst forth in the form of snide comments. (*latent*) _salient_ **3.** When you tell a story, be sure to give a good description of the most ———— events. (*salient*)

vaunt **4.** The self-absorbed actor never passed up an opportunity to ———— his limited talents. (*vaunt*)

flagrantly **5.** The student ———— violated the teacher's rules against chewing gum in class by blowing bubbles. (*flagrant*)

unobtrusively **6.** The investigator slipped into the party ———— to observe the guests. (*unobtrusively*)

sequestered **7.** The production crew was ———— in the hut until the storm passed and they were able to resume filming. (*sequester*)

furtively **8.** The cat crept ———— toward the goldfish bowl. (*furtive*)

surreptitiously **9.** The thief entered the darkened house ————, but was surprised by the hidden police officers. (*surreptitious*)

ostensibly **10.** He complimented Tara's mom, ———— to make a good impression on both women. (*ostensible*)

FIND THE EXAMPLE

Choose the answer that best describes the action or situation.

_d_ **1.** The *ostensible* purpose of laws against speeding
a. to cause pain   **b.** to take money   **c.** to support police   **d.** to ensure safety

_b_ **2.** One of the most common examples of *subterfuge*
a. new pencil   **b.** magic trick   **c.** private tutorial   **d.** hockey game

_c_ **3.** A characteristic of a *salient* fact
a. subtlety   **b.** confusion   **c.** obviousness   **d.** slyness

_a_ **4.** A *surreptitious* act
a. jewel heist   **b.** stage show   **c.** poetry reading   **d.** silly advertising

_a_ **5.** A quality that a *flagrant* act would NOT have
a. subtlety   **b.** obviousness   **c.** negativity   **d.** offensiveness

_d_ **6.** Someone likely to be *furtive*
a. athlete   **b.** actor   **c.** salesperson   **d.** spy

_b_ **7.** A place in which people are most likely to be *sequestered*
a. stadium   **b.** small room   **c.** crowded street   **d.** commuter train

_b_ **8.** Something you might *vaunt*
a. past failures   **b.** awards won   **c.** bad luck   **d.** embarrassing moments

_a_ **9.** Something that moves *unobtrusively*
a. a stalking cat   **b.** an enraged hippo   **c.** a loud SUV   **d.** a landslide

_d_ **10.** A *latent* talent that a former basketball player might discover at age fifty
a. rebounding ability   **b.** dribbling ability   **c.** athletic ability   **d.** chess ability

Words from French

WORD LIST

adroit	blasé	cliché	clientele	entrepreneur
forte	gauche	naive	nonchalant	rendezvous

Almost a thousand years ago, William the Conqueror and his French-speaking army conquered England. This resulted in great changes to the English language, as numerous French words became part of the English vocabulary. All of the words on this list come from French words, though some of the etymologies continue back to Latin.

adroit

1. adroit (ə-droit´) *adjective* from French *à droit,* "to the right"
Skillful and quick in the use of the hands or the mind
• In basketball, guards must be especially **adroit** dribblers.

adroitness *noun* The mayor showed great **adroitness** in avoiding embarrassing topics during news conferences.

2. blasé (blä-zā´) *adjective* from French *blaser*
a. Bored or unimpressed because of overexposure; jaded
• The spoiled child had been to so many theme parks that she was **blasé** about the prospects of visiting yet another.
b. Unconcerned; carefree
• I was worried about the cook's **blasé** attitude toward keeping the kitchen clean.
c. Extremely sophisticated; worldly
• The **blasé** diplomat had been entertained by powerful people around the world.

3. cliché (klē-shā´) *noun* from French *clicher,* "to stereotype"
A trite or an overused expression, idea, or practice
• "It was a dark and stormy night" is a **cliché,** so you probably shouldn't start your story with it.

clichéd *adjective* The **clichéd** plot of the movie was as unoriginal as it was predictable and boring.

4. clientele (klī´ən-tĕl´) *noun* from French *clientèle,* taken from Latin *cliens,* "dependent follower"
A group of customers or patrons
• The restaurant mailed promotional coupons to its regular **clientele.**

5. entrepreneur (ŏn´trə-prə-nûr´) *noun* from Old French *entreprendre,* "to undertake"
A person who founds, organizes, operates, and assumes the risk for a business
• The **entrepreneur** began her career selling handmade bags at a local flea market; she now owns a boutique and an online store.

entrepreneurial *adjective* His **entrepreneurial** skills eventually led him from part-time clerk to founder and CEO.

Point out that many French words are pronounced differently from what their spellings might suggest. Have students pronounce *blasé, cliché, forte, naive,* and *rendezvous.*

6. **forte** (fôr´tā´) *noun* from Old French *fort,* "strong"
Something in which a person excels; a strong point
• Hector's **forte** has always been math.

7. **gauche** (gōsh) *adjective* from French *gauche,* "awkward" (literally, "left-handed"), taken from Old French *gauchir,* "to turn aside; to walk clumsily"
Tactless; socially awkward
• Trevor's **gauche** complaint about the food offended the hostess and the other guests at the table.

   gaucheness *noun* Matilda showed her **gaucheness** by shouting, "Wow, this sure is fancy!" at the elegant party.

8. **naive** (nī-ēv´) *adjective* from French *naïve,* taken from Latin *natus,* "to be born"
Trusting due to lack of experience or sophistication; innocently unaware or unrealistic
• The **naive** tourists didn't know that the prices were negotiable, so they ended up paying twice as much as everyone else.

   naiveté (nī´ēv-tā´) *noun* His willingness to believe in the smooth-talking stranger's get-rich-quick scheme showed his **naiveté.**

9. **nonchalant** (nŏn´shə-länt´) *adjective* from French, taken from Latin *non,* "not" + *calere,* "to be warm; to heat up"
Seeming to be coolly unconcerned or indifferent
• The astronaut remained **nonchalant** even in the face of danger.

   nonchalance *noun* We all knew Vera's **nonchalance** was an act to cover up her embarrassment.

10. **rendezvous** (rän´dā-vōō´) from Old French *rendre,* "to present" + *vous,* "yourselves"
   a. *noun* An arranged meeting
      • Mrs. Caldwell and her friend arranged a three o'clock **rendezvous** at the corner of Mason and Vine Streets.
   b. *verb* To meet at an agreed time and place
      • The hikers went their separate ways after agreeing to **rendezvous** at the campsite in six hours.

> Note that the origins of *adroit* and *gauche* reflect a common language bias in favor of right over left.

> Note that the plural of *rendezvous* is *rendezvous.*

WORD ENRICHMENT

Clicking clichés

Cliché comes from the French verb *clicher,* "to stereotype," and originates in the printing business. When printers made copies of something, they used to put molds into hot metal, which made a clicking sound. Thus "clicking" became associated with something produced over and over again.

WRITE THE CORRECT WORD

Write the correct word in the space next to each definition.

__rendezvous__ **1.** an arranged meeting

__naive__ **2.** overly trusting; innocent

__clientele__ **3.** a group of customers

__forte__ **4.** a strong point

__blasé__ **5.** unimpressed; jaded

__adroit__ **6.** highly skilled

__nonchalant__ **7.** seemingly unconcerned

__entrepreneur__ **8.** a business founder

__gauche__ **9.** tactless; awkward

__cliché__ **10.** an overused expression

COMPLETE THE SENTENCE

Write the letter for the word that best completes each sentence.

__c__ **1.** It's not really my _____, but I'll give it a try.
    a. rendezvous   **b.** entrepreneur   **c.** forte   **d.** clientele

__a__ **2.** How can you be so _____ when the boat is leaking?
    a. nonchalant   **b.** naive   **c.** gauche   **d.** entrepreneurial

__d__ **3.** He might seem _____, but I'm sure that under the surface he's upset.
    a. clichéd   **b.** gauche   **c.** entrepreneurial   **d.** blasé

__b__ **4.** Only a(n) _____ person would even think such a thing, let alone say it out loud.
    a. forte   **b.** gauche   **c.** adroit   **d.** rendezvous

__d__ **5.** *Chez Henri* and *Joe's Grub Shack* are two restaurants with very different _____.
    a. rendezvous   **b.** nonchalance   **c.** clichés   **d.** clienteles

__c__ **6.** Though unoriginal, _____ often have some truth behind them.
    a. entrepreneurs   **b.** clienteles   **c.** clichés   **d.** fortes

__a__ **7.** Romeo and Juliet weren't the only people to have a secret _____ in the play.
    a. rendezvous   **b.** forte   **c.** cliché   **d.** gaucheness

__b__ **8.** The skillful pianist could play any piece _____.
    a. gauchely   **b.** adroitly   **c.** naively   **d.** blasé

__d__ **9.** Don't be _____, Jamie; despite what they say, the check could not have been lost in the mail three times.
    a. nonchalant   **b.** adroit   **c.** blasé   **d.** naive

__c__ **10.** Although people thought he was just a dreamer, he proved his ideas were worthwhile when he became a successful _____.
    a. cliché   **b.** rendezvous   **c.** entrepreneur   **d.** clientele

Challenge: Though it can sometimes be challenging to do so, a good host can remain _____ in the face of the most _____ behavior.
__a__   **a.** nonchalant…gauche   **b.** naive…adroit   **c.** blasé…entrepreneurial

Wristies? No Kidding!

(1) When people picture an inventor, what they imagine is often a *cliché*: a wild-eyed man with unruly gray hair, frantically laboring away in a lab cluttered with test tubes full of strange, bubbling liquids. In contrast, however, K. K. Gregory became an inventor when she was just a ten-year-old elementary-school student!

In 1993, Gregory was building a snow fort with her little brother. While she played, snow kept getting between the bottom of her gloves and the ends of her jacket sleeves, making her cold. She went into her house and sewed some fleece material together to make two long tubes, like sleeves. She then cut a slit near the ends for her thumbs. The tubes, which she wore on her arms and under her gloves, kept snow off her wrists and helped her stay warm. That week, Gregory showed her Girl Scout troop the invention. It was a big hit, and they encouraged her to make more.

And make more she did. In fact she went to a lawyer and learned that her idea had not been patented. She applied for a patent and trademarked her product, deciding to call them "Wristies." **(2)** She then set herself to the task of finding the right *clientele*.

(3) Many people thought that the idea of a ten-year-old running a successful business was hopelessly *naive*. Undaunted, Gregory aimed high, eventually selling Wristies to national businesses that employed outdoor workers.

(4) Being a young *entrepreneur* wasn't easy. Her mother had to drive her to meetings. **(5)** Though the young inventor herself made arrangements to *rendezvous* with business contacts, when people saw mother and daughter arrive, they often assumed that young Gregory was just tagging along because her mother couldn't find a babysitter. **(6)** In the face of these slights, Gregory had no choice but to remain *nonchalant*. **(7)** But with her *adroit* sales techniques, she eventually overcame such age barriers. Soon, Wristies were being sold in stores nationwide. Gregory even became the youngest person to present a product on a cable home-shopping channel; she sold 2,700 pairs of Wristies in just six minutes.

Meanwhile, some of Gregory's jealous classmates insulted and teased her about her company. **(8)** Their *gauche* comments hurt, but Gregory was cheered by the positive responses she received elsewhere. **(9)** Although people are sometimes *blasé* about business success stories, this child inventor sparked wide interest. Gregory was invited to appear on popular television shows. Major newspapers and magazines reported her story.

(10) Gregory ran her company until she was sixteen, at which time she decided to pursue her other *forte*, indoor rock climbing. In 2000, she earned a spot on the U.S. Climbing Team and competed in Austria. Sales of Wristies continue to grow under her mother's direction. U.S. soldiers and toll collectors are among the new users and fans of Wristies.

As a college student, Gregory has taken courses in environmental science, humanities, and documentary filmmaking. Between her studies and rock climbing, Gregory gives talks at schools about her unique experiences. She wants to give young people the faith and courage to invent their own dreams, just as she did.

Each sentence below refers to a numbered sentence in the passage. Write the letter of the choice that gives the sentence a meaning that is closest to the original sentence.

____c____ **1.** When people picture an inventor, what they imagine is often a _____.
    a. customer base   **b.** business leader   **c.** stereotype   **d.** meeting

____d____ **2.** She then set herself to the task of finding the right _____.
    a. expression   **b.** strong point   **c.** businessperson   **d.** customer base

____a____ **3.** Many people thought that the idea of a ten-year-old running a successful business was _____.
    a. unrealistic   **b.** jaded   **c.** tactless   **d.** overused

____d____ **4.** Being a young _____ wasn't easy.
    a. trite expression   **b.** customer   **c.** strong point   **d.** business owner

b **5.** The young inventor made arrangements to _____ with business contacts.
   a. overuse   **b.** meet   **c.** be innocent   **d.** appear unconcerned

a **6.** In the face of these slights, Gregory had no choice but to remain _____.
   a. cool and calm   **b.** highly skilled   **c.** very sophisticated   **d.** overused and tired

c **7.** But with her _____ sales techniques, she overcame such age barriers.
   a. worldly   **b.** calm   **c.** skillful   **d.** tactless

b **8.** Their _____ comments hurt, but Gregory was cheered by the positive responses she received elsewhere.
   a. skillful   **b.** tactless   **c.** worldly   **d.** trite

a **9.** People are sometimes _____ business success stories.
   a. bored by   **b.** disbelieving of   **c.** enchanted by   **d.** innocent about

d **10.** Gregory ran her company until she was sixteen, at which time she decided to pursue her other _____, indoor rock climbing.
   a. business meeting   **b.** business interest   **c.** customer base   **d.** strong point

Indicate whether the statements below are TRUE or FALSE according to the passage.

F **1.** K. K. Gregory read about a product similar to Wristies.

T **2.** K. K. Gregory not only invented Wristies, but handled much of the business side of selling her invention, thus becoming something of a celebrity.

F **3.** Because she had already made so much money, K. K. Gregory decided to skip college.

FINISH THE THOUGHT

Complete each sentence so that it shows the meaning of the italicized word.

1. It's good to be *nonchalant* when _____ Answers will vary. _____

_____

2. She was so *gauche* that _____ Answers will vary. _____

_____

WRITE THE DERIVATIVE

Complete the sentence by writing the correct form of the word shown in parentheses. You may not need to change the form that is given.

gaucheness **1.** His _____ didn't surprise me because I knew he'd grown up without the opportunity to learn manners. (*gauche*)

blasé **2.** It's hard to appear _____ when being chased by an angry 200-pound ostrich. (*blasé*)

naiveté	**3.** Con artists prey on the _____ of their victims. *(naive)*
forte	**4.** Marla was a good defender, but her real _____ was scoring goals. *(forte)*
clichéd	**5.** By now, the "damsel in distress" plot is not only _____, but outdated. *(cliché)*
entrepreneurial	**6.** Our _____ success has created enough wealth that we can now fund many of the charities that we feel are important. *(entrepreneur)*
clientele	**7.** The tailor's _____ consists mainly of local businessmen. *(clientele)*
adroitness	**8.** It takes a fair amount of _____ to steer a boat gently into its mooring. *(adroit)*
rendezvous	**9.** Does calling it a "_____" sound more sophisticated than just calling it a "meeting"? *(rendezvous)*
nonchalance	**10.** Unlike Jake, who always seems anxious, Asa is the model of _____. *(nonchalant)*

FIND THE EXAMPLE

Choose the answer that best describes the action or situation.

d   **1.** A *gauche* thing to do at a party
     a. shake hands   **b.** compliment food   **c.** eat cheese   **d.** insult the host

b   **2.** A description of the facial expression of a *nonchalant* person
     a. wide-eyed   **b.** relaxed   **c.** grimacing   **d.** flushed

c   **3.** An activity that requires *adroitness*
     a. sleeping   **b.** watching TV   **c.** playing tennis   **d.** eating toast

d   **4.** A *cliché*
     a. Eat the gumbo.   **b.** I am here.   **c.** Todd is smart.   **d.** Haste makes waste.

a   **5.** Person most likely to be *naive*
     a. kindergartener   **b.** professor   **c.** CIA agent   **d.** diplomat

a   **6.** A chef's *forte*
     a. cooking   **b.** basketball   **c.** sculpting   **d.** cello

a   **7.** A good spot for a friendly *rendezvous*
     a. coffee shop   **b.** garbage dump   **c.** jail cell   **d.** freeway

c   **8.** Something usually possessed by successful *entrepreneurs*
     a. tardiness   **b.** athletic talent   **c.** creativity   **d.** ability to copy

d   **9.** A *blasé* approach to homework
     a. start early   **b.** check your work   **c.** read carefully   **d.** get to it eventually

c   **10.** Most likely the main *clientele* of a pizza parlor near a high school
     a. lawyers   **b.** pepperoni   **c.** students   **d.** beverages

Taking Tests

SAT Critical Reading Tests

The new SAT, first administered in 2005, has a Critical Reading section that presents both short and long reading passages, each of them followed by a set of multiple-choice questions. The strategies outlined below can help you approach a critical reading test with confidence and answer questions successfully.

Strategies

1. *Scan the passage and the test items first.* This will enable you to look for specific information as you read.

2. *Read at an appropriate rate.* Read through the passage once to get the overall idea. Then reread it slowly to make sure you understand it.

3. *Determine the main idea as you read.* The main idea may or may not be directly stated in the passage, but identifying it is critical to understanding what you read.

4. *Identify supporting details.* Details that support main points are often queried in test items.

5. *Be prepared to make inferences and draw conclusions.* These may involve making predictions or generalizations, or they may be logical conclusions drawn.

6. *Be prepared to make judgments.* Critical reading involves making evaluative judgments about ideas, fact and opinions, or an author's attitude, style, or tone.

7. *Refer to the passage to find information.* You do not need to memorize information from the passage, and may go back to it if necessary.

Practice

Read the following passage. Answer the questions based on what is stated or implied in the passage. For each question, choose the best answer and write the letter of the answer you choose in the space provided.

Though you have probably heard of the Seven Wonders of the World, do you know what they are? The Seven Wonders of the World were widely known for many centuries but have recently faded into near-oblivion. One reason for their decline may be the indisputable fact that six of the seven wonders no longer exist.

The original seven wonders were all constructed in ancient times and were all located in the Mediterranean and Middle East. Apparently, a Greek scholar at the ancient library of Alexandria created the first list of wonders in about 290 BC. An engineer named Philo of Byzantium drew up the most widely acknowledged list about 40 years later. Among other things, these lists reflected a growing sense of human achievement and appreciation for man-made structures. Prior to this time, most achievements and "wonders" were attributed to mythological gods and goddesses. The lists also reflected a growing tendency among people in Middle Eastern and Mediterranean cultures to travel beyond the confines of their own societies.

For those who yearned to know what was on the other side of the hill, the Seven Wonders constituted the "A-List" of attractions. Of the seven, three were built by the ancient Greeks as offerings to gods or goddesses. These include the 40-foot gold and ivory Statue of Zeus at Olympia, which was a religious sanctuary south of Athens and the site of the ancient Olympic Games; the Colossus of Rhodes, a 110-foot bronze statue of the sun god Helios; and the Temple of Artemis, an enormous marble structure, dedicated to the goddess of the moon and the hunt.

The other four wonders could be found in North Africa and the Middle East. These four structures tended more toward human concerns, and two of them were tombs for human remains. The Mausoleum at Halicarnassus was a tomb that stood 140 feet tall. It was constructed in 350 BC for King Mausolos (hence the word *mausoleum*) in modern-day Turkey. Next was the Pharos, or Lighthouse, of Alexandria, a limestone tower that stood 445 feet tall. The flame that burned in the lighthouse could be seen by sailors for many miles. The Hanging Gardens of Babylon were commissioned by King Nebuchadnezzar II in about 550 BC. The ancient city of Babylon was about 50 miles south of Baghdad in modern-day Iraq. The Pyramids of Giza in Egypt are the seventh and final wonder—and the only one still in existence. Several Egyptian pharaohs oversaw the construction of the pyramids, which were built as repositories for the royal remains. All the other wonders have disintegrated, but the pyramids still stand and can be seen to this day.

_____b_____ **1.** Which of these titles best fits this passage?
    a. "Powerful Gods and Goddesses"
    b. "Marvels of the Ancient World"
    c. "Visiting the Pyramids at Giza"
    d. "Structures Built by the Greeks"
    e. "Mediterranean and Middle Eastern Cultures"

_____e_____ **2.** The passage mentions "the *indisputable* fact that six of the seven wonders no longer exist." The word *indisputable* means
    a. without any apparent cause.
    b. never recognized before.
    c. to be avoided if possible.
    d. causing a deep sense of loss.
    e. not open to question.

_____d_____ **3.** Which detail from the passage supports the idea that some of the Seven Wonders "tended more toward human concerns"?
    a. The Pyramids of Giza still stand and can be seen today.
    b. The Colossus of Rhodes was a 110-foot statue of the sun god Helios.
    c. An engineer named Philo of Byzantium drew up the list of wonders.
    d. The Hanging Gardens were built for Nebuchadnezzar's wife.
    e. Four of the wonders were in North Africa and the Middle East.

_____c_____ **4.** The author's phrase, "those who yearned to know what was on the other side of the hill," refers to people who
    a. liked to hike and climb mountains.
    b. could not stay in one place for long.
    c. wanted to travel and see the world.
    d. felt an urge to change the landscape.
    e. feared anything that was unknown.

_____d_____ **5.** The author of this passage seems to think that the Seven Wonders were
    a. objects of little interest to ancient societies.
    b. evidence of human vanity.
    c. myths invented by scholars long ago.
    d. remarkable feats of human achievement.
    e. symbols of religious worship.

Sleepiness and Laziness

WORD LIST

dilatory	languid	lethargy	melancholy	quiescent
repose	sloth	somnambulate	soporific	stupor

There are many reasons why one might feel tired or lazy. The words in this lesson describe those sleepy, lazy feelings and behaviors.

1. **dilatory** (dĭl´ə-tôr´ē) *adjective* from Latin *dilator,* "delayer"
   Intended to delay; tending to postpone or delay
   • Russ was so **dilatory** in returning the books to the library that the late fees were more than fifty dollars.

   dilatoriness *noun* Reggie was known for his **dilatoriness,** so it was not surprising that he arrived late to the lunch meeting.

2. **languid** (lăng´gwĭd) *adjective* from Latin *languere,* "to be weak or faint"
   Lacking energy, spirit, or force; slow
   • They enjoyed the warm days and **languid** breezes on the tropical island.

   languish *verb* After she **languished** in her room for an hour, she finally felt ready to join the family for dinner.

   languor (lăng´gər) *noun* Jacques enjoyed the **languor** of long Sunday mornings spent on the couch, reading the newspaper.

3. **lethargy** (lĕth´ər-jē) *noun* from Greek *lethe,* "forgetfulness" + *argos,* "idle"
   A severe lack of energy and enthusiasm; apathy and inactivity
   • Unable to pull himself out of his **lethargy,** the man missed two days of work.

   lethargic *adjective* The newborn colt was so **lethargic** that we feared it would not survive.

4. **melancholy** (mĕl´en-kŏl´ē) from Greek *melan-,* "black" + *khole,* "bile"
   a. *noun* Deep sadness or depression; gloom
      • The girl fell into a state of **melancholy** when she learned she'd be spending her vacation alone at the boarding school.
   b. *adjective* Sad and gloomy; pensive
      • When I think about the end of summer, I am suddenly in a **melancholy** mood.

5. **quiescent** (kwē-ĕs´ənt) *adjective* from Latin *quies,* "quiet"
   Being still, quiet, or inactive
   • Although the preschoolers were **quiescent** for the moment, the teacher knew that could end at any time.

   quiescence *noun* The volcano's **quiescence** was ended by a sudden eruption.

Point out that *stupor* and *languid* can refer to inactive states brought on by illness.

languid

Whereas *languid* can refer to a person, an animal, a mood, or the weather, *lethargy* refers only to people and animals.

6. **repose** (rĭ-pōz´) from Latin *re-*, "back" + *pausare*, "to rest"
   a. *noun* Rest; relaxation; peacefulness
      • She indulged in an hour of **repose** before she went to the party.
   b. *verb* To lie down; to rest
      • On hot summer days, I like to **repose** in my hammock.

7. **sloth** (slôth) *noun* from Middle English *slowth*, "slow"
   Laziness; avoiding work or effort
      • It was hard to keep his **sloth** a secret when he watched television in
      the lounge for five hours each day.

   slothful *adjective* Georgiana's **slothful** approach to her work soon got
   her fired from her job.

A *sloth* is also a type of slow-moving mammal, found in South and Central America.

8. **somnambulate** (sŏm-năm´byə-lāt´) *verb* from Latin *somnus*,
   "sleep" + *ambulare*, "to walk"
   To sleepwalk
      • Thomas often ends up in the kitchen when he **somnambulates.**

   somnambular *adjective* **Somnambular** people can easily injure
   themselves.

   somnambulism *noun* Bea spoke to a specialist about
   her **somnambulism.**

9. **soporific** (sŏp´ə-rĭf´ĭk) from Latin *sopor*, "a deep sleep"
   a. *adjective* Causing or tending to cause sleep
      • Hank discovered that slow music often had a **soporific** effect
      on him.
   b. *noun* A medicine that causes sleep
      • The physician prescribed a **soporific** to the patient who suffered
      from insomnia.

10. **stupor** (stōō´pər) *noun* from Latin *stupere*, "to be stunned"
    A confused condition of reduced consciousness, often brought on by
    shock or illness; a daze
      • My fever was so high that I was in a **stupor** and couldn't think clearly.

    stupefy *verb* The grueling trail and hot sun **stupefied** the hikers.

WORD ENRICHMENT

The four humors

The etymology of the word *melancholy* shows the word's interesting
history. Ancient medical theory suggested that there were four bodily fluids:
black bile, yellow bile, phlegm, and blood. These fluids were thought to
rule bodily health as well as personal temperament. Black bile could cause
depression, or *melancholy.* Blood caused a *sanguine,* or confident, optimistic
temperament. Yellow bile contributed to a *choleric,* or easily irritated,
bad-tempered personality. Finally, phlegm made a person *phlegmatic,* or
calm, sluggish, and unemotional.

Although no longer used in medical theory or psychology, the words
melancholy, sanguine, choleric, and *phlegmatic* retain these meanings in
modern English.

WRITE THE CORRECT WORD

Write the correct word in the space next to each definition.

___sloth___	**1.** laziness	___repose___	**6.** to lie down
___melancholy___	**2.** sadness; gloom	___dilatory___	**7.** tending to postpone
___quiescent___	**3.** still; quiet	___stupor___	**8.** a confused condition
___soporific___	**4.** causing sleep	___languid___	**9.** lacking energy; slow
___lethargy___	**5.** a lack of energy and enthusiasm	___somnambulate___	**10.** to sleepwalk

COMPLETE THE SENTENCE

Write the letter for the word that best completes each sentence.

___c___ **1.** Because of his extreme _____, Jorge decided to stay in bed all day.
a. dilatoriness   **b.** somnambulism   **c.** lethargy   **d.** repose

___b___ **2.** Because Margot tended to _____, she had to make sure the door at the top of the stairs was closed each night.
a. languish   **b.** somnambulate   **c.** sloth   **d.** repose

___d___ **3.** I feel _____ whenever I think of the friends I left behind when I moved away.
a. languid   **b.** dilatory   **c.** slothful   **d.** melancholy

___b___ **4.** The day felt warm and _____, so we sat outside and drank ice tea.
a. dilatory   **b.** languid   **c.** repose   **d.** soporific

___d___ **5.** He tried to think clearly, but the phone call had awakened him from a deep sleep, and he couldn't shake his _____.
a. repose   **b.** dilatoriness   **c.** quiescence   **d.** stupor

___a___ **6.** Consistent with her usual _____, she once again left her room in a total mess and spent the day relaxing.
a. sloth   **b.** melancholy   **c.** soporific   **d.** somnambulism

___d___ **7.** After babysitting the energetic children, Garret needed a few hours of _____.
a. somnambulism   **b.** dilatoriness   **c.** stupor   **d.** repose

___c___ **8.** If the disease is _____, additional treatment will not be necessary.
a. languid   **b.** lethargic   **c.** quiescent   **d.** slothful

___a___ **9.** The hum of the plane engine had a _____ effect, lulling many of the passengers to sleep.
a. soporific   **b.** quiescent   **c.** dilatory   **d.** melancholy

___b___ **10.** The man's _____ payments led to the foreclosure of his mortgage.
a. languid   **b.** dilatory   **c.** lethargic   **d.** quiescent

Challenge: For the first week after his dog died, Justin was in a stupor, but his shock soon transformed to _____, and then he became _____ for the entire month.

___b___ **a.** dilatoriness...soporific   **b.** melancholy...lethargic   **c.** repose...somnambular

The Long Sleep

(1) For many people, the start of winter is a *melancholy* time. Autumn colors fade, and the days grow short and cold. But biologists who study bears during hibernation welcome winter. **(2)** Studying how bears stay healthy during their winter *repose* may shed light on various human medical conditions, ranging from gallstones to heart disease.

Bears begin preparing for their hibernation during the peak of summer, while berries and nuts are in abundance. They eat as much as they can to build up their body fat for the winter. Because hibernating bears don't eat, all their energy comes from breaking down this stored body fat. During the period before hibernation, a bear can gain as much as thirty pounds a week, and its fur doubles in thickness, adding considerable insulation.

(3) In the warm months, bears are *quiescent* only during afternoon naps and at night. **(4)** But come fall, they become more *languid*. Food becomes scarce and with the little energy that remains, bears slowly dig their dens and pad them with bark and leaves. **(5)** Humans have the freedom of choice to be *dilatory* about their winter preparations. But for a bear, failing to prepare a safe place to hibernate could mean certain death.

(6) The shorter winter days and the lack of food have a *soporific* effect on bears, so once their dens are ready, they bed down. For many years, scientists believed bears simply went into a deep sleep and did not stir until spring. Then, researchers actually observed bear behavior by placing heat-sensitive infrared cameras in their dens. **(7)** They found that bears stretch and move about their dens in a *somnambular* state. Female bears also give birth while hibernating, usually in January. **(8)** Despite their *lethargy*, they nurse their young in the den until spring.

(9) While some hibernating bears were in a *stupor*, scientists drew their blood in order to study it. The blood samples revealed that the bears' cholesterol levels double in winter, probably because they are living off stored fat. Yet bears do not develop hardened arteries or gallstones, as humans with high cholesterol do. Understanding how hibernating bears avoid these illnesses could lead to new treatments for humans suffering from these conditions.

(10) In an interesting twist, recent research indicates that some black bears are becoming obese as they develop the *slothful* habits of humans. "Urban" bears that live near cities are one-third less active and 30 percent heavier than "forest" bears. Rather than roaming the forest in search of food, urban bears dine on food in dumpsters from restaurants. Because this food is plentiful year-round, these bears do not hibernate and could end up developing heart disease.

Still, the majority of bears hibernate, and humans may be able to gain valuable medical knowledge by studying how they achieve this feat.

Each sentence below refers to a numbered sentence in the passage. Write the letter of the choice that gives the sentence a meaning that is closest to the original sentence.

__c__ **1.** For many people, the start of winter is a _____ time.
   a. lazy   **b.** slow   **c.** sad   **d.** welcome

__b__ **2.** Studying how bears stay healthy during their winter _____ may shed light on various human medical conditions.
   a. hunting season   **b.** rest   **c.** expeditions   **d.** daze

__a__ **3.** In the warm months, bears are _____ only during naps and at night.
   a. inactive   **b.** confused   **c.** active   **d.** dreamers

__d__ **4.** But come fall, they become _____.
   a. more active   **b.** more confused   **c.** sadder   **d.** slower

_____c_____ **5.** Humans have the freedom of choice to _____ their winter preparations.
    a. travel before   **b.** be quiet about   **c.** delay   **d.** be sad about

_____b_____ **6.** The shorter winter days and the lack of food have a _____ effect on bears.
    a. delayed   **b.** sleep-inducing   **c.** strongly negative   **d.** very pronounced

_____a_____ **7.** The scientists found that bears stretch and move about in a _____ state.
    a. sleepwalking   **b.** relaxed   **c.** nervous   **d.** sad

_____c_____ **8.** Despite their _____, they nurse their young until spring.
    a. curiosity   **b.** mothering   **c.** inactivity   **d.** hungriness

_____d_____ **9.** While some hibernating bears were in a _____, scientists drew their blood.
    a. depression   **b.** den   **c.** nap   **d.** daze

_____a_____ **10.** In an interesting twist recent research indicates that some black bears are becoming obese as they develop the _____ habits of humans.
    a. lazy   **b.** active   **c.** drinking   **d.** sleeping

Indicate whether the statements below are TRUE or FALSE according to the passage.

_____T_____ **1.** Bears begin preparing for hibernation in the summer.

_____F_____ **2.** Hibernating bears do not move until spring.

_____F_____ **3.** Bears eat during hibernation.

WRITING EXTENDED RESPONSES

Bear hibernation takes much preparation. In an essay of at least three paragraphs, describe your own sleep habits. Are you a heavy or a light sleeper? Are you an early or a late riser? Do you sleepwalk? Use at least three lesson words in your essay and underline them.

WRITE THE DERIVATIVE

Complete the sentence by writing the correct form of the word shown in parentheses. You may not need to change the form that is given.

_____dilatoriness_____ **1.** Because of the waiter's _____, his customers never left him very large tips. *(dilatory)*

_____soporific_____ **2.** Such foods as warm milk are said to have a mild _____ effect. *(soporific)*

_____languor_____ **3.** There was _____ in the overall mood of the people walking through the plaza on the warm night. *(languid)*

_____quiescence_____ **4.** After receiving months of treatment, the patient was relieved to learn that the disease had lapsed into _____. *(quiescent)*

_____somnambular_____ **5.** Some _____ people actually walk out of their homes in the middle of the night. *(somnambulate)*

<u>reposing</u> **6.** Although he said he was working, I found him _____ on the lounge chair, with a bag of popcorn. *(repose)*

<u>stupefying</u> **7.** Even though the fireworks were set off several blocks away, the noise from the explosions was still _____. *(stupor)*

<u>slothful</u> **8.** I was feeling _____, so I left my dishes in the sink for someone else to wash. *(sloth)*

<u>melancholy</u> **9.** The man felt a wave of _____ when he realized that his childhood home had fallen into a state of disrepair. *(melancholy)*

<u>lethargic</u> **10.** The frogs became _____ in the cool weather. *(lethargy)*

FIND THE EXAMPLE

Choose the answer that best describes the action or situation.

<u>a</u> **1.** Something that is always done by people who *somnambulate*
  a. walk   **b.** cry   **c.** talk   **d.** eat

<u>b</u> **2.** A good place to *repose*
  a. ladder   **b.** bed   **c.** sidewalk   **d.** trampoline

<u>c</u> **3.** Something that may result from *sloth*
  a. waking early   **b.** being on time   **c.** arriving late   **d.** planning

<u>d</u> **4.** What a person in a *melancholy* mood would most likely do
  a. scream   **b.** smile   **c.** laugh   **d.** cry

<u>b</u> **5.** How a *languid* person would most likely feel
  a. efficient   **b.** tired   **c.** strong   **d.** helpful

<u>d</u> **6.** A likely result of someone's *dilatory* arrival at the airport
  a. time to waste   **b.** sleeplessness   **c.** hunger   **d.** missed flight

<u>a</u> **7.** Something a *lethargic* person lacks
  a. energy   **b.** vision   **c.** thoughts   **d.** a frown

<u>d</u> **8.** The way someone is most likely to feel while in a *stupor*
  a. quick   **b.** alert   **c.** afraid   **d.** confused

<u>c</u> **9.** Something that would most likely have a *soporific* effect
  a. yelling   **b.** coffee   **c.** a warm bath   **d.** loud music

<u>a</u> **10.** What a *quiescent* audience would be most likely to do
  a. sit quietly   **b.** sleepwalk   **c.** clap   **d.** sing along

Liking and Disliking

WORD LIST

abhor	affinity	animosity	ardent	disdain
enamor	estrange	kudos	pejorative	repugnance

The words in this lesson can be used to express various degrees of liking and disliking. Do you merely dislike, or do you *abhor*, doing the dishes? Are you *enamored* by a certain musician, or do you simply find his or her music decent? As you study the words, think about how you might apply each word to something you like or dislike.

Have students classify the words into those that indicate *like* or *love* for something and those that indicate *dislike*. Ask them to explain their classifications.

1. **abhor** (ăb-hôr´) *verb* from Latin *ab-*, "away from" + *horrere*, "to shudder"
   To hate intensely; to detest; to regard with horror or loathing
   • Lynn **abhors** cats; if you have one as a pet, she will refuse to visit you.

   abhorrent *adjective* I find racial discrimination to be **abhorrent**.

   abhorrence *noun* He glared with **abhorrence** at the youths who had vandalized the gravestones.

2. **affinity** (ə-fĭn´ĭ-tē) *noun* from Latin *affinis*, "related by marriage"
   A natural attraction, liking, or feeling of kinship
   • He had an **affinity** for the outdoors and loved to take long hikes.

3. **animosity** (ăn´ə-mŏs´ĭ-tē) *noun* from Latin *animus*, "soul; spirit"
   Bitter hostility; open hatred
   • The teams displayed great **animosity** toward each other during the game.

4. **ardent** (är´dnt) *adjective* from Latin *ardere*, "to burn"
   Passionate; showing strong enthusiasm or devotion
   • Mrs. McElvain, an **ardent** supporter of the arts, donated all the paintings in her private collection to the museum.

   ardor *noun* My grandfather's **ardor** for swimming continued well into his "golden years"; he did laps in the pool every morning.

   > *Ardent* feelings can also be negative. For example, one might *ardently abhor* rats.

5. **disdain** (dĭs-dān´) from Latin *de-*, "not" + *dignus*, "worthy"
   a. *verb* To regard or treat with contempt or scorn; to despise
      • The gourmet chef **disdained** fast-food restaurants.
   b. *noun* Scorn; contempt and aloofness
      • The waitress had **disdain** for the customer who left no tip.

   disdainful *adjective* Gerald's **disdainful** expression made it clear that he did not think the opera's soloists were very good.

6. **enamor** (ĭ-năm´ər) *verb* from Old French *en-*, "put into" + *amour*, "love"
   To inspire with love; to captivate
   • She was so **enamored** with the speaker that she waited in line for an hour to get his autograph.

   > *Enamor* is most often used in the passive construction, as in "She was *enamored*."

7. **estrange** (ĭ-strānj´) *verb* from Latin *extraneare*, "to treat as a stranger; disown"
To destroy affection or friendliness; to alienate; to make hostile
   • An unfortunate misunderstanding **estranged** the two friends.

   estrangement *noun* The woman's seven-year **estrangement** from her brother ended when she was invited to his wedding.

8. **kudos** (kōō´dōz´) *noun* from Greek *kudos*, "magical glory"
Praise for exceptional achievement
   • The architect received **kudos** for his creative and cost-effective design for the new library.

kudos

9. **pejorative** (pĭ-jôr´ə-tĭv) *adjective* from Latin *peiorare*, "to make worse"
Disrespectful; insulting; belittling
   • Many people feel the word *housewife* is an old-fashioned, **pejorative** term.

> *Pejorative* commonly refers to language, such as words or remarks.

10. **repugnance** (rĭ-pŭg´nəns) *noun* from Latin *repugnare*, "to fight against"
Extreme dislike; disgust
   • The attorney was filled with **repugnance,** as he read the violent offender's criminal record.

   repugnant *adjective* "Torture is a morally **repugnant** practice," Mr. Ali said emphatically.

ANALOGIES

On the answer line, write the letter of the answer that best completes each analogy. Refer to Lessons 18–20 if you need help with any of the lesson words.

__a__   **1.** Repose is to quiescent as _____ .
     a. disdain is to scornful   **c.** lethargic is to energetic
     b. disgust is to repugnant   **d.** kudos is to insults

__c__   **2.** Animosity is to love as _____ .
     a. disdain is to repugnance   **c.** nonchalant is to ardent
     b. sloth is to snail   **d.** dilatory is to adroit

__d__   **3.** Pejorative is to complimentary as _____ .
     a. rendezvous is to place
     b. adroit is to athlete
     c. somnambulate is to sleepwalker
     d. abhor is to adore

__a__   **4.** Cliché is to expression as _____ .
     a. predictable is to plot   **c.** blasé is to bored
     b. finale is to movie   **d.** languid is to stupor

WRITE THE CORRECT WORD

Write the correct word in the space next to each definition.

repugnance	**1.** disgust		enamor	**6.** to inspire with love
estrange	**2.** to alienate		ardent	**7.** passionate
pejorative	**3.** insulting; belittling		abhor	**8.** to hate intensely
kudos	**4.** praise		affinity	**9.** natural attraction
animosity	**5.** bitter hostility		disdain	**10.** to treat with contempt

COMPLETE THE SENTENCE

Write the letter for the word that best completes each sentence.

b **1.** The toddler's _____ for water was apparent; she was able to swim independently after just one lesson.
   a. kudos   **b.** affinity   **c.** abhorrence   **d.** repugnance

c **2.** The reunion made him feel closer to his cousins and less _____ from his parents.
   a. ardent   **b.** enamored   **c.** estranged   **d.** kudos

d **3.** Movies that contain a lot of gratuitous violence are _____ to me.
   a. estranged   **b.** disdainful   **c.** enamored   **d.** abhorrent

a **4.** His _____ interest in literature was evidenced by his 4,000-book library.
   a. ardent   **b.** disdainful   **c.** repugnant   **d.** pejorative

c **5.** She felt great _____ toward her coach after he embarrassed her at the game.
   a. pejorative   **b.** kudos   **c.** animosity   **d.** affinity

d **6.** The awful odor coming from the oil refinery was _____.
   a. disdainful   **b.** pejorative   **c.** ardent   **d.** repugnant

a **7.** The executive received _____ from her boss after the successful presentation.
   a. kudos   **b.** disdain   **c.** abhorrence   **d.** animosity

b **8.** The maintenance manager felt that *janitor* was a(n) _____ term for his job.
   a. enamored   **b.** pejorative   **c.** ardent   **d.** estranged

c **9.** The man was _____ of the red sports car the moment he saw it on the lot.
   a. estranged   **b.** ardent   **c.** enamored   **d.** kudos

a **10.** In his harsh review of her performance, the critic's _____ for the actor was obvious.
   a. disdain   **b.** affinity   **c.** kudos   **d.** ardor

Challenge: The spokesperson insisted that _____ terms be avoided at all costs, because these words not only display but can also evoke _____.
c   **a.** estranged…kudos   **b.** enamored…animosity   **c.** pejorative…disdain

Osceola, Seminole Warrior

In 1835, as part of a government land-management, effort U.S. Indian Agent Wiley Thompson proposed a treaty that would require Native Americans to leave their Florida homeland. Some of the Seminole tribal chiefs agreed. **(1)** But according to legend, one man stepped forth and *disdainfully* plunged his dagger into the treaty. He was Osceola, a leader of the Seminole people. Osceola is remembered for his heroic resistance to forced relocation. **(2)** His brave efforts earned him *kudos* from his people, but betrayal from the U.S. army.

Osceola was born in Alabama between 1800 and 1806. He was the son of a Creek mother who moved to Florida and settled among the Seminoles. **(3)** Although he was not born among them, Osceola developed an *affinity* for his adopted people. **(4)** Always *enamored* with physical strength and bravery, Osceola was a natural warrior. Rather than inheriting a position of authority, he earned one through his courage and leadership. He gained respect by adhering to a strict code of behavior. **(5)** He *abhorred* dishonorable treatment of women and children, declaring that he made war only on men.

Sadly, U.S. policies often amounted to war on all Native Americans, including women and children. When the United States acquired Florida from Spain in 1821, officials urged the Native Americans living there to move west. The Indian Removal Act of 1830 ordered all Native Americans in the east to relocate to lands west of the Mississippi River. Unfortunately, many U.S. officials ignored the agreements that promised compensation for, and help with, these relocations. Native Americans received little more than cruelty and callousness from the U.S. government. During the Cherokee nation's famous ordeal, now known as the Trail of Tears, more than a quarter of their people—men, women, and children—died from the hardships of the journey west. Many Seminoles, however, refused to leave their native land in Florida.

At the meeting in 1835, Wiley Thompson hoped to convince the Seminole chiefs to agree to relocate. **(6)** Osceola surprised both his tribe and U.S. officials by *ardently* urging armed resistance. In response, Thompson threatened to move the Seminoles by force. **(7)** Although Thompson and Osceola had previously been friendly, this meeting created tremendous *animosity* between them. **(8)** Afterward, another incident caused the two men to become further *estranged*. **(9)** Claiming that Osceola had burst into his office and made *pejorative* comments to him, Thompson imprisoned Osceola. He then humiliated Osceola by forcing him to sign a treaty agreeing to relocation, in order to gain his freedom.

Osceola signed the treaty but vowed revenge. In the first of two daring raids, the Seminoles invaded Fort King, where Thompson was stationed, and killed him. They then ambushed a unit of U.S. troops. For two years, aided by two able lieutenants, Wild Cat and a freed slave named "Black Seminole" John Horse, Osceola successfully fought the powerful U.S. army.

(10) Then, in a morally *repugnant* act, Osceola was betrayed. U.S. General Thomas Jessup requested that he and Osceola meet beneath a flag of truce. But when Osceola arrived, he was arrested and put in prison. Three months later, he died. Yet, his spirit of resistance to injustice lived on. The Seminoles fought fiercely for five more years before succumbing to defeat.

Each sentence below refers to a numbered sentence in the passage. Write the letter of the choice that gives the sentence a meaning that is closest to the original sentence.

_____ **a** **1.** One man stepped forth and _____ plunged his dagger into the treaty.
     a. scornfully   **b.** insultingly   **c.** dramatically   **d.** passionately

_____ **c** **2.** His brave efforts earned him _____ from his people.
     a. disapproval   **b.** disgust   **c.** praise   **d.** affection

_____ **d** **3.** Although he was not born among them, Osceola developed a(n) _____ for his adopted people.
     a. bitter hostility   **b.** extreme dislike   **c.** strong enthusiasm   **d.** feeling of kinship

___a___ 4. Always _____ with physical strength and bravery, Osceola was a natural warrior.
  a. captivated   **b.** bothered   **c.** inspired   **d.** worried

___c___ 5. He _____ dishonorable treatment of women and children.
  a. banned   **b.** disapproved of   **c.** hated intensely   **d.** warned against

___d___ 6. Osceola surprised both his tribe and U.S. officials by _____ urging armed resistance.
  a. cautiously   **b.** destructively   **c.** loudly   **d.** passionately

___c___ 7. Although Thompson and Osceola had previously been friendly, this meeting created tremendous _____ between them.
  a. concern   **b.** horror   **c.** hostility   **d.** disgust

___b___ 8. Afterward, another incident caused the two men to become further _____.
  a. critical   **b.** alienated   **c.** unhappy   **d.** scornful

___a___ 9. Claiming that Osceola had burst into his office and made _____ comments to him, Thompson imprisoned Osceola.
  a. insulting   **b.** thoughtful   **c.** confusing   **d.** loathsome

___c___ 10. Then, in a morally _____ act, Osceola was betrayed.
  a. religious   **b.** balanced   **c.** disgusting   **d.** honorable

Indicate whether the statements below are TRUE or FALSE according to the passage.

___F___ 1. Osceola was the son of a Seminole chief.

___T___ 2. Most Native Americans in the East were ordered by the U.S. government to move west.

___T___ 3. Osceola fought against U.S. forces to protect the Seminoles' homeland.

FINISH THE THOUGHT

Complete each sentence so that it shows the meaning of the italicized word.

1. He and his cousin were *estranged* because _____ Answers will vary. _____

_____

2. The snob *disdained* _____ Answers will vary. _____

_____

WRITE THE DERIVATIVE

Complete the sentence by writing the correct form of the word shown in parentheses. You may not need to change the form that is given.

___repugnant___ 1. He thought the anchovy pizza was _____. *(repugnance)*

___kudos___ 2. The class received _____ for its volunteer work. *(kudos)* affinity   **3.** The girl had excellent logic skills and an _____ for playing chess. (*affinity*)

animosity   **4.** The dissatisfied townspeople displayed _____ toward the mayor. (*animosity*)

enamored   **5.** He loved different cultures and was _____ with travel to foreign places. (*enamor*)

disdainful   **6.** The student was _____ of school rules and usually arrived late to class. (*disdain*)

ardor   **7.** He had great _____ for music and loved attending concerts. (*ardent*)

pejorative   **8.** Please refrain from making _____ comments about the visitors. (*pejorative*)

abhorrent   **9.** The _____ dictator was responsible for many deaths. (*abhor*)

estrangement   **10.** The man learned later that his _____ from coworkers was one of the reasons preventing him from getting a promotion. (*estrange*)

FIND THE EXAMPLE

Choose the answer that best describes the action or situation.

b   **1.** A hobby most likely to *enamor* a creative person
    a. stamp collecting   **b.** painting   **c.** eating   **d.** driving

d   **2.** Something most people find *repugnant*
    a. cheese   **b.** mushrooms   **c.** broccoli   **d.** mold

a   **3.** Something an athlete is most likely to be *ardent* about
    a. exercise   **b.** fashion   **c.** cooking   **d.** traveling

c   **4.** The word most likely to be used in a *pejorative* comment
    a. worker   **b.** backpacker   **c.** fool   **d.** goldfish

b   **5.** A good destination for someone who *disdains* cold weather
    a. Iceland   **b.** Florida   **c.** Alaska   **d.** Canada

d   **6.** A person's most likely behavior toward someone he or she is *estranged* from
    a. warm welcome   **b.** praise   **c.** consideration   **d.** avoidance

c   **7.** Something a student might receive *kudos* for
    a. anger   **b.** lateness   **c.** good grades   **d.** poor grades

a   **8.** Something a vegetarian would most likely *abhor*
    a. meat   **b.** vegetables   **c.** fruit   **d.** cereal

c   **9.** A profession that someone who has an *affinity* for books might choose
    a. painter   **b.** gardener   **c.** librarian   **d.** pilot

d   **10.** The way you might feel about someone you have *animosity* toward
    a. neutral   **b.** giving   **c.** friendly   **d.** hostile

Strength and Defense

WORD LIST

assail	asylum	bulwark	citadel	fortitude
invincible	mettle	resilient	stalwart	stamina

To some, the words *strength* and *defense* suggest military might or conflict. Other people associate the words with sports or physical health. This lesson presents words that refer to different aspects of these topics.

1. **assail** (ə-sāl´) *verb* from Latin *ad-*, "onto" + *salire*, "to jump"
To attack; to assault
   • Working as a pack, the hyenas **assailed** the zebra from every side.

   assailant *noun* The victim identified his **assailant** in the police lineup.

> *Assail* can refer to physical or mental attacks. One can *assail a point of view,* for example.

2. **asylum** (ə-sī´ləm) *noun* from Greek *a-*, "without" + *sulon*, "right of seizure"
   a. A place offering protection and safety, often from persecution; a shelter
      • In many countries, foreign embassies offer **asylum** to persecuted people.
   b. An institution for the care of people who require organized supervision or assistance
      • The Mount St. Mary's Convent and Orphan **Asylum** was founded in 1863 to care for and educate orphans.

> At one time, people were placed in *asylums* if they were considered to have a mental disorder. This usage of *asylum*, however, now has a negative connotation and is used infrequently.

3. **bulwark** (bŏŏl´wərk) *noun* from Middle German *bole*, "plank" + *werc*, "work"
   a. A wall or an embankment used as protection
      • The soldiers hastily erected a **bulwark** of planks and logs.
   b. A strong defense of any type
      • The first ten amendments to the U.S. Constitution serve as a **bulwark** for civil liberties.

4. **citadel** (sĭt´ə-dəl) *noun* from Latin *civis*, "citizen"
A fortress in a commanding position in or near a city
   • A thousand-year-old **citadel**, standing on a hill, overlooks the Iraqi city of Kirkuk.

a citadel

5. **fortitude** (fôr´tĭ-tōōd´) *noun* from Latin *fortis*, "strong"
Strength of mind that allows one to endure pain or adversity with courage
   • The crew of the *Endurance* had enough **fortitude** to survive a frigid winter in the Antarctic.

Point out that *bulwark, citadel,* and *asylum* are actual places of defense or refuge.

6. **invincible** (ĭn-vĭn´sə-bəl) *adjective* from Latin *in-*, "not" + *vincibilis*, "conquerable"
Incapable of being overcome or defeated
   • After a series of successful military campaigns, Alexander the Great seemed **invincible.**

   invincibility *noun* Ken Jennings demonstrated **invincibility** on seventy-four *Jeopardy* programs, but finally lost on the seventy-fifth.

7. **mettle** (mĕt´l) *noun* from Latin *metallon*, "metal"
   a. Courage and strength of mind; spirit
      • The bold scout showed his **mettle** by riding ahead of the wagon train into dangerous territory.
   b. Innate or inherent quality of character and temperament
      • "What we throw at you today will certainly test your **mettle**," said the drill instructor, with an ominous grin.

8. **resilient** (rĭ-zĭl´yənt) *adjective* from Latin *resilire*, "to leap back"
Able to recover or spring back quickly
   • The **resilient** patient was walking just a few days after her major surgery.

   resilience *noun* Refugees often demonstrate great **resilience**, starting new lives soon after escaping the horrors of war.

9. **stalwart** (stôl´wərt) from Old English *statholwierthe*, "steadfast"
   a. *adjective* Strong and dependable
   • The **stalwart** gatekeeper kept the enemy from crossing the castle's bridge.
   b. *noun* A person who is strong and dependable
   • The general said, "Give me a few good **stalwarts**, and we'll be able to take the town."

10. **stamina** (stăm´ə-nə) *noun* from Latin *stamen*, "thread"
Endurance; ability to withstand prolonged physical or mental effort
   • The swimmer needed great **stamina** to complete one hundred laps in the Olympic-sized swimming pool.

> *Stamina* can refer to physical or mental strength, whereas *fortitude* refers to mental strength.

WORD ENRICHMENT

Stamína and the fates

According to Greek and Roman mythology, the three Fates were goddesses who determined each person's destiny by controlling the thread of life (*stamen*, or *stamina*, plural) that guides each human from birth to death. Each of the Fates played a different role in controlling human destiny: One spun the "thread of life"; one measured it; the third cut it, thus ensuring the death of mortals. The three Fates have counterparts in Norse mythology, a fact that reflects the importance of weaving throughout human history.

This mythological etymology has a scientific offshoot, too. The word *stamen* also refers to the threadlike reproductive organs in flowers. Note how this "thread" also has to do with the continuity of life.

WRITE THE CORRECT WORD

Write the correct word in the space next to each definition.

asylum	1. a safe place	bulwark	6. a strong defense
mettle	2. courage	stalwart	7. faithful and firm
fortitude	3. mental strength	assail	8. to attack
resilient	4. able to recover quickly	invincible	9. too strong to be defeated
citadel	5. a fortress	stamina	10. endurance

COMPLETE THE SENTENCE

Write the letter for the word that best completes each sentence.

b 1. The Pilgrims needed great _____ to endure their harsh living conditions.
    a. asylum   **b.** fortitude   **c.** bulwark   **d.** assailant

a 2. Because of her emotional _____, she was never unhappy for very long.
    a. resilience   **b.** citadel   **c.** stalwart   **d.** asylum

c 3. The boy cried bitterly after being _____ with names and insults.
    a. resilient   **b.** invincible   **c.** assailed   **d.** mettle

a 4. Mountain-biking requires great _____.
    a. stamina   **b.** stalwart   **c.** assailant   **d.** bulwark

d 5. Jared proved his _____ when he safely steered the schooner through the storm.
    a. asylum   **b.** citadel   **c.** bulwark   **d.** mettle

b 6. The company's policies are a _____ against discrimination of any kind.
    a. citadel   **b.** bulwark   **c.** mettle   **d.** fortitude

d 7. The _____ is now a museum with a commanding view of the city.
    a. mettle   **b.** stamina   **c.** assailant   **d.** citadel

c 8. After winning every game of the season, the team seemed _____.
    a. asylum   **b.** resilient   **c.** invincible   **d.** assailing

d 9. The Cuban refugees sought _____ in the United States.
    a. stamina   **b.** invincibility   **c.** mettle   **d.** asylum

b 10. _____ people are not easily swayed from their convictions.
    a. Assailed   **b.** Stalwart   **c.** Bulwark   **d.** Asylum

Challenge: The enemy prisoners held in the _____ begged to be granted political _____.

b   **a.** fortitude…stamina   **b.** citadel…asylum   **c.** bulwark…resilience

Women of the Revolution

"We may destroy all of the men in America, and we shall still have all we can do to defeat the women."

With these words, British General Lord Cornwallis paid tribute to the American women of the Revolutionary War. **(1)** These heroes mended uniforms, nursed the wounded, supplied food, and offered *asylum* to soldiers. But they also fought and spied on the enemy.

Disguised as "Robert Shurtleff," Deborah Sampson enlisted as a soldier with the Continental army. **(2)** Her regiment was sent to West Point, New York, where an impressive *citadel* had been erected. There she fought alongside male soldiers. **(3)** Perhaps to preserve the secret of her identity, Sampson had the *fortitude* to insist upon tending to her own leg wound. The fact that she was a woman remained undiscovered through two more injuries—a sword cut to her head and a bullet in her thigh. **(4)** The *resilient* patriot continued to serve as a soldier, until her identity was discovered due to a terrible fever.

Fearless Nancy Morgan Hart lends her name to a present-day county in Georgia. **(5)** Living in the isolated backcountry, Hart served as a *bulwark* of the revolutionary effort, at a time when many women and children had fled these dangerous regions. **(6)** One day, six enemy soldiers *assailed* her home, shot her last turkey, and demanded that she cook it for their dinner. Cook it she did—but then she grabbed a gun and held them at bay while her daughter signaled for help. In another bold act, she threw lye through the cracks in her cabin wall and blinded an enemy soldier who was spying on her.

(7) Emily Geiger of South Carolina showed her *mettle* when she carried a message through fifty miles of dangerous enemy territory. The patriots had hoped that this seventeen-year-old would not look suspicious riding sidesaddle through the countryside. But the

British stopped her and sent for a woman to search her. Meanwhile, Geiger took the letter she was carrying and ate it piece by piece! Finding no evidence of spying, the British apologized and released her. Geiger calmly proceeded on her way. When she arrived at her destination, she delivered the important message, which she had memorized before eating.

(8) A slave called Mammy Kate was a woman whose devotion proved no less impressive than her *stamina*. **(9)** Her *stalwart* loyalty to her master, Georgia Governor Stephen Heard, has become legendary. When he was arrested by British troops, Mammy Kate was determined to rescue him. She rode to the prison where he was held and offered to do washing for the British soldiers. Her work was so beautifully done that she soon became a popular laundress. But her last load was the best: Under the guise of taking clothes from the prison, she carried Heard, in the basket above her head, to freedom!

Colonial women served as soldiers, spies, and liberators in the American Revolution. **(10)** They, along with their husbands, sons, fathers, and brothers, showed the world that the mighty British army was not *invincible*. And in so doing, they helped establish the United States of America.

Each sentence below refers to a numbered sentence in the passage. Write the letter of the choice that gives the sentence a meaning that is closest to the original sentence.

___c___ **1.** These heroes offered _____ to soldiers.
    a. restaurants   **b.** forts   **c.** safe places   **d.** sleeping bags

___a___ **2.** Her regiment was sent to West Point, New York, where an impressive_____ had been erected.
    a. fortress   **b.** monument   **c.** office   **d.** embankment

___b___ **3.** Sampson had the_____ to insist upon tending to her own leg wound.
    a. peace of mind   **b.** mental strength   **c.** knowledge   **d.** creativity

c **4.** The _____ patriot continued to serve as a soldier until her identity was discovered.
  a. slowly healing   **b.** always outspoken   **c.** quick to recover   **d.** very cautious

d **5.** Hart served as a _____ of the revolutionary effort.
  a. clever persuader   **b.** gifted historian   **c.** useful analyst   **d.** strong defender

d **6.** One day, six enemy soldiers _____ her home.
  a. visited   **b.** set fire to   **c.** complimented   **d.** attacked

a **7.** Emily Geiger of South Carolina showed her _____ when she carried a message through fifty miles of dangerous enemy territory.
  a. courage   **b.** coins   **c.** willingness   **d.** trickery

c **8.** Mammy Kate was a woman whose devotion proved no less impressive than her _____ .
  a. stature   **b.** intelligence   **c.** endurance   **d.** skills

b **9.** Her _____ loyalty to her master has become legendary.
  a. flexible   **b.** firm   **c.** fragile   **d.** questionable

a **10.** They showed the world that the mighty British army was not _____ .
  a. unbeatable   **b.** fast   **c.** easy to overcome   **d.** strong

Indicate whether the statements below are TRUE or FALSE according to the passage.

F **1.** Women did not take part in the American Revolutionary War.

T **2.** Emily Geiger probably had a very good memory.

T **3.** At least one British general had a high opinion of the role that American women played in the revolution.

WRITING EXTENDED RESPONSES

In the passage, you read about several female heroes of the Revolutionary War. What kinds of qualities are necessary to do what these people did? In an expository essay, describe the characteristics needed for the type of heroism these women displayed. Your essay should be a minimum of three paragraphs long. Use at least three lesson words in your essay and underline them.

WRITE THE DERIVATIVE

Complete the sentence by writing the correct form of the word shown in parentheses. You may not need to change the form that is given.

asylum **1.** The political prisoners escaped across the border and asked for _____ in the neighboring country. (*asylum*)

mettle **2.** Any one of the ten events in the decathlon would test the _____ of most athletes. (*mettle*) __stamina__   **3.** Finishing a triathlon requires great _____. (*stamina*)

__resilience__   **4.** The human body often shows great _____ in healing itself after an injury. (*resilient*)

__assailant__   **5.** The sheriff apprehended the lone _____. (*assail*)

__bulwarks__   **6.** In the Netherlands, dikes were built to be _____ against the sea. (*bulwark*)

__invincibility__   **7.** Belief in one's own _____ usually leads to downfall. (*invincible*)

__stalwarts__   **8.** The fishermen were _____ who could be counted on to do their jobs in any kind of weather. (*stalwart*)

__fortitude__   **9.** Whether you are a member of a persecuted group or not, it takes great _____ to stand up to the persecutors. (*fortitude*)

__citadel__   **10.** The cracked and crumbling walls of the old _____ showed the ravages of time. (*citadel*)

FIND THE EXAMPLE

Choose the answer that best describes the action or situation.

__d__   **1.** Something you need *stamina* to do
    a. clean your desk   **b.** wash the dishes   **c.** watch a game   **d.** run ten miles

__a__   **2.** Something an *assailant* does
    a. attacks   **b.** soothes   **c.** nurtures   **d.** feeds

__c__   **3.** Something that could be a *citadel*
    a. lake   **b.** beach   **c.** fort   **d.** motel

__d__   **4.** Something an *invincible* person would never do
    a. win   **b.** tie   **c.** eat   **d.** lose

__b__   **5.** An example of a *stalwart*
    a. lazy foe   **b.** loyal supporter   **c.** lab partner   **d.** funny clown

__b__   **6.** The most important purpose of *asylum*
    a. punishment   **b.** protection   **c.** education   **d.** revenge

__a__   **7.** Something very *resilient*
    a. rubber band   **b.** cracked egg   **c.** broken glass   **d.** ripe tomato

__c__   **8.** The key characteristic of *fortitude*
    a. physical ability   **b.** artistic talent   **c.** mental strength   **d.** fast healing

__d__   **9.** One way to show your *mettle*
    a. run and hide   **b.** experience success   **c.** blame others   **d.** overcome problems

__b__   **10.** Your probable reaction if someone called you a *bulwark* of the community
    a. to cry bitterly   **b.** to feel pride   **c.** to take offense   **d.** to fight back

Prefixes, Roots, and Suffixes

The Prefixes circum-, peri-, semi-, and hemi-

The meaning of an unknown word may be determined by contextual clues in the surrounding sentence or by the *word elements* that are within words. These word elements, which often come from Ancient Greek and Latin, are of three types. *Prefixes* come before a word or root; *roots* are the central portion of a word; *suffixes* attach to the end of a word or root. Some roots can stand alone. These kinds of roots are known as *base words*. Others, known as *combining roots,* must be combined with other word elements to become English words. In addition, a single element may serve more than one function, such as serving as both a prefix and a root. *Circum-,* which is usually a prefix, may also be used as a root.

The elements in this lesson have to do with *around* and *half. Circum-* (from Latin) and *peri-* (from Greek) both mean "around." The word *circle* comes from *circum-,* and if you were to walk the *perimeter* of a yard, you would be walking around the outside edges of it.

Semi- (from Latin) and *hemi-* (from Greek) mean "half" and can also mean "partial." A *semirigid* substance is partially rigid and partially flexible. A *hemisphere* is half of a sphere—or half of the earth. *Semi* can also mean "two," or "occurring twice." For example, a *semiannual* meeting is held two times per year.

Prefix	Meaning	Language Origin	Word	Word Meaning
circum-	around	Latin	circumnavigate	travel around the world
peri-	around	Greek	perimeter	measurement around
semi-	half, partial, two	Latin	semiarid	quite dry, with low rainfall
hemi-	half, partial	Greek	hemisphere	half of a sphere

Practice

You can combine the use of context clues with your knowledge of this prefix to make intelligent guesses about the meanings of words. All of the sentences below contain a word formed with the prefixes *circum-, peri-, semi-,* or *hemi-.* Read the sentences and try to infer what the word in italics means. Then check your definition with the one you find in the dictionary, remembering to choose the definition that best fits the sentence.

1. The blood *circulates* around the body.

My definition _____

Dictionary definition _____ to move in or flow through a circle or circuit

2. The *semiaquatic* animal spent time on land and water.

My definition _____

Dictionary definition ___ adapted for living or growing in or near water; not entirely aquatic

3. In medieval times, *peripatetic* bands of entertainers went throughout the countryside to entertain.

My definition _____

Dictionary definition <u>walking about or from place to place; traveling on foot</u>

4. <u>Cordylanthus</u> is a *hemiparasite* associated with plants.

My definition _____

Dictionary definition <u>a plant that gets part of its nourishment from its host</u>

5. Somehow the manager always managed to *circumvent* usual channels and go directly to the company president to air his complaints.

My definition _____

Dictionary definition _____ to go around; bypass _____

6. Some people prefer hard cheeses such as parmesan and cheddar, however I like *semisoft* varieties.

My definition _____

Dictionary definition _____ of medium softness; or firm, but easily sliced _____

7. A puncture of the *pericardium* sac can cause serious injury to the heart.

My definition _____

Dictionary definition _____ the membranous sac that encloses the heart _____

8. Despite the *hemialgia* she suffered from in her right side, she felt no pain on her left side.

My definition _____

Dictionary definition _____ pain affecting one half of the body _____

9. A wall *circumscribed* some medieval towns, both protecting them and limiting their growth.

My definition _____

Dictionary definition _____ encircled _____

10. His check was issued *semimonthly*.

My definition _____

Dictionary definition _____ occurring or issued twice a month _____

The Root -ject-

WORD LIST

abject	conjecture	dejected	interject	jettison
jetty	jut	objectionable	projectile	trajectory

The root -ject- means "throw" and comes from the Latin verb *iacere*. The root is an example of how word elements describing physical movement have entered the English language and are used in many different ways. For example, the prefix *in-* means "in"; giving an *injection* can be thought of as "throwing something in" to the body. Similarly, the prefix *re-* means "back"; when we *reject* something, we literally or figuratively "throw it back." This lesson presents ten more -ject- words.

Discuss with students how prefixes and the root *ject* combine to make the following common words: *eject, project,* and *inject*.

1. **abject** (ăb´jĕkt´) *adjective* from Latin *ab-*, "away from" + *ject*, "throw"
   a. Of the most miserable kind; brought to a low state; wretched
   • The **abject** poverty of the native inhabitants stunned the tourists.
   b. Of the most despicable kind; deserving of great scorn
   • Overseeing the court-martial, the judge said, "Your **abject** cowardice has brought shame to our nation."

2. **conjecture** (kən-jĕk´chər) from Latin *con-*, "with" + *ject*, "throw"
   a. *noun* A judgment or statement based on little or no evidence; a guess
   • It was pure luck that his **conjecture** was correct.
   b. *verb* To infer from insufficient evidence; to guess
   • We can only **conjecture** how many lives would have been saved had people received warning that the storm was approaching.

3. **dejected** (dĭ-jĕk´tĭd) *adjective* from Latin *de-*, "down" + *ject*, "throw"
   Depressed; in low spirits
   • The Cortez family was **dejected** after they had to cancel their vacation.

   deject *verb* Rainy, gray weather **dejects** some people.

   dejection *noun* The fans' joy turned to **dejection** after their team lost the game in the final seconds.

4. **interject** (ĭn´tər-jĕkt´) *verb* from Latin *inter-*, "between" + *ject*, "throw"
   To insert between other elements
   • She **interjected** a defensive comment between her professor's criticisms about her thesis.

   interjection *noun* A sudden, short utterance, usually expressing emotion
   • The word *wow* is an **interjection**.

5. jettison (jĕt´ĭ-sən) *verb* from Latin *ject,* "throw"
To cast overboard or off; to discard
- After takeoff, the spacecraft **jettisoned** its empty fuel tanks.

6. jetty (jĕt´ē) *noun* from Latin *ject,* "throw"
A structure that projects into the water and protects the shore
- The wharf served as a **jetty** that helped protect the beach from eroding.

7. jut (jŭt) from Latin *ject,* "throw"
  a. *verb* To project out; to extend outward beyond a main part
    - The edge of the cliff **jutted** out over the sea.
  b. *noun* Something that projects out
    - The **jut** of his chin gave him a distinctive profile.

8. objectionable (əb-jĕk´shə-nə-bəl) *adjective*
from Latin *ob-,* "before; toward" + *ject,* "throw"
Offensive; arousing disapproval
- Many people find the smell of cigarette smoke **objectionable.**

object *verb* After the city council **objected** to her policies, the town manager decided to resign.

objection *noun* At the meeting, many residents stated their **objections** to the plan for a new power plant.

9. projectile (prə-jĕk´təl) *noun* from Latin *pro-,* "forward" + *ject,* "throw"
An object that is fired, thrown, or self-propelled
- Bullets are deadly **projectiles.**

project *verb* To thrust forward or cast outward
- She **projected** the arrow with perfect accuracy.

10. trajectory (trə-jĕk´tə-rē) *noun* from Latin *trans-,* "across" + *ject,* "throw"
  a. The path of a moving object
    - The airplane's **trajectory** took it over a large lake and a metropolitan area.
  b. A chosen or taken course
    - The **trajectory** of her career was dancing, directing, then producing.

> *Jettison* need not refer to a physical action. A TV network could *jettison* an unpopular show.

a jetty

> As a verb, *project* has many other meanings, including "to cause to appear on a surface," "to form a plan for," and "to predict."

WORD ENRICHMENT

The direction of unhappiness

    Down, downcast, and *low* (as in "feeling low") can all be used to describe unhappiness. The meanings and etymologies of many words related to sadness are also related to the direction "down." *Dejected* has word parts that combine to mean "cast down" or "thrown down." Another word with similar root meanings is *depressed* ("pressed down"), a synonym of *dejected.*

    In contrast, many words that refer to happiness are related to the direction "up." Examples include *lift* (as in "lift one's spirits"), *buoyed, elated,* and *uplifted.*

WRITE THE CORRECT WORD

Write the correct word in the space next to each definition.

interject	**1.** to insert	abject	**6.** miserable
trajectory	**2.** a moving object's path	jettison	**7.** to discard
conjecture	**3.** a guess	dejected	**8.** in low spirits
jut	**4.** to stick out	projectile	**9.** an object moving forward
jetty	**5.** a shore-protector that projects into the water	objectionable	**10.** arousing disapproval

COMPLETE THE SENTENCE

Write the letter for the word that best completes each sentence.

___a___ **1.** Explanations of why people behave the way they do are often little more than _____.
   a. conjectures   **b.** projectiles   **c.** dejections   **d.** interjections

___c___ **2.** The _____ flew though the air with incredible speed.
   a. interjection   **b.** jetty   **c.** projectile   **d.** conjecture

___d___ **3.** To ponder a topic with a truly open mind, you must be prepared to _____ your previous beliefs.
   a. interject   **b.** object   **c.** jut   **d.** jettison

___b___ **4.** The librarian defended the book against charges that the content was _____.
   a. dejected   **b.** objectionable   **c.** interjected   **d.** abject

___b___ **5.** Mom complained that Stella _____ the word *like* into almost every sentence.
   a. dejects   **b.** interjects   **c.** jettisons   **d.** objects

___d___ **6.** The _____ outside the harbor is a popular fishing spot.
   a. jut   **b.** projectile   **c.** conjecture   **d.** jetty

___c___ **7.** The _____ of the fireworks took them out over the open water, where they exploded with dazzling colors.
   a. conjecture   **b.** objection   **c.** trajectory   **d.** jetty

___a___ **8.** The _____ nature of the suffering I witnessed brought tears to my eyes.
   a. abject   **b.** interjected   **c.** conjectured   **d.** jutting

___a___ **9.** The small strip of land _____ out into the lake is too thin and low for a campsite.
   a. jutting   **b.** interjecting   **c.** conjecturing   **d.** jettisoning

___c___ **10.** The puppy looked so lonely and _____ that I just had to pick it up and pet it.
   a. objectionable   **b.** interjected   **c.** dejected   **d.** jettisoned

Challenge: The _____ failure of the party's candidates in recent elections caused its leadership to _____ the advisers who had shaped the overall strategy.
___c___   **a.** conjectured…jut   **b.** object…deject   **c.** abject…jettison

Escape from Vietnam

(1) Viem Nguyen (pronounced "win") can only *conjecture* what his life would have been like if it hadn't been for the war in Vietnam. **(2)** The war set his life on a *trajectory* that took him from the country of his birth to the United States. His journey, like those of so many other refugees, was filled with hardships.

When the Vietnam War ended in 1975, conditions in that country were harsh. **(3)** Many people lived in *abject* poverty. Nguyen's family had special problems because his father had fought on the side of the United States. To punish him, the government sentenced the father to six months in jail. **(4)** Even after he was released, the Vietnamese government continued to discriminate against his father and his family for what they considered *objectionable* political beliefs. For example, Nguyen had to achieve higher exam scores to enter college than did the children of other families. **(5)** *Dejected* about his future in Vietnam, Nguyen decided to escape.

But trying to escape was as frustrating as it was risky. **(6)** People were illegally sneaking out of Vietnam on small, overcrowded boats, but sometimes the fugitives were stopped by the police before they could leave the *jetty*. **(7)** Or guards on the shore would fire bullets and other *projectiles* at fleeing boats. Pirates sometimes kidnapped and killed people, or sunk their boats.

Careful planning was essential. In fact, Nguyen made ten attempts before he actually escaped in 1982. The successful journey began as he carefully made his way to the seacoast, avoiding the police. **(8)** As he approached the shore, he saw a small, open fishing boat *jutting* out of the water. Forty-three people piled on, and it silently slid away. Farther out to sea, they rolled uncontrollably back and forth in rough waters, fearing for their lives. **(9)** People had to *jettison* belongings to keep the boat afloat. Four long days later, they landed in Malaysia.

Nguyen was one of the lucky ones. A boat that had left before Nguyen's was lost at sea for fifty-two days, and many of the people aboard died. Another boat, which left after Nguyen's, was captured by the Vietnamese police.

Nguyen lived in refugee camps in Malaysia and the Philippines before he was allowed to come to the United States. He was sent to Chicago, where he had to get used to long, snow-filled winters.

(10) Nguyen now speaks fluent English, although he sometimes *interjects* Vietnamese words and phrases. He graduated from college and has a good job. In the adopted country that he risked so much to enter, Nguyen has found the opportunity to live with dignity.

Each sentence below refers to a numbered sentence in the passage. Write the letter of the choice that gives the sentence a meaning that is closest to the original sentence.

___d___ **1.** Viem Nguyen can only _____ what his life would have been like if it hadn't been for the war in Vietnam.
    a. remember   **b.** predict   **c.** explain   **d.** guess

___c___ **2.** The war set his life on a(n) _____ that took him from the country of his birth to the United States.
    a. boat   **b.** road trip   **c.** path   **d.** adventure

___a___ **3.** Many people lived in _____ poverty.
    a. miserable   **b.** slight   **c.** projecting   **d.** discarded

___c___ **4.** The Vietnamese government continued to discriminate against his father and his family for what they considered _____ political beliefs.
    a. commendable   **b.** sad   **c.** offensive   **d.** mistaken

_____d_____ **5.** _____ about his future in Vietnam, Nguyen decided to escape.
   a. Excited   **b.** Hopeful   **c.** Offended   **d.** Depressed

_____b_____ **6.** Sometimes the fugitives were stopped by the police before they could leave the _____ .
   a. hotel   **b.** pier   **c.** terminal   **d.** ticket window

_____d_____ **7.** Or guards on the shore would fire bullets and other _____ at fleeing boats.
   a. signals   **b.** guesses   **c.** gestures   **d.** objects

_____c_____ **8.** As he approached the shore, he saw a small, open fishing boat _____ the water.
   a. gliding on   **b.** burning on   **c.** sticking out of   **d.** floating beneath

_____c_____ **9.** People had to _____ belongings to keep the boat afloat.
   a. eat or drink   **b.** propel or fire   **c.** toss overboard   **d.** use up

_____a_____ **10.** Nguyen now speaks fluent English, although he sometimes _____ Vietnamese words and phrases.
   a. inserts   **b.** confuses   **c.** forgets   **d.** guesses

Indicate whether the statements below are TRUE or FALSE according to the passage.

_____F_____ **1.** Most Vietnamese people were quite wealthy and comfortable after the war ended.

_____T_____ **2.** Viem Nguyen believed that he could have a good life if he could escape Vietnam.

_____T_____ **3.** Escaping from Vietnam, even after the war ended in 1975, was not easy.

FINISH THE THOUGHT

Complete each sentence so that it shows the meaning of the italicized word.

1. *Jutting* out from the skyline,_____ Answers will vary. _____

_____

2. I find it *objectionable* when people _____ Answers will vary. _____

_____

WRITE THE DERIVATIVE

Complete the sentence by writing the correct form of the word shown in parentheses. You may not need to change the form that is given.

_____jetties_____ **1.** The twin _____ on either side of the channel helped create a protected area from all but the worst storms. *(jetty)*

_____abject_____ **2.** Due to a lack of planning, our project was an _____ failure. *(abject)*

__trajectory__	3. The _____ of Halley's comet takes it around the sun roughly every seventy-six years. (*trajectory*)
__jettisoned__	4. After the plane lost one of its engines, the crew _____ some of the cargo to lighten the load. (*jettison*)
__Conjecturing__	5. _____ about other people's personal business is a favorite pastime for many people with too much time on their hands. (*conjecture*)
__projectile__	6. The pitcher went into his wind-up, and suddenly, the baseball became a 100-mph _____. (*projectile*)
__dejection__	7. I hope I haven't done anything to contribute to your _____. (*dejected*)
__objected__	8. At the family meeting, the children _____ to how the household chores had been assigned. (*objectionable*)
__jut__	9. The cast made her arm _____ out at a strange angle. (*jut*)
__Interjections__	10. _____ from the audience annoyed the speaker. (*interject*)

FIND THE EXAMPLE

Choose the answer that best describes the action or situation.

___c___ 1. Something most likely to have a *trajectory*
   a. houseplant   **b.** curb   **c.** rocket   **d.** building

___a___ 2. A word NOT usually paired with *abject*
   a. achievement   **b.** poverty   **c.** failure   **d.** cowardice

___b___ 3. The first thing one would probably *jettison* from a sinking boat
   a. necessary tools   **b.** excess baggage   **c.** the crew   **d.** the boat

___c___ 4. The one most likely to look *dejected*
   a. winning athlete   **b.** happy child   **c.** lonely puppy   **d.** lottery winner

___d___ 5. NOT a good *projectile*
   a. arrow   **b.** rubber ball   **c.** paper airplane   **d.** cotton ball

___d___ 6. Something a *jetty* might be designed to protect
   a. big wave   **b.** flying birds   **c.** mountain range   **d.** docked boats

___a___ 7. An *interjection*
   a. Yikes!   **b.** Hello, Joe.   **c.** Pass the soup.   **d.** a raspy cough

___b___ 8. Something that *juts* out from trees
   a. pinecones   **b.** branches   **c.** trunks   **d.** wind

___a___ 9. Something many people find *objectionable*
   a. deliberate cruelty   **b.** career success   **c.** good manners   **d.** high quality

___d___ 10. NOT an example of a *conjecture*
   a. Ty will never pass.   **b.** He will win.   **c.** I'll be president.   **d.** Earth is round.

The Root -cred-

WORD LIST

accredit	credence	credential	credibility	creditable
credulous	creed	discredit	incredulous	miscreant

The root *-cred-*, which means "to believe," is derived from the Latin verb *credere*. Many English words contain this root. For example, businesses extend *credit* to their customers because they *believe* that the debt will be repaid. When we find a story hard to believe, we may call it *incredible*. This lesson presents other words that are based on the root *-cred-*.

1. **accredit** (ə-krĕdʹĭt) *verb* from Latin *ad-*, "to" + *cred*, "believe"
   a. To officially recognize or approve as having met certain standards
   • A national board **accredits** teacher preparation programs at universities.
   b. To credit with; to attribute to
   • To **accredit** only Liz with the success of the project would be to overlook the valuable contributions of her assistants.

   accredited *adjective* To practice medicine in the United States, physicians have to graduate from an **accredited** medical school.

2. **credence** (krēdʹns) *noun* from Latin *cred,* "believe"
   Acceptance as true or valid; belief
   • I don't give any **credence** to common superstitions.

   > Credence is often used in the expression *give credence to.*

3. **credential** (krĭ-dĕnʹshəl) *noun* from Latin *cred,* "believe"
   Something that gives one confidence or authority; evidence of one's qualifications
   • The judge's **credentials** included fifteen years on the Ohio Court of Appeals.

credential

4. **credibility** (krĕdʹə-bĭlʹĭ-tē) *noun* from Latin *cred,* "believe"
   Believability; reliability; the power to inspire belief
   • The factual errors in the article damaged the writer's **credibility.**

   credible *adjective* Jury members believed that the defendant's alibi was **credible** because several witnesses had confirmed his whereabouts.

5. **creditable** (krĕdʹĭ-tə-bəl) *adjective* from Latin *cred,* "believe"
   a. Deserving of limited praise; sufficiently good
   • The substitute tenor gave a **creditable** performance, but I would have preferred to hear the singer who was originally scheduled.
   b. Worthy of belief
   • "The dog ate my homework" is hardly a **creditable** excuse.

Discuss with students the meanings of the prefixes that are added to the root *cred* to form the words *miscreant, discredit,* and *incredulous.*

6. credulous (krĕj´ə-ləs) *adjective* from Latin *cred*, "believe"
Easily deceived; believing too readily; gullible
• The **credulous** man fell victim to yet another get-rich-quick scheme.

credulity *noun* The woman's **credulity** led her to believe
advertisements that made the most ridiculous claims.

credulousness *noun* Young children who believe in the tooth fairy
display a charming **credulousness.**

7. creed (krēd) *noun* from Latin *cred*, "believe"
A system of beliefs, principles, or opinions
• All members of the U.S. Army are expected to learn and live by the
  Soldier's Creed.

Creed is often used to refer to a system of religious beliefs.

8. discredit (dĭs-krĕd´ĭt) from Latin *dis-*, "deprive of" + *cred*, "believe"
a. *verb* To damage in reputation; to disgrace
  • The company was **discredited** after its chief executive was charged
    with knowingly reporting inflated sales figures.
b. *verb* To cause to be distrusted or doubted
  • The man's testimony was **discredited** by three witnesses.
c. *noun* Lack of trust or belief; doubt
  • Her mismanagement of the project should cast no **discredit** on
    her coworkers.

9. incredulous (ĭn-krĕj´ə-ləs) *adjective* from Latin *in-*, "not"
+ *cred*, "believe"
Disbelieving; showing disbelief; skeptical
• They were **incredulous** when they heard that their shabbily dressed
  neighbor had made a fortune in the stock market.

incredulity *noun* The student's insistence that she wrote the scholarly
paper herself was met with **incredulity** by her teacher.

10. miscreant (mĭs´krē-ənt) *noun* from Latin *mis-*, "bad; wrong"
+ *cred*, "believe"
An evildoer; a villain
• At the end of the play, the **miscreant** was sent to prison, and the hero
  rode off into the sunset.

Miscreant once referred to a person who objected to or refused to follow religious beliefs.

ANALOGIES

On the answer line, write the letter of the answer that best completes
each analogy. Refer to Lessons 21–23 if you need help with any of the
lesson words.

_____a_____ **1.** Objectionable is to acceptable as _____.
  a. dejected is to happy   **c.** discredited is to discarded
  b. invincible is to strong   **d.** accredited is to qualifications

_____b_____ **2.** Credulous is to gullible as _____.
  a. jut is to harbor   **c.** fortitude is to weakness
  b. trajectory is to path   **d.** resilient is to fragile

_____d_____ **3.** Stalwart is to fortitude as _____.
  a. incredulous is to belief **c.** abject is to uplifted
  b. invincible is to weakness **d.** believable is to credibility

WRITE THE CORRECT WORD

Write the correct word in the space next to each definition.

credibility	1. believability	creed	6. a system of beliefs
incredulous	2. showing disbelief; skeptical	discredit	7. to cause to be doubted
credence	3. acceptance as true	credulous	8. easily deceived
creditable	4. deserving of limited praise	miscreant	9. a villain
accredit	5. to officially recognize	credential	10. a qualification that gives authority

COMPLETE THE SENTENCE

Write the letter for the word that best completes each sentence.

__b__ 1. The politician tried to _____ his opponent in an effort to win the election.
    a. accredit   b. discredit   c. credential   d. creed

__c__ 2. The thief who stole from the poor was the worst kind of _____.
    a. creed   b. credulity   c. miscreant   d. credence

__a__ 3. I made a(n) _____ effort on my report, but I knew I could have done more.
    a. creditable   b. credulous   c. accredited   d. discredited

__d__ 4. Morna was _____ when Harry told her that he saw aliens from outer space.
    a. creditable   b. accredited   c. discredited   d. incredulous

__c__ 5. In order to get his real-estate license, he had to complete a(n) _____ program.
    a. discredited   b. incredulous   c. accredited   d. credulous

__b__ 6. She politely refused the hamburger because her _____ prohibited consuming beef.
    a. credibility   b. creed   c. credence   d. credentials

__a__ 7. Her _____ was in question after her boss learned that she had lied on her résumé.
    a. credibility   b. creed   c. credulousness   d. incredulity

__d__ 8. My little brother was _____ enough to believe that my ghost stories were true.
    a. creditable   b. incredulous   c. credible   d. credulous

__b__ 9. I don't usually give much _____ to the gossip I hear at school.
    a. credential   b. credence   c. discredit   d. creed

__c__ 10. The doctor's diplomas and other _____ hung in the office where patients could see them.
    a. accredits   b. creeds   c. credentials   d. miscreants

Challenge: I didn't give _____ to the biography because its author's _____ had come into question when some information in his previous book proved to be fabricated.
__c__   a. accredits…creed   b. credulity…credence   c. credence…credibility

Raining Cats and Dogs?

(1) You would no doubt be *incredulous* if someone told you that, in England, it sometimes rains fish, or that in Kansas City, Missouri, a downpour of frogs once pelted the surprised residents. **(2)** Most people are not likely to give *credence* to such fantastic tales, especially when the tales travel by word of mouth. **(3)** After all, *credulity* is not a trait for which people wish to be known.

Amazingly, however, these stories are actually true! **(4)** *Creditable* sources, such as the national weather institutes of many countries, have reported that unusual weather events can cause rather unexpected precipitation. **(5)** Showers of tadpoles, fish, frogs, crabs, salamanders, and (perhaps most unpleasant) slimy jellyfish have all been reported by meteorologists with the most respected *credentials*.

(6) Scientists on the faculties of *accredited*, well-respected universities explain that fish storms may be caused by waterspouts, which are small tornadoes that form over water. A waterspout's powerful winds can suck up water, along with the creatures that live in it, and carry the creatures for miles before expelling them.

In 2000, the seaside resort of Great Yarmouth, England, was bombarded with sprats, a type of small fish. Sounds fishy, doesn't it? **(7)** Most people who heard about the event probably thought it was more likely that some *miscreants* had littered the town with smelly sea creatures.

But England's weather institute reported that this fish fall was a natural event. Such things, experts explained, are often reported around the world. In fact, accounts of fish and frogs falling from the sky date back to the first century. In the world's first encyclopedia, the Roman scientist Pliny the Elder wrote that the residents of one town fled when frogs began to rain down on them.

(8) Today, scientists cannot verify Pliny's claims, but many *credible* accounts of more recent fish showers can be found in respected newspapers. **(9)** Reputable news reporters follow a journalistic *creed* which states, among other core values, that "the public journal is a public trust." This means that reporters have an obligation to readers to make sure that what they report is both true and confirmed by reliable sources.

Still, don't believe everything that you hear or read. **(10)** Some accounts of bizarre weather, such as one tale of falling cows, have been *discredited*. The fishermen who claimed that the heavens pelted them with cattle were just repeating a story that originated in a Russian comedy show.

So there is no need to fear rain containing cows, dogs, or cats. But the next time it rains, you might want to bring an umbrella, just in case fish or frogs fall from the sky!

Each sentence below refers to a numbered sentence in the passage. Write the letter of the choice that gives the sentence a meaning that is closest to the original sentence.

___b___ **1.** You would no doubt be _____ if someone told you that, in England, it sometimes rains fish.
   a. horrified   **b.** skeptical   **c.** deceived   **d.** delighted

___a___ **2.** Most people are not likely to give _____ to such fantastic tales, especially when the tales travel by word of mouth.
   a. acceptance   **b.** praise   **c.** confidence   **d.** thought

___d___ **3.** After all, _____ is not a trait for which people wish to be known.
   a. recognition   **b.** bitterness   **c.** believability   **d.** gullibility

___b___ **4.** _____ sources, such as the national weather institutes of many countries, have reported that unusual weather events can cause rather unexpected precipitation.
   a. Questionable   **b.** Believable   **c.** Skeptical   **d.** Foreign

_____a_____ **5.** Showers of tadpoles, fish, frogs, and slimy jellyfish have all been reported by meteorologists with the most respected _____ .
  a. qualifications   **b.** recognition   **c.** reputations   **d.** manners

_____c_____ **6.** Scientists on the faculties of _____ , well-respected universities explain that fish storms may be caused by waterspouts.
  a. national   **b.** praiseworthy   **c.** approved   **d.** truthful

_____c_____ **7.** Most people who heard about the event probably thought it was more likely that some _____ had littered the town with smelly sea creatures.
  a. fishermen   **b.** townspeople   **c.** evildoers   **d.** authorities

_____d_____ **8.** Today, scientists cannot verify Pliny's claims, but many _____ accounts of more recent fish showers can be found in respected newspapers.
  a. amusing   **b.** damaging   **c.** ordinary   **d.** reliable

_____b_____ **9.** Reputable news reporters follow a journalistic _____ which states, among other core values, that "the public journal is a public trust."
  a. lifestyle   **b.** system of beliefs   **c.** style of language   **d.** set of qualifications

_____c_____ **10.** Some accounts of bizarre weather, such as one tale of falling cows, have been _____ .
  a. amazing   **b.** shown true   **c.** shown false   **d.** trustworthy

Indicate whether the statements below are TRUE or FALSE according to the passage.

_____F_____ **1.** All reports of animals raining from the sky have been discredited by meteorologists as false.

_____T_____ **2.** People in the ancient world recorded events of animals falling from the sky.

_____F_____ **3.** Amazingly, the skies have sometimes rained cows.

WRITING EXTENDED RESPONSES

The passage you just read describes some seemingly fantastic weather events. Suppose a friend told you a similar type of story. In an essay of at least three paragraphs, tell how you would decide whether this story was true. Give examples of two reliable sources of information that you might consult to confirm the story, and tell why they are trustworthy. (Or, indicate why your friend's sources should not be trusted, and explain why.) Use at least three lesson words in your essay and underline them.

WRITE THE DERIVATIVE

Complete the sentence by writing the correct form of the word shown in parentheses. You may not need to change the form that is given.

_____discredited_____ **1.** In the sixteenth century, Copernicus _____ the idea that the sun revolves around the earth. *(discredit)*

_____credible_____ **2.** I found her argument to be persuasive and _____ . *(credibility)*

accredits	**3.** A special board _____ all the state's lawyers. *(accredit)*
creeds	**4.** The _____ of many religions dictate that followers must donate money or time to those who are less fortunate than themselves. *(creed)*
credulity	**5.** His _____ made him the perfect victim for the con man's scheme. *(credulous)*
incredulous	**6.** I was _____ when I read about a man who survived alone on a desert island for years. *(incredulous)*
creditable	**7.** Georgette made a _____ effort, and her name was mentioned in the acknowledgments. *(creditable)*
Miscreants	**8.** _____ may often get more media attention than law-abiding people. *(miscreant)*
credence	**9.** I didn't give too much _____ to the things he said in anger. *(credence)*
credentials	**10.** After many years of schooling, he finally acquired the necessary _____ for his dream job. *(credential)*

FIND THE EXAMPLE

Choose the answer that best describes the action or situation.

c **1.** Something that might be *accredited*
  a. a play **b.** the weather **c.** a university **d.** a villain

d **2.** Something that makes up a *creed*
  a. stones **b.** a degree **c.** actions **d.** beliefs

a **3.** The subject of a story that would be most likely to cause *incredulity*
  a. monster **b.** pet **c.** bank **d.** marriage

b **4.** An example of a *credential*
  a. credit card **b.** college degree **c.** term paper **d.** shopping list

a **5.** Something one might say to someone who has done a *creditable* job
  a. Nice job. **b.** Fantastic! **c.** Unacceptable! **d.** This is all wrong.

b **6.** Something that might cause one's reputation to be *discredited*
  a. an experiment **b.** a nasty rumor **c.** a portrait **d.** an award

d **7.** An example of something that is *credible*
  a. gossip **b.** tall tale **c.** funny joke **d.** evidence

a **8.** A fairy tale character who is an example of a *miscreant*
  a. Big Bad Wolf **b.** Goldilocks **c.** Cinderella **d.** Snow White

c **9.** Something a *credulous* person might believe in
  a. gravity **b.** Saturn **c.** Martians **d.** history

b **10.** Something you would probably NOT give *credence* to
  a. diploma **b.** myth **c.** bank statement **d.** newspaper article

The Root -vert-

WORD LIST

aversion	avert	diversify	diversion	inadvertently
incontrovertible	invert	irreversible	revert	vertigo

The Latin root *-vert-*, also spelled *-vers-*, means "to turn." It comes from the Latin verb *vertere*. Almost everywhere you turn, you'll find common words based on this root. For example, an *extrovert* is "turned outward" toward others, while an *introvert* is "turned inward" toward one's self. Think about how the meanings of the lesson words have to do with turning.

1. aversion (ə-vûr´zhən) *noun* from Latin *ab-*, "away" + *vers*, "turn"
  a. An intense dislike
    • She developed an **aversion** to boating after she fell into the ocean.
  b. The avoidance of something considered unpleasant or painful
    • My **aversion** to potato salad started right after I got sick from eating it.

  averse *adjective* Having a strong dislike or opposition
  • Although I prefer R & B, I'm not **averse** to going to a jazz or blues concert now and then.

2. avert (ə-vûrt´) *verb* from Latin *ab-*, "away from" + *vert*, "turn"
  a. To turn away
    • They **averted** their eyes during the violent parts of the movie.
  b. To ward off (something about to happen); to prevent
    • By making sure the gas was turned off, Pat **averted** disaster.

3. diversify (dĭ-vûr´sə-fī´) *verb* from Latin *dis-*, "aside" + *vers*, "turn"
  To give variety to; to vary
  • Seamus's teacher wanted him to **diversify** his interests by reading poetry and history, in addition to science fiction.

  diversity *noun* The company wanted to increase the **diversity** of its workforce by hiring people of various backgrounds.

  diverse *adjective* Students in my school come from **diverse** cultures.

4. diversion (dĭ-vûr´zhən) *noun* from Latin *dis-*, "aside" + *vers*, "turn"
  a. An action or a ploy that turns attention away
    • I created a **diversion** by engaging Mr. Hibbard in conversation, while my sister ran across his lawn to retrieve our ball.
  b. Something that distracts the mind and relaxes or entertains
    • Watching the game was a welcome **diversion** after working.
  c. The act or instance of turning aside
    • The road construction caused a temporary **diversion** of traffic away from State Street.

Pantomiming often helps students remember the meanings of words. Have students act out the words *aversion, avert, divert, invert,* and *vertigo.*

> *Diversify* also means "to spread investments widely to limit losses in the event of a fall in a certain market."

diverse

divert *verb* The mother pointed at the posters on the wall to **divert** the child's attention from the doctor's needle.

diversionary *adjective* Some people think that the president's proposal is a **diversionary** tactic meant to shift attention away from recent failures.

5. **inadvertently** (ĭn´əd-vûr´tnt-lē) *adverb* from Latin *in-*, "not" + *ad-*, "toward" + *vert*, "turn"
Accidentally; unintentionally
  • I left without my keys, **inadvertently** locking myself out of the house.

inadvertent *adjective* Though Jessica had committed a hard foul, the referee realized it was **inadvertent** and did not eject her from the game.

6. **incontrovertible** (ĭn-kŏn´trə-vûr´tə-bəl) *adjective* from Latin *in-*, "not" + *contra-*, "against" + *vert*, "turn"
Unquestionable; impossible to dispute
  • The lab provided **incontrovertible** evidence that the suspect was innocent of the crime.

incontrovertibility *noun* The **incontrovertibility** of the damage caused by pollution has led to laws that protect the environment.

7. **invert** (ĭn-vûrt´) *verb* from Latin *in-*, "in" + *vert*, "turn"
To turn upside down or inside out; to reverse the position or order of
  • If you **invert** that glass, the water will spill out.

inversion *noun* The **inversion** of just two words in a sentence can subtly or drastically change its meaning.

8. **irreversible** (ĭr´ĭ-vûr´sə-bəl) *adjective* from Latin *in-*, "not" + *re-*, "back" + *vers*, "turn"
Impossible to reverse
  • Muscle loss in the elderly was once thought to be completely **irreversible,** but researchers have disproved that theory.

9. **revert** (rĭ-vûrt´) *verb* from Latin *re-*, "back" + *vert*, "turn"
To return to a former condition, practice, subject, or belief
  • In 1997, after ninety-nine years as a British colony, the city of Hong Kong **reverted** to Chinese sovereignty.

reversion *noun* The police chief promised that there would be no **reversion** to the corrupt practices of the past.

10. **vertigo** (vûr´tĭ-gō´) *noun* from Latin *vert*, "turn"
The sensation of dizziness
  • Harvey experienced **vertigo** whenever he looked down from tall buildings or bridges.

WRITE THE CORRECT WORD

Write the correct word in the space next to each definition.

vertigo	**1.** dizziness		_invert_	**6.** to turn upside down
aversion	**2.** intense dislike		_incontrovertible_	**7.** unquestionable
irreversible	**3.** impossible to reverse		_revert_	**8.** to return to a former condition
inadvertently	**4.** unintentionally		_diversify_	**9.** to vary
diversion	**5.** a distraction		_avert_	**10.** to turn away from

COMPLETE THE SENTENCE

Write the letter for the word that best completes each sentence.

___c___ **1.** Taking a hike with Ray was a nice _____ from my chores.
   a. aversion   **b.** diversity   **c.** diversion   **d.** inversion

___d___ **2.** I stayed in bed all day with _____ and a high fever.
   a. diversion   **b.** inversion   **c.** aversion   **d.** vertigo

___a___ **3.** The paw prints are _____ evidence that a raccoon knocked over our trash can.
   a. incontrovertible   **b.** averted   **c.** reverted   **d.** diversified

___b___ **4.** The sound of someone whispering his name caused him to _____ his attention from the lecture.
   a. diversify   **b.** avert   **c.** revert   **d.** invert

___c___ **5.** He thought he was paying his teacher a compliment, but he had _____ insulted her.
   a. reversibly   **b.** aversively   **c.** inadvertently   **d.** diversely

___d___ **6.** The student wanted to _____ her music studies by learning about jazz and blues, too.
   a. revert   **b.** invert   **c.** divert   **d.** diversify

___b___ **7.** If you _____ the letters in the word *time*, you get the word *emit*.
   a. diversify   **b.** invert   **c.** revert   **d.** aversion

___a___ **8.** I hope my brother won't _____ to his old ways during his visit.
   a. revert   **b.** diversify   **c.** avert   **d.** invert

___c___ **9.** The mechanic determined that the damage to the engine was _____.
   a. aversive   **b.** vertigo   **c.** irreversible   **d.** reverted

___c___ **10.** He's had a(n) _____ to peanut butter ever since eating a few peanuts gave him a rash.
   a. diversion   **b.** inversion   **c.** aversion   **d.** vertigo

Challenge: The police officer's _____ statements about the confidential details of the case ended up causing _____ damage to his reputation.
___b___
   a. aversive...diversionary   **b.** inadvertent...irreversible   **c.** inverse...diversified

Walking a Tightrope

Seventy feet above the ground, the high-wire walker freezes dramatically on the platform. As thousands watch, he slowly moves forward. A half-inch cable is all that separates him from disaster. He calmly continues either walking, dancing, or biking along the wire, as though he has lived up there his whole life. **(1)** He even *inverts* his body and performs a headstand on his thin, lofty perch. **(2)** Breathless audience members stare upward, imagining the *vertigo* they would feel if they were in his position. **(3)** Those with an *aversion* to heights can't help but look away. **(4)** Others gasp *inadvertently.* How does he perform these amazing feats?

(5) It may seem like magic, but high-wire walking is based on *incontrovertible* principles of physics. If the performer's weight is balanced directly above the wire, gravity will not pull him to the side and then down to the ground. But even the most skilled tightrope walkers find that their weight shifts from side to side as they move across the wire. **(6)** They must correct these shifts before the effect becomes *irreversible* and they lose their balance completely.

The poles that many performers carry help them keep their balance. These poles may be forty feet long and weigh as much as thirty pounds. When walkers feel their weight tilting to one side, they can correct the imbalance immediately by moving the pole in the opposite direction. **(7)** The pole helps the performer *revert* to a balanced, completely upright position.

(8) Created as a thrilling *diversion* for the public, high-wire walking dates back several thousand years. In ancient China, it was performed over knives. **(9)** The high-wire artists of today have developed increasingly *diversified* acts. Balanced on a thin wire, performers ride unicycles, stand on one another's shoulders, and even jump rope. Some combine wire walking with trapeze performances featuring twists and midair somersaults. Others rig a cable from the top of one skyscraper to another and then walk across the windy void between the buildings!

In addition to tightropes, some performers walk on slack wire ropes. These curved aerial pathways are generally rigged lower to the ground. These performers usually don't use balancing poles while walking the "looser" ropes. With their hands free, the artists can juggle a variety of items, such as clubs, rings, balls, knives, and even flaming torches.

High-wire performers train for years to develop their skills. **(10)** Conscientious equipment maintenance and consistent practice help them *avert* accidents. It takes constant attention and perfectionism—not to mention a working knowledge of physics—to perform these dangerous but crowd-pleasing feats.

Each sentence below refers to a numbered sentence in the passage. Write the letter of the choice that gives the sentence a meaning that is closest to the original sentence.

c **1.** He even _____ his body and performs a headstand on his thin, lofty perch.
    a. turns away   **b.** turns back   **c.** turns upside down   **d.** turns attention from

b **2.** Breathless audience members stare upward, imagining the _____ they would feel if they were in his position.
    a. fear   **b.** dizziness   **c.** emotions   **d.** dislike

d **3.** Those with a(n) _____ of heights can't help but look away.
    a. understanding   **b.** love   **c.** sneaky ploy   **d.** strong dislike

d **4.** Others gasp _____ .
    a. without question   **b.** with dizziness   **c.** with variation   **d.** without meaning to

___a___ **5.** It may seem like magic, but high-wire walking is based on _____ principles of physics.
     a. unquestionable   **b.** varied   **c.** accidental   **d.** dizzying

___b___ **6.** They must correct these shifts before the effect _____ and they lose their balance completely.
     a. is noticed   **b.** can't be undone   **c.** is variable   **d.** can't be questioned

___d___ **7.** The pole helps the performer _____ to a balanced, completely upright position.
     a. turn away   **b.** jump   **c.** walk   **d.** return

___a___ **8.** Created as a thrilling _____ for the public, high-wire walking dates back several thousand years.
     a. pastime   **b.** dislike   **c.** conversation   **d.** turning away

___c___ **9.** The high-wire artists of today have developed increasingly _____ acts.
     a. difficult   **b.** disliked   **c.** varied   **d.** dizzying

___b___ **10.** Conscientious equipment maintenance and consistent practice help them _____ accidents.
     a. question   **b.** avoid   **c.** dislike   **d.** reverse

Indicate whether the statements below are TRUE or FALSE according to the passage.

___T___ **1.** High-wire walking dates back several thousand years.

___F___ **2.** Principles of physics and gravity have no bearing on high-wire walking.

___F___ **3.** The balancing pole used by some high-wire walkers is for show only.

FINISH THE THOUGHT

Complete each sentence so that it shows the meaning of the italicized word.

1. I have an *aversion* to _____ Answers will vary.

_____

2. My favorite *diversion* is _____ Answers will vary.

_____

WRITE THE DERIVATIVE

Complete the sentence by writing the correct form of the word shown in parentheses. You may not need to change the form that is given.

___irreversibly___ **1.** Due to the earthquake, the building was _____ damaged. (*irreversible*)

___diverted___ **2.** All incoming airline flights were _____ because of the blizzard. (*diversion*)

inadvertently	**3.**	In the school's crowded hallway, I _____ bumped her with my overstuffed backpack. *(inadvertently)*
incontrovertible	**4.**	It is an _____ fact that the sun is the center of our solar system, but in 1633, Galileo was thrown in jail for declaring this. *(incontrovertible)*
reversion	**5.**	"A _____ to the bad old days is something we will not accept," said the leader of the newly independent nation. *(revert)*
vertigo	**6.**	Many amusement-park rides give me _____. *(vertigo)*
averse	**7.**	You hurt his feelings; of course he's _____ to hanging out with you. *(aversion)*
inversion	**8.**	A temperature _____ is a pollution-trapping condition in which air temperature increases instead of decreases with rising altitude. *(invert)*
diversity	**9.**	There is a great _____ of birds in the Florida swamplands. *(diversify)*
averted	**10.**	The pilot _____ a terrible accident by landing the disabled plane in a cornfield instead of on the busy highway. *(avert)*

FIND THE EXAMPLE

Choose the answer that best describes the action or situation.

b **1.** Something that a vegetarian would most likely have an *aversion* to
   a. carrots   **b.** beef   **c.** peanuts   **d.** lettuce

b **2.** An *incontrovertible* fact
   a. 2 + 2 = 22   **b.** 2 + 2 = 4   **c.** People are smart.   **d.** Ghosts are mean.

d **3.** Someone who would most likely try to avoid *reverting* to old habits
   a. runner   **b.** firefighter   **c.** composer   **d.** dieter

a **4.** The area or group that is likely to have the most *diversity*
   a. large city   **b.** tiny town   **c.** one family   **d.** college fraternity

c **5.** Something that someone would do *inadvertently*
   a. drive   **b.** write   **c.** sneeze   **d.** hike

b **6.** A process that is *irreversible*
   a. walking   **b.** aging   **c.** freezing   **d.** sitting

c **7.** Something that is often *inverted*
   a. soccer goal   **b.** friend   **c.** hourglass timer   **d.** car

d **8.** An activity that would most likely cause *vertigo*
   a. lying   **b.** eating   **c.** drawing   **d.** spinning

b **9.** Something that would most likely be a *diversion* from stress
   a. loud noises   **b.** soothing music   **c.** anger   **d.** coughing

d **10.** Something that would most likely *avert* a burglary
   a. doormat   **b.** sparrow   **c.** egg   **d.** alarm

Prefixes, Roots, and Suffixes

The Prefixes *auto-, equi-,* and *iso-*

The prefixes in this lesson refer to concepts of "self," as well as "equal." *Auto-, aut-* is taken from ancient Greek, and can refer to either "self" or "same." One common word using this prefix is *automobile,* a contraption that "moves" by "itself."

The prefix *equi-,* or *equ-,* also comes from Latin and means "equal." At times, *equi-* can refer to the equality, or balance, of forces. A person with *equanimity* is a person who is calm and even-tempered. In fact, the common word *equal* comes from this prefix.

The prefix *iso-* also means "equal." An *isosceles* triangle has two sides that are equal in length. Below is a chart of the meanings and origins of these prefixes.

Prefix	Meaning	Language Origin	Word	Word Meaning
auto-, aut-	self	Greek	autobiography	story of one's own life
equi-, equ-	equal	Latin	equidistant	at equal distances
iso-	equal	Greek	isochromatic	having the same color

Practice

You can combine the use of context clues with your knowledge of these prefixes to make intelligent guesses about the meanings of words. All of the sentences below contain a word formed with the prefixes *auto, equi,* or *iso-.* Read the sentences and write down what you think the word in italics means. Then check your definition with the one that you find in the dictionary, remembering to choose the definition that best fits in the sentence.

1. At the time of the *equinox,* we have twelve hours of day and twelve of night.

   My definition _____

   Dictionary definition <u>either of the two times during a year when day and night are of approximately equal length</u>

2. Some fruit-bearing trees, such as apple and peach trees, produce *autotoxins.*

   My definition _____

   Dictionary definition <u>a poison that acts on the organism in which it is generated</u>

3. Let's hope the tightrope walker never loses her *equilibrium.*

   My definition _____

   Dictionary definition <u>a condition in which all acting influences are canceled by others, resulting in a stable, balanced, or unchanging system</u>

4. Joseph Stalin was as an *autocrat* who deprived his people of personal freedoms and power.

My definition _____

Dictionary definition _____ a ruler having unlimited power; a despot _____

_____

5. *Isothermal* clothing is designed to maintain a constant body pressure for the wearer, regardless of variation in outside temperature.

My definition _____

Dictionary definition of, related to, or indicating equal or constant _____

temperatures

6. People who want to be *autonomous* and make decisions independently typically need to be self supporting.

My definition _____

Dictionary definition not controlled by others or by outside forces; _____

independent

7. Surprisingly, the temperatures in these two very different zones are *isometric*.

My definition _____

Dictionary definition of or exhibiting equality in dimensions or measurement _____

_____

8. Heather felt that the politician's speech was full of *equivocal* statements and she didn't know how she should interpret them.

My definition _____

Dictionary definition open to two or more interpretations and often _____

intended to mislead

Review Word Elements

Reviewing word elements helps you to remember them and use them in your reading. Below, write the meaning of the word elements you have studied.

Word	Word Element	Type of Element	Meaning of Word Element
circumnavigate	*circum-*	prefix	around
interject	*ject*	root	throw
credibility	*cred*	root	belief
semisoft	*semi-*	prefix	half; partial
invert	*vert*	root	turn
perimeter	*peri-*	prefix	around
hemisphere	*hemi-*	prefix	half

The Roots -cede- and -grad-

WORD LIST

cede	concede	deceased	egress	gradation
gradient	predecessor	regress	transgress	unprecedented

Both roots in this lesson deal with movement. The root -cede- means "go or withdraw" or "yield or surrender," and can also be spelled -cess- and -ceas-. It comes from the Latin verb *cedere*. The root -grad- means "go" or "step," and can also appear as -gress-. It comes from the Latin verb *gradis*. Many English words are formed from these roots. If you *precede* someone, you go before him or her. An *excessive* amount goes beyond the usual. When we *progress*, we go forward. As you study the words in this lesson, notice the various ways these roots can be spelled.

1. cede (sēd) *verb* from Latin *cede*, "yield"
a. To yield; to give up control over
  • When Roberto got an afterschool job, he **ceded** his position as editor of the yearbook to another student.
b. To surrender possession of, especially by treaty
  • Sweden was forced to **cede** Finland to Russia in 1809.

2. concede (kən-sēd´) *verb* from Latin *com-*, "very" + *cede*, "yield"
a. To admit, often reluctantly, that something is true or right
  • United Nations officials **conceded** that they had not made much progress in alleviating poverty worldwide.
b. To acknowledge defeat
  • Refusing to **concede** the election, the candidate demanded a recount.
c. To yield or grant rights or privileges
  • The principal finally **conceded** off-campus lunch privileges to seniors.

concession *noun* To avoid a strike, company management granted workers **concessions** in the form of pay increases for overtime work.

> *Concession* also means "the selling of goods in a specific area," as in a *concession* stand.

3. deceased (dĭ-sēst´) from Latin *de-*, "away" + *ceas*, "go"
a. *adjective* Dead; no longer living
  • All four of my grandparents are **deceased.**
b. *noun* A dead person
  • A memorial service was held for the **deceased.**

4. egress (ē´grĕs´) from Latin *e-*, "out" + *gress*, "go"
a. *noun* A path or an opening for going out; an exit
  • The lost campers searched for an **egress** from the dense forest.
b. *noun* The act of coming or going out; emergence
  • The baby alligators' **egress** from their eggs was slow and laborious.
c. *verb* To go out; to emerge
  • Scuba divers who panic and try to **egress** from the water too quickly risk getting "the bends."

Point out the prefixes that have been added to the roots to form several words in this lesson. Discuss how the meanings of *egress, regress, transgress,* and *deceased* relate to their word parts.

5. **gradation** (grā-dā´shən) *noun* from Latin *grad*, "step"
   a. A systematic progression; a series of gradual changes
      • The orchestra's volume rose in **gradation,** until it reached a crescendo.
   b. A passing, by almost imperceptible degrees, from one tone or shade to another.
      • The collection of paint samples showed all the **gradations** of blue, from light blue to dark navy.

A *gradation* can also be one stage within a progression or series of changes.

gradations

6. **gradient** (grā´dē-ənt) *noun* from Latin *grad*, "step"
   A rate of inclination; a slope
      • The road had such a steep **gradient** that it was difficult for drivers of large trucks to keep their speed in check on the downhill.

7. **predecessor** (prĕd´ĭ-sĕs´ər) *noun* from Latin *pre-*, "before" + *cess*, "go"
   Someone or something that comes before another
      • The new governor emphasized the need to improve the state's public education system more than her **predecessor** had.

The opposite of a *predecessor* is a *successor,* someone who comes after another.

8. **regress** (rĭ-grĕs´) *verb* from Latin *re-*, "back" + *grad*, "go"
   To go back to a previous, often worse or less developed, state; to revert
   • When the trainer went on vacation, the athletes **regressed** to their former lazy habits.

   regression *noun* The mother was discouraged by her four-year-old's apparent **regression** when he became attached to his blanket again.

9. **transgress** (trăns-grĕs´) *verb* from Latin *trans-*, "across" + *gress*, "go"
   a. To go beyond a limit or boundary
      • Lions often attack other lions that **transgress** into their territory.
   b. To break a law or code by overstepping limits
      • Without realizing it, the driver **transgressed** Manhattan's motor vehicle rules by making a right turn at a red light.

   transgression *noun* The football player's frequent off-the-field **transgressions** got him dismissed from the team.

10. **unprecedented** (ŭn-prĕs´ĭ-dĕn´tĭd) *adjective* from Latin *un-*, "not" + *pre-*, "before" + *ced*, "go"
    Not done or known before; without previous example
       • The legal battles resulting from the 2000 U.S. presidential election were **unprecedented.**

A *precedent* is a previous decision that may be followed in other cases.

WORD ENRICHMENT

Synonyms of *cede*

   Cede has many synonyms such as the words *yield* and *surrender,* which imply "giving way to pressure." Another synonym is *waive,* meaning "to voluntarily give up a claim or right." *Renounce* means "to formally announce that one is giving something up," as in "to *renounce* the right to the throne." *Relinquish* can indicate that one is giving something up either voluntarily or due to pressure, depending on the context.

WRITE THE CORRECT WORD

Write the correct word in the space next to each definition.

regress	**1.** to revert	_transgress_	**6.** to break a law
gradation	**2.** a series of gradual changes	_predecessor_	**7.** the one who came before
gradient	**3.** a slope	_unprecedented_	**8.** never done before
egress	**4.** to emerge or go out	_deceased_	**9.** not alive
cede	**5.** to give up	_concede_	**10.** to admit reluctantly

COMPLETE THE SENTENCE

Write the letter for the word that best completes each sentence.

___b___ **1.** The _____ from light to shadow in the painting was very subtle and effective.
    a. regression   **b.** gradation   **c.** transgression   **d.** egression

___d___ **2.** The new principal faces the challenge of following in the footsteps of a successful _____.
    a. transgressor   **b.** regression   **c.** gradient   **d.** predecessor

___a___ **3.** The settlers _____ the fort when they saw that it was surrounded by enemy troops.
    a. ceded   **b.** deceased   **c.** regressed   **d.** transgressed

___d___ **4.** Winning five straight championships is _____; no team has ever done it.
    a. conceded   **b.** transgressed   **c.** egressed   **d.** unprecedented

___b___ **5.** The steep _____ of the mountain made the hike difficult.
    a. regression   **b.** gradient   **c.** predecessor   **d.** egression

___c___ **6.** All the heroes of the Spanish-American War of 1898 are now _____.
    a. ceded   **b.** unprecedented   **c.** deceased   **d.** transgressed

___a___ **7.** Sometimes it is hard to _____ that you have made a mistake.
    a. concede   **b.** egress   **c.** regress   **d.** transgress

___b___ **8.** Merrill had done a good job of kicking her nail-biting habit, but the stress of final exams caused her to _____.
    a. cede   **b.** regress   **c.** transgress   **d.** egress

___a___ **9.** When entering into a dangerous situation, spies always look for a(n) _____.
    a. egress   **b.** gradient   **c.** regression   **d.** predecessor

___d___ **10.** The soldier was court-martialed for _____ the military code of conduct.
    a. egressing   **b.** conceding   **c.** regressing   **d.** transgressing

Challenge: The disappointed parent had to _____ that his children had _____ school rules when the twins were caught loitering outside during first-period classes.
___c___   **a.** cede…regressed   **b.** egress…unprecedented   **c.** concede…transgressed

Into the Deep Cave

Cocklebiddy Cave, underneath south central Australia's Nullarbor Plain, is one of the world's longest submerged caves. Its depths are dangerous and forbidding, even to experienced spelunkers, or cave explorers. Going into Cocklebiddy requires both expert rock climbing and scuba-diving skills.

(1) Like most caves, Cocklebiddy has steep *gradients* and rocky grottos. **(2)** But its most distinctive feature is the unique *gradation* of lakes that fill its interior. These lakes are located in air-filled caverns, situated in layers that reach deep into the earth.

Similar to a tall building with floors connected by staircases, the levels of Cocklebiddy Cave are joined by narrow channels called *siphons.* About the size of sewer pipes, the siphons are completely filled with water. The deeper they go, the narrower they become. To travel from one level of the cave to a lower level, explorers must dive through the siphons.

(3) In 1983, French explorer Francis Le Guen, along with four companions, investigated areas of Cocklebiddy that had never been explored by their *predecessors.* After two years of planning and collecting state-of-the-art equipment, including thirty-five lightweight fiberglass oxygen tanks and two submarine scooters, the team was ready for their perilous diving adventure.

Reaching the first lake in the cave, they inflated a rubber raft. In the clear water, they observed the entrance to one of the siphons that would take them deeper. It was so narrow that the divers, connected by ropes, had to swim single file.

When the divers reached the second underground lake, they surfaced for a rest and then followed another siphon to a third lake. They repeated this process until the siphons became too narrow for human beings to pass through. At the lowest point they could reach, they were more than three miles beneath the surface. **(4)** This *unprecedented* feat set a cave-diving record.

(5) As even the most experienced caver will *concede,* spelunking involves tremendous danger. Le Guen and his team were forced to separate at times and to spend many hours underwater as they traveled through Cocklebiddy's long siphons. Far beneath the surface of the earth, they endured tremendous water pressure. Le Guen became stuck in a narrow passage, saving himself only by removing some equipment. Some of the other explorers suffered from narcosis, which is a condition caused by excess nitrogen in the bloodstream. **(6)** Narcosis can make divers *regress* to confused, childlike behavior. Still others lost their way and their sense of direction in the dark, underground waters. **(7)** Such confusion is very dangerous, for panicked divers may *transgress* safety guidelines for slow and gradual surfacing, and the divers can end up with a painful and potentially fatal decompression problem, known as the "bends."

But for Le Guen and his team, the thrill of discovery made these risks worthwhile. Hundreds of feet beneath the surface, Le Guen saw a perfectly vaulted, oval cave and another that bristled with rocky teeth. **(8)** He also found the submerged skeletons of bats, possibly *deceased* for thousands of years, proving that these depths had once been accessible from the surface.

(9) Forty-seven hours after they plunged into Cockebiddy, Le Guen's team *egressed,* exhausted but exhilarated. **(10)** Although the record for deep-cave diving has since been *ceded* to others, the 1983 Cocklebiddy adventure remains a famous achievement in the challenging world of spelunking.

Each sentence below refers to a numbered sentence in the passage. Write the letter of the choice that gives the sentence a meaning that is closest to the original sentence.

_b_   **1.** Cocklebiddy has steep _____ and rocky grottos.
     a. caverns   **b.** slopes   **c.** changes   **d.** boundaries

_c_   **2.** But its most distinctive feature is the unique _____ of lakes.
     a. emergence   **b.** shape   **c.** progression   **d.** yield

d **3.** Le Guen and his team investigated areas that had never been explored by _____.
  a. their parents   **b.** rescue teams   **c.** dead people   **d.** previous explorers

a **4.** This _____ feat set a cave-diving record.
  a. never done before   **b.** cave-exploring   **c.** very difficult   **d.** overstepping limits

c **5.** As even the most experienced caver will _____, spelunking involves danger.
  a. believe   **b.** yield   **c.** admit   **d.** incline

b **6.** Narcosis can make divers _____ confused, childlike behavior.
  a. mimic   **b.** revert to   **c.** emerge from   **d.** aware of

c **7.** Panicked divers may _____ safety guidelines for slow surfacing.
  a. surrender to   **b.** change   **c.** break   **d.** revert to

c **8.** The skeletons of bats, possibly _____ for thousands of years, proved that these depths had once been accessible from the surface.
  a. hanging   **b.** infected   **c.** dead   **d.** underwater

d **9.** Le Guen's team _____, exhausted but exhilarated.
  a. changed   **b.** went back   **c.** survived   **d.** emerged

a **10.** The record for deep-cave diving has since been _____ to others.
  a. yielded   **b.** limited   **c.** opened   **d.** forgotten

Indicate whether the statements below are TRUE or FALSE according to the passage.

T **1.** Spelunkers are adventurers who explore and study caves.

F **2.** Divers routinely descend more than five miles beneath the earth's surface.

F **3.** The divers used siphons to drain water out of the underground lakes.

WRITING EXTENDED RESPONSES

Because of numerous tragic accidents, Australia has suspended some deep-cave exploring. Do you think that this type of exploration should be allowed at the explorers' risk, or do you think it should be banned? State your position in a persuasive essay that is at least three paragraphs. Include at least two points and defend each one with supporting details. Use at least three lesson words in your essay and underline them.

WRITE THE DERIVATIVE

Complete the sentence by writing the correct form of the word shown in parentheses. You may not need to change the form that is given.

regression **1.** After the new leader was elected, the people were appalled to see a serious _____ in the protection of endangered species in their country. *(regress)*

concession **2.** The incumbent senator gave her _____ speech following the stunning election upset. *(concede)*

deceased	**3.**	The minister said a prayer for the _____ at the burial service. (_deceased_)
egress	**4.**	The amusement park's most popular ride is designed so that, at the end, passengers _____ into a gift shop full of toys. (_egress_)
predecessor	**5.**	The new CEO promised to handle the company's finances better than his _____ had. (_predecessor_)
gradation or gradations	**6.**	It is interesting to watch the _____ of a lunar eclipse. (_gradation_)
unprecedented	**7.**	Winning the Oscar for best actress three years in a row is _____. (_unprecedented_)
gradients	**8.**	The expert skier preferred the steep _____ of the black-diamond trails. (_gradient_)
ceded	**9.**	In the interest of ending its involvement in World War I, Russia _____ its warm water port in the Balkans. (_cede_)
transgression	**10.**	Jaywalking is a minor _____ of the law. (_transgress_)

FIND THE EXAMPLE

Choose the answer that best describes the action or situation.

b   **1.** An event that would be _unprecedented_
   a. exploring space   **b.** walking on Mars   **c.** splitting atoms   **d.** discovering a new plant

d   **2.** A creature that might _egress_ dramatically from the water
   a. a lobster   **b.** a squid   **c.** a shrimp   **d.** a dolphin

a   **3.** How you might feel if you _conceded_ a chess match
   a. disappointed   **b.** elated   **c.** successful   **d.** indifferent

d   **4.** A place where one is most likely to find someone who is _deceased_
   a. a garden   **b.** a school play   **c.** an inauguration   **d.** a morgue

c   **5.** Something most people would be reluctant to _cede_
   a. daily chores   **b.** the weather   **c.** legal rights   **d.** condemned property

d   **6.** How a marathoner might feel when running up a _gradient_
   a. surprised   **b.** victorious   **c.** bored   **d.** strained

a   **7.** Something that is NOT a _transgression_
   a. studying   **b.** cheating   **c.** lying   **d.** stealing

b   **8.** A _predecessor_ of the telephone
   a. Internet   **b.** telegraph   **c.** DVD   **d.** television

c   **9.** Something that does NOT have _gradations_
   a. sunrise   **b.** mountain range   **c.** flat plain   **d.** springtime

b   **10.** Something that never _regresses_
   a. memory   **b.** time   **c.** tide   **d.** public policy

The Root -cur-

WORD LIST

concurrent	courier	cursory	discursive	incur
incursion	precursor	recourse	recurrent	succor

The root *-cur-* means "run." It comes from the Latin verb *currere,* and can be spelled *-cur-*, *-cor-*, and *-cour-*. Many common English words are formed from this root. For example, something *current* is in continuous, running motion. In another sense, *current* means "running" at the present time. Horses "run" around a *corral.* Even *currency* refers to money that is circulating, or "running" around.

Point out that the words *cursor, cursive,* and *corridor* also contain the root *cur.* Discuss how *cur* relates to the meanings of these words.

1. **concurrent** (kən-kûr´ənt) *adjective* from Latin *com-,* "together" + *cur,* "run"
   Happening at the same time; simultaneous
   • I have two **concurrent** meetings, so I'll have to send someone in my place to attend one of them.

2. **courier** (ko͝or´ē-ər) *noun* from Latin *cour,* "run"
   A messenger carrying information or important documents
   • The **courier** carried copies of the treaty from Washington to Geneva.

courier

A *courier* can also be a spy, a tour guide, or someone who helps plan a trip.

3. **cursory** (kûr´sə-rē) *adjective* from Latin *cur,* "run"
   Done quickly and not thoroughly; hasty
   • After a **cursory** glance at the newspaper, Dad rushed off to work.

4. **discursive** (dĭ-skûr´sĭv) *adjective* from Latin *dis-,* "apart" + *cur,* "run"
   a. Moving from one topic to another without order; rambling
      • Mrs. Flagstad's **discursive** talk had some interesting points, but was hard to follow.
   b. Coming to a conclusion by reasoning; analytical
      • His **discursive** debate presentation was a model of good logic.

   discursiveness *noun* After the tenth time she wandered off the topic, we began to resent the speaker's **discursiveness.**

The two definitions of *discursive* have nearly opposite meanings.

5. **incur** (ĭn-kûr´) *verb* from Latin *in-,* "on" + *cur,* "run"
   To bring about something undesirable as a result of one's own actions
   • After buying a new wardrobe, he found he had **incurred** thousands of dollars of credit card debt.

6. **incursion** (ĭn-kûr´zhən) *noun* from Latin *in-,* "in" + *cur,* "run"
   An aggressive attack or invasion of territory
   • In the 1500s, Scottish outlaws often made **incursions** into England to pillage rich farms.

7. **precursor** (prĭ-kûr´sər) *noun* from Latin *pre-*, "before" + *cur*, "run"
   Something or someone that comes before another; a forerunner
   or predecessor
   • During World War II, Alan Turing's Colossus, a **precursor** to the
     modern computer, was used to break German codes.

8. **recourse** (rē´kôrs´) *noun* from Latin *re-*, "back" + *cour*, "run"
   a. The act of turning to someone or something for help or security
      • Landlords have legal **recourse** when tenants fail to pay rent.
   b. Someone or something that is turned to for help or security
      • When she found out that her grade had dropped, her only
        recourse was to ask whether she could do some extra-credit work.

The phrase *to have recourse to* is common.

9. **recurrent** (rĭ-kûr´ənt) *adjective* from Latin *re-*, "back" + *cur*, "run"
   Happening repeatedly; occurring over and over again
   • The highway has **recurrent** flooding problems due to overflow from
     the nearby lake.

   recur *verb* The pain in my elbow seems to **recur** whenever I
   play tennis.

   recurrence *noun* Her doctor told her to call immediately if she
   experienced any **recurrence** of symptoms.

10. **succor** (sŭk´ər) from Latin *sub-*, "under" + *cor*, "run"
    a. *noun* Assistance in time of need; relief
       • Nations around the world provided **succor** to victims of the tragic
         tsunami of 2004.
    b. *verb* To provide assistance in time of need
       • Many religions teach their followers to **succor** the poor and
         less fortunate.

ANALOGIES

On the answer line, write the letter of the answer that best completes
each analogy. Refer to Lessons 24–26 if you need help with any of the
lesson words.

___a___ **1.** Egress is to exit as _____.
  a. precursor is to forerunner   **c.** ringleader is to circus
  b. inadvertent is to purposeful   **d.** garage is to car

___c___ **2.** Courier is to document as _____.
  a. aversion is to avert   **c.** boat is to cargo
  b. driver is to car   **d.** gradation is to gradual

___d___ **3.** Diversify is to vary as _____.
  a. eraser is to pencil   **c.** breakfast is to lunch
  b. alive is to deceased   **d.** concede is to admit

___b___ **4.** Improve is to regress as _____.
  a. vertigo is to dizziness   **c.** half is to whole
  b. painstaking is to cursory   **d.** food is to plate

WRITE THE CORRECT WORD

Write the correct word in the space next to each definition

recurrent	**1.** happening repeatedly	_succor_	**6.** assistance in a time of need
precursor	**2.** a forerunner	_discursive_	**7.** rambling
incur	**3.** to bring upon oneself	_cursory_	**8.** hasty
courier	**4.** a messenger	_incursion_	**9.** an invasion
concurrent	**5.** simultaneous	_recourse_	**10.** a source of help

COMPLETE THE SENTENCE

Write the letter for the word that best completes each sentence.

___d___ **1.** The _____ was caught in a traffic jam, so the documents didn't arrive in time.
    a. precursor   **b.** recurrence   **c.** incursion   **d.** courier

___a___ **2.** By offering to negotiate, the government hoped to convince the rebels that violence was not their only _____.
    a. recourse   **b.** recurrence   **c.** courier   **d.** precursor

___c___ **3.** Mary's _____ dream about being late to an important event always seems to happen when her life is stressful.
    a. concurrent   **b.** discursive   **c.** recurrent   **d.** incurring

___b___ **4.** Unfortunately, the two courses she needed to take were given at _____ times.
    a. recurrent   **b.** concurrent   **c.** discursive   **d.** cursory

___a___ **5.** The military _____ into enemy territory successfully achieved its goals.
    a. incursion   **b.** precursor   **c.** succor   **d.** discursive

___b___ **6.** Jaleel expected more than a _____ apology from Dara after she lost his favorite book.
    a. concurrent   **b.** cursory   **c.** discursive   **d.** recurrent

___d___ **7.** The teacher said that Colin's essay was too _____ and that it should be revised to provide more focus.
    a. recurrent   **b.** incurred   **c.** concurrent   **d.** discursive

___c___ **8.** The homeless woman came to the shelter for _____ and rest.
    a. recourse   **b.** courier   **c.** succor   **d.** precursor

___a___ **9.** The lyre, an ancient instrument, is a(n) _____ to the modern guitar.
    a. precursor   **b.** courier   **c.** incursion   **d.** discursion

___c___ **10.** By ignoring parking fines, one often _____ even greater financial penalties.
    a. succors   **b.** recurs   **c.** incurs   **d.** incursions

Challenge: After lengthy and stalled negotiations, the police believed that their only _____ was to launch a(n) _____ into the terrorists' hideout in order to rescue the hostages.
___c___   **a.** discourse...recourse   **b.** precursor...courier   **c.** recourse...incursion

The Science of Ancient China

(1) Even a *cursory* survey of the history of science reveals that Chinese technological achievements made between 200 BC and AD 1500 were without equal.
(2) Many of the advancements that modernized Europe in the 1500s had *precursors* in China. Sir Francis Bacon, an English philosopher of science, thought that three Chinese inventions—the magnetic compass, the printing press, and gunpowder—"changed the whole face and state of things throughout the world."

(3) *Recurrent* advanced discoveries showed that China was on the cutting edge of technology in ancient times. Ancient Chinese philosophy books, for example, warn against mixing charcoal, saltpeter, and sulfur.
(4) They state that this combination might *incur* the anger of nature in the form of an explosion. Hundreds of years later, these ingredients were used to make gunpowder. **(5)** Thus, *incursions* using this weapon became a much more effective means of overpowering enemies. It was a full two centuries after the Chinese started using gunpowder that Europeans discovered this powerful weapon.

But the three inventions Bacon wrote about give only a hint of Chinese achievements in science. The wheelbarrow, paper money, stirrups for riding on horses, efficient iron and steel technology, suspension bridges, sternpost rudders on ships, and

ancient compass

even a form of vaccination were also invented by Chinese scientists. As early as 100 BC, the Chinese were efficiently producing paper from wood. **(6)** The *concurrent* Roman writing surfaces were either papyrus or parchment made from animal skins.

(7) Scientists from the West had little opportunity to use Chinese technology as *recourse* to deal with their own technological challenges. After all, communication between the cultures was difficult. Contact was largely limited to a small number of silk and spice traders, who the Chinese government allowed into their country.
(8) Therefore, there were no *couriers* bringing word of Chinese scientific discoveries back to Europe.

In addition to their clever inventions, the Chinese had a sophisticated knowledge of astronomy.
(9) Chinese *discursive* tracts on the stars and the concept of the universe as infinite space would have fascinated Western astronomers, such as Galileo. And when Europeans "invented" the seismograph to predict earthquakes in the 1800s, they were unaware that the Chinese had been using their own version of this technology for almost 1,500 years!

Today, however, knowledge from one part of the world soon spreads to another. To cite just one example, Western physicians are now making use of Eastern medical practices, such as herbal remedies and acupuncture. **(10)** These methods are now commonly used to bring *succor* to those who are sick and suffering.

Each sentence below refers to a numbered sentence in the passage. Write the letter of the choice that gives the sentence a meaning that is closest to the original sentence.

___a___ **1.** Even a(n) _____ survey of the history of science reveals that Chinese technological achievements made between 200 BC and AD 1500 were without equal.
    a. quick   **b.** detailed   **c.** simultaneous   **d.** uninformed

___d___ **2.** Many of the advancements that modernized Europe in the 1500s had _____ in China.
    a. difficulties   **b.** traveled   **c.** research   **d.** forerunners

___c___ **3.** _____ advanced discoveries showed that China was on the cutting edge of technology in ancient times.
    a. Puzzling   **b.** Simultaneous   **c.** Repeated   **d.** Scientific

___b___ **4.** This combination might _____ the anger of nature in the form of an explosion.
    a. assist   **b.** bring about   **c.** help to avoid   **d.** repeat

_b_   **5.** Thus, _____ using this weapon became a much more effective means of
overpowering enemies.
    a. messengers   **b.** invasions   **c.** ramblings   **d.** explosions

_c_   **6.** The _____ Roman writing surfaces were more primitive.
    a. cumbersome   **b.** delicate   **c.** simultaneous   **d.** rambling

_a_   **7.** Scientists from the West had little opportunity to use Chinese technology as a(n)
_____ to deal with their own technological challenges.
    a. resource   **b.** excuse   **c.** experiment   **d.** forerunner

_d_   **8.** Therefore, there were no _____ bringing word of Chinese scientific
discoveries back to Europe.
    a. sources of help   **b.** forerunners   **c.** translators   **d.** messengers

_b_   **9.** Chinese _____ tracts on the stars and the concept of the universe as infinite
space would have fascinated Western astronomers.
    a. astronomical   **b.** analytical   **c.** repeated   **d.** hasty

_c_   **10.** These methods are now commonly used to bring _____ to those who are sick.
    a. medicine   **b.** physicians   **c.** relief   **d.** messages

Indicate whether the statements below are TRUE or FALSE according to the passage.

_T_   **1.** The Chinese made many advances in technology before the Western world did.

_F_   **2.** Galileo used Chinese texts to study the stars.

_F_   **3.** Eastern medical practices are not used in the West.

FINISH THE THOUGHT

Complete each sentence so that it shows the meaning of the italicized word.

1. An example of a _recurrent_ event is _____ Answers will vary. _____

_____

2. When his dog ran away, his only _recourse_ was _____ Answers will vary. _____

_____

WRITE THE DERIVATIVE

**Complete the sentence by writing the correct form of the word shown in
parentheses. You may not need to change the form that is given.**

concurrently   **1.** During rush hour, some trains run _____ to accommodate the large numbers
of commuters. _(concurrent)_

succor   **2.** If you are a compassionate person, you _____ those in need. _(succor)_

<u>courier</u>   **3.** The _____ plotted out the best route for our European trip. *(courier)*

<u>recur</u>   **4.** I promise that this type of error will not _____. *(recurrent)*

<u>cursory</u>   **5.** A _____ glance at the stitching showed that it was not a well-made garment. *(cursory)*

<u>incurred</u>   **6.** By showing up late to work every day, Bronson _____ the ill will of his coworkers. *(incur)*

<u>discursively</u>   **7.** This author writes _____ but powerfully. *(discursive)*

<u>precursors</u>   **8.** Scientists believe that some types of dinosaurs were _____ to modern birds. *(precursor)*

<u>recourse</u>   **9.** Completely surrounded, he had no _____ but to surrender. *(recourse)*

<u>incursions</u>   **10.** Repeated _____ had a devastating effect on the civilians in the area. *(incursion)*

FIND THE EXAMPLE

Choose the answer that best describes the action or situation.

<u>b</u>   **1.** One way to provide *succor*
     a. eat breakfast   **b.** donate clothing   **c.** go to a ball game   **d.** launch an attack

<u>a</u>   **2.** The LEAST *recurrent* event
     a. being born   **b.** taking a test   **c.** waking up   **d.** eating a meal

<u>d</u>   **3.** Of the pairs listed, the most likely to occur *concurrently*
     a. lunch and dinner   **b.** sunrise and sunset   **c.** summer and fall   **d.** history and math class

<u>b</u>   **4.** Something you would most likely read in a *cursory* manner
     a. final exam   **b.** junk mail   **c.** good book   **d.** job application

<u>c</u>   **5.** Something a *courier* is most likely to carry
     a. football   **b.** bag of groceries   **c.** urgent message   **d.** luggage

<u>a</u>   **6.** How you would most likely feel if there was an *incursion* into your home
     a. violated   **b.** indifferent   **c.** curious   **d.** amused

<u>c</u>   **7.** The most likely reason you would turn to someone for *recourse*
     a. to assist them   **b.** to have a chat   **c.** to get help   **d.** to enjoy a snack

<u>c</u>   **8.** Something that was NOT a *precursor* to modern automobiles
     a. covered wagon   **b.** early automobiles   **c.** jet plane   **d.** horseless carriage

<u>d</u>   **9.** Something you would be likely to *incur* if you make fun of people regularly
     a. debt   **b.** honor   **c.** humor   **d.** resentment

<u>a</u>   **10.** Of the words listed, the best word to describe a *discursive* argument
     a. analytical   **b.** boring   **c.** short   **d.** funny

The Roots -sent- and -path-

WORD LIST

apathy	assent	empathy	pathetic	pathology
presentiment	sensational	sensibility	sententious	sentient

The Latin root *-sent-* means "feeling." The root, which can also appear as *-sens-*, is from the Latin word *sentire*, meaning "to perceive" or "to feel." The Greek root *-path-* can mean "feeling," "suffering," or "disease." It comes from the Greek word *pathos*, or "feeling." The words in this lesson are all derived from *-sent-* or *-path-*.

1. **apathy** (ăp´ə-thē) *noun* from Greek *a-*, "without" + *path*, "feeling"
   Lack of feeling; lack of concern or interest
   • Public **apathy** about a political issue may result in low voter turnout.

   apathetic *adjective* Constantly chatting on the phone, the sales clerk seemed **apathetic** about serving his customers.

2. **assent** (ə-sĕnt´) from Latin *ad-*, "toward" + *sent*, "feeling"
   a. *verb* To agree to something
   • The company president **assented** to implementing the new policy.
   b. *noun* Agreement
   • The architect needed her client's **assent** before making expensive structural changes.

3. **empathy** (ĕm´pə-thē) *noun* from Greek *em-*, "in" + *path*, "feeling"
   An identification with and understanding of other people's feelings and situations
   • I'm from overseas, so I have **empathy** for recent immigrants.

   empathetic (or **empathic**) *adjective* The **empathetic** special-education teacher seemed to understand the challenges his students faced.

   empathize *verb* The woman who had permanently injured her leg as a child **empathized** with those who had other physical disabilities.

4. **pathetic** (pə-thĕt´ĭk) *adjective* from Greek *path*, "suffering"
   Arousing compassion or pity
   • The injured dog made a **pathetic** attempt to walk.

5. **pathology** (pă-thŏl´ə-jē) *noun* from Greek *path*, "disease" + *-logy*, "study"
   a. The scientific study of disease
   • **Pathology** advanced greatly after the invention of the microscope.
   b. Signs of disease
   • The **pathology** of multiple sclerosis includes muscle deterioration.
   c. An abnormal, usually negative, state
   • A rising crime rate is an indication of social **pathology.**

   pathologist *noun* **Pathologists** study diseases in bodily tissues.

Point out that some lesson words can be confused with other common words. Discuss *empathy* and *sympathy,* as well as *sensibility* and *sense.* Point out the differences between them.

Pathological describes something that relates to or is caused by a disease. It can also describe a behavior that is faulty or compulsive, as in "a *pathological* liar."

6. presentiment (prĭ-zĕn´tə-mənt) *noun* from Latin *pre-*, "before"
+ *sent*, "feeling"
A sense that something is about to occur
• The dark settings of many mystery novels impart a **presentiment**
of danger.

7. sensational (sĕn-sā´shə-nəl) *adjective* from Latin *sent*, "feeling"
a. Causing strong feelings of curiosity or interest by giving exaggerated
or shocking details
• "Tears Shed After Massive Food Fight!" screamed the **sensational**
headline.
b. Wonderful; outstanding
• The outfielder's **sensational** catch saved the game for the team.

sensationalism *noun* Doctored pictures of "extraterrestrials"
contributed to the **sensationalism** of the tabloid.

> A *sensation* is a feeling.

sensational catch

8. sensibility (sĕn´sə-bĭl´ĭ-tē) *noun* from Latin *sent*, "feeling"
a. Acute intellectual or emotional perception or feeling
• The editor had a sharp **sensibility** for literary style.
b. Awareness and responsiveness toward something; sensitivity
• Eric knew that dyeing his hair blue might offend his grandparents'
sensibilities.
c. The ability to feel or perceive
• Though he had been in a deep sleep, I quickly shook him to
sensibility.

insensible *adjective* Not aware or sensitive to
• "Sir, although I am not **insensible** to the honor of your offer,
I must refuse it," said Mr. Spock.

9. sententious (sĕn-tĕn´shəs) *adjective* from Latin *sent*, "feeling"
a. Energetic and concise in expression; saying meaningful things
precisely
• The **sententious** speaker captivated her audience.
b. Prone to pompous moralizing or giving advice in a
self-righteous way
• My great-uncle's long, **sententious** lecture was filled with advice
about how to behave properly.

sententiousness *noun* The bored and restless congregation didn't
appreciate the **sententiousness** of the sermon.

10. sentient (sĕn´shənt) *adjective* from Latin *sent*, "feeling"
Capable of perceiving and feeling; conscious
• Animals are **sentient** creatures and should be treated as such.

sentience *noun* Will super-advanced computers ever achieve **sentience?**

WRITE THE CORRECT WORD

Write the correct word in the space next to each definition.

empathy	**1.** identification with the feelings of others	**presentiment**	**6.** a feeling that something will occur
pathetic	**2.** arousing pity	**assent**	**7.** agreement
apathy	**3.** a lack of interest	**sententious**	**8.** self-righteous
sentient	**4.** conscious	**sensibility**	**9.** acute perception
pathology	**5.** the study of disease	**sensational**	**10.** outstanding

COMPLETE THE SENTENCE

Write the letter for the word that best completes each sentence.

b   **1.** The art teacher sought to increase her students' _____ to the beauty of nature.
     a. pathology   **b.** sensibility   **c.** apathy   **d.** assent

a   **2.** Jerome did not _____ to the terms of the deal, so he did not sign the contract.
     a. assent   **b.** apathy   **c.** sense   **d.** empathize

c   **3.** The food at the new restaurant is _____; everyone loves it!
     a. pathetic   **b.** sententious   **c.** sensational   **d.** sentient

d   **4.** Shivering in the rain, the kitten looked truly _____.
     a. sensational   **b.** apathetic   **c.** empathetic   **d.** pathetic

d   **5.** Which is more important when it comes to deciding how much respect we owe another species, intelligence or _____?
     a. presentiment   **b.** pathology   **c.** assent   **d.** sentience

b   **6.** After having a(n) _____ of an accident, Glen decided to be extra careful.
     a. pathology   **b.** presentiment   **c.** empathy   **d.** assent

a   **7.** She thinks teens tend to be more politically _____ than older citizens are.
     a. apathetic   **b.** pathetic   **c.** sentient   **d.** pathological

c   **8.** Physicians receive extensive training in the _____ of diseases.
     a. assent   **b.** sensationalism   **c.** pathology   **d.** apathy

c   **9.** Having been in a similar position, the personnel manager had _____ for Mr. Hunter's desire to change his job in the company.
     a. presentiment   **b.** pathology   **c.** empathy   **d.** sensationalism

b   **10.** The preachy lecture was filled with annoyingly _____ advice.
     a. assenting   **b.** sententious   **c.** sentient   **d.** pathological

Challenge: Because animals cannot give or withhold their _____ in situations affecting their welfare, pet owners try to be _____ to the needs of their sentient companions.
c   **a.** apathy…pathetic   **b.** pathology…assenting   **c.** assent…empathic

"Bigfoot Kidnaps Local Girl!"

"Lose 80 Pounds on the All-Chocolate Diet!" **(1)** "Wax Sculpture of Elvis Shows Signs of *Sentience!*" "Celebrity's Identical Twin Actually from Mars!" **(2)** If you've ever stood in line at a grocery store, you have probably noticed a rack of newspapers with *sensational* headlines like these. Outrageous claims are often made in tabloid newspapers. But how did tabloid journalism begin?

At the turn of the century, the term *tabloid* referred to a condensed version of the regular newspaper. These shortened papers had minimal news content and focused on human interest stories. These tabloids also contained many pictures and often presented fictional pieces as well. Over time, these publications have evolved into a profitable form of sensational entertainment.

Some media critics argue that tabloids further the democratic nature of a diverse media. They think that, even though the main purpose of tabloid journalism is entertainment, it can also be informative and thought provoking. **(3)** To these critics, it is *sententious* to say that tabloids are a disgrace to the journalistic principles of honest, objective reporting. **(4)** Although most tabloids certainly violate journalistic *sensibilities* and standards, the tabloids continue to be highly popular among Americans. Why is this?

Many Americans avidly read reputable newspapers every day. **(5)** However, many others are *apathetic* about the goings-on in the world. In the early 1950s, some writers found that if they made up wild stories, more people would read their papers. Many readers believed that a paper wouldn't print a story that wasn't true. Due in part to their audience's naiveté, tabloid newspapers began to flourish.

Today, tabloid journalism takes many forms: newspapers, magazines, eZines, and even television programs. Many current tabloid-media consumers know not to take the stories seriously. **(6)** Still, they may enjoy learning about their favorite celebrity's *pathological* shopping habits—whether the story is true or not. **(7)** Or, people may read a story about a star's difficult childhood, which may generate *empathy* for the star and possibly gain a new fan or two. **(8)** Viewers may be shocked by a television program about people who had *presentiments* of disasters that later came true. The widespread audience of tabloid media attests to the genre's entertainment value.

Celebrities, on the other hand, are often hostile towards tabloid journalism. **(9)** Tabloid journalists sometimes publish candid photographs and stories about a particular star, without his or her *assent.* Frequently, celebrity photos are "creatively interpreted" into sensational stories. For example, a tabloid photographer might take a picture of a supermodel while she is out jogging, with a tired expression, no makeup, and messy hair. **(10)** The tabloid might crop the photo so that you see just her face, and then write an article that portrays the model as a *pathetic* nervous wreck due to some personal scandal that— you guessed it—may or may not be true.

So, the next time you are waiting to pay for your groceries, you might be shocked and scandalized by the tabloid headlines, that is, if you believe them.

Each sentence below refers to a numbered sentence in the passage. Write the letter of the choice that gives the sentence a meaning that is closest to the original sentence.

_____a_____ **1.** "Wax Sculpture of Elvis Shows Signs of _____!"
   a. Consciousness   **b.** Sentimentality   **c.** Melting   **d.** Foreboding

_____d_____ **2.** You have probably noticed a rack of newspapers with _____ headlines like these.
   a. terrible   **b.** pitiful   **c.** agreed-upon   **d.** attention-getting

_____d_____ **3.** To these critics, it is _____ to say that tabloids are a disgrace to journalistic principles.
   a. uninterested   **b.** passionate   **c.** false   **d.** pompous

_____a_____ **4.** Most tabloids violate journalistic _____ and standards.
   a. sensitivities   **b.** morals   **c.** abnormalities   **d.** consciousness

____c____ **5.** However, many others are _____ the goings-on in the world.
    a. open to   **b.** aware of   **c.** uninterested in   **d.** in agreement with

____b____ **6.** Still, they may enjoy learning about their favorite celebrity's _____ shopping habits—whether the story is true or not.
    a. ardent   **b.** disease-like   **c.** life-threatening   **d.** unconscious

____b____ **7.** Or, people may read a story about a star's difficult childhood, which may generate _____ for the star and possibly gain a new fan or two.
    a. lack of feeling   **b.** understanding   **c.** recollection   **d.** self-righteousness

____d____ **8.** Viewers may be shocked by a television program about people who had _____ of disasters that later came true.
    a. diseases   **b.** interests   **c.** agreements   **d.** premonitions

____a____ **9.** Tabloid journalists sometimes publish candid photographs and stories about a particular star, without his or her _____.
    a. agreement   **b.** concern   **c.** understanding   **d.** moralizing

____c____ **10.** The tabloid might crop the photo so that you just see her face, and then write an article that portrays the model as a _____ nervous wreck.
    a. shocking   **b.** pretend   **c.** pitiful   **d.** conscious

Indicate whether the statements below are TRUE or FALSE according to the passage.

____T____ **1.** The way a photograph is used can greatly influence the impression it gives to viewers.

____F____ **2.** Because they are so obviously full of false information, tabloid newspapers are not popular.

____F____ **3.** Tabloids are vital for keeping the population fully informed of important world events.

WRITING EXTENDED RESPONSES

Look at the headlines mentioned at the beginning of the reading passage. Now, come up with a sensational headline of your own and write the news story to go with it. Your story, which can be as realistic or as ridiculous as you want, should be at least three paragraphs long. Make sure your headline and your story are suitable for class. Use at least three lesson words in your story and underline them.

WRITE THE DERIVATIVE

Complete the sentence by writing the correct form of the word shown in parentheses. You may not need to change the form that is given.

__assented__   **1.** The millionaire _____ in writing, enabling the charity to benefit from the sale of her land. (*assent*)

__pathologist__   **2.** The _____ conducted a study of the new disease. (*pathology*)

apathetic   **3.** Carl's friends accused him of being _____ when he said he didn't care who became class president. *(apathy)*

sensationalism   **4.** The veteran journalist thinks that modern-day news media rely too heavily on _____ . *(sensational)*

presentiment   **5.** The soundtrack of a movie will often give you a _____ that something important is about to happen. *(presentiment)*

sentience   **6.** Emergency-room doctors use a variety of methods to determine a patient's _____ . *(sentient)*

Empathizing   **7.** _____ with other people's problems is a sign of kindness. *(empathy)*

sensibilities   **8.** When it comes to art and music, different generations usually have different _____ . *(sensibility)*

pathetic   **9.** My initial attempts to play the trumpet produced _____ results, but eventually I began to get the hang of it. *(pathetic)*

sententiousness   **10.** The _____ of the graduation speaker disappointed the audience. *(sententious)*

FIND THE EXAMPLE

Choose the answer that best describes the action or situation.

d   **1.** One who most needs to be *empathic* toward his or her clients
     a. baker   **b.** plumber   **c.** grocer   **d.** counselor

c   **2.** Something that would LEAST reflect artistic *sensibility*
     a. favorite music   **b.** style of dress   **c.** choice of soda   **d.** selection of art

a   **3.** An example of *apathetic* behavior
     a. ignoring the news   **b.** studying hard   **c.** finding a job   **d.** running for office

a   **4.** Something that is *sentient*
     a. pony   **b.** fencepost   **c.** rock   **d.** flower

b   **5.** One characteristic of *pathology*
     a. normalcy   **b.** abnormality   **c.** commonness   **d.** superiority

c   **6.** Someone whose job most relies on *presentiments*
     a. historian   **b.** newscaster   **c.** fortuneteller   **d.** astronaut

c   **7.** The best way to give your *assent*
     a. say no   **b.** walk away   **c.** say yes   **d.** think carefully

d   **8.** An example of a *sensational* headline
     a. Man Finds Dog   **b.** Kids Win Award   **c.** Building Completed   **d.** Senator Breathes Fire

a   **9.** Another word for *sententious*
     a. preachy   **b.** heavy   **c.** sleepy   **d.** tasty

b   **10.** Something that is most likely to seem *pathetic*
     a. prize bull   **b.** hungry dog   **c.** racehorse   **d.** chicken à la king

Prefixes, Roots, and Suffixes

The Prefixes *sym-*, *syn-*, and *syl-*

The prefixes *sym-*, *syn-*, *syl-* mean "together with" or "the same" and come from ancient Greek. Although these prefixes are quite common, they often have looser meanings. For example, the word *synopsis* has word elements meaning "together" and "view." A *synopsis* is a brief summary or overview, or something where one might "view things together."

Prefix	Meaning	Language Origin	Word	Word Meaning
sym-, syn-, syl-	same, together	Greek	synonym	word with the same meaning

Practice

You can combine the use of context clues with your knowledge of these prefixes to make intelligent guesses about the meanings of words. All of the sentences below contain a word formed with the prefixes *syl-*, *sym-*, or *syn-*. Read the sentences and write down what you think the word in italics means. Then check your definition with the one you find in the dictionary, remembering to choose the definition that best fits in the sentence.

1. Let's *synchronize* our watches so that we can coordinate our activities.

   My definition _____

   Dictionary definition to cause to occur or operate at the same time as something else.

2. I *sympathize* with anybody who has tried to hold down a job while also taking a heavy schedule of classes.

   My definition _____

   Dictionary definition to feel or express compassion, as for another's suffering; commiserate

3. In many movies stars *lip-synch* songs that are actually recorded by others.

   My definition _____

   Dictionary definition to move the lips in synchronization with recorded speech or song

4. The popular column was *syndicated* to over 100 papers across the country.

   My definition _____

   Dictionary definition to sell directly to independent stations

5. Several very successful films are *syntheses* of animation and live action.

   My definition _____

   Dictionary definition the combining of separate elements or substances to form a coherent whole

6. The plants in the carefully planned garden were in perfect *symmetry* on either side of a path that passed through the center.

My definition _____

Dictionary definition _____ exact correspondence of form _____

7. Thousands of physicians attended the *symposium* for pediatric radiologists.

My definition _____

Dictionary definition ___ a meeting or conference for discussion of a topic ___

8. The *syllabus* of the course described each topic and assignment for the semester.

My definition _____

Dictionary definition ___ an outline or summary of the main points of a course ___

Review Word Elements

Reviewing word elements helps you to remember them and use them in your reading. Below, write the meaning of the word elements you have studied.

Word	Word Element	Type of Element	Meaning of Word Element
predecessor	*cede*	root	go; withdraw
semirigid	*semi-*	prefix	half; partial
egress	*grad, gress*	root	go; step
interject	*ject*	root	throw
autonomous	*auto-*	prefix	self
concurrent	*cur*	root	run
isothermal	*iso-*	prefix	equal
aversion	*vert, vers*	root	turn
sentient	*sens, sent*	root	feeling
hemiparasite	*hemi-*	prefix	half
apathy	*path*	root	feeling
equinox	*equi-*	prefix	equal
credence	*cred*	root	belief
perimeter	*peri-*	prefix	around
circumference	*circum-*	prefix	around

Time

WORD LIST

ensue	ephemeral	harbinger	imminent	interim
interminable	perennial	precipitate	provisional	retrospective

How often have you heard phrases such as "Time is of the essence," "There's no time like the present," "Time is money," or "Timing is everything"? Time is constantly in our thoughts and speech. The words in this lesson deal with ways in which people refer to and think about time.

1. **ensue** (ĕn-sōō´) *verb* from Latin *en-*, "put into" + *sequi*, "to follow"
   a. To occur as a consequence or result of something else
   • The floods caused damage to property, but the famine that **ensued** caused extreme hardship for thousands of people.
   b. To take place subsequently; to follow
   • The police report said, "The sun went down, and a riot **ensued**."

   ensuing *adjective* When the Fed lowered interest rates, real-estate analysts predicted an **ensuing** rise in home buying.

2. **ephemeral** (ĭ-fĕm´ər-əl) *adjective* from Greek epi-, "on" + *hemera*, "day"
   Lasting for a very brief time; fleeting; transitory
   • The children squealed with delight as the **ephemeral** bubbles vanished only seconds after they were formed.

   ephemeral bubbles

3. **harbinger** (här´bĭn-jər) from Old French *herbergier*, "to lodge"
   a. *noun* A person or thing that signals or foreshadows what is to come
   • The two leaders' warm handshake was a **harbinger** of successful negotiations.
   b. *verb* To signal the approach of; to warn
   • The sudden ripples in the water in our glasses **harbingered** the beginning of an earthquake.

4. **imminent** (ĭm´ə-nənt) *adjective* from Latin *imminere*, "to hang over"
   About to occur; impending
   • Because the building was in **imminent** danger of collapsing, the police roped off the area around it.

   imminence *noun* The **imminence** of our moving date finally persuaded us that we had to start packing.

5. **interim** (ĭn´tər-ĭm) from Latin *interim*, "in the meantime"
   a. *noun* A period of time between two events
   • In the **interim** between the matinee and the evening performance, the orchestra members ate a quick meal.
   b. *adjective* Temporary; not final
   • Workers and management pledged to abide by the terms of an **interim** agreement while they continued to negotiate a long-term contract.

Point out that the meaning of the words *harbinger, interim,* and *provisional* involve looking forward in time or anticipating a future event. In contrast, *retrospective* involves looking back in time.

Don't confuse *imminent* with *eminent,* which means "distinguished" or "prominent."

6. **interminable** (ĭn-tûr′mə-nə-bəl) *adjective* from Latin *in-*, "not" + *terminare,* "to terminate"
Being or seeming to be without end; endless; tiresomely long
• Even short car trips can seem **interminable** to young children.

7. **perennial** (pə-rĕn′ē-əl) from Latin *per-*, "throughout" + *annus,* "year"
   a. *adjective* Enduring; recurring or long-lasting
      • As her room full of trophies showed, she was a **perennial** golf champ.
   b. *noun* A plant that grows again each year
      • My garden's **perennials** were planted long before I bought the house.

> Unlike *perennial, interminable* usually has a negative connotation.

8. **precipitate** from Latin *praecipitare,* "to throw headlong"
   a. *verb* (prĭ-sĭp′ĭ-tāt′) To cause to happen, especially suddenly or prematurely
      • A few careless remarks **precipitated** the argument.
   b. *verb* (prĭ-sĭp′ĭ-tāt′) To throw forcefully downward
      • The collapsing bridge **precipitated** debris into the lake.
   c. *adjective* (prĭ-sĭp′ĭ-tĭt′) Sudden; unexpected
      • The driver's **precipitate** stop caused the passengers to jerk forward.

   precipitation *noun* Sheila and Joey were responsible for the **precipitation** of a family feud.

> *Precipitation* also refers to any form of water, such as rain or snow, that is "thrown down" from the sky.

9. **provisional** (prə-vĭzh′ə-nəl) *adjective* from Latin *providere,* "to foresee; to provide for"
Serving only for the time being; temporary
• The **provisional** office assistant was so adept at her duties that she was soon hired as a full-time employee.

10. **retrospective** (rĕt′rə-spĕk′tĭv) from Latin *retro-*, "backward" + *specere,* "to look"
    a. *adjective* Looking back on, contemplating, or directed to the past
       • Once, in a **retrospective** mood, my father showed me his high-school yearbook and told me stories about his teenage days.
    b. *noun* An exhibit or a performance of works produced by an artist over a considerable time period
       • The **retrospective** included the painter's most prominent works from 1960 to the present.

    retrospect *noun* In **retrospect,** George realized he should have studied harder for the test.

    retrospect *verb* Both my grandmother and my great-aunt often **retrospect** about their childhood in Argentina.

WORD ENRICHMENT

Going backward

The Latin prefix *retro-*, meaning "backward," is used in many words besides *retrospective.* For example, *retroactive* means "going back to an earlier time." A pay raise granted in April might be *retroactive* to January, meaning workers would get additional pay for hours already worked since January. *Retrogress* is a verb that means "to move backward, or to return to an earlier, inferior state." (*Retrograde* is the adjective form of *retrogress.*) *Retro* is also a word used to describe fashion or décor that is reminiscent of things past.

WRITE THE CORRECT WORD

Write the correct word in the space next to each definition.

harbinger	**1.** signal of a future event	**retrospective**	**6.** contemplating the past
perennial	**2.** enduring; recurring	**imminent**	**7.** about to happen
interminable	**3.** endless	**ephemeral**	**8.** fleeting; short-lived
precipitate	**4.** to cause suddenly	**provisional**	**9.** temporary
ensue	**5.** to occur as a result	**interim**	**10.** a time between two events

COMPLETE THE SENTENCE

Write the letter for the word that best completes each sentence.

a **1.** Enjoy your achievements as they come, because success can be _____.
    a. ephemeral   **b.** imminent   **c.** interminable   **d.** perennial

d **2.** When you have a blister on your foot, even a short walk can seem _____.
    a. precipitate   **b.** retrospective   **c.** provisional   **d.** interminable

c **3.** When the coach retired unexpectedly, the school board appointed a(n) _____ coach until a permanent replacement could be chosen.
    a. retrospective   **b.** interminable   **c.** interim   **d.** imminent

b **4.** The new teacher was hired on a(n) _____ basis until she received certification.
    a. retrospective   **b.** provisional   **c.** ephemeral   **d.** precipitate

b **5.** When a natural disaster occurs, many social and economic problems _____.
    a. precipitate   **b.** ensue   **c.** retrospect   **d.** harbinger

a **6.** Shilo LaMott's _____ album contained songs from her entire music career.
    a. retrospective   **b.** provisional   **c.** precipitate   **d.** imminent

c **7.** Merry-go-rounds seem to be a(n) _____ attraction for young children.
    a. ephemeral   **b.** imminent   **c.** perennial   **d.** ensuing

d **8.** Flocks of migrating birds overhead are _____ of seasonal change.
    a. retrospectives   **b.** precipitation   **c.** imminence   **d.** harbingers

d **9.** A widely published news story about the acceptance of illicit campaign contributions _____ the resignation of the two public officials involved.
    a. ensued   **b.** provisioned   **c.** retrospected   **d.** precipitated

a **10.** The menacing music in the horror film signaled _____ disaster.
    a. imminent   **b.** precipitate   **c.** perennial   **d.** ephemeral

Challenge: The artist's _____ was titled "Look Back in Apathy," and true to the title, little interest from critics or the public _____.
a
    a. retrospective…ensued   **b.** interim…precipitated   **c.** harbinger…retrospected

Out of Kenya

From sleepy villages in Kenya, evidence of a new hero has emerged. Local babies, schools, and even oxen are being named for Barack Obama, Jr. **(1)** Obama's 2004 race for a seat in the U.S. Senate thrust him into global prominence, *precipitating* tremendous media attention for him and his entire extended family.

Barack Obama's relatives have lived in the village of Nyangoma-Kogelo, Kenya, for generations. His father, was a goatherd in his youth, but he was also a brilliant scholar who earned a scholarship to attend the University of Hawaii. There, he married Barack's mother, Ann, who was from Kansas.

When Obama was two, his parents divorced. His father left Hawaii to attend Harvard University. He then returned to his native Kenya, where he became a leading economist in the Finance Ministry. **(2)** His success was a *harbinger* of his son's future accomplishments.

Barack, Jr., was raised in Hawaii by his mother and his maternal grandparents. He spent several years of his childhood in Indonesia. **(3)** He graduated from Columbia University, and then worked as a community organizer, helping to alleviate *perennial* problems, such as poverty and discrimination, in poor urban neighborhoods. Next, he graduated from Harvard Law School, where he earned various academic and extra-curricular honors. **(4)** In the *ensuing* years, Obama worked as a civil rights lawyer, taught at the University of Chicago Law School, and became an Illinois state senator.

Never, however, did Barack Obama forget his Kenyan roots. In 1987, he traveled to Nyangoma-Kogelo for the first time. He visited with relatives who knew him only from his father's treasured photographs. **(5)** He was motivated to visit, in part, by a wish to feel closer to his deceased father, whom Obama knew only from *ephemeral* memories of his childhood.

(6) Visiting the village where his father grew up enabled Obama to gain *retrospective* insight into his father's life. On a second trip to see his relatives, he brought his fiancée, Michelle Robinson, and followed Kenyan tradition by asking for—and receiving—their permission to marry Michelle.

In 2004, when the U.S. Senate race in Illinois thrust Obama onto the national stage, Kenyan relatives followed his campaign closely. They heard him call himself "the skinny little kid with the funny name" who rose to prominence through dedication and hard work. **(7)** Through the autumn, with the election *imminent*, Obama's relatives watched as polls showed him surging ahead of his opponent. **(8)** While some other races were so close that election results were delayed until *provisional* ballots could be verified, Obama won a clear victory with more than 70 percent of the vote.

(9) The *interim* between the election and the inauguration was a busy time for the Obama clan in Kenya. Reporters from around the world came to Nyangoma-Kogelo to learn more about Barack Obama, Jr. **(10)** In fact, some relatives complained about the seemingly *interminable* requests for interviews. Other relatives traveled halfway around the world to see Barack Obama, Jr., sworn in as the only African American in the U.S. Senate. As they stood proudly in the audience, perhaps Obama's relatives thought about how appropriate his name is. In Swahili, *barack* means "blessed."

Each sentence below refers to a numbered sentence in the passage. Write the letter of the choice that gives the sentence a meaning that is closest to the original sentence.

_____a_____ **1.** Obama's 2004 race for a seat in the U.S. Senate thrust him into global prominence, _____ tremendous media attention.
   a. causing   **b.** undermining   **c.** signaling   **d.** following

_____c_____ **2.** His success was a _____ of his son's future accomplishments.
   a. reminder   **b.** termination   **c.** foreshadowing   **d.** performance

_____a_____ **3.** He helped to alleviate _____ problems, such as poverty and discrimination.
   a. recurring   **b.** annoying   **c.** simple   **d.** complex

___d___ **4.** In the _____ years, Obama worked as a civil rights lawyer.
    a. previous   **b.** same   **c.** difficult   **d.** following

___b___ **5.** Obama knew his father only from _____ memories of his childhood.
    a. long-lasting   **b.** fleeting   **c.** recurring   **d.** unreliable

___d___ **6.** Visiting the village where his father grew up enabled Obama to gain _____ insight into his father's life.
    a. very little   **b.** long-lasting   **c.** between events   **d.** looking back

___c___ **7.** Through the autumn, with the election _____, Obama's relatives watched as polls showed him surging ahead of his opponent.
    a. lasting briefly   **b.** nearly over   **c.** about to occur   **d.** happening suddenly

___a___ **8.** Some other races were so close that election results were delayed until _____ ballots could be verified.
    a. temporary   **b.** recurring   **c.** illegal   **d.** fleeting

___c___ **9.** The _____ between the election and the inauguration was a busy one.
    a. hard campaigning   **b.** celebration   **c.** time period   **d.** performance

___b___ **10.** Some relatives complained about the seemingly _____ requests for interviews.
    a. brief   **b.** endless   **c.** impending   **d.** rude

Indicate whether the statements below are TRUE or FALSE according to the passage.

___T___ **1.** Barack Obama, Jr., is highly educated.

___F___ **2.** Obama had little interest in his father's life in Kenya.

___T___ **3.** The Obama clan is supportive of Barack Obama's political career.

FINISH THE THOUGHT

Complete each sentence so that it shows the meaning of the italicized word.

1. The war was *precipitated* by _____ Answers will vary. _____

_____

2. In *retrospect*, I can see that _____ Answers will vary. _____

_____

WRITE THE DERIVATIVE

Complete the sentence by writing the correct form of the word shown in parentheses. You may not need to change the form that is given.

___perennials___ **1.** Most _____ should be planted in the spring or the fall. (*perennial*)

___imminence___ **2.** The darkening skies and plunging barometer hinted at the _____ of the storm. (*imminent*)

ensuing   **3.** With great skill and leadership, the governor handled the disaster and the
_____ public panic. (_ensue_)

retrospect   **4.** In _____, I think I should have included more facts to support my argument.
(_retrospective_)

precipitated   **5.** The Sundance Film Festival has _____ public interest in lesser-known,
independent films. (_precipitate_)

ephemeral   **6.** The post-election spirit of cooperation proved to be _____; once the legislators
returned from the holiday recess, partisanship quickly resurfaced. (_ephemeral_)

harbinger   **7.** The appearance of daffodils is a _____ of spring. (_harbinger_)

provisional   **8.** After the war, a _____ government took over until elections could be held.
(_provisional_)

interminably   **9.** To those defending the Alamo in 1836, Santa Anna's siege went on _____.
(_interminable_)

interim   **10.** The _____ principal was known for his jovial personality. (_interim_)

FIND THE EXAMPLE

Choose the answer that best describes the action or situation.

___d___   **1.** A word that describes something _provisional_
  a. definite   **b.** assured   **c.** bright   **d.** temporary

___c___   **2.** A _harbinger_ of morning
  a. vivid sunset   **b.** lullaby   **c.** light in the east   **d.** hearty laugh

___a___   **3.** Something that deserts _perennially_ lack
  a. water   **b.** heat   **c.** wind   **d.** animals

___a___   **4.** Something that is likely to _ensue_ after unusually heavy rains
  a. flooding   **b.** drought   **c.** snow   **d.** dust storms

___b___   **5.** Description that always applies to an _interim_ solution
  a. effective   **b.** short-lived   **c.** unapproved   **d.** long-lasting

___d___   **6.** Someone who is most likely to be the subject of a _retrospective_
  a. plumber   **b.** teacher   **c.** doctor   **d.** sculptor

___d___   **7.** Something that people are most likely to describe as _interminable_
  a. sleeping   **b.** eating lunch   **c.** breathing   **d.** waiting in line

___a___   **8.** Something that is always _imminent_
  a. tomorrow   **b.** yesterday   **c.** old times   **d.** distant future

___b___   **9.** Something that would likely _precipitate_ a fight
  a. parade   **b.** insult   **c.** smile   **d.** compliment

___d___   **10.** Something that is _ephemeral_
  a. monument   **b.** fact   **c.** jewel   **d.** flower

Levels of Activity or Excitement

WORD LIST

alacrity	composure	ennui	imperturbable	impetuous
incite	indolent	inertia	pandemonium	serenity

Everything, the outside physical world to our own bodies to our innermost emotions, varies in terms of the level of activity or excitement present. The words in this lesson will help you understand and express these aspects of daily life.

1. **alacrity** (ə-lăkʹrĭ-tē) *noun* from Latin *alacer*, "lively"
   a. Cheerful willingness; eagerness
   • Carmella accepted our invitation with **alacrity**.
   b. Speed or quickness
   • His **alacrity** in writing news stories on deadline earned him the nickname "Speedy."

2. **composure** (kəm-pōʹzhər) *noun* from Latin *componere*, "to put together"
   Control over one's emotions; calmness; self-control
   • If you lose your **composure** during an argument, you are likely to lose the argument.

   compose *verb* The bride took a moment to **compose** herself before walking down the aisle.

3. **ennui** (ŏn-wēʹ) *noun* from Old French *ennuyer*, "to annoy; to bore"
   Weary dissatisfaction resulting from lack of interest; boredom
   • Charles Baudelaire wrote about doing seemingly crazy things to relieve soul-deadening **ennui**.

4. **imperturbable** (ĭmʹpər-tûrʹbə-bəl) *adjective* from Latin *im-*, "not" + *per-*, "thoroughly; completely" + *turbare*, "to throw into disorder"
   Unshakably calm
   • The **imperturbable** captain continued to give orders to her crew as the boat began to sink.

5. **impetuous** (ĭm-pĕchʹ oō-əs) *adjective* from Latin *impetus*, "impetus"
   Given to acting without thinking; impulsive; hasty
   • **Impetuous** shoppers can quickly find themselves deep in debt.

6. **incite** (ĭn-sītʹ) *verb* from Latin *incitare*, "to stimulate; to put in motion"
   To provoke to action; stir up; urge on
   • The troublemakers **incited** a food fight.

   incitement *noun* The calls of "Revenge!" were an **incitement** to violence.

Have students classify words as related to activity and excitement (for example, *incite* and *impetuous*) or related to inactivity and boredom (for example, *ennui* and *indolent*). Allow students to explain their choices.

ennui

> Don't confuse *incite* with *insight*—the capacity to determine the true nature of a situation.

7. **indolent** (ĭn′də-lənt) *adjective* from Latin *in-*, "not" + *dolere*, "to feel pain"
Habitually lazy; lethargic
- "You're **indolent** and you don't even know what that means!" barked the irate, sharp-tongued coach at his lazy, out-of-shape player.

indolence *noun* Tyra has so much natural talent for math that **indolence** must be the reason for her poor grades in that class.

8. **inertia** (ĭ-nûr′shə) *noun* from Latin *in-*, "not" + *ars*, "skill"
Resistance to motion, action, or change
- Large organizations often suffer from **inertia,** but once they get moving, they can wield considerable power.

inert *adjective* Unable to move or act
- It was frustrating to lie there, ill and **inert** in bed, while my friends played outside.

> In physics, *inertia* is the tendency of a body at rest to remain at rest, or of a body in motion to remain in motion, unless acted on by an outside force.

9. **pandemonium** (păn′də-mō′nē-əm) *noun* from Greek *pan-*, "all" + *daimonion*, "lesser god; demon"
Wild, noisy uproar; chaos
- **Pandemonium** broke out in the theater when smoke began rising from the balcony.

> John Milton coined the term *pandemonium* in his 1667 epic poem *Paradise Lost*.

10. **serenity** (sə-rĕn′ĭ-tē) *noun* from Latin *serenus*, "clear"
Peacefulness; calmness
- In a famous quotation, people ask to be granted the **serenity** to accept the things that they cannot change.

serene *adjective* The **serene** lake looked like a sheet of glass.

ANALOGIES

On the answer line, write the letter of the answer that best completes each analogy. Refer to Lessons 27–29 if you need help with any of the lesson words.

___c___ **1.** Interminable is to end as _____.
- **a.** impetuous is to quick
- **b.** pathology is to physician
- **c.** imperturbable is to anger
- **d.** inertia is to slowness

___c___ **2.** Pandemonium is to disorder as _____.
- **a.** sensational is to riot
- **b.** assent is to deny
- **c.** composure is to calmness
- **d.** sententious is to numbness

___a___ **3.** Presentiment is to before as _____.
- **a.** retrospective is to after
- **b.** harbinger is to bird
- **c.** imminent is to medicine
- **d.** ensue is to attorneys

___d___ **4.** Empathy is to callous as _____.
- **a.** forest is to path
- **b.** serenity is to angry
- **c.** callous is to hand
- **d.** money is to poor

WRITE THE CORRECT WORD

Write the correct word in the space next to each definition.

composure	**1.** emotional control		serenity	**6.** peacefulness
pandemonium	**2.** chaos; uproar		indolent	**7.** lazy; lethargic
alacrity	**3.** eagerness or speed		impetuous	**8.** hasty; impulsive
incite	**4.** to provoke		imperturbable	**9.** unshakably calm
inertia	**5.** resistance to movement		ennui	**10.** boredom; weary dissatisfaction

COMPLETE THE SENTENCE

Write the letter for the word that best completes each sentence.

____a____ **1.** Overcome by _____, Fred slumped in a chair waiting for his life to happen.
   a. ennui   **b.** alacrity   **c.** pandemonium   **d.** composure

____c____ **2.** The painting of a tranquil landscape conveyed a deep sense of _____.
   a. inertia   **b.** indolence   **c.** serenity   **d.** alacrity

____b____ **3.** People often regret _____ actions.
   a. indolent   **b.** impetuous   **c.** serene   **d.** inert

____b____ **4.** Jake responds with _____ the moment his beloved grandparents need help with anything.
   a. inertia   **b.** alacrity   **c.** incitement   **d.** pandemonium

____a____ **5.** Rita's _____ was momentarily shaken when the rest of us shouted "Surprise!"
   a. composure   **b.** pandemonium   **c.** alacrity   **d.** incitement

____d____ **6.** The people who live next door are _____; nothing seems to bother them.
   a. impetuous   **b.** incited   **c.** inert   **d.** imperturbable

____b____ **7.** The _____ of the massive bureaucracy made major policy changes nearly impossible.
   a. incitement   **b.** inertia   **c.** pandemonium   **d.** alacrity

____d____ **8.** Don't insult him; you'll just _____ him, and then we're all in trouble.
   a. compose   **b.** serene   **c.** inert   **d.** incite

____c____ **9.** Because of his _____, Harry can't handle jobs that require lots of energy and effort.
   a. serenity   **b.** imperturbability   **c.** indolence   **d.** composure

____a____ **10.** The teachers couldn't quiet the _____ in the playground.
   a. pandemonium   **b.** composure   **c.** alacrity   **d.** serenity

Challenge: Normally a person of chronic, impervious _____, Seth played Ping-Pong with an uncharacteristic and almost maniacal _____.
____b____   **a.** composure…inertia   **b.** indolence…alacrity   **c.** serenity…indolence

Blast Off but Keep Cool

If you don't like to be stuck at home for more than a day, imagine spending months confined to a spacecraft. Then picture yourself sharing its tiny living space with several other astronauts who are with you constantly.

(1) Only individuals with exceptional *composure* can handle the stress of such close confinement. That's why candidates need to exhibit more than just knowledge and physical fitness to be chosen as astronauts. Prospective astronauts must also undergo rigorous psychological testing. **(2)** Obviously, a tendency to respond with *alacrity* to immediate challenges is an important characteristic, but less obvious character traits are equally important. This is partly because the routine nature of long-term space missions can eventually lead to near-paralyzing boredom. **(3)** *Ennui* can quickly become dangerous if the astronauts lose interest in completing critical tasks.

For example, in the 1970s, a crew aboard the *Skylab* space station became so depressed when they fell behind schedule that they went on strike. It took a good deal of support and encouragement from mission control to get them back to work. **(4)** As you could probably guess, *indolence* is simply not an option on most space missions.

(5) Astronauts who *incite* conflict can also put their missions at risk. On Russia's 1976 *Soyuz-21* mission, the crew was not getting along. Soon, they began to complain so steadily of a sour odor that the mission was cut short. No cause was ever found, and no other crews ever smelled the odor. Psychologists now suspect that the smell was imaginary, brought on by tension.

Astronauts face many sources of stress. For instance, homesickness can be overwhelming when a person is in space for many months. The danger of hurtling through space can also cause great anxiety. **(6)** And, long periods of limited physical activity can make crewmembers feel almost *inert*.

Of course, the stresses involved in space travel are not limited to the long-term missions. **(7)** The ability to remain *imperturbable* in the face of sudden emergencies is imperative. **(8)** A certain mental and emotional *serenity* is needed to reason through critical problems and respond appropriately. In 1970, when an oxygen tank exploded, the *Apollo 13* crew handled the crisis calmly and rationally. They did not panic, and thus made it safely back to Earth.

Other crews have not behaved so heroically. **(9)** Full-scale *pandemonium* has not yet broken out aboard a spacecraft, but one Russian *Salyut* space-station crew became so angry with mission control that they cut off communications for twenty-four hours. **(10)** Such *impetuous* behavior is reminiscent of a child's temper tantrum, but the results are potentially far more serious.

Space exploration is exciting and important, but it is also costly and dangerous. Missions cannot afford to have a spacecraft— or its crew—break down. Fortunately, experts are refining techniques for selecting individuals who are likely to "keep it together," despite the challenges they may encounter in space.

Each sentence below refers to a numbered sentence in the passage. Write the letter of the choice that gives the sentence a meaning that is closest to the original sentence.

__b__ **1.** Only individuals with exceptional _____ can handle the stress of such close confinement.
  a. eagerness **b.** emotional control **c.** resources **d.** composition skill

__d__ **2.** Obviously, a tendency to respond with _____ to immediate challenges is an important characteristic.
  a. careful reasoning **b.** impulsive action **c.** peaceful slowness **d.** willingness and speed

__c__ **3.** _____ can quickly become dangerous.
  a. Energy **b.** Carefulness **c.** Boredom **d.** Haste

_____c_____ **4.** _____ is simply not an option on most space missions.

    a. Quickness   **b.** Energy   **c.** Laziness   **d.** Boredom

_____d_____ **5.** Astronauts who _____ conflict can also put their missions at risk.

    a. don't ruffle   **b.** impede all   **c.** respond to   **d.** stir up

_____d_____ **6.** And, long periods of limited physical activity can make crewmembers feel almost _____.

    a. eager and happy   **b.** stiff and sore   **c.** bored to tears   **d.** unable to move

_____c_____ **7.** The ability to remain _____ in the face of sudden emergencies is imperative.

    a. eager and excited   **b.** bored and kind   **c.** unshakably calm   **d.** robotically rational

_____c_____ **8.** A certain mental and emotional _____ is needed to reason through critical problems and respond appropriately.

    a. nervousness   **b.** eagerness   **c.** calmness   **d.** slowness

_____b_____ **9.** Full-scale _____ has not yet broken out aboard a spacecraft.

    a. control   **b.** chaos   **c.** animosity   **d.** conflict

_____c_____ **10.** Such _____ behavior is reminiscent of a child's temper tantrum.

    a. lazy   **b.** stirred up   **c.** impulsive   **d.** peaceful

Indicate whether the statements below are TRUE or FALSE according to the passage.

_____F_____ **1.** No astronaut has ever lost his or her temper.

_____T_____ **2.** Long confinement in a spacecraft affects people mentally.

_____T_____ **3.** To handle emergencies, astronauts must be good at problem solving and at remaining calm and rational.

WRITING EXTENDED RESPONSES

You have just read about a few of the traits that are necessary to be an astronaut. Other careers also require certain types of characteristics or personality traits. In an essay, identify a specific career and describe the traits that you think are most important for achieving success in that field. Your essay should be at least three paragraphs long. Use at least three lesson words in your essay and underline them.

WRITE THE DERIVATIVE

Complete the sentence by writing the correct form of the word shown in parentheses. You may not need to change the form that is given.

_____Inertia_____ **1.** _____ seemed to paralyze Louise; she didn't leave her room all day. *(inertia)*

_____Pandemonium_____ **2.** _____ broke out as the last second ticked off the clock and hordes of euphoric fans rushed onto the field. *(pandemonium)*

indolence	**3.**	Because of Kelly's _____, her mom's houseplants withered and died under Kelly's care. (*indolent*)
alacrity	**4.**	With _____ Kim acted on our suggestions. (*alacrity*)
impetuously	**5.**	Mike _____ added two boxes of expensive chocolates to his shopping cart. (*impetuous*)
serene	**6.**	Buddhist monks usually have a _____ demeanor. (*serenity*)
incitement	**7.**	The authorities argued that the Web site provided an _____ to violence. (*incite*)
Compose	**8.**	_____ yourself, Darius—she's just a person like you and me. (*composure*)
ennui	**9.**	Enrique's _____ was so overpowering that anyone near him began to feel listless, apathetic, and bored, too. (*ennui*)
imperturbable	**10.**	Our old dog is _____; even when the baby jumps on him, he doesn't get upset. (*imperturbable*)

FIND THE EXAMPLE

Choose the answer that best describes the action or situation.

b   **1.** The person for whom on-the-job *alacrity* is most important
     a. dog trainer   **b.** lifeguard   **c.** chess player   **d.** accountant

c   **2.** Something most likely to *incite* an argument
     a. clean room   **b.** handshake   **c.** insult   **d.** cuddly cat

d   **3.** Something often used as a symbol for *inertia*
     a. a hunting cheetah   **b.** a diving hawk   **c.** a lacrosse player   **d.** a bump on a log

b   **4.** An *impetuous* act
     a. writing an essay   **b.** kissing a frog   **c.** sweeping a floor   **d.** dressing for school

d   **5.** A possible sign of *ennui*
     a. laughing   **b.** dancing   **c.** running   **d.** yawning

a   **6.** A *serene* scene
     a. wooded hillside   **b.** spewing volcano   **c.** holiday parade   **d.** political rally

b   **7.** Phrase that applies to *indolent* people
     a. high maintenance   **b.** couch potato   **c.** pencil pusher   **d.** go-getter

b   **8.** NOT a sign of *composure*
     a. calm expression   **b.** trembling hands   **c.** soft voice   **d.** thoughtful rationality

c   **9.** Two careers in which *imperturbability* is key
     a. actor, boxer   **b.** clown, chef   **c.** referee, psychiatrist   **d.** wrestler, hog caller

c   **10.** An example of *pandemonium*
     a. orderly fire drill   **b.** polite applause   **c.** food fight   **d.** high five

Density, Weight, and Texture

WORD LIST

attenuate	diaphanous	effulgent	encumber	evanescent
palpable	permeate	pliant	ponderous	viscous

As you know, we are surrounded by objects that have drastically different densities, weights, and textures. The words in this lesson will help you understand and describe some of these differences in sophisticated ways.

Have students name things that are *diaphanous, effulgent, evanescent, palpable, pliant, ponderous,* and *viscous.*

1. **attenuate** (ə-tĕn´yōō-āt´) *verb* from Latin *ad-*, "toward" + *tenuare*, "to make thin"
   a. To make slender, fine, or small
     • The drought **attenuated** the once-mighty river to a thin trickle.
   b. To reduce in force, value, amount, or degree; to weaken
     • The company president never made jokes for fear that being friendly would **attenuate** his authority.

2. **diaphanous** (dī-ăf´ə-nəs) *adjective* from Greek *diaphainein*, "to be transparent"
   a. Of such fine texture as to be transparent
     • The bride wore a delicate gown with **diaphanous** sleeves.
   b. Vague; lacking substance
     • His **diaphanous** dreams of stardom were interrupted when his guitar teacher told him to play a scale.

3. **effulgent** (ĭ-fōōl´jənt) *adjective* from Latin *ex-*, "out" + *fulgere*, "to shine"
   Shining brilliantly; radiant; bright
   • The **effulgent** sequins on her shoes sparkled in the spotlight.

   effulgence *noun* My grandfather's military medals have a certain **effulgence** achieved through frequent polishing.

diaphanous material

4. **encumber** (ĕn-kŭm´bər) *verb* from Old French *encombrer*, "to block up"
   a. To put a heavy load on; to burden or weigh down
     • As I shopped, I gave no thought to how I would manage to walk home while **encumbered** with so many packages.
   b. To hinder; to impede
     • These new laws are **encumbering** my ability to make a profit!

   encumbrance *noun* His debts were a serious **encumbrance** to his attempts to gain financial independence.

5. **evanescent** (ĕv´ə-nĕs´ənt) *adjective* from Latin *e-*, "out" + *vanescere*, "to disappear"
   Vanishing or likely to vanish like vapor; fleeting
   • The actor cherished her **evanescent** moment of fame.

   evanescence *noun* The vapor that comes out of your mouth on a cold day is a good example of **evanescence**.

6. **palpable** (păl´pə-bəl) *adjective* from Latin *palpare*, "to touch gently"
   a. Capable of being handled, touched, or felt
      • The tension in my knotted shoulders was **palpable.**
   b. Obvious; easily perceived; noticeable
      • At the sound of the air-raid siren, a **palpable** fear filled the room.

   palpability *noun* The **palpability** of the mob's rage made it scarier.

7. **permeate** (pûr´mē-āt´) *verb* from Latin *per-*, "through" + *meare*, "to pass"
   a. To spread or flow throughout
      • The fragrance of lilies **permeated** the garden.
   b. To pass through the openings or spaces of
      • A few golden shafts of sunlight **permeated** the leafy canopy formed by the trees.

   permeability *noun* Selective **permeability,** the ability of membranes to let some things, but not others, pass through them, is what keeps you alive.

   permeable *adjective* A window screen is supposed to be **permeable** by air, but not by bugs.

> The opposite of *permeable* is *impermeable*.

8. **pliant** (plī´ənt) *adjective* from Latin *plicare*, "to fold"
   a. Easily bent or flexed
      • **Pliant** willow twigs are excellent for weaving baskets.
   b. Easily altered or modified; adaptable
      • "What a **pliant** tool this is," she exclaimed as she quickly converted the screwdriver to a chisel.
   c. Yielding easily to influence or domination
      • Maura was too **pliant** to resist her friends' persuasion to go shopping, even though she had a lot of homework to do.

   pliancy *noun* The **pliancy** of clay makes it good for sculpting.

> *Compliant* is a synonym of the third definition of *pliant*. Also, *pliantness* is an alternative way to say *pliancy*.

9. **ponderous** (pŏn´dər-əs) *adjective* from Latin *pondus*, "weight"
   a. Heavy; difficult to carry due to weight or bulk
      • The little boy could barely stand under the weight of his **ponderous** backpack.
   b. Lacking grace and fluency
      • The audience yawned through the clumsy, **ponderous** speech.

10. **viscous** (vĭs´kəs) *adjective*
    Sticky and thick; resistant to flow
    • Once gelatin has been cooked and chilled, it is **viscous** at room temperature.

    viscosity *noun* The **viscosity** of blood increases as it starts to clot.

WORD ENRICHMENT

Weighty words

As you have already seen, the word *ponderous* comes from the Latin word *pondus*, meaning "weight." The word *ponder* does, too. When you *ponder* something, you think about something "heavy" and "weigh" it in your mind. The word *pound*, though not from Latin, comes from an Old English root also meaning "weight."

WRITE THE CORRECT WORD

Write the correct word in the space next to each definition.

diaphanous	1. thin and transparent	viscous	6. sticky; thick
encumber	2. to weigh down	ponderous	7. heavy; bulky
pliant	3. bendable	permeate	8. to spread through
effulgent	4. radiant; shiny	evanescent	9. fleeting
palpable	5. obvious; noticeable	attenuate	10. to make thinner

COMPLETE THE SENTENCE

Write the letter for the word that best completes each sentence.

d 1. The _____ rhinestones on her denim jacket glinted in the sun.
   a. pliant   **b.** attenuated   **c.** encumbered   **d.** effulgent

a 2. The curtains were so _____ that they looked almost like a fine mist.
   a. diaphanous   **b.** palpable   **c.** pliant   **d.** ponderous

b 3. _____ by a heavy pack, the scout could barely make it up the steep trail.
   a. Permeated   **b.** Encumbered   **c.** Palpated   **d.** Attenuated

c 4. The excitement in the stands was _____ as the home team scored its second run.
   a. diaphanous   **b.** viscous   **c.** palpable   **d.** ponderous

c 5. In general, liquids become more _____ as they cool.
   a. effulgent   **b.** attenuated   **c.** viscous   **d.** diaphanous

a 6. Heat makes many metals more _____.
   a. pliant   **b.** evanescent   **c.** ponderous   **d.** encumbered

b 7. The spirit of revolution _____ the countryside when the king was deposed.
   a. attenuated   **b.** permeated   **c.** encumbered   **d.** pondered

c 8. The _____ of her good moods often caught her friends by surprise.
   a. diaphanousness   **b.** permeation   **c.** evanescence   **d.** attenuation

d 9. The new treatment _____ the symptoms of the disease.
   a. ponders   **b.** palpates   **c.** permeates   **d.** attenuates

a 10. The _____ medical textbook was more than 800 pages long.
   a. ponderous   **b.** diaphanous   **c.** effulgent   **d.** pliant

Challenge: The less _____ a liquid is, the more likely it is to _____ the surrounding environment; that is one reason why spills of some types of oil are more harmful to ecosystems than spills of other types of oil.

c   **a.** palpable…encumber   **b.** effulgent…attenuate   **c.** viscous…permeate

An Amazing Creation

It's stronger than the material used to make bulletproof vests. It absorbs tension without breaking. **(1)** It is so *diaphanous* that it's almost invisible. **(2)** You can hold it in your hand without feeling any *palpable* weight. What could it be? If you guessed a spider web, you are correct.

These amazing creations can be found almost everywhere. **(3)** You might notice *effulgent* webs dancing in the wind as you walk along a country road on a sunny day. You can also find these precise constructions indoors, in places such as attics, basements, and quiet corners. **(4)** The airy webs may seem *evanescent,* but in actuality, they're built quite soundly.

(5) Spiders produce silk, a liquid protein that hardens as it is *attenuated* into fine thread. They spin their silk from spinnerets, tube-shaped organs that expel silk, much as toothpaste is expelled from a tube. But why do spiders make silk?

(6) Spiders use their *pliant* webs to capture prey. The webs function as nets that trap living meals, which the spiders then wrap up in more silk. They also use their venom to paralyze their prey, which are usually insects, but, depending on the species of spider, can include small mammals, birds, or other creatures.

Many spiders also use their silk to weave egg sacs. Some species abandon the sac; others dutifully guard it. **(7)** Still others carry the *ponderous* sac around until the eggs are ready to hatch. **(8)** Apparently, that burden is not too much of an *encumbrance.*

Of special interest to scientists are orb spiders. They spin the familiar shiny webs often seen in gardens. These webs are made of different types of silk. **(9)** There is the *viscous* kind that captures prey. But of most interest is the "dragline" silk, used to make what looks like the spokes of a wheel. The diameter of a strand of dragline silk is far thinner than a human hair. The material is very light, but for its size, it is stronger than steel. In fact, a strand the thickness of your thumb could support a jumbo jet! Bridge engineers have studied dragline silk's strength and its ability to absorb tension. There are many potential uses for this amazing material, including artificial connective tissue, medical stitches, body armor, and biodegradable fishing lines.

Researchers are also studying the antiseptic properties of spider webs. For thousands of years, people have used spider webs to cover wounds. More recently, biologists have discovered why this practice has proven so beneficial: Orb spiders cover their webs with antiseptic chemicals. **(10)** These antibiotics can *permeate* a wound and help prevent infection.

Considering the many potential uses for spider silk, putting spiders to work producing it probably would be highly beneficial for humans. But efforts to create spider farms have failed; in close proximity, spiders tend to fight or even eat one another.

Believe it or not, scientists might soon be able to manufacture spider silk from goats' milk. Goats can be genetically modified to produce milk containing complex proteins found in spider silk. These protein strands can then be separated out of the milk, made into a powder, and spun into silk. In this way, we may be able to harness the amazing properties of spider silk without actually relying on the spiders themselves.

Each sentence below refers to a numbered sentence in the passage. Write the letter of the choice that gives the sentence a meaning that is closest to the original sentence.

___c___ **1.** It is so _____ that it's almost invisible.
  a. heavy and bulky **b.** brilliant and shiny **c.** thin and transparent **d.** flexible and loose

___d___ **2.** You can hold it in your hand without feeling any _____ weight.
  a. thinning **b.** thick **c.** burdensome **d.** noticeable

___a___ **3.** You might notice _____ webs dancing in the wind.
  a. shiny **b.** heavy **c.** vaporous **d.** flexible

___d___ **4.** The airy webs may seem _____, but in actuality, they're built quite soundly.
  a. bright **b.** long **c.** bulky **d.** fleeting

___d___ **5.** The silk hardens as it is _____ into fine thread.
    a. weighted   **b.** unraveled   **c.** bent   **d.** thinned

___a___ **6.** Spiders use their _____ webs to capture prey.
    a. flexible   **b.** sticky   **c.** transparent   **d.** shiny

___c___ **7.** Still others carry the _____ sac around until the eggs are ready to hatch.
    a. empty   **b.** see-through   **c.** heavy   **d.** shining

___d___ **8.** Apparently, that burden is not too much of a _____.
    a. vapor   **b.** trap   **c.** chore   **d.** hindrance

___b___ **9.** There is the _____ kind that captures prey.
    a. transparent, clear   **b.** thick, sticky   **c.** thin, weak   **d.** flexible, bendy

___a___ **10.** These antibiotics can _____ a wound and help prevent infection.
    a. spread through   **b.** irritate   **c.** infect   **d.** partially heal

Indicate whether the statements below are TRUE or FALSE according to the passage.

___T___ **1.** Genetic engineering may allow scientists to make substances similar to spider silk without relying on spiders.

___T___ **2.** A cable made of dragline spider silk would be stronger than a similar cable made of steel.

___F___ **3.** The ancient belief that spider webs could help heal wounds was primitive nonsense.

FINISH THE THOUGHT

Complete each sentence so that it shows the meaning of the italicized word.

1. The *ponderous* weight _____ Answers will vary. _____

_____

2. The *diaphanous* material _____ Answers will vary. _____

_____

WRITE THE DERIVATIVE

Complete the sentence by writing the correct form of the word shown in parentheses. You may not need to change the form that is given.

___ponderous___ **1.** Trying to get that _____ couch up the stairs was not easy. (*ponderous*)

___viscosity___ **2.** Motor oil loses its _____ over time. (*viscous*)

___attenuated___ **3.** After feeling ill from a flu vaccine, Kevin half-joked, "Doc, I think I'm more _____ than the virus in the vaccine ever was." (*attenuate*) _diaphanous_   **4.** The _____ fabric was perfect to use for making a veil. (_diaphanous_)

evanescent   **5.** The bright sun began to evaporate the _____ fog. (_evanescent_)

encumbrance   **6.** Which is a greater _____ to human happiness, war or poverty? (_encumber_)

pliancy   **7.** When it comes to playing a cello, the _____ of the bow is important. (_pliant_)

permeability   **8.** A tea bag's _____ is what makes it work. (_permeate_)

effulgence   **9.** The night sky was aglow with the stars' _____. (_effulgent_)

palpable   **10.** His fear was as _____ as the pain and pressure in his chest. (_palpable_)

FIND THE EXAMPLE

Choose the answer that best describes the action or situation.

___d___   **1.** Something that has _effulgence_
   a. textbook   **b.** loaf of bread   **c.** chalkboard   **d.** diamond ring

___a___   **2.** Something NOT known for its _evanescence_
   a. tree   **b.** fog   **c.** smoke   **d.** cloud

___d___   **3.** Something that can _permeate_ a room
   a. pencil   **b.** roach   **c.** table   **d.** aroma

___d___   **4.** Something _ponderous_
   a. feather   **b.** comic book   **c.** kitten   **d.** piano

___b___   **5.** A _viscous_ substance
   a. water   **b.** molasses   **c.** gasoline   **d.** air

___d___   **6.** Something most likely to be an _encumbrance_ during a job search
   a. academic success   **b.** athletic victories   **c.** successful career   **d.** felony conviction

___c___   **7.** Something _palpable_
   a. idea   **b.** principle   **c.** fatigued muscles   **d.** fictional character

___d___   **8.** Something that is often _diaphanous_
   a. winter coat   **b.** clown shoes   **c.** firefighter jacket   **d.** ballerina tutu

___a___   **9.** A way to _attenuate_ a blob of bread dough
   a. stretch it   **b.** thicken it   **c.** add to it   **d.** leave it alone

___b___   **10.** The thing most likely to be _pliant_
   a. wooden stick   **b.** flower stem   **c.** steel bar   **d.** concrete pillar

Prefixes, Roots, and Suffixes

The Prefixes *anti-* and *counter-*

The prefixes *anti-* and *counter-* both mean "opposite" or "against." The prefix *anti-*, also spelled *ant-*, comes from Greek. An *antifreeze* prevents liquids in a car's engine from freezing. Some words formed with *anti-* are hyphenated, such as *anti-inflammatory*. The prefix *counter-*, also spelled *contra-*, comes from Latin. The common word *counteract* means "to act against something," effectively canceling it out.

Prefix	Language Origin	Meaning	Word	Word Meaning
anti-, ant-	Greek	against, opposite	*anti*allergic	preventing or relieving allergies
counter, contra	Latin	against,	*counter*measure	a measure taken against another

Practice

You can combine the use of context clues with your knowledge of these prefixes to make intelligent guesses about the meanings of words. All of the sentences below contain a word formed with the prefixes *anti-, ant-, counter-,* or *contra-.* Read the sentences and write down what you think the word in italics means. Then check your definition with the one you find in the dictionary, remembering to choose the definition that best fits in the sentence.

1. Right is the *antithesis* of wrong.

My definition _____

Dictionary definition _____ direct contrast; opposition _____

2. Taking this medicine is *contraindicated* if you are about to drive or operate heavy equipment.

My definition _____

Dictionary definition _____ to indicate the inadvisability of _____

3. The writer *antagonized* government officials with his critical attacks on their policies.

My definition _____

Dictionary definition _____ to incur the dislike of _____

4. The senator's defeat in the election was a miserable *anticlimax* to a dazzling career.

My definition _____

Dictionary definition a decline viewed in disappointing contrast to previous events

5. It is often *counterproductive* to work when you are tired.

My definition _____

Dictionary definition _tending to hinder rather than to serve one's purpose_

6. His betrayal was the beginning of my *antipathy* toward him.

My definition _____

Dictionary definition _a strong feeling of aversion or repugnance_

7. The workers were confused when the manager *countermanded* her previous order.

My definition _____

Dictionary definition _to cancel or reverse_

8. The attorney presented a *counterproposal*, which the other attorney wisely accepted on behalf of his client.

My definition _____

Dictionary definition _a proposal offered to nullify or substitute for a pervious one_

Review Word Elements

Write the meaning of each italicized word element.

Word	Word Element	Type of Element	Meaning of Word Element
autocrat	*auto-*	prefix	self
synonym	*syn-*	prefix	same
regress	*grad*	root	go; step
dejected	*ject*	root	throw
discredit	*cred*	root	belief
perimeter	*peri-*	prefix	around
circumference	*circum-*	prefix	around
empathy	*path*	root	feeling
equitable	*equi-*	prefix	equal
cursory	*cur*	root	run
isothermal	*iso-*	prefix	equal
revert	*vert*	root	turn
presentiment	*sens*	root	feeling
hemiparasite	*hemi-*	prefix	half
predecessor	*cede*	root	go; withdraw
semirigid	*semi-*	prefix	half; partial

Contents

For your convenience, the lesson **Tests** and **Bonus** activities that accompany
Vocabulary for Achievement, Fourth Course, are available as reproducible
masters in this section. Answers are printed in color on the front of each
reproducible master for ease in locating.

This section also contains recordkeeping charts that may be reproduced for each of
your classes. These will help you keep track of student progress on **lesson exercises,**
Bonus activities, and **Tests.**

Tests

There are fifteen multiple-choice tests, each covering two consecutive lessons.
This format ensures that students can demonstrate proficiency with a wider set
of vocabulary words than is found in a single lesson.

Test formats resemble those of the lesson exercises. Each test is divided into two
parts of ten items each, allowing for the testing of all words in the two lessons. Part A
focuses on recognizing and recalling definitions, whereas Part B emphasizes placing
words within the context of sentences.

Bonuses

Twelve **Bonus** activities offer students further opportunities for reinforcement and
enrichment. These activities consist of crossword puzzles, word searches, sentence
completions, scrambled words, and other word-game formats. Depending on
classroom needs, use these activities as added practice, as reviews of previously
mastered words, or as extra-credit assignments.

Fourth Course

Student Record

Class Period _____

	Lesson 1 Exercises	Lesson 2 Exercises	Lesson 3 Exercises	Lesson 4 Exercises	Lesson 5 Exercises	Lesson 6 Exercises	Lesson 7 Exercises	Lesson 8 Exercises	Lesson 9 Exercises	Lesson 10 Exercises	Lesson 11 Exercises	Lesson 12 Exercises	Lesson 13 Exercises	Lesson 14 Exercises	Lesson 15 Exercises	Lesson 16 Exercises	Lesson 17 Exercises	Lesson 18 Exercises	Lesson 19 Exercises	Lesson 20 Exercises	Lesson 21 Exercises	Lesson 22 Exercises	Lesson 23 Exercises	Lesson 24 Exercises	Lesson 25 Exercises	Lesson 26 Exercises	Lesson 27 Exercises	Lesson 28 Exercises	Lesson 29 Exercises	Lesson 30 Exercises
1.																														
2.																														
3.																														
4.																														
5.																														
6.																														
7.																														
8.																														
9.																														
10.																														
11.																														
12.																														
13.																														
14.																														
15.																														
16.																														
17.																														
18.																														
19.																														
20.																														
21.																														
22.																														
23.																														
24.																														
25.																														
26.																														
27.																														
28.																														
29.																														
30.																														
31.																														
32.																														
33.																														
34.																														
35.																														

	Bonus: Lessons 1 & 2	Bonus: Lessons 3 & 4	Bonus: Lessons 5 & 6	Bonus: Lessons 7 & 8	Bonus: Lessons 9 & 10	Bonus: Lessons 11 & 12	Bonus: Lessons 13, 14, & 15	Bonus: Lessons 16, 17, & 18	Bonus: Lessons 19, 20, & 21	Bonus: Lessons 22, 23, & 24	Bonus: Lessons 25, 26, & 27	Bonus: Lessons 28, 29, & 30	Test: Lessons 1 & 2	Test: Lessons 3 & 4	Test: Lessons 5 & 6	Test: Lessons 7 & 8	Test: Lessons 9 & 10	Test: Lessons 11 & 12	Test: Lessons 13 & 14	Test: Lessons 15 & 16	Test: Lessons 17 & 18	Test: Lessons 19 & 20	Test: Lessons 21 & 22	Test: Lessons 23 & 24	Test: Lessons 25 & 26	Test: Lessons 27 & 28	Test: Lessons 29 & 30	SAT Practice Test
1.																												
2.																												
3.																												
4.																												
5.																												
6.																												
7.																												
8.																												
9.																												
10.																												
11.																												
12.																												
13.																												
14.																												
15.																												
16.																												
17.																												
18.																												
19.																												
20.																												
21.																												
22.																												
23.																												
24.																												
25.																												
26.																												
27.																												
28.																												
29.																												
30.																												
31.																												
32.																												
33.																												
34.																												
35.																												

BONUS: LESSONS 1 AND 2

(pages 1–12)

Use the following clues to identify the vocabulary words and write the words on the line to the right. Then circle each vocabulary word in the word-search box below. The words may overlap and may read in any direction.

1. The invention of new words (7 letters)

2. Something that is _____ is lacking in security or stability. (10 letters)

3. An expression that contains contradictory terms (8 letters)

4. A word formed from the first letter of each word in a series (7 letters)

5. A sense of doubt or uneasiness (5 letters)

6. Decisive; putting an end to doubt, question, or uncertainty (10 letters)

7. If you are anxious or fearful about the future, then you are _____. (12 letters)

8. A _____ is a nickname indicating affection or familiarity. (10 letters)

9. _____ plans are not fully worked out or agreed upon. (9 letters)

10. A word part, such as a prefix or suffix (5 letters)

11. Typical of informal language usage (10 letters)

12. Without exception or qualification (11 letters)

1. coinage
2. precarious
3. oxymoron
4. acronym
5. qualm
6. conclusive
7. apprehensive
8. diminutive
9. Tentative
10. affix
11. colloquial
12. categorical

Challenge

Locate and circle the eight additional vocabulary words in the word-search box.

dubious
indeterminate
metonymy
palindrome
portmanteau word
spoonerism
unequivocal
vacillate

```
P O R T M A N T E A U W O R D I O C S
U N A R O P R E T E N T A T I V E O U
N E G A N I O C A T E G O R I C A L O
E W C A D I M I N U T I V E F E L L I
Q S P O O N E R I S M L A U Q U I O R
U N A C R O N Y M B Y E R V K A O Q A
I C I E T R O B R E S U O I B U D U C
V E J P R S A O E R T P A I B V C I E
O V A C I L L A T E I O R E A M O A R
C A S U O K E R E I P I N J V E T L P
A F F I X I B Y D R E B I Y P A R J O
L E V I S U L C N O C O X Y M O R O N
T F G E A P A L I N D R O M E Y E W Q
A P P R E H E N S I V E L O V F R L K
```

BONUS: LESSONS 1 AND 2

(pages 1–12)

Use the following clues to identify the vocabulary words and write the words on the line to the right. Then circle each vocabulary word in the word-search box below. The words may overlap and may read in any direction.

1. The invention of new words (7 letters)   1. _____

2. Something that is _____ is lacking in security or stability. (10 letters) 2. _____

3. An expression that contains contradictory terms (8 letters)   3. _____

4. A word formed from the first letter of each word in a series (7 letters) 4. _____

5. A sense of doubt or uneasiness (5 letters)   5. _____

6. Decisive; putting an end to doubt, question, or uncertainty (10 letters) 6. _____

7. If you are anxious or fearful about the future, then you are _____. (12 letters) 7. _____

8. A _____ is a nickname indicating affection or familiarity. (10 letters) 8. _____

9. _____ plans are not fully worked out or agreed upon. (9 letters)   9. _____

10. A word part, such as a prefix or suffix (5 letters)   10. _____

11. Typical of informal language usage (10 letters)   11. _____

12. Without exception or qualification (11 letters)   12. _____

Challenge
Locate and circle the eight additional vocabulary words in the word-search box.

dubious
indeterminate
metonymy
palindrome
portmanteau word
spoonerism
unequivocal
vacillate

P	O	R	T	M	A	N	T	E	A	U	W	O	R	D	I	O	C	S
U	N	A	R	O	P	R	E	T	E	N	T	A	T	I	V	E	O	U
N	E	G	A	N	I	O	C	A	T	E	G	O	R	I	C	A	L	O
E	W	C	A	D	I	M	I	N	U	T	I	V	E	F	E	L	L	I
Q	S	P	O	O	N	E	R	I	S	M	L	A	U	Q	U	I	O	R
U	N	A	C	R	O	N	Y	M	B	Y	E	R	V	K	A	O	Q	A
I	C	I	E	T	R	O	B	R	E	S	U	O	I	B	U	D	U	C
V	E	J	P	R	S	A	O	E	R	T	P	A	I	B	V	C	I	E
O	V	A	C	I	L	L	A	T	E	I	O	R	E	A	M	O	A	R
C	A	S	U	O	K	E	R	E	I	P	I	N	J	V	E	T	L	P
A	F	F	I	X	I	B	Y	D	R	E	B	I	Y	P	A	R	J	O
L	E	V	I	S	U	L	C	N	O	C	O	X	Y	M	O	R	O	N
T	F	G	E	A	P	A	L	I	N	D	R	O	M	E	Y	E	W	Q
A	P	P	R	E	H	E	N	S	I	V	E	L	O	V	F	R	L	K

BONUS: LESSONS 3 AND 4

(pages 13–18, 21–26)

Unscramble the letters of each italicized word and write the word on the answer line to the right.

1. The boy's calm *edanorem* endears him to his elderly relatives, who like quiet gatherings.

2. This sumptuous banquet is sure to *tiastea* even the hungriest diner.

3. When you attend a formal event, you must display a certain level of *rodeumc*.

4. That mansion, filled with valuable antiques and works of art, is a showcase of *enolucep*.

5. The island had a(n) *nipracivol* government.

6. Volunteering at the local soup kitchen is a(n) *nevolebnet* act.

7. Some suburban areas have seen a large increase in the population of *ralfe* animals.

8. My brother's latest *dinogsera* dream is to own a baseball team.

9. The politician regretted his *repminatete* outburst during the debate.

10. Camila's *floigapter* spending habits put her deeply into debt.

11. Online advertisers often use *lyiw* approaches to get people to visit their Web sites.

12. The magician seemed to *gubelie* both children and adults at the birthday party.

13. Due to the *bitaronecex* of rental prices, Winston has to share his apartment with three roommates.

14. The exchange student was very respectful of the *remos* and culture of her host family.

15. There was such a(n) *feruits* of dessert choices that it seemed impossible to choose just one.

16. Janelle thought it was *yeulsemn* for her grandmother to drive a motorcycle.

17. Adam had nothing but *obeigln* thoughts toward the driver who cut him off.

18. I asked the librarian to recommend a good mystery that didn't have *guatuosirt* violence.

19. Caroline listened with amusement while her co-worker *eaairzgdng* his position in the company.

20. Because of his *aifslmtrouui* skills, the artist was known not only as a painter and a sculptor, but also as a writer.

1. demeanor
2. satiate
3. decorum
4. opulence
5. provincial
6. benevolent
7. feral
8. grandiose
9. intemperate
10. profligate
11. wily
12. beguile
13. exorbitance
14. mores
15. surfeit
16. unseemly
17. ignoble
18. gratuitous
19. aggrandize
20. multifarious

BONUS: LESSONS 3 AND 4

(pages 13–18, 21–26)

Unscramble the letters of each italicized word and write the word on the answer line to the right.

1. The boy's calm *edanorem* endears him to his elderly relatives, who like quiet gatherings.

   1. _____

2. This sumptuous banquet is sure to *tiastea* even the hungriest diner.

   2. _____

3. When you attend a formal event, you must display a certain level of *rodeumc*.

   3. _____

4. That mansion, filled with valuable antiques and works of art, is a showcase of *enolucep*.

   4. _____

5. The island had a(n) *nipracivol* government.

   5. _____

6. Volunteering at the local soup kitchen is a(n) *nevolebnet* act.

   6. _____

7. Some suburban areas have seen a large increase in the population of *ralfe* animals.

   7. _____

8. My brother's latest *dinogsera* dream is to own a baseball team.

   8. _____

9. The politician regretted his *repminatete* outburst during the debate.

   9. _____

10. Camila's *floigapter* spending habits put her deeply into debt.

    10. _____

11. Online advertisers often use *lyiw* approaches to get people to visit their Web sites.

    11. _____

12. The magician seemed to *gubelie* both children and adults at the birthday party.

    12. _____

13. Due to the *bitaronecex* of rental prices, Winston has to share his apartment with three roommates.

    13. _____

14. The exchange student was very respectful of the *remos* and culture of her host family.

    14. _____

15. There was such a(n) *feruits* of dessert choices that it seemed impossible to choose just one.

    15. _____

16. Janelle thought it was *yeulsemn* for her grandmother to drive a motorcycle.

    16. _____

17. Adam had nothing but *obeigln* thoughts toward the driver who cut him off.

    17. _____

18. I asked the librarian to recommend a good mystery that didn't have *guatuosirt* violence.

    18. _____

19. Caroline listened with amusement while her co-worker *eaairzgdng* his position in the company.

    19. _____

20. Because of his *aifslmtrouui* skills, the artist was known not only as a painter and a sculptor, but also as a writer.

    20. _____

BONUS: LESSONS 5 AND 6

(pages 27–38)

Use the clues to spell out the words on the answer blanks. Then identify the mystery person at the bottom of the page by writing the numbered letters on the lines with the corresponding numbers.

1. Gentle, easily manageable

1. d o c i l e
   4

2. State of lacking or doing without something

2. d e p r i v a t i o n
   12

3. Acting with confidence and force

3. a s s e r t i v e
   2

4. Showy, flashy, dramatic

4. f l a m b o y a n t
   9

5. To influence; to change

5. a f f e c t
   8

6. To go forward or onward

6. p r o c e e d
   15

7. To settle in a country or region where one is not a native

7. i m m i g r a t e
   5

8. Fearless; unwaveringly courageous

8. i n t r e p i d
   3

9. Of a peaceful nature; calm

9. p a c i f i c
   6   11

10. Impartial; free of bias

10. d i s i n t e r e s t e d
    1

11. Relaxed and easygoing

11. m e l l o w
    10

12. Not embarrassed; composed

12. u n a b a s h e d
    7

13. A raid; damage or destruction

13. d e p r e d a t i o n
    13

14. Loud, harsh, rasping, grating, or shrill

14. s t r i d e n t
    14

15. To leave one country or region and settle in another

15. e m i g r a t e
    16

S A N D R A   D A Y   O'C O N N O R
1 2 3 4 5 6   7 8 9   10 11 12 13 14 15 16

BONUS: LESSONS 5 AND 6

(pages 27–38)

Use the clues to spell out the words on the answer blanks. Then identify the mystery person at the bottom of the page by writing the numbered letters on the lines with the corresponding numbers.

1. Gentle, easily manageable
2. State of lacking or doing without something
3. Acting with confidence and force
4. Showy, flashy, dramatic
5. To influence; to change
6. To go forward or onward
7. To settle in a country or region where one is not a native
8. Fearless; unwaveringly courageous
9. Of a peaceful nature; calm
10. Impartial; free of bias
11. Relaxed and easygoing
12. Not embarrassed; composed
13. A raid; damage or destruction
14. Loud, harsh, rasping, grating, or shrill
15. To leave one country or region and settle in another

BONUS: LESSONS 7 AND 8

(pages 41–52)

Use the clues to complete the crossword puzzle.

The crossword grid contains the following filled answers:

- 1 Across: CONCILIATORY
- 3 Across: IMPORTUNE
- 7 Across: PATRONIZE
- 10 Across: EXTRICATE
- 13 Across: PEDANTIC
- 16 Across: EDIFY
- 17 Across: DIDACTIC
- 19 Across: MITIGATE

- 1 Down: CONDUCIVE
- 2 Down: RENOVATE
- 4 Down: PUNDIT
- 5 Down: ERUDITE
- 6 Down: AEGIS
- 8 Down: INDOCTRINATE
- 9 Down: ESOTERIC
- 11 Down: ELUCIDATE
- 12 Down: PEDAGOGY
- 14 Down: AMENDS
- 15 Down: MEDIATE
- 18 Down: IMBUE

Across

1. Peace-making; appeasing

3. To annoy with repeated and insistent requests

7. To support or sponsor

10. To free from difficulty or entanglement

13. Too concerned with book learning or formal rules

16. To instruct for intellectual, moral, or spiritual improvement

17. Intended to teach

19. To make less severe; to soften, lessen, or moderate

Down

1. Tending to cause or bring about; favorable to

2. To restore something to an earlier condition, as by repairing or remodeling

4. A person of great learning about a particular topic

5. Possessing great knowledge and scholarship

6. Protection; sponsorship; guidance

8. To instruct in a particular body of principles or ideology

9. Understood only by an elite, scholarly, or exclusive group

11. To explain or make clear

12. The art or profession of teaching

14. To make up for a wrong or a mistake; compensation

15. To help opposing sides reach an agreement

18. To inspire or influence thoroughly

BONUS: LESSONS 7 AND 8

(pages 41–52)

Use the clues to complete the crossword puzzle.

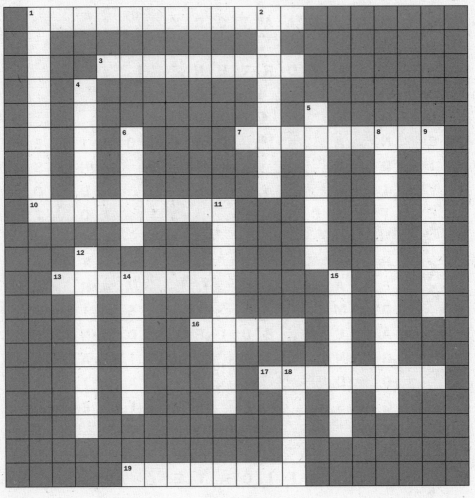

Across

1. Peace-making; appeasing
3. To annoy with repeated and insistent requests
7. To support or sponsor
10. To free from difficulty or entanglement
13. Too concerned with book learning or formal rules
16. To instruct for intellectual, moral, or spiritual improvement
17. Intended to teach
19. To make less severe; to soften, lessen, or moderate

Down

1. Tending to cause or bring about; favorable to
2. To restore something to an earlier condition, as by repairing or remodeling
4. A person of great learning about a particular topic
5. Possessing great knowledge and scholarship
6. Protection; sponsorship; guidance
8. To instruct in a particular body of principles or ideology
9. Understood only by an elite, scholarly, or exclusive group
11. To explain or make clear
12. The art or profession of teaching
14. To make up for a wrong or a mistake; compensation
15. To help opposing sides reach an agreement
18. To inspire or influence thoroughly

BONUS: LESSONS 9 AND 10

(pages 53–58, 61–66)

Use the following clues to identify the vocabulary words and write the words on the line to the right. Then circle each vocabulary word in the word-search box below. The words may overlap and may read in any direction.

1. Someone who is economical and thrifty can also be called _____. (6 letters)

2. To punish or criticize severely (8 letters)

3. In indirect or subtle expression of something is also called _____. (8 letters)

4. A general decline in business activity (9 letters)

5. To speak of in a disrespectful or slighting way, to belittle (9 letters)

6. Something that is _____ is bitter or sharp in tone. (11 letters)

7. To decrease or cause to decrease in value or price (10 letters)

8. Abusive or strongly critical language (9 letters)

9. _____ means poor, or lacking basic necessities. (8 letters)

10. Generous; liberal in giving (10 letters)

11. To _____ is to irritate or torment repeatedly. (6 letters)

12. Capable of meeting financial obligations (7 letters)

1. **frugal**
2. **chastise**
3. **innuendo**
4. **recession**
5. **disparage**
6. **acrimonious**
7. **depreciate**
8. **invective**
9. **Indigent**
10. **munificent**
11. **harass**
12. **solvent**

Challenge

Locate and circle the eight additional vocabulary words in the word-search box.

austerity
debunk
derogatory
equity
impugn
pecuniary
remunerate
vilify

D	E	R	O	G	A	T	O	R	Y	D	E	N	E	K	I	E	V	A
I	P	E	C	U	N	I	A	R	Y	E	O	E	T	D	O	S	H	P
S	C	M	Q	J	O	I	B	I	O	A	U	S	T	E	R	I	T	Y
G	H	U	U	U	P	N	E	E	P	R	T	H	E	P	E	T	N	I
P	A	N	N	O	I	S	S	E	C	E	R	E	I	R	J	S	E	N
A	S	E	R	O	M	T	L	I	M	P	U	G	N	E	R	A	C	N
H	A	R	A	S	S	I	Y	N	I	R	K	O	O	C	S	H	I	U
E	G	A	R	A	P	S	I	D	N	Y	A	P	F	I	O	C	F	E
A	R	T	P	A	A	A	P	I	N	F	R	U	G	A	L	F	I	N
C	D	E	B	U	N	K	E	G	E	I	D	V	D	T	V	E	N	D
M	K	E	L	E	W	T	M	E	U	L	R	I	X	E	E	K	U	O
O	L	E	R	E	E	I	A	N	D	I	O	N	S	V	N	D	M	I
S	O	Y	I	N	V	E	C	T	I	V	E	T	A	S	T	O	I	M
A	C	R	I	M	O	N	I	O	U	S	P	A	P	A	L	E	C	O

BONUS: LESSONS 9 AND 10

(pages 53–58, 61–66)

Use the following clues to identify the vocabulary words and write the words on the line to the right. Then circle each vocabulary word in the word-search box below. The words may overlap and may read in any direction.

1. Someone who is economical and thrifty can also be called _____. (6 letters)   1. _____

2. To punish or criticize severely (8 letters)   2. _____

3. In indirect or subtle expression of something is also called _____. (8 letters)   3. _____

4. A general decline in business activity (9 letters)   4. _____

5. To speak of in a disrespectful or slighting way, to belittle (9 letters)   5. _____

6. Something that is _____ is bitter or sharp in tone. (11 letters)   6. _____

7. To decrease or cause to decrease in value or price (10 letters)   7. _____

8. Abusive or strongly critical language (9 letters)   8. _____

9. _____ means poor, or lacking basic necessities. (8 letters)   9. _____

10. Generous; liberal in giving (10 letters)   10. _____

11. To _____ is to irritate or torment repeatedly. (6 letters)   11. _____

12. Capable of meeting financial obligations (7 letters)   12. _____

Challenge
Locate and circle the eight additional vocabulary words in the word-search box.

austerity
debunk
derogatory
equity
impugn
pecuniary
remunerate
vilify

```
D E R O G A T O R Y D E N E K I E V A
I P E C U N I A R Y E O E T D O S H P
S C M Q J O I B I O A U S T E R I T Y
G H U U P N E E P R T H E P E T N I
P A N N O I S S E C E R E I R J S E N
A S E R O M T L I M P U G N E R A C N
H A R A S S I Y N I R K O O C S H I U
E G A R A P S I D N Y A P F I O C F E
A R T P A A A P I N F R U G A L F I N
C D E B U N K E G E I D V D T V E N D
M K E L E W T M E U L R I X E E K U O
O L E R E E I A N D I O N S V N D M I
S O Y I N V E C T I V E T A S T O I M
A C R I M O N I O U S P A P A L E C O
```

BONUS: LESSONS 11 AND 12

(pages 67–78)

Unscramble the letters of each italicized word and write the word on the answer line to the right.

1. An artist at the fair drew a charming *uracatecir* of my little sister.

   1. __caricature__

2. There was a great *raydispit* between the work the painter had promised and what he delivered.

   2. __disparity__

3. Sometimes the chef *ideatevs* from a recipe to create something new.

   3. __deviates__

4. The orchestra took a(n) *chisiwalm* detour when it suddenly switched from Beethoven to the Beatles.

   4. __whimsical__

5. The talk show host likes to *ernbat* with his celebrity guests about the latest news in the entertainment world.

   5. __banter__

6. I thought it was completely *clurosuid* when my neighbor dressed her dog in a little track suit and sneakers.

   6. __ludicrous__

7. I noticed a(n) *rucenoceng* between the books I love to read and the books that my English teacher recommends for leisure reading.

   7. __congruence__

8. A(n) *geroenetohuse* crowd, made up of various ages and social backgrounds, attended the New Year's celebration in the city.

   8. __heterogeneous__

9. My music teacher can tell how much I've practiced by listening to the *ncenua* of my playing.

   9. __nuance__

10. My brother has a(n) *roldl* sense of humor that always surprises people.

    10. __droll__

11. Some teachers give detentions to students who make *tlipafnp* remarks in class.

    11. __flippant__

12. Harry felt that his starting pay was not *ecomusrantem* with the long training that he had endured to become a doctor.

    12. __commensurate__

13. Maria was being *ticfousae* when she said that only aliens should bother applying to college.

    13. __facetious__

14. Seth enjoyed the fact that his *iitwimcst* made all his friends laugh.

    14. __witticism__

15. The student council's decision to vote on a uniform dress code was *namotuntat* to approving the idea.

    15. __tantamount__

16. To encourage a healthier lifestyle, my doctor uses the *yoangal* of a car that needs fuel and proper maintenance in order to last a long time.

    16. __analogy__

17. The buildings in the lovely old town had a(n) *umngeehsooo* look to them, because new ones were built in the old style.

    17. __homogeneous__

18. Jasmine's brother was so funny that there was constant *lhiaytri* at our table, much to the annoyance of the other diners.

    18. __hilarity__

19. Ellie named her kitten *himtr* because it always seemed happy, and its silly antics made the family laugh.

    19. __Mirth__

20. My idea of a vacation is the *hitensaist* of relaxation, since it involves little sleep and an abundance of physical exercise.

    20. __antithesis__

BONUS: LESSONS 11 AND 12

(pages 67–78)

Unscramble the letters of each italicized word and write the word on the answer line to the right.

1. An artist at the fair drew a charming *uracatecir* of my little sister.

    1. _____

2. There was a great *raydispit* between the work the painter had promised and what he delivered.

    2. _____

3. Sometimes the chef *ideatevs* from a recipe to create something new.

    3. _____

4. The orchestra took a(n) *chisiwalm* detour when it suddenly switched from Beethoven to the Beatles.

    4. _____

5. The talk show host likes to *ernbat* with his celebrity guests about the latest news in the entertainment world.

    5. _____

6. I thought it was completely *clurosuid* when my neighbor dressed her dog in a little track suit and sneakers.

    6. _____

7. I noticed a(n) *rucenoceng* between the books I love to read and the books that my English teacher recommends for leisure reading.

    7. _____

8. A(n) *geroenetohuse* crowd, made up of various ages and social backgrounds, attended the New Year's celebration in the city.

    8. _____

9. My music teacher can tell how much I've practiced by listening to the *ncenua* of my playing.

    9. _____

10. My brother has a(n) *roldl* sense of humor that always surprises people.

    10. _____

11. Some teachers give detentions to students who make *tlipafnp* remarks in class.

    11. _____

12. Harry felt that his starting pay was not *ecomusrantem* with the long training that he had endured to become a doctor.

    12. _____

13. Maria was being *ticfousae* when she said that only aliens should bother applying to college.

    13. _____

14. Seth enjoyed the fact that his *iitwimcst* made all his friends laugh.

    14. _____

15. The student council's decision to vote on a uniform dress code was *namotuntat* to approving the idea.

    15. _____

16. To encourage a healthier lifestyle, my doctor uses the *yoangal* of a car that needs fuel and proper maintenance in order to last a long time.

    16. _____

17. The buildings in the lovely old town had a(n) *umngeehsooo* look to them, because new ones were built in the old style.

    17. _____

18. Jasmine's brother was so funny that there was constant *lhiaytri* at our table, much to the annoyance of the other diners.

    18. _____

19. Ellie named her kitten *himtr* because it always seemed happy, and its silly antics made the family laugh.

    19. _____

20. My idea of a vacation is the *hitensaist* of relaxation, since it involves little sleep and an abundance of physical exercise.

    20. _____

BONUS: LESSONS 13, 14, AND 15

(pages 81–98)

Use the clues to complete the crossword puzzle.

¹M	E	T	I	C	U	L	O	U	²S		³U	N	M	I	N	D	F	⁴U	L
I								O								N
S								V				⁵F				S
⁶D	E	S	P	O	T			E				I				C
E						⁷R	U	F	F	I	A	N				R
⁸M	I	N	U	⁹T	I	A		E				I				U
E			R		¹⁰D	I	L	I	G	E	N	C	E			P
A			E			G				K				U
N			P			N				Y				L
O			I											O
R			D					¹¹J	U	D	¹²I	C	I	O	U	S
			A							M			S
	¹³A	U	T	O	¹⁴C	R	¹⁵A	T	I	C		P
		I		U		U			R	
	¹⁶C	O		L		T			U		¹⁷E
	A	N		P		O			D		X
	S	A		¹⁸E	X	O	N	E	R	A	T	E
	T	B			N			N		O
¹⁹F	E	U	D	A	L		M		T		R
	E			E		Y				T

Across

1. Extremely careful and precise
3. Failing to give due care or attention; inattentive
6. A ruler with absolute power
7. A gangster or thug
8. Small, minor, or trivial details
10. Attentive care; carefulness
11. Having or exhibiting good, sound judgment
13. Ruling with unlimited power or authority
18. To free from blame
19. A system in which people were given protection and the use of land in return for loyalty, payments, and services to a lord

Down

1. A minor offense; a misdeed
2. A king, queen, or other noble
4. Lacking moral restraint; scornful of what is right or honorable
5. Difficult to please; insisting on getting exactly what one wants
9. Anxiety; a state of alarm, dread, or fear
12. Unwise, done or prone to doing things without careful thought
14. Deserving of blame or punishment for being wrong, evil, or harmful
15. Independence; self-determination or self-governance
16. A social class separated from others by profession, wealth, or hereditary rank
17. To obtain by force or threat

BONUS: LESSONS 13, 14, AND 15

(pages 81–98)

Use the clues to complete the crossword puzzle.

Across

1. Extremely careful and precise
3. Failing to give due care or attention; inattentive
6. A ruler with absolute power
7. A gangster or thug
8. Small, minor, or trivial details
10. Attentive care; carefulness
11. Having or exhibiting good, sound judgment
13. Ruling with unlimited power or authority
18. To free from blame
19. A system in which people were given protection and the use of land in return for loyalty, payments, and services to a lord

Down

1. A minor offense; a misdeed
2. A king, queen, or other noble
4. Lacking moral restraint; scornful of what is right or honorable
5. Difficult to please; insisting on getting exactly what one wants
9. Anxiety; a state of alarm, dread, or fear
12. Unwise, done or prone to doing things without careful thought
14. Deserving of blame or punishment for being wrong, evil, or harmful
15. Independence; self-determination or self-governance
16. A social class separated from others by profession, wealth, or hereditary rank
17. To obtain by force or threat

BONUS: LESSONS 16, 17, AND 18

(pages 101–118)

Unscramble the letters of each italicized word and write the word on the answer line to the right.

1. When the Senate committee presented its report, the chairwoman highlighted the *esnatil* points.

   1. ____**salient**____

2. "I wonder if Courtney will *nesedcodnc* to visit us now that she is famous," I said jokingly.

   2. ____**condescend**____

3. That successful restaurant was started by a(n) *prernuentree* who was willing to try something unusual.

   3. ____**entrepreneur**____

4. Gabriella made *poestururtisi* glances at her watch, hoping the meeting would end soon.

   4. ____**surreptitious**____

5. Although I have never been fond of squid, I pretended to enjoy the meal in *eredencef* to our hosts.

   5. ____**deference**____

6. Many New Yorkers feel that their city will always *natedopmier* in the worlds of culture and finance.

   6. ____**predominate**____

7. The cat licked its paw in a(n) *nanoncahtl* way to hide the fact that it was eyeing my tuna salad.

   7. ____**nonchalant**____

8. The attorney's *idarto* strategies usually result in courtroom victory for her clients.

   8. ____**adroit**____

9. The judge decided to *esuteqers* the jury while they decided the fate of the accused.

   9. ____**sequester**____

10. Joel behaved like a(n) *copshanty* by running errands for our boss and constantly praising her, all in order to get a promotion.

    10. ____**sycophant**____

11. Showing a(n) *nagraftl* disregard for the promise he made to his father, Wilson continued to play video games instead of doing his homework.

    11. ____**flagrant**____

12. The two friends exchanged *tivfuer* looks as they anticipated their escape from the boring party.

    12. ____**furtive**____

13. I will plan a(n) *zenvorused* with my pen pal when she visits this area next month.

    13. ____**rendezvous**____

14. The store's loyal *letceneli* continued to shop there, ignoring the giant chain store.

    14. ____**clientele**____

15. My brother's *hisvals* devotion to work left him with no time or energy to spend with his friends.

    15. ____**slavish**____

16. It is normal for wolves to *rleogv* before the alpha male, or leader of the wolf pack.

    16. ____**grovel**____

17. Grandma Moses didn't discover her *ntalte* artistic talent until she was in her seventies.

    17. ____**latent**____

18. The mouse crept *torybslunvuie* through the field, hoping to avoid the notice of the owl flying overhead.

    18. ____**unobtrusively**____

19. The little girl was *ivane* enough to believe her brother when he said that an alien lived in his closet.

    19. ____**naive**____

20. I couldn't believe I was talking to such a(n) *tasugu* person as a prince.

    20. ____**august**____

BONUS: LESSONS 16, 17, AND 18

(pages 101–118)

Unscramble the letters of each italicized word and write the word on the answer line to the right.

1. When the Senate committee presented its report, the chairwoman highlighted the *esnatil* points.

   1. _____

2. "I wonder if Courtney will *nesedcodnc* to visit us now that she is famous," I said jokingly.

   2. _____

3. That successful restaurant was started by a(n) *prernuentree* who was willing to try something unusual.

   3. _____

4. Gabriella made *poesturtsi* glances at her watch, hoping the meeting would end soon.

   4. _____

5. Although I have never been fond of squid, I pretended to enjoy the meal in *eredencef* to our hosts.

   5. _____

6. Many New Yorkers feel that their city will always *natedopmier* in the worlds of culture and finance.

   6. _____

7. The cat licked its paw in a(n) *nanoncahtl* way to hide the fact that it was eyeing my tuna salad.

   7. _____

8. The attorney's *idarto* strategies usually result in courtroom victory for her clients.

   8. _____

9. The judge decided to *esuteqers* the jury while they decided the fate of the accused.

   9. _____

10. Joel behaved like a(n) *copshanty* by running errands for our boss and constantly praising her, all in order to get a promotion.

    10. _____

11. Showing a(n) *nagraftl* disregard for the promise he made to his father, Wilson continued to play video games instead of doing his homework.

    11. _____

12. The two friends exchanged *tivfuer* looks as they anticipated their escape from the boring party.

    12. _____

13. I will plan a(n) *zenvorused* with my pen pal when she visits this area next month.

    13. _____

14. The store's loyal *letceneli* continued to shop there, ignoring the giant chain store.

    14. _____

15. My brother's *hisvals* devotion to work left him with no time or energy to spend with his friends.

    15. _____

16. It is normal for wolves to *rleogv* before the alpha male, or leader of the wolf pack.

    16. _____

17. Grandma Moses didn't discover her *ntalte* artistic talent until she was in her seventies.

    17. _____

18. The mouse crept *torybslunvuie* through the field, hoping to avoid the notice of the owl flying overhead.

    18. _____

19. The little girl was *ivane* enough to believe her brother when he said that an alien lived in his closet.

    19. _____

20. I couldn't believe I was talking to such a(n) *tasugu* person as a prince.

    20. _____

BONUS: LESSONS 19, 20, AND 21

(pages 121–138)

Use the clues to spell out the words on the answer blanks. Then identify the mystery person at the bottom of the page by writing the numbered letters on the lines with the corresponding numbers.

1. A severe lack of energy and enthusiasm

   1. l e t h a r g y
      (2 under g)

2. Bitter hostility; open hatred

   2. a n i m o s i t y
      (7 under i)

3. A fortress in a commanding position in or near a city

   3. c i t a d e l
      (14 under a)

4. Causing or tending to cause sleep

   4. s o p o r i f i c
      (6 under s)

5. To destroy affection or friendliness

   5. e s t r a n g e
      (3 under g)

6. Endurance; ability to withstand prolonged physical or mental effort

   6. s t a m i n a
      (19 under s, 15 under m)

7. Being still, quiet, or inactive

   7. q u i e s c e n t
      (17 under u, 4 under n)

8. A natural attraction, liking, or feeling of kinship

   8. a f f i n i t y
      (1 under f)

9. Strength of mind that allows one to endure pain or adversity with courage

   9. f o r t i t u d e
      (13 under f, 20 under t)

10. Lacking energy, spirit, or force; slow

    10. l a n g u i d
        (9 under a, 22 under g)

11. Passionate; showing strong enthusiasm or devotion

    11. a r d e n t
        (10 under t)

12. Incapable of being overcome or defeated

    12. i n v i n c i b l e
        (21 under i, 8 under i, 23 under e)

13. Rest; relaxation; peacefulness

    13. r e p o s e
        (11 under r, 16 under o)

14. To hate intensely, to detest; to regard with horror or loathing

    14. a b h o r
        (12 under a, 24 under r)

15. Praise for exceptional achievement

    15. k u d o s
        (5 under k, 18 under s)

F	R	A	N	K		S	I	N	A	T	R	A
1	2	3	4	5		6	7	8	9	10	11	12

,

F	A	M	O	U	S		S	I	N	G	E	R
13	14	15	16	17	18		19	20	21	22	23	24

BONUS: LESSONS 19, 20, AND 21

(pages 121–138)

Use the clues to spell out the words on the answer blanks. Then identify the mystery person at the bottom of the page by writing the numbered letters on the lines with the corresponding numbers.

1. A severe lack of energy and enthusiasm

1. __ __ __ __ __ __ __ __
                   2

2. Bitter hostility; open hatred

2. __ __ __ __ __ __ __ __ __
         7

3. A fortress in a commanding position in or near a city

3. __ __ __ __ __ __
              14

4. Causing or tending to cause sleep

4. __ __ __ __ __ __ __ __ __ __
      6

5. To destroy affection or friendliness

5. __ __ __ __ __ __ __
                 3

6. Endurance; ability to withstand prolonged physical or mental effort

6. __ __ __ __ __ __
   19   15

7. Being still, quiet, or inactive

7. __ __ __ __ __ __ __ __
      17   4

8. A natural attraction, liking, or feeling of kinship

8. __ __ __ __ __ __ __
      1

9. Strength of mind that allows one to endure pain or adversity with courage

9. __ __ __ __ __ __ __ __ __
   13   20

10. Lacking energy, spirit, or force; slow

10. __ __ __ __ __ __
      9   22

11. Passionate; showing strong enthusiasm or devotion

11. __ __ __ __ __ __ __
                10

12. Incapable of being overcome or defeated

12. __ __ __ __ __ __ __ __ __
      21   8   23

13. Rest; relaxation; peacefulness

13. __ __ __ __ __
   11   16

14. To hate intensely, to detest; to regard with horror or loathing

14. __ __ __ __ __
   12   24

15. Praise for exceptional achievement

15. __ __ __ __ __
   5   18

__ __ __ __ __   __ __ __ __ __ __ __ ,
1 2 3 4 5   6 7 8 9 10 11 12

__ __ __ __ __ __   __ __ __ __ __ __
13 14 15 16 17 18   19 20 21 22 23 24

BONUS: LESSONS 22, 23, AND 24

(pages 141–158)

Use the following clues to identify the vocabulary words and write the words on the lines to the right. Then circle each vocabulary word in the word-search box below. The words may overlap and may read in any direction.

1. A judgment based on little or no evidence (10 letters)

2. A _____ is a structure that protects the shore. (5 letters)

3. An evildoer; a villain (9 letters)

4. _____ is the sensation of dizziness. (7 letters)

5. Depressed; in low spirits (8 letters)

6. To _____ someone is to damage his or her reputation. (9 letters)

7. Something that turns attention away (9 letters)

8. Of the most miserable kind; brought to a low state (6 letters)

9. One who is disbelieving or skeptical is _____. (11 letters)

10. To give variety to; to vary (9 letters)

11. To officially recognize or approve (8 letters)

12. To turn away from; toward off; to prevent (5 letters)

1. conjecture
2. jetty
3. miscreant
4. Vertigo
5. dejected
6. discredit
7. diversion
8. abject
9. incredulous
10. diversify
11. accredit
12. avert

Challenge
Locate and circle the eight additional vocabulary words in the word-search box.

aversion
credential
creed
invert
jettison
jut
projectile
revert

```
C R E D E N T I A L T I D E R C S I D
A H L I L E R R L A P T A H A E M I E
F A E S I J I E E J V N O S I T T E J
R K J E T T Y L J E F E K G F O A R E
I L P U C O N J E C T U R E E F D E C
P D I V E R S I O N D L I S N G K O T
O G A B J E C T D E E J U T I S E H E
T E R E O E N K E V E R T I G O P E D
D I V E R S I F Y A L A R D A O N R R
R N S L P I T A W L I P S E I A E E P
A V L E T N A E R C S I M R P K P V O
P E C A W S U O L U D E R C N I E E V
T R E L Q B B P E D E E R C A N W R E
E T H W A A E E O B U D I A V E R T M
```

BONUS: LESSONS 22, 23, AND 24

(pages 141–158)

Use the following clues to identify the vocabulary words and write the words on the lines to the right. Then circle each vocabulary word in the word-search box below. The words may overlap and may read in any direction.

1. A judgment based on little or no evidence (10 letters)   1. _____

2. A _____ is a structure that protects the shore. (5 letters)   2. _____

3. An evildoer; a villain (9 letters)   3. _____

4. _____ is the sensation of dizziness. (7 letters)   4. _____

5. Depressed; in low spirits (8 letters)   5. _____

6. To _____ someone is to damage his or her reputation. (9 letters)   6. _____

7. Something that turns attention away (9 letters)   7. _____

8. Of the most miserable kind; brought to a low state (6 letters)   8. _____

9. One who is disbelieving or skeptical is _____. (11 letters)   9. _____

10. To give variety to; to vary (9 letters)   10. _____

11. To officially recognize or approve (8 letters)   11. _____

12. To turn away from; toward off; to prevent (5 letters)   12. _____

Challenge
Locate and circle the eight additional vocabulary words in the word-search box.

aversion
credential
creed
invert
jettison
jut
projectile
revert

```
C R E D E N T I A L T I D E R C S I D
A H L I L E R R L A P T A H A E M I E
F A E S I J I E E J V N O S I T T E J
R K J E T T Y L J E F E K G F O A R E
I L P U C O N J E C T U R E E F D E C
P D I V E R S I O N D L I S N G K O T
O G A B J E C T D E E J U T I S E H E
T E R E O E N K E V E R T I G O P E D
D I V E R S I F Y A L A R D A O N R R
R N S L P I T A W L I P S E I A E E P
A V L E T N A E R C S I M R P K P V O
P E C A W S U O L U D E R C N I E E V
T R E L Q B B P E D E E R C A N W R E
E T H W A A E E O B U D I A V E R T M
```

BONUS: LESSONS 25, 26, AND 27

(pages 161–178)

Use the clues to complete the crossword puzzle.

```
¹S E N S A ²T I O N A L
E           R
N   ³U   ⁴P A T H O L O ⁵G Y
S   N   N           R   ⁶R
I   P   S   ⁷D ⁸E C E A S E D
B   R   G   G       D   C
I   E   R   R       A   O
L   C   E   E       T   U   ⁹G
I   E   S   S       I   R   R
T   D   S   S       O   S   A
Y   E       ¹⁰S     N   E   D
    N   ¹¹S  U           ¹²I N C U R
¹³P A T H E T I C       E
    E   N   ¹⁴C O N ¹⁵C U R R E N T
    D   T   O   O       T
    I   R   N
  ¹⁶A S S E N T   C
    N   ¹⁷P R E D E C E S S O R
¹⁸E M P A T H Y   D
            ¹⁹S E N T E N T I O U S
```

Across

1. Causing strong feeling of curiosity or interest by giving exaggerated or shocking details
4. The scientific study of disease
7. Dead; no longer living
12. To bring about something undesirable as a result of one's own actions
13. Arousing pity
14. Happening at the same time; simultaneous
16. To agree to something
17. Someone or something that comes before another
18. An identification with and understanding of other people's feelings and situations
19. Energetic in expression; saying meaningful things precisely

Down

1. Acute intellectual or emotional perception or feeling
2. To go beyond a limit or boundary
3. Not done or known before; without previous example
5. A systematic progression; a series of gradual changes
6. The act of turning to someone or something for help or security
8. A path or an opening for going out; an exit
9. A rate of inclination; a slope
10. Assistance in time of need; relief
11. Capable of perceiving and feeling; conscious
15. To admit, often reluctantly, that something is true or right

BONUS: LESSONS 25, 26, AND 27

(pages 161–178)

Use the clues to complete the crossword puzzle.

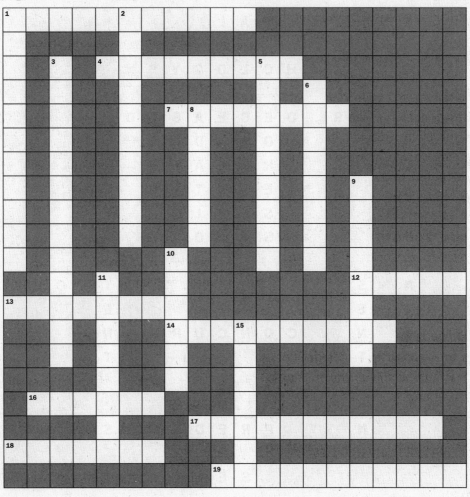

Across

1. Causing strong feeling of curiosity or interest by giving exaggerated or shocking details

4. The scientific study of disease

7. Dead; no longer living

12. To bring about something undesirable as a result of one's own actions

13. Arousing pity

14. Happening at the same time; simultaneous

16. To agree to something

17. Someone or something that comes before another

18. An identification with and understanding of other people's feelings and situations

19. Energetic in expression; saying meaningful things precisely

Down

1. Acute intellectual or emotional perception or feeling

2. To go beyond a limit or boundary

3. Not done or known before; without previous example

5. A systematic progression; a series of gradual changes

6. The act of turning to someone or something for help or security

8. A path or an opening for going out; an exit

9. A rate of inclination; a slope

10. Assistance in time of need; relief

11. Capable of perceiving and feeling; conscious

15. To admit, often reluctantly, that something is true or right

BONUS: LESSONS 28, 29, AND 30

(pages 182–198)

Unscramble the letters of each italicized word and write the word on the answer line to the right.

1. During the debate, the participants tried to maintain their *oscomurep* so that they would not lose points.

2. The smells of perfume *mepateer* the air in the cosmetics department.

3. The wait for the airplane to take off felt *binterelinam* because I was eager to get my vacation started.

4. There was complete *demopniuman* in the stadium after our team scored the winning goal.

5. When our teacher announced that we had won the trip to Washington, D.C., the excitement in our classroom was *labpapel*.

6. We agreed that the warm, sunny day was a(n) *bringareh* of spring.

7. I was struck with an overwhelming *ainrite* that made it impossible to accomplish anything, including my homework.

8. I am sorry to *cubernem* you with more work, but please read the next two chapters of *A Separate Peace* by tomorrow.

9. The feeling of excitement that comes at midnight on each New Year's Eve is *hemealper*.

10. Sitting by the lake on a quiet summer evening always gives me a feeling of *tisnyere*.

11. The museum had a(n) *spetctirveero* exhibit that featured paintings from Picasso's entire career.

12. After spending a week alone, I experienced a profound sense of *nueni*.

13. The fashion designer draped the *piasanoduh* fabric on the model so that it flowed gracefully whenever she moved.

14. The question of where to put garbage is a(n) *enrinlepa* problem for city planners.

15. The mason wrestled with one particularly *derpouson* stone that he wanted to place in the wall.

16. The *emiirnt* coach gave Alex much more playing time than his regular coach did.

17. With the *imeitnnm* arrival of the hurricane, everyone helped get boats out of the water and windows boarded up.

18. The lifeguard moved with *raiycatl* when he heard the shouts of a swimmer in trouble.

19. The air traffic controller was *arurlbpteeibm* as she calmly guided the pilot of the crippled aircraft to a safe landing.

20. At the zoo, I watched in fascination as the giant snake wrapped its *ipnlat* body around the tree branch.

1. **composure**
2. **permeate**
3. **interminable**
4. **pandemonium**
5. **palpable**
6. **harbinger**
7. **inertia**
8. **encumber**
9. **ephemeral**
10. **serenity**
11. **retrospective**
12. **ennui**
13. **diaphanous**
14. **perennial**
15. **ponderous**
16. **interim**
17. **imminent**
18. **alacrity**
19. **imperturbable**
20. **pliant**

BONUS: LESSONS 28, 29, AND 30

(pages 182–198)

Unscramble the letters of each italicized word and write the word on the answer line to the right.

1. During the debate, the participants tried to maintain their *oscomurep* so that they would not lose points.

    1. _____

2. The smells of perfume *mepateer* the air in the cosmetics department.

    2. _____

3. The wait for the airplane to take off felt *binterelinam* because I was eager to get my vacation started.

    3. _____

4. There was complete *demopniuman* in the stadium after our team scored the winning goal.

    4. _____

5. When our teacher announced that we had won the trip to Washington, D.C., the excitement in our classroom was *labpapel*.

    5. _____

6. We agreed that the warm, sunny day was a(n) *bringareh* of spring.

    6. _____

7. I was struck with an overwhelming *ainrite* that made it impossible to accomplish anything, including my homework.

    7. _____

8. I am sorry to *cubernem* you with more work, but please read the next two chapters of *A Separate Peace* by tomorrow.

    8. _____

9. The feeling of excitement that comes at midnight on each New Year's Eve is *hemealper*.

    9. _____

10. Sitting by the lake on a quiet summer evening always gives me a feeling of *tisnyere*.

    10. _____

11. The museum had a(n) *spetctirveero* exhibit that featured paintings from Picasso's entire career.

    11. _____

12. After spending a week alone, I experienced a profound sense of *nueni*.

    12. _____

13. The fashion designer draped the *piasanoduh* fabric on the model so that it flowed gracefully whenever she moved.

    13. _____

14. The question of where to put garbage is a(n) *enrinlepa* problem for city planners.

    14. _____

15. The mason wrestled with one particularly *derpouson* stone that he wanted to place in the wall.

    15. _____

16. The *emiirnt* coach gave Alex much more playing time than his regular coach did.

    16. _____

17. With the *imeitnnm* arrival of the hurricane, everyone helped get boats out of the water and windows boarded up.

    17. _____

18. The lifeguard moved with *raiycatl* when he heard the shouts of a swimmer in trouble.

    18. _____

19. The air traffic controller was *arurlbpteeibm* as she calmly guided the pilot of the crippled aircraft to a safe landing.

    19. _____

20. At the zoo, I watched in fascination as the giant snake wrapped its *ipnlat* body around the tree branch.

    20. _____

TEST: LESSONS 1 AND 2

(pages 1–12)

Part A Choosing the Best Definition

On the answer line, write the letter of the best definition of the italicized word.

1. Claire had *qualms* about her flute solo in the upcoming concert.
   a. new ideas   **c.** regrets
   b. doubts   **d.** memories

1. _____

2. Scientists now have *conclusive* evidence that shows the dangers of secondhand smoke.
   a. well-publicized   **c.** fairly strong
   b. preliminary   **d.** decisive

2. _____

3. All winter long, Gus *vacillated* about whether to play baseball or join the track team in the spring.
   a. made a decision   **c.** swung back and forth
   b. asked advice   **d.** talked endlessly

3. _____

4. One example of a *coinage* is the word "dot-com," referring to a company that relies on the Internet for most of its business.
   a. an invented word   **c.** a word related to money
   b. big business   **d.** words with hyphens

4. _____

5. Coach Sullivan was *unequivocal* in his demand that every member of the team attend every practice.
   a. very strict   **c.** very clear
   b. defiant   **d.** casual

5. _____

6. Many dictionaries include *colloquial* words and phrases.
   a. foreign   **c.** unusual; rare
   b. frequently confused or misunderstood   **d.** characteristic of informal language

6. _____

7. *Affix* the labels, seal the envelopes, and take them to the post office before 5:00 P.M.
   a. match   **c.** write
   b. attach   **d.** remove

7. _____

8. When the voting machine malfunctioned, an *indeterminate* number of votes were lost.
   a. vast   **c.** unimportant
   b. very small   **d.** not known

8. _____

9. Marita has always been *apprehensive* about air travel, but she decided to go anyway.
   a. disapproving   **c.** uninformed
   b. fearful   **d.** indifferent

9. _____

10. When several students asked for extra time to finish their tests, Mr. Bloom's *categorical* answer was "no."
   a. furious   **c.** absolute
   b. apologetic   **d.** immediate

10. _____

TEST: LESSONS 1 AND 2

(pages 1–12)

Part B Choosing the Best Word

On the answer line, write the letter of the word that best completes the sentence.

11. The "sweat of his brow" is a familiar _____ for "hard work."
    a. spoonerism   **c.** metonymy
    b. category   **d.** affix

11. _____

12. Theo said it was okay to eat the pie that was cooling on the table, but I was _____ and thought we should check with his mother first.
    a. dubious   **c.** colloquial
    b. precarious   **d.** diminutive

12. _____

13. The National Aeronautics & Space Administration is usually referred to by the _____ NASA, which is much easier to say.
    a. oxymoron   **c.** portmanteau word
    b. acronym   **d.** vacillation

13. _____

14. Isn't it strange that the words *mom* and *dad* are both _____?
    a. portmanteau words   **c.** palindromes
    b. acronyms   **d.** spoonerisms

14. _____

15. "Roaring pain" is a _____ for the phrase "pouring rain."
    a. spoonerism   **c.** coinage
    b. colloquialism   **d.** metonymy

15. _____

16. Kevin told his parents that he was too old to be referred to by the childish _____ *Kevvie.*
    a. qualm   **c.** acronym
    b. palindrome   **d.** diminutive

16. _____

17. Our vacation plans are still a bit _____, but we hope to make them final by the end of this week.
    a. colloquial   **c.** tentative
    b. apprehensive   **d.** conclusive

17. _____

18. "Smog," a combination of the words "smoke" and "fog," is an example of a _____.
    a. palindrome   **c.** portmanteau word
    b. diminutive   **d.** colloquialism

18. _____

19. Two riders on one bicycle can make for a rather _____ ride.
    a. categorical   **c.** dubious
    b. unequivocal   **d.** precarious

19. _____

20. The _____ "deafening silence" is the best way to describe the response to the principal's dramatic announcement.
    a. oxymoron   **c.** metonymy
    b. conclusion   **d.** coinage

20. _____

TEST: LESSONS 3 AND 4

(pages 13–18, 21–26)

Part A Choosing the Best Definition

On the answer line, write the letter of the best definition of the italicized word.

1. The new president wants to *aggrandize* the company by advertising that it does
well in overseas markets.
   a. criticize
   c. make legal
   b. make greater
   d. hide from view

   1. _____

2. It's not a good idea to approach a *feral* cat because it is likely to scratch or bite you.
   a. mother
   c. wild
   b. injured
   d. unknown

   2. _____

3. The duchess's gracious *demeanor* at the royal reception charmed all of the guests
and put them at ease.
   a. conversation
   c. entertainment
   b. generosity
   d. behavior

   3. _____

4. Mr. Lopez criticizes his students' *intemperate* use of the word "like."
   a. excessive
   c. harmful
   b. unnecessary
   d. unworthy

   4. _____

5. Doreen was surprised when her coworker was fired for *unseemly* behavior.
   a. unfriendly
   c. dishonest
   b. inappropriate
   d. childish

   5. _____

6. *Satiated* by a three-course dinner, I went to bed without my usual midnight snack.
   a. fully satisfied
   c. nourished
   b. made ill
   d. exhausted

   6. _____

7. The garden's *multifarious* plants attracted visitors from quite far away.
   a. exotic
   c. diverse
   b. seasonal
   d. awesome

   7. _____

8. We stopped ordering supplies from that company because of the *exorbitance* of
their prices.
   a. unfairness
   c. wastefulness
   b. extreme variability
   d. unreasonable expense

   8. _____

9. The new wing of the museum was paid for by a *benevolent* businessman.
   a. wealthy
   c. infamous
   b. well-intentioned
   d. highly competitive

   9. _____

10. The *wily* coach confused the opposing team by changing his defensive strategy
halfway through the game.
    a. cunning
    c. kindly
    b. winning
    d. reckless

    10. _____

TEST: LESSONS 3 AND 4

(pages 13–18, 21–26)

Part B Choosing the Best Word

On the answer line, write the letter of the word that best completes the sentence.

11. Nora has _____ plans for traveling around the world, but I'll be surprised if she ever saves enough money to go anywhere.
   a. feral **b.** provincial **c.** ignoble **d.** grandiose

11. _____

12. Max got a stomachache from the _____ of Halloween candy that he ate.
   a. opulence **b.** surfeit **c.** exorbitance **d.** wiliness

12. _____

13. The factory foreman was _____ and spiteful in his punishment of the workers for such a small mistake.
   a. ignoble **b.** opulent **c.** grandiose **d.** multifarious

13. _____

14. From a very early age, the young prince learned to act with _____ whenever he was in public.
   a. demeanor **b.** exorbitance **c.** decorum **d.** surfeit

14. _____

15. Harold's _____ spending on his recent vacation almost depleted his savings.
   a. decorous **b.** profligate **c.** beguiling **d.** feral

15. _____

16. The saleswoman _____ Marissa into buying cosmetics that she really didn't need.
   a. aggrandized **b.** surfeited **c.** beguiled **d.** satiated

16. _____

17. The high ceilings, carved columns, and lush plants gave the hotel lobby a feeling of great _____.
   a. benevolence **b.** mores **c.** wiliness **d.** opulence

17. _____

18. In the eighteenth century, many people in Britain thought American colonists were backward and _____.
   a. intemperate **b.** exorbitant **c.** gratuitous **d.** provincial

18. _____

19. The _____ of frontier culture ensured that neighbors helped one another by working together at barn raisings and quilting bees.
   a. grandiosity **b.** exorbitance **c.** mores **d.** intemperance

19. _____

20. That television show wasted a lot of time with _____ car chases and violence that did not contribute to the storyline.
   a. gratuitous **b.** wily **c.** multifarious **d.** opulent

20. _____

TEST: LESSONS 5 AND 6

(pages 27–38)

Part A Choosing the Best Definition

On the answer line, write the letter of the best definition of the italicized word.

1. Normally *complaisant,* Griffin surprised his friend by refusing to support her latest scheme.
   a. difficult to get along with   **c.** wanting to please
   b. dramatic and flashy   **d.** lacking confidence

1. _____

2. Club members agreed to *proceed* with the plan and meet again in a month.
   a. gather   **c.** contribute
   b. come before   **d.** go forward

2. _____

3. Esperanza, *intrepid* as ever, has signed up to take chemistry, physics, and calculus, all in one quarter.
   a. fearless   **c.** unrealistic
   b. boastful   **d.** forgetful

3. _____

4. The potato famine caused many people to *emigrate* from Ireland in the late 1840s.
   a. come to settle in a new country   **c.** leave a country and move to another
   b. lose a job   **d.** start over in a new profession

4. _____

5. *Strident* voices called for the prime minister's resignation whenever he appeared in public.
   a. impartial   **c.** foreign
   b. loud and harsh   **d.** emotional

5. _____

6. Somalia has endured the *depredations* of civil unrest and warfare for many years.
   a. lack of necessities   **c.** damage and destruction
   b. humiliation   **d.** inconvenience

6. _____

7. The ambassador's *pacific* speech made people believe that war could be avoided.
   a. supportive   **c.** self-assured
   b. familiar   **d.** peaceful

7. _____

8. Several *disinterested* observers monitored the elections in the new democracy.
   a. not interested   **c.** inexperienced
   b. unbiased   **d.** not critical

8. _____

9. When he spoke with the store manager, James tried to be *assertive* yet polite.
   a. acting with confidence   **c.** grown-up or mature
   b. overly proud   **d.** willing to please

9. _____

10. Members of the commission hope to *effect* a change in the laws regarding cell phone use while driving.
   a. evaluate   **c.** bring about
   b. prevent   **d.** influence

10. _____

TEST: LESSONS 5 AND 6

(pages 27–38)

Part B Choosing the Best Word

On the answer line, write the letter of the word that best completes the sentence.

11. Watching a crackling, flickering campfire always puts me in a completely
_____ mood.
   a. mellow   **b.** flamboyant   **c.** intrepid   **d.** disinterested

11. _____

12. Acting quite _____ when she was caught in a lie, Samantha immediately changed
her story.
   a. docile   **b.** unabashed   **c.** uninterested   **d.** flamboyant

12. _____

13. When my ancestors _____ to the United States, they had many hopes
and dreams.
   a. effected   **b.** emigrated   **c.** asserted   **d.** immigrated

13. _____

14. The _____ young man pushed to the head of the line and demanded
immediate service.
   a. pacific   **b.** complaisant   **c.** brazen   **d.** mellow

14. _____

15. The little boy I babysit for after school every day is really _____ and shy.
   a. strident   **b.** unabashed   **c.** docile   **d.** assertive

15. _____

16. Most commuters will not be _____ by the roadwork, which will be done early
in the morning, before rush hour.
   a. preceded   **b.** affected   **c.** immigrated   **d.** effected

16. _____

17. Several seasons of poor crops caused great _____ among the farm families in
the region.
   a. depredation   **b.** precedence   **c.** deprivation   **d.** brazenness

17. _____

18. My friend Nicole's loud voice and _____ style attracts attention wherever
she goes.
   a. disinterested   **b.** uninterested   **c.** mellow   **d.** flamboyant

18. _____

19. At the sports banquet, the presentation of awards will _____ the serving
of dessert.
   a. proceed   **b.** deprive   **c.** precede   **d.** pacify

19. _____

20. During the long speech, Ethan wiggled in his seat and looked out the window,
completely _____ in the speaker's views.
   a. brazen   **b.** uninterested   **c.** strident   **d.** disinterested

20. _____

TEST: LESSONS 7 AND 8

(pages 41–52)

Part A Choosing the Best Definition

On the answer line, write the letter of the best definition of the italicized word.

1. Carly tried to *mediate* a dispute between two of her friends, and now they are angry at her, too.
   a. express a point of view   **c.** create a distraction
   b. help reach agreement   **d.** make less severe

   1. _____

2. Dr. Arnot's presentation *edified* me about the latest research on nutrition and health.
   a. instructed   **c.** influenced
   b. confused   **d.** surprised

   2. _____

3. Spending time in a foreign country is *conducive* to learning a second language.
   a. customary   **c.** unnecessary
   b. recommended   **d.** favorable

   3. _____

4. The speaker made some interesting points, but his *didactic* tone annoyed many people in the audience.
   a. knowledgeable   **c.** moralizing
   b. boastful   **d.** informal

   4. _____

5. A good teacher must have an excellent understanding of a particular subject, and must be well versed in *pedagogy*.
   a. leadership   **c.** psychology
   b. knowledge about education   **d.** public speaking

   5. _____

6. Sometimes one person's small *conciliatory* act can bring an end to a longstanding feud.
   a. appeasing   **c.** secret
   b. well planned   **d.** insignificant

   6. _____

7. Everyone in the neighborhood *patronizes* the farmers' market because of its fresh produce.
   a. sells at   **c.** enjoys
   b. shops at   **d.** talks about

   7. _____

8. Growing up in a family of musicians has *imbued* me with a passion for music.
   a. inspired   **c.** set free
   b. embarrassed   **d.** showed

   8. _____

9. A dip in the lake might *mitigate* the itchiness of all those mosquito bites.
   a. forget   **c.** overlook
   b. increase   **d.** lessen

   9. _____

10. *Pundits* from different political parties often disagree on important issues.
    a. friends and neighbors   **c.** people of great learning
    b. elected leaders   **d.** news reporters

    10. _____

TEST: LESSONS 7 AND 8

(pages 41–52)

Part B Choosing the Best Word

On the answer line, write the letter of the word that best completes the sentence.

11. A good education does not _____ pupils; instead it teaches them to think for themselves.
   a. indoctrinate   **b.** amend   **c.** extricate   **d.** imbue

11. _____

12. I tried to read the journal article, but it was full of _____ language I could not understand.
   a. edified   **b.** importunate   **c.** esoteric   **d.** conciliatory

12. _____

13. A great deal of important research is done under the _____ of the American Cancer Society.
   a. pundit   **b.** pedagogy   **c.** aegis   **d.** amends

13. _____

14. Vinny decided to _____ himself from the group when the conversation became heated.
   a. indoctrinate   **b.** extricate   **c.** patronize   **d.** mediate

14. _____

15. The man's dry, _____ speaking style was totally inappropriate at the merry neighborhood cookout.
   a. imbued   **b.** conducive   **c.** conciliatory   **d.** pedantic

15. _____

16. "After we _____ the school, there will be Internet access in every room," the principal told a group of parents.
   a. mitigate   **b.** elucidate   **c.** edify   **d.** renovate

16. _____

17. Hitting a home run in the ninth inning made _____ for her three strikeouts earlier in the game.
   a. mediation   **b.** amends   **c.** pedagogy   **d.** aegis

17. _____

18. Can you _____ the famous scientific formula, $e = mc^2$, for us?
   a. edify   **b.** renovate   **c.** patronize   **d.** elucidate

18. _____

19. My _____ neighbor often travels to Europe to lecture at anthropology conferences.
   a. erudite   **b.** pedagogical   **c.** conducive   **d.** conciliatory

19. _____

20. The child _____ his father to buy something in each aisle of the grocery store.
   a. extricated   **b.** mediated   **c.** importuned   **d.** mitigated

20. _____

TEST: LESSONS 9 AND 10

(pages 53–58, 61–66)

Part A Choosing the Best Definition

On the answer line, write the letter of the best definition of the italicized word.

1. The family's *munificent* gift to the city will be used to create a public park.
   a. fortunate   **c.** unusual
   b. surprising   **d.** generous

    1. _____

2. Ella tried to use rumor and *innuendo* to turn my friends against me, but her plan failed.
   a. mockery   **c.** bribes
   b. outright lies   **d.** negative hints

    2. _____

3. *Indigent* farm laborers move to find work as the seasons change.
   a. unskilled   **c.** poor
   b. numerous   **d.** immigrant

    3. _____

4. Too many politicians use negative campaign ads to *vilify* their opponents.
   a. keep up with   **c.** make fun of
   b. describe   **d.** slander

    4. _____

5. The actor employs an agent to deal with the *pecuniary* details of his contracts.
   a. tedious and boring   **c.** relating to money
   b. minor; unimportant   **d.** difficult to understand

    5. _____

6. As the protestor was led away, his loud, bitter *invective* shocked the crowd.
   a. life story   **c.** sobbing
   b. abusive language   **d.** violent behavior

    6. _____

7. A hiker *chastised* the group of teenagers for leaving litter along the trail.
   a. criticized   **c.** assisted
   b. reported   **d.** pursued

    7. _____

8. The executive is known for treating her staff with *equity* and respect.
   a. good pay   **c.** encouragement
   b. privacy   **d.** fairness

    8. _____

9. The doctor used recent research in his article to *debunk* some old-fashioned ideas about a healthful diet.
   a. claim credit for   **c.** expose as false
   b. weigh the merit of   **d.** speak in support of

    9. _____

10. Mr. Moreno does not tolerate any *derogatory* comments in his classroom.
   a. untrue   **c.** helpful
   b. insulting   **d.** exaggerated

    10. _____

TEST: LESSONS 9 AND 10

(pages 53–58, 61–66)

Part B Choosing the Best Word

On the answer line, write the letter of the word that best completes the sentence.

11. Jermaine decided to buy a used car because expensive new cars _____ in value very quickly.
    a. debunk   **b.** depreciate   **c.** impugn   **d.** remunerate

  11. _____

12. Despite a season of poor sales, I'm happy to report that the company remains _____.
    a. pecuniary   **b.** derogatory   **c.** solvent   **d.** acrimonious

  12. _____

13. When the stranger _____ his honor, the duke challenged him to a duel at dawn.
    a. chastised   **b.** depreciated   **c.** harassed   **d.** impugned

  13. _____

14. Because of the current _____, Ashley was reluctant to leave her job, even though she disliked it.
    a. recession   **b.** equity   **c.** munificence   **d.** invective

  14. _____

15. The company will _____ you generously if you agree to work during the holiday weekend.
    a. chastise   **b.** disparage   **c.** debunk   **d.** remunerate

  15. _____

16. During the debate, the candidate lost her temper, and her language and tone became increasingly _____.
    a. recessive   **b.** acrimonious   **c.** indigent   **d.** munificent

  16. _____

17. Our parents warned us not to _____ our little cousin's piano playing.
    a. chastise   **b.** harass   **c.** disparage   **d.** debunk

  17. _____

18. During times of _____, when city budgets are reduced, schools and libraries seem to suffer the biggest cuts.
    a. austerity   **b.** innuendo   **c.** solvency   **d.** remuneration

  18. _____

19. My friend's _____ habits enabled him to save enough money to travel through South America for an entire summer.
    a. solvent   **b.** disparaging   **c.** frugal   **d.** munificent

  19. _____

20. Our neighbor's dog likes to run up to the fence and _____ anyone who walks by.
    a. depreciate   **b.** remunerate   **c.** harass   **d.** debunk

  20. _____

TEST: LESSONS 11 AND 12

(pages 67–78)

Part A Choosing the Best Definition

On the answer line, write the letter of the best definition of the italicized word.

1. Amit didn't say "I'm sorry," but the roses he sent were *tantamount* to an apology.
   a. related   **c.** in addition
   b. impressive   **d.** equivalent

  1. _____

2. I thought the play was *hilarious,* and everyone in the theater seemed to agree.
   a. original   **c.** ridiculous
   b. very funny   **d.** mean-spirited

  2. _____

3. Our neighborhood included a *homogenous* group of houses.
   a. of the same age   **c.** similar
   b. unwelcoming   **d.** sociable

  3. _____

4. Alisha's storytelling skills and *droll* sense of humor entertained us all the
   way home.
   a. ridiculous   **c.** complicated
   b. amusing in an odd way   **d.** very quiet and low-key

  4. _____

5. One writer made an *analogy* between a computer and the human brain.
   a. distinction   **c.** fable
   b. joking remark   **d.** comparison

  5. _____

6. The guests enjoyed a delightful meal and lots of holiday *mirth.*
   a. traditions and customs   **c.** gift-giving
   b. delicious, festive food   **d.** good spirits and laughter

  6. _____

7. "Cool new shoes! Why are you wearing only one?" was Sophie's *flippant* comment,
   when she saw her brother in his walking cast.
   a. worded incorrectly   **c.** humorous in a disrespectful way
   b. deliberately wrong   **d.** uninformed

  7. _____

8. The artist's *caricature* emphasized the girl's enormous eyes and long eyelashes.
   a. exaggerated image   **c.** teasing remarks
   b. collection of related works   **d.** comparison showing a similarity

  8. _____

9. Expecting to hear a debate, we were surprised by the *congruence* between the
   two speakers.
   a. contrast   **c.** dissatisfaction
   b. passion   **d.** harmony

  9. _____

10. The man peppered his speech with *witticisms* that kept the audience grinning.
    a. wild stories   **c.** clever remarks
    b. mistakes   **d.** imitations

  10. _____

TEST: LESSONS 11 AND 12

(pages 67–78)

Part B Choosing the Best Word

On the answer line, write the letter of the word that best completes the sentence.

11. Synonyms such as *break, crack, shatter, split,* and *smash* have certain _____ in meaning.
    a. witticism   **b.** nuances   **c.** antitheses   **d.** mirth

11. _____

12. Several listeners were offended by your _____ remark about people and their pets.
    a. tantamount   **b.** whimsical   **c.** commensurate   **d.** facetious

12. _____

13. The members of our dance class make up quite a _____ group, ranging in age from 14 to 77 and with varying levels of experience.
    a. heterogeneous   **b.** droll   **c.** homogeneous   **d.** ludicrous

13. _____

14. Johnny's worn, old-fashioned clothes are the _____ of his wife's flashy, up-to-the-minute style.
    a. caricature   **b.** analogy   **c.** antithesis   **d.** whim

14. _____

15. Going for a swim in this freezing weather seems like a _____ idea to me!
    a. ludicrous   **b.** facetious   **c.** commensurate   **d.** congruent

15. _____

16. Determined to improve his grades, Colin almost never _____ from his new study schedule.
    a. caricatures   **b.** banters   **c.** homogenizes   **d.** deviates

16. _____

17. The ad for this job does not reveal how much it pays, saying only that the salary will be _____ with experience.
    a. heterogeneous   **b.** disparate   **c.** commensurate   **d.** flippant

17. _____

18. The panelists engaged in lighthearted _____ during the break, but became serious as soon as the program resumed.
    a. congruence   **b.** banter   **c.** antithesis   **d.** analogy

18. _____

19. When I was a child, I loved to make up _____ stories about talking animals.
    a. analogous   **b.** flippant   **c.** homogeneous   **d.** whimsical

19. _____

20. "Equal pay for equal work" is the rallying cry of those determined to eliminate the _____ between men's and women's incomes.
    a. disparity   **b.** nuance   **c.** congruence   **d.** banter

20. _____

TEST: LESSONS 13 AND 14

(pages 81–92)

Part A Choosing the Best Definition

On the answer line, write the letter of the best definition of the italicized word.

1. In traditional Indian society, members of the lowest *caste* were the "untouchables."   1. _____
    a. government   **c.** reward
    b. ruling family   **d.** social class

2. It is *imprudent* to give out your name, telephone number, or street address in an   2. _____
online chat room.
    a. unwise   **c.** customary
    b. not practical   **d.** unnecessary

3. Svetlana impressed the music director with her *diligence* in preparing for the concert.   3. _____
    a. concerns   **c.** calmness
    b. hard work   **d.** good sense

4. An *autocratic* ruler inspires more fear and resentment than loyalty or respect.   4. _____
    a. less powerful   **c.** corrupt
    b. leading by example   **d.** wielding unlimited power

5. Zach turned on his CD player, *unmindful* of others who were reading   5. _____
and studying.
    a. annoyed by   **c.** putting up with
    b. without consideration   **d.** following orders

6. A group of generals *usurped* control from the newly elected representatives.   6. _____
    a. bought   **c.** took by force
    b. surrendered   **d.** imitated

7. Adolf Hitler established a *totalitarian* government with the help of   7. _____
military police.
    a. having complete control   **c.** unpopular; despised
    b. freely elected   **d.** violent; warlike

8. The pilot made a *meticulous* check of his fuel supply, engine, and other   8. _____
vital equipment.
    a. required   **c.** hasty
    b. very careful   **d.** superficial

9. The company executives spend their workdays in lavish offices on the tenth floor,   9. _____
uninvolved in the *minutia* of filling orders and packing boxes.
    a. time pressures   **c.** minor details
    b. difficulties   **d.** paid labor

10. Filled with *trepidation*, Chen began to climb the ladder to the high-dive platform.   10. _____
    a. eagerness   **c.** glee
    b. false boldness   **d.** nervous fear

TEST: LESSONS 13 AND 14

(pages 81–92)

Part B Choosing the Best Word

On the answer line, write the letter of the word that best completes the sentence.

11. The emperor, a _____ who was hated and feared by his subjects, maintained power by means of a strong and loyal army.
   a. caste   **b.** hegemony   **c.** despot   **d.** minutiae

11. _____

12. Joel's twin sister was a _____ eater, yet he loved all kinds of exotic foods.
   a. finicky   **b.** meticulous   **c.** diligent   **d.** totalitarian

12. _____

13. Division managers have complete _____ to hire or fire staff members and to set team goals and priorities.
   a. autonomy   **b.** sovereign   **c.** trepidation   **d.** diligence

13. _____

14. A successful restaurant owner must be _____ about cleanliness and food safety.
   a. unmindful   **b.** sovereign   **c.** slovenly   **d.** fastidious

14. _____

15. The city-states of ancient Greece, including Athens and Sparta, were _____ ruled by wealthy aristocrats.
   a. castes   **b.** oligarchies   **c.** despots   **d.** autocrats

15. _____

16. Ling made the _____ choice to snack on an apple and a slice of cheese instead of a sugary candy bar.
   a. autocratic   **b.** finicky   **c.** judicious   **d.** feudal

16. _____

17. Queen Elizabeth is the British _____, but Parliament actually makes the laws that govern the country.
   a. autonomy   **b.** imprudence   **c.** oligarchy   **d.** sovereign

17. _____

18. Raymond's _____ appearance did not make a good first impression during his job interview.
   a. imprudent   **b.** slovenly   **c.** meticulous   **d.** judicious

18. _____

19. Millions of people celebrated the end of Soviet _____ over the Balkan states.
   a. trepidation   **b.** minutiae   **c.** hegemony   **d.** diligence

19. _____

20. Serfs living under the _____ system during the Middle Ages lived hard lives with little or no freedom.
   a. unmindful   **b.** fastidious   **c.** feudal   **d.** autocratic

20. _____

TEST: LESSONS 15 AND 16

(pages 93–98, 101–106)

Part A Choosing the Best Definition

On the answer line, write the letter of the best definition of the italicized word.

1. This new evidence *exonerates* the man who was first arrested for the crime.
   a. proves guilty
   b. raises suspicion about
   c. agrees with
   d. frees from blame

   1. _____

2. An *august* group of world leaders attended the signing of a historic peace treaty.
   a. assorted
   b. inspiring awe
   c. antagonistic
   d. perspiring from heat

   2. _____

3. In *deference* to your wishes, we'll go to the early show and then to dinner.
   a. opposition
   b. lucky coincidence
   c. anticipation
   d. respectful yielding

   3. _____

4. A successful and famous chef would never *condescend* to wash dishes in the kitchen.
   a. be required
   b. find time
   c. lower herself
   d. expect

   4. _____

5. Every year, *unscrupulous* employees steal thousands of dollars' worth of equipment from the company's storage room.
   a. blundering
   b. ill-mannered
   c. dishonest
   d. maltreated

   5. _____

6. Allison crossed the street to avoid walking by the *ruffian* who was standing on the corner.
   a. beggar
   b. stray dog
   c. worker
   d. troublemaker

   6. _____

7. The governor does not like *sycophants;* he only hires people who speak their minds.
   a. people who flatter
   b. corrupt people
   c. incompetent people
   d. original thinkers

   7. _____

8. I forgot to put a quarter in the parking meter, and that *misdemeanor* cost me twenty-five dollars.
   a. minor offense
   b. omission
   c. poor excuse
   d. lowly job

   8. _____

9. With a *supercilious* look, the executive assistant informed us that no one sees Ms. Etheredge without an appointment.
   a. weary
   b. triumphant
   c. regretful
   d. disdainful

   9. _____

10. Danni *purloined* the salary list from our boss's office and passed it among the employees.
    a. stole
    b. uncovered
    c. borrowed
    d. copied

    10. _____

TEST: LESSONS 15 AND 16

(pages 93–98, 101–106)

Part B Choosing the Best Word

On the answer line, write the letter of the word that best completes the sentence.

11. The defendant is a gangster who has _____ money from many business owners in the city.
   a. exonerated   **b.** condescended   **c.** extorted   **d.** condemned

11. _____

12. Someone sprayed paint on the wall, and whoever is found to be _____ will be punished.
   a. culpable   **b.** supercilious   **c.** august   **d.** incorrigible

12. _____

13. The aging star surrounded himself with _____ to fulfill his every need.
   a. misdemeanors   **b.** ruffians   **c.** scruples   **d.** lackeys

13. _____

14. The cruel dictator enjoyed seeing her enemies _____ .
   a. subjugate   **b.** grovel   **c.** predominate   **d.** purloin

14. _____

15. Felice's _____ devotion to her boss made her blind to his many faults.
   a. august   **b.** culpable   **c.** slavish   **d.** supercilious

15. _____

16. The former state treasurer, accused of _____ in his handling of the organization's funds, was forced out of office.
   a. subjugation   **b.** malfeasance   **c.** deference   **d.** exoneration

16. _____

17. The art show includes prints, sketches, and sculptures, but I would say that oil paintings _____ .
   a. defer   **b.** condescend   **c.** extort   **d.** predominate

17. _____

18. Total _____ of the native population was the goal of the invading army.
   a. deference   **b.** subjugation   **c.** misdemeanor   **d.** malfeasance

18. _____

19. My aunt and uncle have given my cousin many chances to change his behavior, but he seems to be _____ .
   a. incorrigible   **b.** slavish   **c.** unscrupulous   **d.** sycophantic

19. _____

20. The celebrity's thoughtless remarks were _____ by the media and the public.
   a. purloined   **b.** predominated   **c.** groveled   **d.** condemned

20. _____

TEST: LESSONS 17 AND 18

(pages 107–118)

Part A Choosing the Best Definition

On the answer line, write the letter of the best definition of the italicized word.

1. By the age of ten, Deion was *adroit* in the use of carpentry tools such as saws and drills.
   a. skillful
   b. showing off
   c. clumsy
   d. interested

   1. _____

2. While his friend was in the other room, Brandon made a *furtive* phone call to check on some last-minute arrangements for the surprise party.
   a. prearranged
   b. secretive
   c. essential
   d. hasty

   2. _____

3. The police commissioner never misses an opportunity to *vaunt* her success in reducing the city's crime rate.
   a. add to
   b. cover up
   c. boast of
   d. explain

   3. _____

4. The teacher believes that his new student has a *latent* ability to excel in math.
   a. present but not active
   b. exciting
   c. obvious or apparent
   d. unique

   4. _____

5. Trevor's *forte* has always been putting great meals together, and now he has his own catering business.
   a. pet peeve
   b. secret task
   c. dream
   d. strong point

   5. _____

6. Agricultural officials have *sequestered* some cattle until they can test them for diseases.
   a. taken
   b. isolated
   c. kept alive
   d. arrested

   6. _____

7. The group will *rendezvous* at the airport at 9:00 A.M. on Saturday, August 17th.
   a. join a secret club
   b. board an airplane
   c. meet by arrangement
   d. return from a trip

   7. _____

8. The speaker's *salient* point is that global warming is a problem that people all over the world should address now.
   a. troubling
   b. arguable
   c. final
   d. essential

   8. _____

9. A guest *unobtrusively* poured the awful-tasting coffee into a large vase of flowers.
   a. ungratefully
   b. in a dramatic manner
   c. awkwardly
   d. without attracting attention

   9. _____

10. Business travelers often become quite *blasé* about all of the places they get to visit.
    a. boastful
    b. unimpressed
    c. secretive
    d. annoyed

    10. _____

Test: Lessons 17 and 18   T29

TEST: LESSONS 17 AND 18

(pages 107–118)

Part B Choosing the Best Word

On the answer line, write the letter of the word that best completes the sentence.

11. Checking on a homework assignment was Marcy's _____ reason for telephoning her friend.
   a. gauche   **b.** ostensible   **c.** blasé   **d.** flagrant

11. _____

12. Dozens of fairy tales end with the _____, "and they lived happily ever after."
   a. cliché   **b.** subterfuge   **c.** vaunt   **d.** clientele

12. _____

13. You seem remarkably _____ about having your wisdom teeth removed tomorrow.
   a. salient   **b.** furtive   **c.** nonchalant   **d.** latent

13. _____

14. The new hair salon is having a special half-price promotion in hopes of building up its _____.
   a. rendezvous   **b.** forte   **c.** entrepreneur   **d.** clientele

14. _____

15. The senator didn't know the microphone was still on when he made the _____ comment about the president.
   a. ostensible   **b.** gauche   **c.** unobtrusive   **d.** adroit

15. _____

16. Vic was cut from the hockey team after his _____ display of poor sportsmanship.
   a. flagrant   **b.** surreptitious   **c.** naive   **d.** nonchalant

16. _____

17. To get his father to drive him to town, Troy used _____, claiming he needed to go to the library.
   a. clientele   **b.** subterfuge   **c.** latency   **d.** entrepreneur

17. _____

18. Hector maintained a _____ belief that his dad could do almost anything.
   a. flagrant   **b.** blasé   **c.** furtive   **d.** naive

18. _____

19. A successful young _____ started this software company, while she was still in high school.
   a. entrepreneur   **b.** cliché   **c.** rendezvous   **d.** forte

19. _____

20. While their parents were admiring the scenery, Roberta gave her sister a _____ pinch.
   a. gauche   **b.** clichéd   **c.** surreptitious   **d.** salient

20. _____

TEST: LESSONS 19 AND 20

(pages 121–132)

Part A Choosing the Best Definition

On the answer line, write the letter of the best definition of the italicized word.

1. Maria turned the pages of the magazine in a *dilatory* manner as she waited for her appointment to begin.
   a. efficient
   b. careless
   c. cheery
   d. slow; delaying

   1. _____

2. There is some *animosity* between the local residents and the students who come to the city to attend the university.
   a. communication
   b. hostility
   c. misunderstanding
   d. gentle teasing

   2. _____

3. Sometimes young children *somnambulate,* but they usually grow out of it.
   a. stumble
   b. pretend
   c. stutter
   d. sleepwalk

   3. _____

4. Noticing Sela's flushed face and unusual *lethargy,* her track coach sent her to the nurse's office.
   a. lack of energy
   b. hostility
   c. worry
   d. sadness

   4. _____

5. After a weekend of *sloth,* I looked around my apartment and cringed at the sight of the unmade bed, unwashed dishes, and piles of dirty clothes.
   a. activity
   b. illness
   c. guests
   d. laziness

   5. _____

6. The book review included many *pejorative* comments about the author's latest novel.
   a. negative
   b. inaccurate
   c. upsetting
   d. uninformed

   6. _____

7. A bitter argument about the company's finances *estranged* the former partners.
   a. embarrassed
   b. alienated
   c. depressed
   d. ruined

   7. _____

8. Since Mel has an *affinity* for animals, he should volunteer at the new animal shelter.
   a. natural liking
   b. dread
   c. long experience
   d. dislike

   8. _____

9. "How can anyone find pleasure in such *melancholy* music?" I asked my father.
   a. old-fashioned
   b. gloomy
   c. not original
   d. horrible

   9. _____

10. The whirring fan and the warmth of the room had a *soporific* effect on all of us.
    a. confusing; puzzling
    b. comforting; reassuring
    c. inducing gloom
    d. causing sleepiness

    10. _____

TEST: LESSONS 19 AND 20

(pages 121–132)

Part B Choosing the Best Word

On the answer line, write the letter of the word that best completes the sentence.

11. The volcano, which had been _____ for years, has recently begun to show
some activity.
  a. languid   **b.** melancholy   **c.** dilatory   **d.** quiescent

11. _____

12. The babysitter turned away in _____ when he saw the pile of diapers.
  a. disdain   **b.** repugnance   **c.** repose   **d.** affinity

12. _____

13. Mrs. Gomez _____ herself to all the neighborhood children by serving them
popsicles on hot summer afternoons.
  a. estranged   **b.** somnambulated   **c.** disdained   **d.** enamored

13. _____

14. I awoke in a confused _____ when the phone rang at 2:00 A.M.
  a. melancholy   **b.** stupor   **c.** repugnance   **d.** kudos

14. _____

15. Sam, who is the most _____ sports fan I know, is desperately trying to get tickets
to one of the playoff games.
  a. lethargic   **b.** dilatory   **c.** quiescent   **d.** ardent

15. _____

16. I _____ the taste of cooked spinach, but I don't mind eating it raw, especially
in salads.
  a. abhor   **b.** estrange   **c.** repose   **d.** enamor

16. _____

17. Erin, the lead in the school play, received enthusiastic _____ from her classmates.
  a. animosity   **b.** sloth   **c.** quiescence   **d.** kudos

17. _____

18. Our old cat loves to _____ in a square of sunshine on our porch each morning.
  a. somnambulate   **b.** repose   **c.** disdain   **d.** abhor

18. _____

19. We spent a _____ afternoon poking around the pond in our canoe, enjoying the
warm sunshine and light breeze.
  a. pejorative   **b.** languid   **c.** somnambulant   **d.** repugnant

19. _____

20. The queen showed her _____ for the visitor by refusing to speak with him.
  a. ardor   **b.** lethargy   **c.** stupor   **d.** disdain

20. _____

TEST: LESSONS 21 AND 22

(pages 133–138, 141–146)

Part A Choosing the Best Definition

On the answer line, write the letter of the best definition of the italicized word.

1. It takes great *stamina* to run a marathon, or even to walk the twenty-six-mile distance.   1. _____
  a. determination   **c.** nutrition
  b. optimism   **d.** endurance

2. After the launch, we watched the *trajectory* of the rocket until it disappeared above the clouds.   2. _____
  a. amusing show or display   **c.** path of a moving body
  b. round shape   **d.** unusual color

3. After his *abject* apology, I forgave him and even started to feel a bit sorry for him.   3. _____
  a. wretched   **c.** long-winded
  b. rehearsed   **d.** polite

4. We took a guided tour of the *citadel*, which was constructed in the Middle Ages.   4. _____
  a. tomb   **c.** city
  b. fortress   **d.** church

5. Celia really showed her *mettle* by taking charge of the situation when the canoe capsized, and all our camping supplies started to float away.   5. _____
  a. ability to work   **c.** medical training
  b. strength of character   **d.** emergency preparedness

6. Would any of you find it *objectionable* if I turned off the television so we could listen to my new CD?   6. _____
  a. appropriate   **c.** offensive
  b. pleasing   **d.** strange

7. In an effort to conserve fuel, the pilot told his passengers to *jettison* the cargo.   7. _____
  a. pack tightly   **c.** make secure
  b. discard   **d.** minimize

8. Fearing punishment from political enemies in his homeland, the man asked for political *asylum* in the United States.   8. _____
  a. reward   **c.** protection
  b. trial   **d.** support

9. For the garden, choose hardy plants that are *resilient* and can weather a few dry spells.   9. _____
  a. attractive   **c.** familiar
  b. bright in color   **d.** able to spring back

10. As I watched the shark *assail* the other fish, I was glad that they were in a glass tank.   10. _____
  a. tickle   **c.** judge
  b. attack   **d.** welcome

TEST: LESSONS 21 AND 22

(pages 133–138, 141–146)

Part B Choosing the Best Word

On the answer line, write the letter of the word that best completes the sentence.

11. Fans were not allowed to bring glass bottles into the stadium because the bottles could become dangerous _____.
    a. trajectories   **b.** bulwarks   **c.** projectiles   **d.** stalwarts

11. _____

12. _____ about the results of the math test, Travis spent the afternoon in his bedroom with the door shut.
    a. Objectionable   **b.** Dejected   **c.** Invincible   **d.** Stalwart

12. _____

13. In the harbor, a sea wall made of huge rocks serves as an effective _____ against the pounding waves.
    a. projectile   **b.** stamina   **c.** bulwark   **d.** asylum

13. _____

14. I asked the people behind us to please stop _____ their opinions during the movie, so that we could enjoy it.
    a. assailing   **b.** conjecturing   **c.** jutting   **d.** interjecting

14. _____

15. Undergoing a long series of unpleasant medical treatments takes quite a bit of _____.
    a. fortitude   **b.** citadel   **c.** conjecture   **d.** jut

15. _____

16. Among the group of judges, Carlos Escala has a reputation as the most _____ defender of First Amendment rights.
    a. stalwart   **b.** abject   **c.** dejected   **d.** resilient

16. _____

17. In the evening, we strolled out onto the _____ and chatted with a man who was fishing there.
    a. asylum   **b.** mettle   **c.** stamina   **d.** jetty

17. _____

18. A rickety old dock _____ into the water right in front of our cottage.
    a. jettisons   **b.** juts   **c.** interjects   **d.** objects

18. _____

19. To many of us, the basketball team looked _____ because they had exceptionally tall, muscular players.
    a. objectionable   **b.** dejected   **c.** invincible   **d.** abject

19. _____

20. My _____ is that one candidate will be a clear frontrunner long before the convention.
    a. stalwart   **b.** fortitude   **c.** citadel   **d.** conjecture

20. _____

TEST: LESSONS 23 AND 24

(pages 147–158)

Part A Choosing the Best Definition

On the answer line, write the letter of the best definition of the italicized word.

1. I used to run every day, but I've *diversified* my exercise routine to include swimming.
   a. modified
   b. given more variety to
   c. reversed
   d. made more intense

1. _____

2. In the United States we have laws that ban discrimination on the basis of a person's race, *creed*, or national origin.
   a. ethnic group
   b. neighborhood
   c. gender
   d. system of beliefs

2. _____

3. If you're interested in the job, send a summary of your *credentials* to my office.
   a. supporters
   b. qualifications
   c. life story
   d. statistics

3. _____

4. While Carson was home sick, he found that surfing the Internet was a great *diversion*.
   a. hobby or interest
   b. method of communicating
   c. waste of time
   d. something that entertains

4. _____

5. I was *incredulous* when my uncle told me that he had a sure way to win the lottery.
   a. deceived
   b. jealous
   c. disbelieving
   d. thrilled

5. _____

6. Charlize *inadvertently* mentioned to Brian that we were planning a surprise party for him.
   a. finally
   b. casually
   c. unintentionally
   d. unfortunately

6. _____

7. Her first novel was a *creditable* piece of work, and readers who enjoyed it expect even better things when her second book is released next month.
   a. outstanding
   b. deserving of limited praise
   c. believable
   d. having great popularity

7. _____

8. When the cake has cooled, *invert* it onto a serving plate and decorate it with icing.
   a. turn upside down
   b. slide slowly
   c. return quickly
   d. place carefully

8. _____

9. Age is one part of life that is *irreversible*.
   a. easy to repair
   b. preventable
   c. not able to be turned back
   d. minor

9. _____

10. At the top of the observation tower, Quinton was overcome with a feeling of *vertigo*.
   a. regret
   b. being lost
   c. disbelief
   d. dizziness

10. _____

TEST: LESSONS 23 AND 24

(pages 147–158)

Part B Choosing the Best Word

On the answer line, write the letter of the word that best completes the sentence.

11. How much _____ do you give to the idea of life on other planets?   **11.** _____
    a. diversity   **b.** diversion   **c.** vertigo   **d.** credence

12. A political rival tried to _____ the candidate by questioning his motives, his   **12.** _____
values, and even his patriotism.
    a. discredit   **b.** credential   **c.** avert   **d.** diversify

13. Gavin has a college degree in biology, and he is also an _____ physical therapist.   **13.** _____
    a. incontrovertible   **b.** aversive   **c.** irreversible   **d.** accredited

14. Teresa has a strong _____ to swallowing pills so she buys chewable vitamins.   **14.** _____
    a. incredulity   **b.** discredit   **c.** aversion   **d.** creed

15. My _____ sister actually believed me when I told her I had been offered a job   **15.** _____
modeling for a fashion magazine.
    a. creditable   **b.** credulous   **c.** diverse   **d.** inadvertent

16. After my grandfather stopped tilling and weeding his garden, it quickly _____   **16.** _____
to grass and weeds.
    a. accredited   **b.** inverted   **c.** reverted   **d.** averted

17. School officials are investigating the incident and are determined to identify and   **17.** _____
punish the _____.
    a. aversion   **b.** miscreant   **c.** credence   **d.** credibility

18. Scientists have found _____ evidence that dinosaurs once roamed the earth.   **18.** _____
    a. credulous   **b.** incredulous   **c.** irreversible   **d.** incontrovertible

19. Tabloid newspapers that publish wildly improbable, sensationalist stories may be   **19.** _____
entertaining, but they do not have much _____.
    a. credibility   **b.** inversion   **c.** credential   **d.** vertigo

20. George slammed on the brakes and narrowly _____ an accident.   **20.** _____
    a. diverted   **b.** averted   **c.** discredited   **d.** reverted

TEST: LESSONS 25 AND 26

(pages 161–172)

Part A Choosing the Best Definition

On the answer line, write the letter of the best definition of the italicized word.

1. Since Mrs. Klein needed the papers immediately, her lawyer sent them by *courier*.
   a. messenger
   b. email
   c. air travel
   d. fax

   1. _____

2. "The Wall" in Washington, D.C., memorializes thousands of *deceased* servicemen and women who served in the Vietnam War.
   a. courageous
   b. honored
   c. dead
   d. wounded

   2. _____

3. Our hike was difficult because of the extreme heat and the *gradient* of the trail.
   a. poor condition
   b. steepness
   c. rough surface
   d. slipperiness

   3. _____

4. Most likely, the candidate will wait until the last moment to *concede* the election.
   a. give up
   b. decide on
   c. discuss
   d. take part in

   4. _____

5. When I moved into my new office, I discovered that my *predecessor* had spilled some sticky food in several of the desk drawers.
   a. assistant
   b. son or daughter
   c. boss or supervisor
   d. one who comes before

   5. _____

6. My mother finally decided to speak to our neighbor about her dog's *recurrent* barking.
   a. annoying
   b. happening recently
   c. loud
   d. happening repeatedly

   6. _____

7. Lou was surprised to learn that he had *incurred* a $5.00 penalty for returning a video late.
   a. failed to pay
   b. forgotten
   c. brought about
   d. canceled

   7. _____

8. Many non-governmental organizations provide *succor* to those who are less fortunate.
   a. shelter
   b. assistance
   c. cash
   d. sympathy

   8. _____

9. The Northeast has had an *unprecedented* amount of rain this spring.
   a. inadequate
   b. causing problems
   c. fairly large
   d. without previous example

   9. _____

10. Feeling that the comic had *transgressed* by telling jokes in bad taste, my father switched the television channel.
    a. gone beyond limits
    b. reached
    c. gradually changed
    d. worsened

    10. _____

TEST: LESSONS 25 AND 26

(pages 161–172)

Part B Choosing the Best Word

On the answer line, write the letter of the word that best completes the sentence.

11. Hikers and campers should be aware that bears sometimes make _____ into campsites and picnic areas.
    a. couriers   **b.** regressions   **c.** precursors   **d.** incursions

11. _____

12. When a child is sick, he will often _____ to long-abandoned, comforting habits from an earlier age.
    a. recur   **b.** concede   **c.** egress   **d.** regress

12. _____

13. The author's rambling, _____ style is somewhat amusing, but I prefer a book with more action and less description.
    a. concurrent   **b.** deceased   **c.** discursive   **d.** succored

13. _____

14. These gorgeous tulips have a lovely color _____ from pale pink to deep crimson.
    a. succor   **b.** incursion   **c.** egress   **d.** gradation

14. _____

15. Marla was a strong debater who rarely _____ a point to her opponent.
    a. succored   **b.** ceded   **c.** regressed   **d.** incurred

15. _____

16. Vijay hasn't decided which of the _____ graduation parties he will attend.
    a. cursory   **b.** discursive   **c.** concurrent   **d.** unprecedented

16. _____

17. Going on strike is usually a union's last _____ for obtaining fair salaries and improved working conditions.
    a. predecessor   **b.** recourse   **c.** concession   **d.** gradient

17. _____

18. After the show, you may _____ through any of the five exits.
    a. transgress   **b.** incur   **c.** egress   **d.** cede

18. _____

19. Before the history exam, Lisa studied her class notes thoroughly but gave the textbook only the most _____ review.
    a. discursive   **b.** cursory   **c.** unprecedented   **d.** recurrent

19. _____

20. A few, light flurries on Saturday evening were a _____ to the blizzard that began on Sunday morning.
    a. precursor   **b.** courier   **c.** transgression   **d.** gradation

20. _____

TEST: LESSONS 27 AND 28

(pages 173–178, 181–186)

Part A Choosing the Best Definition

On the answer line, write the letter of the best definition of the italicized word.

1. Our media class discussed why television news programs seem to focus on *sensational* stories.
   a. outstanding   c. worrisome
   b. pitiful   d. shocking

   1. _____

2. Lee had a *presentiment* about the pop quiz, so he reviewed the chapter before class.
   a. nagging worry   c. conversation with others
   b. thoughtful moment   d. sense that something will occur

   2. _____

3. The flowers in my garden seem all the more precious because they are so *ephemeral*.
   a. colorful   c. common
   b. short-lived   d. stunning

   3. _____

4. Some members of the audience dozed during the senator's *interminable* speech.
   a. not prepared   c. endless
   b. preachy   d. complicated

   4. _____

5. No one knew what was behind the chairman's *precipitate* resignation from the board.
   a. sudden   c. forced
   b. emotional   d. temporary

   5. _____

6. Buddhists try to avoid harming all *sentient* creatures, including insects.
   a. existing in nature   c. able to feel and perceive
   b. useful   d. non-human

   6. _____

7. The drama director *assented* to our request to end rehearsal fifteen minutes early.
   a. disregarded   c. agreed
   b. respected   d. criticized

   7. _____

8. Dr. Lawton, a medical researcher, specializes in the *pathology* of a rare form of cancer.
   a. cure   c. spread
   b. study of a disease   d. care and comfort

   8. _____

9. Many residents packed up some of their essential belongings and fled from the coast to escape from the *imminent* storm.
   a. violent   c. soon to occur
   b. seasonal   d. unexpected

   9. _____

10. Having changed schools myself, I felt some *empathy* for the new girl in class.
    a. understanding   c. regret
    b. admiration   d. envy

    10. _____

TEST: LESSONS 27 AND 28

(pages 173–178, 181–186)

Part B Choosing the Best Word

On the answer line, write the letter of the word that best completes the sentence.

11. When I saw the boy's _____ expression, I couldn't help feeling sorry for him.
   a. interminable   **b.** pathetic   **c.** sensational   **d.** perennial

11. _____

12. After the artist's death, the museum organized a _____ of his work.
   a. perennial   **b.** presentiment   **c.** harbinger   **d.** retrospective

12. _____

13. Explaining to a child why something is dangerous or unwise is usually more effective than _____ lecturing.
   a. imminent   **b.** interim   **c.** sententious   **d.** ephemeral

13. _____

14. The party needs a candidate who can excite people and reverse the trend toward greater _____ among voters.
   a. sensibility   **b.** apathy   **c.** empathy   **d.** assent

14. _____

15. A _____ government was formed to rule the territory and maintain order until elections could be held.
   a. provisional   **b.** pathetic   **c.** retrospective   **d.** sentient

15. _____

16. In one of my favorite comedies, twin girls switch identities, and the confusion that _____ is really funny.
   a. ensues   **b.** harbingers   **c.** assents   **d.** precipitates

16. _____

17. Last week my neighbor sighted a robin, the traditional _____ of spring.
   a. interim   **b.** imminence   **c.** apathy   **d.** harbinger

17. _____

18. Ms. Martinez, the _____ director, will run the department meetings for the next few months.
   a. imminent   **b.** interminable   **c.** interim   **d.** precipitate

18. _____

19. Film ratings such as "PG" and "PG-13" are intended to help parents protect their children's _____ .
   a. pathologies   **b.** presentiments   **c.** sensibilities   **d.** retrospectives

19. _____

20. Sandra, a _____ optimist, sees something good in every situation.
   a. pathological   **b.** perennial   **c.** sententious   **d.** provisional

20. _____

TEST: LESSONS 29 AND 30

(pages 187–198)

Part A Choosing the Best Definition

On the answer line, write the letter of the best definition of the italicized word.

1. Georgia, as *imperturbable* as ever, cheerfully swept up the pieces when a guest broke her new teapot.
   a. generous
   b. unshakably calm
   c. absentminded
   d. easily influenced

   1. _____

2. We had planned to go to the beach, but because of the rain we endured a day of *ennui* in the cramped cottage.
   a. distasteful chores
   b. relaxed ease
   c. cranky squabbling
   d. weary boredom

   2. _____

3. The salesman suggested that I buy a *diaphanous* scarf to wear with my new outfit.
   a. wooly, warm, fuzzy
   b. expensive
   c. almost transparent
   d. brightly colored

   3. _____

4. Have you noticed how the smell of stale popcorn *permeates* the theater?
   a. evokes memories of
   b. vanishes from
   c. spreads throughout
   d. perfumes

   4. _____

5. Many artists have tried in vain to capture an *effulgent* sunrise in their paintings.
   a. shining
   b. gorgeous
   c. realistic
   d. tranquil

   5. _____

6. This jacket is made of high quality leather that is smooth and extremely *pliant.*
   a. costly
   b. flexible
   c. rare
   d. desirable

   6. _____

7. My uncle was so *attenuated* by his long illness that at first glance I didn't recognize him.
   a. made thinner
   b. wrinkled
   c. aged
   d. made heavier

   7. _____

8. Small children adore blowing *evanescent* bubbles and watching them drift away.
   a. slow-moving
   b. clear like glass
   c. shining
   d. vanishing quickly

   8. _____

9. Josiah sat on a rock at the edge of the lake, observing the sunset and enjoying the *serenity* of the summer evening.
   a. warmth
   b. peacefulness
   c. fragrance
   d. escape

   9. _____

10. Martina applied for the management job with *alacrity* as soon as it was advertised.
    a. reluctance
    b. eagerness
    c. trepidation
    d. diligence

    10. _____

TEST: LESSONS 29 AND 30

(pages 187–198)

Part B Choosing the Best Word

On the answer line, write the letter of the word that best completes the sentence.

11. In the film, an _____ young man runs off to marry a woman he has only known a few months and quickly regrets it.
a. evanescent   **b.** imperturbable   **c.** effulgent   **d.** impetuous

11. _____

12. Juan struggled to keep his _____ when he heard the bad news at work.
a. viscosity   **b.** ennui   **c.** composure   **d.** alacrity

12. _____

13. It took a long time to clean up the _____ honey that had spilled in the kitchen cabinet.
a. viscous   **b.** ponderous   **c.** serene   **d.** indolent

13. _____

14. The hotheaded leader tried to _____ the union members to vote for an immediate strike against the company.
a. attenuate   **b.** incite   **c.** encumber   **d.** compose

14. _____

15. When the bus driver noticed the _____ distress among the passengers, he pulled the bus over to the side of the road.
a. viscous   **b.** diaphanous   **c.** pliant   **d.** palpable

15. _____

16. _____ kept Sally in a low-paying, boring job long after her colleagues had moved on to better opportunities.
a. Inertia   **b.** Pandemonium   **c.** Serenity   **d.** Composure

16. _____

17. Ellie skipped along the sidewalk, but her older sister trudged along slowly because she was _____ by her heavy backpack.
a. permeated   **b.** encumbered   **c.** attenuated   **d.** composed

17. _____

18. After a few minutes, Audrey put the _____ textbook aside and opened up a science-fiction paperback by her favorite author.
a. impetuous   **b.** effulgent   **c.** imperturbable   **d.** ponderous

18. _____

19. There was _____ in the stadium when the home team clinched the championship.
a. incitement   **b.** inertia   **c.** pandemonium   **d.** ennui

19. _____

20. You'll need to change your _____ summertime habits when school starts again in September.
a. palpable   **b.** indolent   **c.** viscous   **d.** evanescent

20. _____

PRACTICE TEST FOR THE NEW SAT

PART A Sentence Completion

Each sentence below has one or two blanks. Read the sentence and choose the word or set of words that best fits the meaning of the sentence as a whole. Write the letter of the answer you choose.

_____ **1.** As a result of the oil shortage, oil companies will be charging _____ prices for heating oil next winter.

    a. benevolent   **c.** solvent   **e.** decorous
    b. gratuitous   **d.** exorbitant

_____ **2.** My favorite _____ was a statement by Mark Twain: "Man is the only animal that blushes—or needs to."

    a. witticism   **c.** lethargy   **e.** rendezvous
    b. citadel   **d.** nuance

_____ **3.** A team of hackers _____ hundreds of people's identities from a database that was supposed to be secure, and then used them to make credit purchases.

    a. bantered   **c.** conceded   **e.** purloined
    b. sequestered   **d.** vaunted

_____ **4.** Leighton was only being _____ when he suggested that the coach let the team mascot play quarterback in the final game of the season.

    a. cursory   **c.** facetious   **e.** furtive
    b. salient   **d.** soporific

_____ **5.** Tiania showed remarkable _____ by taking care of her mother for the last six weeks of her mother's life.

    a. sloth   **c.** latency   **e.** fortitude
    b. asylum   **d.** incorrigibility

_____ **6.** Mr. Carney gave a _____ talk that touched on all sorts of ideas, but his claims of being a genius stretched the limits of _____.

    a. resilient . . . trajectory   **c.** discursive . . . credibility   **e.** serene . . . conjecture
    b. provisional . . . empathy   **d.** concurrent . . . imminence

_____ **7.** Animal rights activists have announced that lobsters are _____ creatures and should be treated as such, but Dr. Mendez will not even _____ to respond to what he considers to be a ridiculous statement.

    a. sentient . . . condescend   **c.** pathetic . . . defer   **e.** adroit . . . grovel
    b. diligent . . . exonerate   **d.** culpable . . . extort

_____ **8.** After the conquest of the Aztec empire and the _____ of its people, Hernando Cortés moved northward to search for the _____ Seven Cities of Gold.

    a. apprehension . . . tentative   **c.** emigration . . . intrepid   **e.** precedence . . . opulent
    b. malfeasance . . . colloquial   **d.** subjugation . . . legendary

Part B Comprehension

Each passage in this section is followed by questions based on its content. Choose the best answer to each question based on what is stated or implied in the passage. Write the letter of the answer you choose.

Throughout history, civilizations have grown and matured through their contacts with other groups, and cultures have borrowed ideas and information from one another. The United States may be the epitome of cultural borrowing, since this is a relatively young country created by people from other countries. For example, many of our government buildings are modeled after Greek and Roman architecture, and our coins include the Latin phrase *e pluribus unum,* which means "out of many, one." Our form of government is derived from the governments of ancient Greece, as well as philosophical principles from England and France. Even our language is filled with words borrowed from other cultures. We get the word *pajamas* from India, *tortillas* from Mexico, and *August* from the Roman Emperor Augustus Caesar. *Chipmunk* and *squash* are Native American words. *Assassin* and *zero* come from Arabic. As you can see, borrowing ideas from other cultures makes our culture richer and more interesting.

9. Which detail from the passage best supports the idea that American English has been influenced by other cultures?
   a. The United States is a relatively young country.
   b. Our government buildings are modeled after Greek and Roman architecture.
   c. U.S. coins include the Latin phrase *e pluribus unum.*
   d. Our form of government is derived from the governments of ancient Greece.
   e. We get the word *pajamas* from India and *tortillas* from Mexico.

10. The author of this passage seems to believe that
   a. the United States is too young to have any creditable form of culture.
   b. American culture has greatly benefited by borrowing from other cultures.
   c. the most useful ideas have been borrowed from ancient Greece.
   d. American culture no longer needs to accommodate other cultures' ideas.
   e. the United States has become the most powerful culture in history.

Scientists have documented the recent decline in the populations of amphibians worldwide, especially in the numbers of frogs and toads. These scientists think that people should be alarmed by this decline, but is this development a red flag we should pay attention to? More than 1,300 species of amphibians face possible extinction in the near future as a result of pesticides, the destruction of natural habitats, and the effects of air and water pollution. The depletion of the ozone layer in the atmosphere has increased the levels of radiation that reach Earth. Apparently, radiation harms amphibians more than other creatures because they have extremely thin skin. However, the problems affecting amphibians do not necessarily mean that other species, such as humans, will soon be in dire straits, too.

11. According to this passage, many scientists believe that
   a. the decline in amphibian populations is a warning for other species.
   b. there are more than enough species of amphibians that will survive.
   c. humans should end the use of pesticides to control insects.
   d. the destruction of natural habitat is a trend that can be reversed.
   e. amphibians must adapt to environmental changes by growing thicker skin.

12. The statement that other species "will soon be in dire straits" means that other species will
   a. need new habitats.
   b. begin to look like amphibians.
   c. adapt to environmental changes.
   d. be in great danger.
   e. increase populations.

In 1999, President William Clinton issued an official pardon for a soldier named Henry O. Flipper, who allegedly committed a crime in 1881. But who was Henry Flipper, and what did he supposedly do? Flipper's story reflects some of the enormous changes that occurred in the United States in the 1800s. Henry Flipper was born into slavery in 1856, but he was emancipated after the Civil War. Flipper attended college in Atlanta, Georgia, and later became the first African American to graduate from West Point Military Academy. Flipper entered the army as an officer and was assigned to a post in the West. His job was to help protect railroads and stagecoaches from hostile attacks. In 1881, a new commander named Shafter was assigned to the fort where Flipper served. He clearly did not like Flipper. Soon after his arrival, Shafter accused Flipper of stealing money and had him arrested. After months of legal struggles, Flipper was found not guilty of theft, but he was forced to resign from the army. He carried the burden of false accusation and discrimination with him for the remainder of his life. He died long before President Clinton finally removed that burden.

_____ **13.** The passage says that Flipper was *emancipated* after the Civil War. The word *emancipated* means
  a. enlisted in the army.
  b. enrolled in school.
  c. freed from slavery.
  a. discriminated against.
  e. accused of a crime.

_____ **14.** The author mentions President Clinton in this passage because she wants to
  a. persuade readers to support the president of the United States.
  b. compare President Clinton with the new fort commander.
  c. blame Clinton for allowing such a disgraceful event to take place.
  d. criticize President Clinton for his interference in this case.
  e. show that Flipper was officially cleared of guilt.

According to recent reports, an overwhelmingly large number of American children suffer from obesity. As a consequence of fast-food diets, lack of exercise, and over-consumption of sweets, more children than ever before are seriously overweight. Health experts know that obesity can have detrimental effects on many different aspects of children's lives—physical, social, and emotional. It can also lead to heart attacks, strokes, and diabetes. We cannot afford to let this epidemic continue. We have got to change what our children eat and how they live before this problem takes a serious toll, not only on individuals, but on our society as a whole.

_____ **15.** The author's main purpose in this passage is to
  a. compare American children with children in other countries.
  b. persuade readers to help solve a serious problem.
  c. entertain readers with anecdotes about American children.
  d. give statistical information about obesity.
  e. explain why American children become overweight.

_____ **16.** The author of this passage probably would agree with the idea that
  a. Americans have become addicted to fast-food restaurants.
  b. the problem of obesity has been greatly exaggerated.
  c. Americans are generally healthier than people of other nations.
  d. adults should not be expected to supervise what children eat.
  e. Americans cannot be expected to pay for the health costs associated with obesity.

Passage 1

The school committee needs to live up to its responsibility to ensure the health and safety of all students by imposing an immediate ban on peanuts and peanut products in all of the city's schools. Peanuts and tree nuts are the leading cause of fatal and near-fatal food-induced anaphylaxis. The right of non-allergic children to enjoy their daily peanut-butter-and-jelly sandwiches is far superseded by the absolute right of allergic children—and their parents—to a safe school environment. Let's be clear about the issue: peanuts and peanut products are potentially lethal for allergic children. Since they are the equivalent to poison for some students, responsible leadership requires that we acknowledge this subtler but no less important threat to some children in our care. Let's vote right now to ban all peanut products from the public schools.

Passage 2

As school committee members, we are responsible for all of the city's children, and any decision must take into account the best interests of all children and all families. Banning peanuts is an unfair and drastic solution that benefits only a tiny minority of our students and imposes a potential hardship on hundreds of others. Such a ban would be impractical and impossible to enforce, and could lead to pressure for bans on other food allergens, including milk, eggs, soy, wheat, and shellfish. A better solution would involve education of school personnel to handle potential problems, a written emergency plan, a strict "no food-sharing" policy, and a supervised "allergy" lunch table for at-risk children.

_____ 17. The author of Passage 1 mentions poison mainly in order to
a. accuse those who bring peanuts to school.
b. remind listeners that some rules are necessary.
c. support a proposal to create a written emergency plan.
d. discredit those who disagree with her point of view.
e. impress her audience with the seriousness of the problem.

_____ 18. Both Passage 1 and Passage 2 are mainly intended to
a. analyze.
b. describe.
c. entertain.
d. persuade.
e. inform.

_____ 19. The author of Passage 1 uses the words "fatal," "potentially lethal," and "threat" to alarm readers. What words does the author of Passage 2 use to refer to the same events in a much less alarming way?
a. "best interests"
b. "potential problems"
c. "drastic solution"
d. "impractical and impossible"
e. "tiny minority"

_____ 20. The author of Passage 2 would most likely describe himself as adhering to the principle of
a. minority rules.
b. excessive responsibility.
c. safety at all costs.
d. strong authority.
e. individual freedom.

An Unlíkely Queen

Long before Venus and Serena Williams climbed to the summit of women's tennis, there was a tall, thin girl named Althea Gibson who lived in Harlem, New York. Gibson shattered the color barrier in women's tennis nearly 50 years ago by becoming the first African-American woman to win the British National Championships at Wimbledon, England, and the United States national competition, the U.S. Open, at Forest Hills, New York.

However, as *The New York Times* noted at the time of Gibson's death in September 2003, she "was an unlikely queen of the lawns of Wimbledon and Forest Hills." For one thing, as a young girl, she constantly cut school, stayed out late at night, and ran away from home. For another, she came of age in a world apart from the manicured lawns and whites-only country clubs where top-ranked tennis players of that era learned the game.

Fortunately, Gibson did have one thing going for her: her family's apartment happened to be on a block designated a play street. In the 1930s, when Gibson was growing up, volunteers from the Police Athletic League cordoned off certain streets and turned them into makeshift playgrounds where youngsters were coached in different sports. That's how nine-year-old Althea Gibson came to learn paddle tennis, a variation of court tennis. Gibson was apparently a natural athlete who excelled at every sport she tried. She won the citywide paddle tennis championship when she was 12.

Gibson caught the eye of some members of the Cosmopolitan Tennis Club, a mostly upper-middle class black club in Harlem. They bought her the best racquets, schooled her in tournament tennis, and taught her proper etiquette.

For a period of time, Gibson found shelter in a Catholic girls' home. Later she got her own apartment, supporting herself with low-paying jobs. Finally, in 1942, at the age of 15, she won her first tournament, the New York State girls' championship. The state tournament was backed by the American Tennis Association (ATA). This group was set up by black players as a counterpart to the whites-only United States Lawn Tennis Association.

Four years later, Gibson lost in the finals of the ATA national championship. However, she attracted the attention of some wealthy black tennis buffs who were determined to integrate mainstream tennis. She went to live with the family of one of them, a doctor in Wilmington, North Carolina. At the age of 19, Gibson returned to high school. She practiced tennis on the doctor's private court in her free time. The one-time dropout graduated three years later near the top of her class and won a scholarship to Florida A&M University.

Meanwhile, Gibson was vaulting to the top of the tennis ranks. In 1947, she became the queen of the black tennis circuit, winning the first of ten straight ATA national championships. That was the year Jackie Robinson broke the color barrier in major league baseball. In 1949, 21-year-old Althea Gibson crashed the barriers of race *and* class that had defined the genteel world of women's tennis by reaching the semifinals in the Eastern Indoor Championships and later the national championships. Gibson's size—a rangy 5 feet 10$\frac{1}{2}$ inches—and her game—powerful serves and long reaches—were similar to that of the Williams sisters.

Though she performed well at the ATA tournaments, Gibson's first few years on the circuit were marked by frustration. She failed to win a major national championship. After briefly flirting with the idea of joining the Army, she was chosen by the U.S. State Department to go on a goodwill tennis tour of Asia.

Somehow, that experience lifted her game to the next level. She won 16 of her first 18 tournaments in 1956, among them the French national championship, her first Grand Slam event. Over the next two years, she dominated the sport, winning twice at Wimbledon and Forest Hills. As Queen Elizabeth II handed this "unlikely queen of the lawns" her first Wimbledon trophy, Gibson said, "At last. At last."

Plagued by chronic health problems and financial difficulties the last two decades of her life, Gibson became a virtual recluse in her apartment in New Jersey. But she did her best to reach out to young black players. In 1997, some friends arranged for Venus Williams to speak to Gibson by phone. "Be who you are," Gibson told her, "and let your racquet do the talking."

_____ **21.** Which sentence best states the author's main point in this passage?
  a. Althea Gibson lived in a Catholic girls' home.
  b. Few women ever experience the recognition Althea Gibson received when she won the British and U.S. tennis championships.
  c. Tennis great Althea Gibson achieved some remarkable feats.
  d. Venus and Serena Williams might be great tennis players, but Althea Gibson was the best of all time.
  e. Althea Gibson was a great tennis player, but she was not as successful in school.

_____ **22.** The passage says, "Volunteers from the Police Athletic League *cordoned* off certain streets." The word *cordoned* means
  a. repaved.
  b. drew lines on.
  c. planted with grass.
  d. purchased with money.
  e. closed to traffic.

_____ **23.** Gibson was called an "unlikely queen of lawn tennis" because she
  a. did not come from the world of privileged white players.
  b. was nearly six feet tall and rangy.
  c. showed no interest in tennis before she was a teenager.
  d. was so good at so many different sports.
  e. played on a private tennis court in North Carolina.

_____ **24.** According to this passage, what did Althea Gibson and Jackie Robinson have in common?
  a. Both grew up in Harlem.
  b. Both broke the color barrier in a professional sport.
  c. Both won national tennis championships.
  d. Both returned to finish high school later in life.
  e. Both learned their sports in California.

_____ **25.** What experience helped Althea Gibson overcome her own frustrations and finally win a major national championship?
  a. She met a doctor from Wilmington, North Carolina.
  b. She joined the U.S. Army.
  c. She toured Asia for the U.S. State Department.
  d. She graduated from Florida A&M University.
  e. She met Jackie Robinson.

_____ **26.** How was Althea Gibson's tennis experience different from that of Venus and Serena Williams?
  a. She grew up in a well-to-do neighborhood.
  b. She completed her education before taking up tennis.
  c. She played only in tournaments for African Americans.
  d. She did not have any African-American role models to talk with.
  e. She had a powerful serve and a long reach.

_____ **27.** The author of this passage seems to feel that Althea Gibson
  a. missed some great opportunities in her life.
  b. should be admired for what she achieved.
  c. did not behave appropriately in the tennis world.
  d. deserves credit for making Venus Williams a great player.
  e. never quite lived up to everyone's expectations.

_____ **28.** Which detail from the passage supports the idea that Althea Gibson had to overcome many disadvantages to accomplish what she did?

 a. She won the British national championship at Wimbledon, England.

 b. Gibson "was an unlikely queen of the lawns of Wimbledon and Forest Hills."

 c. She came of age in a world apart from the manicured lawns and whites-only country clubs where top-ranked tennis players of that era learned the game.

 d. Gibson caught the eye of some members of the Cosmopolitan Tennis Club, a mostly upper-middle class black club in Harlem.

 e. They bought her the best racquets, schooled her in tournament tennis, and taught her proper etiquette.

_____ **29.** The passage says, "Gibson became a virtual *recluse* in her apartment in New Jersey." A *recluse* is a person who

 a. lives apart from society.

 b. announces sports events.

 c. attracts fans and followers.

 d. is not employed.

 e. needs medical help.

_____ **30.** According to the author, how did Gibson "completely reinvent herself as a cultivated young woman"?

 a. She moved from the streets of Harlem to a Catholic girls' home.

 b. She changed from a losing player to a tournament champion.

 c. She moved from New York to North Carolina.

 d. She left tennis and traveled on a tour of Asia.

 e. She went from high school dropout to college graduate.

Answer Key

TEST: LESSONS 1 & 2

Part A	Part B
1. b	11. c
2. d	12. a
3. c	13. b
4. a	14. c
5. c	15. a
6. d	16. d
7. b	17. c
8. d	18. c
9. b	19. d
10. c	20. a

TEST: LESSONS 7 & 8

Part A	Part B
1. b	11. a
2. a	12. c
3. d	13. c
4. c	14. b
5. b	15. d
6. a	16. d
7. b	17. b
8. a	18. d
9. d	19. a
10. c	20. c

TEST: LESSONS 3 & 4

Part A	Part B
1. b	11. d
2. c	12. b
3. d	13. a
4. a	14. c
5. b	15. b
6. a	16. c
7. c	17. d
8. d	18. d
9. b	19. c
10. a	20. a

TEST: LESSONS 9 & 10

Part A	Part B
1. d	11. b
2. d	12. c
3. c	13. d
4. d	14. a
5. c	15. d
6. b	16. b
7. a	17. c
8. d	18. a
9. c	19. c
10. b	20. c

TEST: LESSONS 5 & 6

Part A	Part B
1. c	11. a
2. d	12. b
3. a	13. d
4. c	14. c
5. b	15. c
6. c	16. b
7. d	17. c
8. b	18. d
9. a	19. c
10. c	20. b

TEST: LESSONS 11 & 12

Part A	Part B
1. d	11. b
2. b	12. d
3. c	13. a
4. b	14. c
5. d	15. a
6. d	16. d
7. c	17. c
8. a	18. b
9. d	19. d
10. c	20. a

TEST: LESSONS 13 & 14

Part A	Part B
1. d	11. c
2. a	12. a
3. b	13. a
4. d	14. d
5. b	15. b
6. c	16. c
7. a	17. d
8. b	18. b
9. c	19. c
10. d	20. c

TEST: LESSONS 15 & 16

Part A	Part B
1. d	11. c
2. b	12. a
3. d	13. d
4. c	14. b
5. c	15. c
6. d	16. b
7. a	17. d
8. a	18. b
9. d	19. a
10. a	20. d

TEST: LESSONS 17 & 18

Part A	Part B
1. a	11. b
2. b	12. a
3. c	13. c
4. a	14. d
5. d	15. b
6. b	16. a
7. c	17. b
8. d	18. d
9. d	19. a
10. b	20. c

TEST: LESSONS 19 & 20

Part A	Part B
1. d	11. d
2. b	12. b
3. d	13. d
4. a	14. b
5. d	15. d
6. a	16. a
7. b	17. d
8. a	18. b
9. b	19. b
10. d	20. d

TEST: LESSONS 21 & 22

Part A	Part B
1. d	11. c
2. c	12. b
3. a	13. c
4. b	14. d
5. b	15. a
6. c	16. a
7. b	17. d
8. c	18. b
9. d	19. c
10. b	20. d

TEST: LESSONS 23 & 24

Part A	Part B
1. b	11. d
2. d	12. a
3. b	13. d
4. d	14. c
5. c	15. b
6. c	16. c
7. b	17. b
8. a	18. d
9. c	19. a
10. d	20. b

TEST: LESSONS 25 & 26

Part A	Part B
1. a	11. d
2. c	12. d
3. b	13. c
4. a	14. d
5. d	15. b
6. d	16. c
7. c	17. b
8. b	18. c
9. d	19. b
10. a	20. a

TEST: LESSONS 27 & 28

Part A	Part B
1. d	11. b
2. d	12. d
3. b	13. c
4. c	14. b
5. a	15. a
6. c	16. a
7. c	17. d
8. b	18. c
9. c	19. c
10. a	20. b

TEST: LESSONS 29 & 30

Part A	Part B
1. b	11. d
2. d	12. c
3. c	13. a
4. c	14. b
5. a	15. d
6. b	16. a
7. a	17. b
8. d	18. d
9. b	19. c
10. b	20. b

PRACTICE TEST FOR THE NEW SAT

Part A	Part B
1. d	9. e
2. a	10. b
3. e	11. a
4. c	12. d
5. e	13. c
6. c	14. e
7. a	15. b
8. d	16. a
	17. e
	18. d
	19. b
	20. e
	21. c
	22. e
	23. a
	24. b
	25. c
	26. d
	27. b
	28. c
	29. a
	30. e